# Lessons in Development

A Comparative Study of Asia and Latin America

THE INTERNATIONAL CENTER FOR ECONOMIC GROWTH is a non-profit institute founded in 1985 to stimulate international discussions on economic policy, economic growth, and human development. The Center sponsors research, publications, and conferences in cooperation with an international network of correspondent institutes, which distribute publications of both the Center and other network members to policy audiences around the world. The Center's research and publications program is organized around five series: Sector Studies; Country Studies; Studies in Human Development and Social Welfare; Occasional Papers; and Reprints.

The Center is affiliated with the Institute for Contemporary Studies, and has headquarters in Panama and a home office in San Francisco, California.

For further information, please contact the International Center for Economic Growth, 243 Kearny Street, San Francisco, California, 94108, USA. Phone (415) 981-5353; FAX: (415) 986-4878.

# ICEG Board of Overseers

# Lessons in Development

## A Comparative Study of Asia and Latin America

Edited by
Seiji Naya, Miguel Urrutia, Shelley Mark,
and Alfredo Fuentes

International Center for Economic Growth

Affiliated with the Institute for Contemporary Studies

Publication signifies that the Center believes a work to be a competent treatment worthy of public consideration. The findings, interpretations, and conclusions of a work are entirely those of the author and should not be attributed to ICEG, its affiliated organizations, its board of overseers, or organizations that support ICEG.

Inquiries, book orders, and catalogue requests should be addressed to ICS Press, 243 Kearny Street, San Francisco, California, 94108. (415) 981-5353. FAX: (415) 986-4878.

Distributed to the trade by Kampmann National Book Network, Lanham, Maryland.

**Library of Congress Cataloging-in-Publication Data**

Lessons in development : a comparative study of Asia and Latin America / edited by Seiji Naya . . . [et al.].
  p.  cm.
    Papers presented at the Conference on Comparative Development Experiences of Asia and Latin America, held in Honolulu in April 1988.
    Includes bibliographical references.
    ISBN 1-55815-052-8
    1. Asia—Economic policy—Congresses. 2. Latin America—Economic policy—Congresses. 3. Asia—Commercial policy—Congresses. 4. Latin America—Commercial policy—Congresses. 5. Asia—Economic integration—Congresses. 6. Latin America—Economic integration—Congresses. 7. Asia—Foreign economic relations—Latin America—Congresses. 8. Latin America—Foreign economic relations—Asia—Congresses. I. Naya, Seiji. II. Conference on Comparative Development Experiences of Asia and Latin America (1988: Honolulu, Hawaii)
HC412.L44 1989
338.95—dc20                                                        89-19996
                                                                          CIP

# Contents

# List of Tables and Figures

# Appendix Tables

# Preface

The past twenty years have been difficult for many developing countries. Wide fluctuations in commodity prices, the rapid accumulation of external debt, and changes in world trade and macroeconomic conditions have been among the many problems they have had to face. The Asian developing countries were able to adjust to these changing conditions and have been among the most rapidly growing countries in the world; and prospects for future growth remain bright. Developing countries in other regions, including many Latin American countries, have been less successful; many are beset with problems, including huge debt burdens, high inflation rates, and overall economic stagnation. To be sure, there are exceptions in both Asia and Latin America, but the phenomenal performance of many Asian developing countries stands out as an anomaly of the 1970s and 1980s.

Recognizing the above, Miguel Urrutia of the Inter-American Development Bank and Seiji Naya of the East-West Center invited researchers from Asia and Latin America to discuss this phenomenon. The conference, Comparative Development Experiences of Asia and Latin America, was successful and this volume is the product of the conference. I believe that the volume provides some insight as to why economic performance differs between the countries through comparisons of the development strategies and performances of the countries in Asia and Latin America.

The International Center for Economic Growth (ICEG) is pleased to be a part of the endeavor, as the theme links several important parts of the Center's activities. The major focus of the Center for the last two years has been in Latin American affairs; more recently the Center has begun to look at development problems in other parts of the world. This comparative analysis of two very important regions examines the strengths and weaknesses of various development strategies in a way that scholars, technocrats, government officials and business executives from both regions can utilize. The Center is extremely grateful for the contributions and cooperation of the East-West Center's Resource

Systems Institute, the Inter-American Development Bank, the Institute for Latin American Integration, and the Asian Development Bank. Without their support, ideas, and dedication, this important book may not have been possible. Finally, I would like to thank The Pew Charitable Trusts for its generous contribution to this project.

Nicolás Ardito-Barletta
General Director
International Center
for Economic Growth

Panama City, Panama
July 1989

# Acknowledgments

Current interest and research in economic development has focused on differences in growth rates among developing economies. Whether these differences have been due to institutional, policy, external, or other forces has been the subject of much debate. Particular attention has been directed toward differential rates, as exhibited by the relatively rapid growth of countries in East and Southeast Asia, on the one hand, and the more sluggish growth trends of some of the richly endowed Latin American countries, on the other. In April 1988, the East-West Center's Resource Systems Institute (RSI) convened a meeting in Honolulu of economists and policymakers to examine these issues. The conference came about as the result of discussions between Seiji Naya, Director of RSI, and Miguel Urrutia, Manager of the Economic and Social Development Department of the Inter-American Development Bank (IADB). Research contributions and financial support were also received from the Institute for Latin American Integration (INTAL) and the Asian Development Bank (ADB). Four institutions involved in economic research on the development process in Asia and Latin America came together with the common purpose of studying comparisons and contrasts in the recent experience of that process.

This volume includes edited versions of all the papers presented at the meeting. An introductory chapter attempts to capture the essence of the discussions that took place at the conference. The concluding chapters provide further summaries and also represent views on the current state of affairs and the future outlook. If there was any tilt by the end of the meeting, it was probably toward a consensus that more outward-looking and market-oriented policies can adjust better to external uncertainty and thus enhance internal growth. However, formulation of these policies requires cognizance of behavioral factors and the uniqueness of individual countries, and implementation will depend on their structural and institutional characteristics.

The editors wish to thank the authors and the discussants for their timely and insightful contributions to the project. The lively discussions that occurred clearly indicated that many hypotheses remain to be tested and numerous lessons to be learned through communication and interaction. The editors also would like to thank the staff of the Development Policy Program of RSI, and most especially Pearl Imada and Janis Togashi, for their tireless efforts toward the production of this volume. Wesley Oasa also provided valuable assistance. David Puhlick copyedited the manuscript with the assistance of Patricia Wilson.

Seiji Naya
Miguel Urrutia
Shelley Mark
Alfredo Fuentes

# List of Abbreviations

| | |
|---|---|
| ADB | Asian Development Bank |
| AIC | ASEAN Industrial Complementation |
| AIJV | ASEAN Industrial Joint Venture |
| AIP | ASEAN Industrial Project |
| ANCOM | Andean Common Market |
| ASEAN | Association of Southeast Asian Nations |
| ASEAN-4 | The four larger members of ASEAN (Indonesia, Malaysia, the Philippines, and Thailand) |
| ASEBEX | ASEAN export earnings stabilization |
| BOP | Balance of payments |
| CACM | Central American Common Market |
| CARICOM | Caribbean Community |
| CARIFTA | Caribbean Free Trade Area |
| CCCN | Customs Cooperation Council Nomenclature (Republic of Korea) |
| CECLA | Comisión Especial de Coordinación Latinoamericana (Special Commission for Latin American Coordination) |
| CET | Common External Tariff |
| CIPEC | Consejo Intergubernamental de Países Exportadores de Cobre (Intergovernmental Council of Copper-Exporting Nations) |
| COIME | Committee on Industry, Minerals, and Energy |
| DFI | Direct foreign investment |
| EC | European Community |
| ECLA | United Nations Economic Commission for Latin America |

| | |
|---|---|
| ECLAC | United Nations Economic Commission for Latin America and the Caribbean |
| ECOWAS | Economic Community of West African States |
| ERSO | Electronics and Research Service Organization (Taiwan) |
| ESCAP | Economic and Social Commission for Asia and the Pacific |
| FAR | Fondo Andino de Reservas (Andean Reserve Fund) |
| FIRA | Foreign Investment Review Act (Canada) |
| GATT | General Agreement on Tariffs and Trade |
| GDP | Gross domestic product |
| GSP | Generalized System of Preferences |
| GSTP | Generalized System of Tariff Preferences |
| IADB | Inter-American Development Bank |
| IMF | International Monetary Fund |
| INTAL | Instituto para la Integración de América Latina (Institute for Latin American Integration) |
| JETRO | Japan External Trade Organization |
| JTA | Japan Tariff Association |
| JUNAC | Junta del Acuerdo de Cartagena (Board of the Cartagena Agreement) |
| KIET | Korean Institute of Electronics Technology |
| LAFTA | Latin American Free Trade Association |
| LAIA | Latin American Integration Association |
| MFA | Multifibre Agreement |
| MOP | Margin of preference |
| NICs | Newly industrializing countries |
| ODA | Official development assistance |
| OECD | Organisation for Economic Co-operation and Development |
| OPIC | Overseas Private Investment Corporation |
| PAR | Preferencia arancelaria regional (Regional tariff preference) |

| PBEC | Pacific Basin Economic Committee |
| PECC | Pacific Economic Cooperation Committee |
| PTA | Preferential Trading Arrangement |
| RSI | Resource Systems Institute (East-West Center) |
| SAARC | South Asian Association for Regional Cooperation |
| SELA | Sistema Económico Latinoamericano (Latin American Economic System) |
| SPID | Sectoral Programs for Industrial Development |
| TFP | Total factor productivity |
| TNC | Transnational corporation |
| UNCTAD | United Nations Conference on Trade and Development |
| UNDP | United Nations Development Programme |
| UNIDO | United Nations Industrial Development Organisation |

# Part One

# Introduction and Overview

*Seiji Naya*
*Suby Roy*
*Pearl Imada*

# Introduction

Among the fundamental and difficult questions of modern economic development is how to explain differential rates of economic growth between countries and regions. The question becomes especially intriguing when looking at the development experiences of Asia and Latin America, two important regions in the present world economy. Asia has been experiencing remarkable economic growth in the last twenty-five years, while for many complicated reasons Latin America has seemed unable to fulfill its economic potential.

This volume contains papers presented at the Conference on Comparative Development Experiences of Asia and Latin America, which took place in Honolulu in April 1988. The papers compare and contrast recent economic developments and policymaking in these two regions, which may be of use to policymakers, scholars, technocrats, and others interested in them. Part One contains a general economic survey of each region, two studies of external economic policies, and a case study comparison of two significant countries, Brazil and the Republic of Korea (hereafter Korea). Part Two contains three studies on efforts at regional cooperation and integration in Southeast Asia, Latin America, and South Asia, respectively. Part Three contains three chapters on economic relationships between Asia and Latin America, and between the regions and the main economic powers in the Pacific, namely, the

United States and Japan. Part Four consists of a set of concluding remarks by Miguel Urrutia and a concluding essay by Helen Hughes. A statistical appendix is provided at the end of the volume to assist the reader wishing further references.

In examining and analyzing the economies of two such vast and complex continents, it is to be expected that fineness of vision has to be traded for a wider perspective. Asia is vast and diverse on its own terms even when, as here, the perspective is limited to a fourfold division along the following lines: (1) the newly industrializing countries (NICs), namely, Hong Kong, Korea, Singapore, and Taiwan; (2) the four larger members of the Association of Southeast Asian Nations (ASEAN-4), namely, Indonesia, Malaysia, the Philippines, and Thailand; (3) the South Asian subcontinent of Bangladesh, India, Pakistan, Nepal, and Sri Lanka; and (4) China. A similar classification scheme can be conceived for Latin America, as suggested by Miguel Urrutia in his concluding remarks: (1) the large resource-rich countries, including Argentina, Brazil, and Mexico; (2) the small labor-abundant countries of El Salvador, Guatemala, Haiti, and Honduras; (3) the remaining countries of the South American continent and the Caribbean that are resource-rich but tend to have small markets, such as Bolivia, Chile, Colombia, Costa Rica, the Dominican Republic, Ecuador, Paraguay, Peru, Trinidad, and Venezuela; and (4) the small, highly urbanized economies of Barbados, Panama, and Uruguay. There are of course similarities within each subregion of Latin America and Asia, and possible lessons to be learned from comparisons between the subregions, but there are also obvious and major differences within each subregion and these need to be kept in mind.

In view of these observations, the task set for this volume is a difficult one. While differences must not be ignored, generalizations will need to be made if any comparison or contrast is to be made at all. One major question motivating several of the chapters of this volume is whether the differences in growth rates between Asia and Latin America have been more the result of domestic economic policies or of international events and conditions. The purpose of this Introduction is to focus attention on certain aspects of this comparative question and also to present some of the more significant comments and insights that were made during the discussions of the papers presented at the conference.

## Economic Growth Factors

A number of generalizations that describe and explain the differences in growth rates between Asia and Latin America have become quite common in academic and popular discussion. These generalizations are implicit in several of the chapters. The first is perhaps the most general of all.

GENERALIZATION 1: *In the late 1970s and through the 1980s, Asia has experienced rapid growth, while Latin America has stagnated.*

This is a broadly true statement and is reported by a number of authors in Part One of the book. Asian growth, however, has not been uniform but patchy. A "flying geese" pattern of development (see figure 3.3 in chapter 3) has been used by several Japanese economists (Akamatsu 1962a, 1962b; Kojima 1978) to describe Asian development as being smooth and harmonious, with one country following the next in producing and exporting simple labor-intensive products and then advancing to more complex industrial ones. While the flying geese pattern is a useful metaphor, there is probably much less symmetry in the pattern of Asian development than is suggested by the model. The economic performance of the Asian NICs over the past twenty-five years has indeed been spectacular, surpassing that of any other group of countries in modern times, and almost the same can be said of some countries in Southeast Asia such as Thailand. But the economic performance of other countries in Asia, especially the Philippines and the South Asian countries, has been less impressive. In fact, several Asian countries have experienced very small or negative growth, while some Latin American countries, including Colombia, have experienced respectable growth rates.

As early as the 1950s, however, it had seemed to many observers that some of the larger Latin American countries, in particular Brazil, Mexico, Argentina, and Venezuela, were poised for rapid long-term growth. Indeed, the term "NICs" was initially coined in reference to these Latin American countries more than to the Asian NICs, and most Latin American countries started with higher per capita incomes than are now found in Asia outside the NICs. As noted by Edmar Bacha in his paper (see chapter 2, this volume), if the Latin American economies had continued to grow rapidly, the relevant chapters in this book would have been reporting quite a different set of opinions about Latin America. Therefore, the basic question that arises is why the growth of Latin American countries slowed.

GENERALIZATION 2: *The Asian countries identified in the 1960s as potential NICs succeeded, but those so identified in Latin America did not.*

Among the numerous explanations of this differential growth is that the Asian NICs have been united by a quasi-Confucian ethic. In chapter 3 of this volume, Edward Chen argues that emphasis on a few Confucian values, such as loyalty, respect for elders, and a strong work ethic, was a key factor in the growth of the Asian NICs. This suggestion is similar to the religious and sociological explanations for the growth of the West in the last century. Certainly an observer is impressed with the continuation of traditional values in social and family life in many parts of Asia, continuation that may have contributed to the greater orderliness that is found there. This may be an important factor that has a bearing, for instance, on differences in industrial organization in Asia and the West. For example, it has been pointed out that the labor force of the Asian NICs exhibits more self-discipline than that of any other in the world economy. Yet the question of cultural influence is a complicated and technical one that needs to be (and is being) seriously addressed by cultural and political historians. It is not something on which economists can speak with comparative advantage.

Instead, the kind of explanation that the economist finds more appealing tends to be the following:

GENERALIZATION 3: *Asia has had more market-oriented and less-regulated economic policies than Latin America. There have been more incentives encouraging entrepreneurship and private initiative in Asia; there also has been greater confidence in and between the government and the private sector.*

This again is a broadly true statement that requires some qualification. The Asian NICs are well known for their policies emphasizing market- and private-sector development. At the same time, the policies of the Asian NICs (except Hong Kong's) are not laissez-faire policies, and in fact their governments do a great deal to determine the shape and direction of their economies' development. Chen proposes that this be called "neoclassical interventionism," since the policies adopted are based on neoclassical principles, with greater reliance on incentives and the market system. That is, the government intervenes, but only in a manner that—insofar as these policies are intended either to correct market distortions or achieve certain social goals—will facilitate the market system. The ASEAN-4 countries also have emphasized market-oriented policies, though less so than the Asian NICs.

On the other hand, the governments of the South Asian countries have traditionally intervened in every facet of the production process. Here the government, through its public enterprises, is a large producer of a wide range of goods. Several of these South Asian countries, like many Latin American ones, are in the process of easing regulations, but most are finding it a difficult task. How far, how fast, and in what order to liberalize are questions that must be further addressed. The task is made more difficult because in Latin America and South Asia, as Ryokichi Hirono, a discussant at the conference, pointed out, unlike in the NICs and the ASEAN-4 countries, there is a wariness and a mutual lack of confidence between the government and the private sector.

GENERALIZATION 4: *Asia has had more outward-looking trade and exchange-rate policies than Latin America.*

As noted by Somsak Tambunlertchai, a discussant at the conference, despite extensive government intervention, trade regimes in the NICs have generally been left to market forces. In fact, Hong Kong and Singapore are virtually free-trade economies, while the level of protection in Taiwan is also very low. Although tariff levels are somewhat higher in Korea, they are still generally lower than those of other developing countries. Further, protected industries in Korea were required to become competitive and begin exporting within a short period of time. This meant that efficiency and competition have been promoted rather than suppressed.

One reason the NICs moved against the conventional wisdom and toward outward-looking policies was that their small markets and lack of natural resources made import-substitution policies untenable. Unlike the resource-rich and larger countries in both Latin America and Asia, the NICs had few other options.

In contrast, most developing countries, including the Southeast Asian, South Asian, and Latin American countries, followed the economic wisdom of that time and allowed their industries to hide behind high tariff walls. This provided a quick spurt of growth that did not last once the domestic market was satiated. The large profits that were gained by inefficient domestic producers in a protected market invariably led to the creation of special-interest groups supporting the continuation of such policies. Because of the foreign exchange received from producing and exporting primary commodities, the ASEAN-4 and Latin American countries were able to sustain expensive import-substitution policies. However, such policies supported overvalued exchange rates, which discriminated against manufactured exports.

Further, commodity exporters were affected by the problem of booming sectors. With high commodity prices, other exporting industries were hurt by the appreciating domestic currencies. For example, the textile industry in Colombia went into crisis in the early 1980s despite efforts by the government to prevent revaluation of the domestic currency.

The ASEAN-4 countries, however, moved to reduce the bias against exports in the mid-1970s. Several of them depreciated their currencies and lowered overall levels of protection. Exports of manufactured goods boomed and helped cushion the effect of lower commodity prices in the 1980s.

More generally, there may have been a basic difference between parts of Asia and Latin America in their perceptions of export opportunities. For example, in Latin America the predominance of commodity exports and the low income elasticity of demand for commodities has generated more pessimism than has been the case in East or Southeast Asia. In contrast, despite the slower growth of world trade and the fact that the NICs and ASEAN-4 economies have faced at least as much, and possibly more, Western protectionism in the 1970s and 1980s than have Latin American economies, there seems to have been less "export pessimism" in Asia than in Latin America.

GENERALIZATION 5: *Asia has been more concerned with macroeconomic stability than Latin America, especially with respect to inflation and debt management.*

A few Asian countries have experienced repressed inflation and shortages and have not followed prudent borrowing or debt-management policies. Most of them, however, have adopted pragmatic policies and approaches with respect to debt management and inflationary expectations, in contrast to the less-restrained expenditure policies of Latin America. To this may be added the relatively higher rates of real saving in East and Southeast Asia than in Latin America. Furthermore, in contrast to many Latin American countries, saving rates have increased since 1970 in all East and Southeast Asian countries except the Philippines. Because of moderate levels of inflation, realistic interest rates, and the strong economic performance of the region, capital flight has not been a problem in Asia.

Augustine Tan, a discussant at the conference, pointed out that the nominal growth of the Latin American economies in the 1960s and 1970s was being financed by extensive borrowing, with the borrowed funds too often being used not for productive investment but to pay for public sector consumption. The financial sectors of the Latin American countries were flooded by a large supply of capital available for borrowing in the 1970s, and the low or even negative real interest rates signaled the Latin American countries to borrow more rather than to produce for export.

Moreover, while economists in Asia would agree that high rates of real inflation are inimical to real economic growth due to the uncertainties and unanticipated transfers that inflation causes, the same may not be true of Latin America. It was argued that, until only very recently, there has been relatively little consensus among Latin American economists and government officials with respect to economic policies, and that there has not been the same sense of direction in Latin America with respect to macroeconomic policy that is found in the NICs. However, because of the serious distortions caused by inflation and hyperinflation (despite indexation of wages and prices), there is emerging a growing consensus among Latin American economists on the importance of lower inflation rates to economic growth.

GENERALIZATION 6: *Efforts at regional cooperation succeed when they are not too ambitious; they should work to create trust and information capital.*

Latin America has the longest experience of regional cooperation beginning with the Central American Common Market (CACM) and the Latin American Free Trade Association (LAFTA) in the late 1950s and early 1960s. As the names suggest, these were ambitious attempts to form large markets with no tariff barriers. Asia has had a shorter history of regional cooperation. The Association of Southeast Asian Nations (ASEAN) was formed in 1967 without such ambitious goals. More recently, in 1985, the South Asian Association for Regional Cooperation (SAARC) was formed. These attempts at cooperation have taken different forms and have met with various degrees of success. In evaluating the success of regional cooperation efforts, the most important benefit that is often neglected as being too obvious is that regional cooperation contributes to the prevention of unnecessary war. For example, by reducing the prospect of war within Western Europe to zero, economic cooperation in Europe has contributed to the general welfare of the region. The same could be said for the cooperation schemes within ASEAN, and perhaps to a lesser extent for those in Latin America; but the same cannot be said as yet for South Asia, where tensions between India and Pakistan continue.

Efforts at regional cooperation can lead to more and better contacts, information, and channels of communication, all of which may reduce transaction costs and increase the stock of what may be called the "information capital" available to traders and potential traders. Such an invisible stock of trust or information capital can be very valuable. Bureaucracies may be needed to maintain this stock. While there is the danger that these new bureaucracies, once created, will develop lives of their own that are independent of their original purposes, the net gain may nevertheless be positive. Wars and civil wars destroy not only physical and human capital but this invisible and intangible kind of capital as well. For instance, with the breakup of the economic union in South Asia forty years ago, an invaluable stock of information capital was lost, and it is proving extremely difficult for SAARC to now rebuild that informational base. The same may be said with respect to Indochina, North and South Korea, and so on.

Attempts at integration often face the problem of intraregional trade expansion being limited by lack of complementarity in the export structures of the regional partners. Exports are often concentrated in primary products that are destined for Western markets. The question of how the structure of production can be expanded to allow for greater trade is central to most regional integration schemes. The Latin American experience clearly shows the problems of pursuing industrial programs of agreed-upon specialization, where regional production of certain goods is designated to selected countries. ASEAN's attempt at a regional industrial scheme also failed. Two major lessons that can be drawn from these experiences are the importance of a slow approach to integration as well as the need to maintain openness with the rest of the world.

Finally, two generalizations were voiced pertaining to the state of politics in Asia and Latin America.

GENERALIZATION 7: *Asia has had more political stability than Latin America.*

In the Asian countries, there have been few changes in government leadership in the past ten years and in some cases twenty years. For example, Lee Kuan Yew has been the leader of Singapore's government for almost thirty years, and Suharto governed Indonesia for more than twenty years.

In addition to the generally long tenure of political regimes in Asia, the economic policies followed have generally reflected a pragmatism on the part of the government that, typically, has extended into the next regime despite differences in political ideology. For example, even when political coups occurred in Thailand in the 1970s and Korea in the 1980s, economic policies remained basically unchanged.

GENERALIZATION 8: *Latin America has had more of a trend toward democratization than Asia.*

Of course there are major exceptions to this. The large and vibrant Indian democracy thrives as it has done for half a century, democratic institutions continue in Sri Lanka even in the midst of civil war, and the Philippines experienced an important democratic revolution only a few years ago. At the same time, dictatorships continue in some Latin American countries. Yet for a variety of reasons, the last decade has witnessed a broad trend toward political democratization in Latin America. While Latin American economists (of all persuasions) seem frank enough to be highly critical of many aspects of the management of economic policies in their part of the world, they take some pride in these recent political trends. Asian economists on the other hand are sometimes a little complacent and self-congratulatory with respect to the economic successes in their region, and they may need to move increasingly toward improvements in the nature of their political institutions.

Each of the eight generalizations given above contains an important element of truth (although the reader is reminded of the difficulties that are involved in making large-scale comparisons and contrasts). The development experiences of Asia and Latin America are likely to remain important subjects of academic and policy interest, and it is hoped that this volume will contribute to that discussion. While numerous questions clearly remain, the volume provides a foundation upon which further research into the development process and experiences of Asia and Latin America can be built.

# 1

# Economic Trends in Asia

This chapter describes the overall economic development of Asia (excluding Japan) in the 1970s and 1980s, and examines some of the major external and domestic factors that have contributed to it. An overall assessment is first presented, followed by an examination of groups of countries with common features: the Asian newly industrializing countries (NICs), the four larger members of the Association of Southeast Asian Nations (the ASEAN-4), and South Asia. China is treated separately. Countries for which data are not available—in particular Afghanistan, Cambodia, Laos, and Vietnam—have been excluded.

Asia's economic performance in the 1970s and 1980s has been remarkable. As compared to overall growth in gross domestic product (GDP) of about 5.0 percent in the 1960s, overall GDP growth increased by 6.5 percent in the 1970s and by 6.6 percent in the 1980s (Asian Development Bank 1987). Large countries such as China, India, and Indonesia have become self-sufficient in food grains, and the region has emerged as a major exporter of edible oils and several agricultural raw materials. The principal impetus to growth was provided by rapid growth in manufacturing, which in turn was greatly facilitated by a relatively favorable environment for exports, especially during the 1970s.

The structure of production has undergone major changes since 1970. Outside South Asia, the share of industrial production now exceeds that of agriculture in the total GDP of the Asian developing

countries (see table A.4 in the statistical appendix). Industrial production is becoming increasingly diversified, although in many countries
light industry based on the processing of domestic raw materials still
predominates. With some exceptions, the share of the service sector has
continued to expand, and in several countries this sector now accounts
for the largest share of GDP. Agriculture, however, continues to be the
major source of employment except in the NICs.

The efforts of many countries to maintain high growth rates in the
face of an adverse international environment contributed to growth in
external borrowing, the latter accelerating during the 1980s. Consequently, external public debt grew rapidly, particularly after the second
oil shock. In recent years, the debt service payments of several countries have been large, although all countries except the Philippines
have been able to meet their debt-service obligations. Thus debt service
is not a major concern in most of Asia. In fact, Asia is the only developing region where commercial banks continue to provide fresh loans
without any major support from the International Monetary Fund
(IMF) or the World Bank.

## The Newly Industrializing Countries

Since the beginning of the 1960s, the NICs (Hong Kong, South Korea
[hereafter Korea], Singapore, and Taiwan) have been the fastest-growing countries in Asia, and perhaps in the world. In the 1960s, their GDP
growth averaged more than 9.7 percent a year and in the 1970s between 8.0 and 9.0 percent a year (table A.2). However, their growth was
especially low from 1980 to 1985 because of the second oil price shock
and depressed demand for their exports in industrialized countries.
Singapore was the most adversely affected because, in addition to low
export demand, a government policy of high wages and escalating
rents led to the closure of many foreign firms. Since 1986, however,
these countries have again shown rapid growth, with Singapore averaging 9.0 percent and the other three NICs more than 10.0 percent.

This high growth in GDP has been accompanied by changes in the
structure of production in the NICs. Between 1970 and 1986, the share
of agriculture in GDP fell dramatically in Korea and Taiwan—representing only 12 percent and 6 percent, respectively, in 1986 (table
A.4). On the other hand, the share of industry has increased rapidly,
and in 1986 accounted for 42 percent of GDP in Korea and 55 percent

in Taiwan. The share of the service sector in both countries has remained stable at around 42 to 45 percent. In Hong Kong and Singapore there has been little change in the production structure since 1970. The service sector continues to account for about 60 percent of GDP, with industry accounting for the balance. The role of agriculture in both of these city-states is negligible.

With the dramatic fall in the share of agriculture in total GDP, the share of the labor force employed in agriculture has also shrunk (table 1.1). In 1986 agriculture accounted for 24 percent of the labor force in Korea, 17 percent in Taiwan, and only about 1 percent each in Hong Kong and Singapore. The industrial labor force has grown rapidly, and

### Table 1.1
### Employed Labor Force in Asian Countries, by Sector Share, 1970–86 (%)

| Country | 1970 Agriculture | Industry | Service | 1986 Agriculture | Industry | Service |
|---|---|---|---|---|---|---|
| **NICs** | | | | | | |
| Hong Kong[a] | 1.9 | 37.3 | 60.8 | 1.5 | 35.0 | 63.5 |
| Korea | 50.4 | 14.3 | 35.2 | 23.6 | 25.9 | 50.5 |
| Singapore | 3.4 | 22.3 | 74.3 | 0.9 | 25.7 | 73.4 |
| Taiwan | 35.4 | 22.0 | 42.7 | 17.0 | 34.2 | 48.7 |
| **ASEAN-4** | | | | | | |
| Indonesia[b] | 61.6 | 8.4 | 30.1 | 54.7 | 9.9 | 35.4 |
| Malaysia | 53.2 | 11.6 | 35.2 | 34.3 | 15.5 | 50.2 |
| Philippines[c] | 53.8 | 11.9 | 34.3 | 49.3 | 10.3 | 40.4 |
| Thailand[d] | 72.2 | 7.7 | 20.1 | 59.2 | 11.3 | 29.5 |
| **South Asia** | | | | | | |
| Bangladesh[e] | 73.9 | 6.8 | 19.3 | 64.0 | 8.5 | 27.6 |
| Burma[c] | 66.7 | 6.8 | 26.5 | 65.8 | 9.1 | 25.0 |
| India[f] | 73.0 | 12.0 | 15.0 | 70.0 | 13.0 | 17.0 |
| Nepal | na | na | na | na | na | na |
| Pakistan | 57.0 | 15.4 | 27.6 | 50.6 | 13.7 | 35.8 |
| Sri Lanka[g] | 50.4 | 1.5 | 40.0 | 43.5 | 10.8 | 43.7 |
| **Other Asia** | | | | | | |
| China[h] | 74.5 | 12.2 | 13.3 | 62.5 | 17.0 | 20.5 |

na = Not available.
a. 1971.
b. 1976 and 1985.
c. 1985.
d. 1972 and 1985.
e. 1973 and 1985.
f. 1970 and 1980.
g. 1971 and 1981.
h. 1977 and 1985.
SOURCE: Asian Development Bank, *Key Indicators of Developing Member Countries of ADB*, April 1984 and July 1987.

in 1986 accounted for 35 percent of the total labor force in Hong Kong, 34 percent in Taiwan, and 26 percent each in Korea and Singapore. The largest share of the labor force in all NICs was employed by the service sector.

Export-led industrial development has been the engine of growth in all of the NICs. The compounded annual growth in exports during the decade 1970–80 ranged from 23 percent in Hong Kong to 36 percent in Korea (table A.8). Imports also increased rapidly at a compounded annual rate, ranging from about 23 percent for Hong Kong to 29 percent for Taiwan during the same period (table A.9). But the growth in both exports and imports fell dramatically between 1980 and 1985. Growth in exports was slow because of reduced demand and increased barriers to imports in industrialized countries. Imports were drastically reduced so as not to strain foreign exchange resources.

It may be noted that investment in the NICs has been financed primarily by domestic saving (table A.5). In fact, domestic saving has exceeded investment, and the inflow of external resources has been only a fraction of the increase in the NICs' international reserves. Most of their foreign inflows have been in the form of direct investment. Thus reliance on external borrowing has been rather limited. The aftermath of the two oil shocks and efforts to expand heavy industry led Korea to borrow heavily from both official and commercial sources abroad. As a result, the country's total external debt increased rapidly to US$44 billion at the end of 1986 (table A.13). This became a matter of concern not only to the international lending community, but also to the Korean government.

Since 1986, the picture has changed dramatically. The impact of the devaluation of the U.S. dollar relative to the yen and the major European currencies has stimulated the NICs' exports greatly. Hong Kong and Korea, both of which had current account deficits until 1985, experienced growing surpluses in 1986 and 1987. The current account surplus of Hong Kong was US$4 billion in 1986 and US$10 billion in 1987, while the corresponding figures for Korea were US$5 billion and US$12 billion. Taiwan saw its current account surplus increase sharply from US$9.2 billion in 1985 to US$16 billion in 1986, and to $26 billion in 1987. Singapore was the only country among the NICs with its current account virtually in balance. It is worth noting that most of the NICs' surplus was from its trade with the United States. This is evidenced by the fact that in 1987 the United States had a trade deficit of

US$6 billion with Hong Kong, US$10 billion with Korea, US$2 billion with Singapore, and US$20 billion with Taiwan.

## The ASEAN-4

During the 1970s, the performance of the ASEAN-4 countries, or quasi-NICs (Indonesia, Malaysia, the Philippines, and Thailand), was quite impressive. The annual GDP growth rate of these countries during the period ranged from about 6 percent for the Philippines to 8 percent for Indonesia (table A.2). Although industrial production increased at a fairly high rate, the major stimulus to growth came from the excellent performance of the agricultural and mineral sectors. This situation, however, changed dramatically in all of these countries during the 1980s. Between 1980 and 1987 the average GDP growth rate of the ASEAN-4 was nearly half of that in the 1970s. This resulted from a combination of several factors that are discussed later.

The production structure in the ASEAN-4 has undergone significant change since 1970 (table A.4). With the exception of the Philippines, the share of agriculture in total output steadily declined between 1970 and 1986, while that of industry and services increased. In the Philippines, the sharp fall in industrial production since 1983 was responsible for the decline in the share of industry, which was accompanied by an increase in the share of agriculture. In Indonesia, the fall in the production and price of crude oil contributed to a reduction in the share of industry in recent years. Despite these adverse developments, the share of industry in total GDP in all the ASEAN-4 in 1986 greatly exceeded the share of agriculture. However, in all of these countries the service sector accounted for the largest share of GDP, ranging from 42 percent in Indonesia, Malaysia, and the Philippines to 53 percent in Thailand.

Although agriculture now accounts for less than a quarter of total GDP in most of the ASEAN-4, the proportion of labor employed in agriculture in 1986 ranged from 34 percent in Malaysia to 59 percent in Thailand (table 1.1). The share of total labor employed in industry has shown a modest increase since 1970, and in 1986 it ranged from some 10 percent in the Philippines and Indonesia to 16 percent in Malaysia. Except in Malaysia, agriculture continues to absorb the greatest amount of labor, followed by services and industry.

The rapid growth in the output and price of oil and other primary commodities greatly expanded the exports of the Southeast Asian countries during the 1970s (table A.8). The greatest increase was experienced by oil-exporting Indonesia (35 percent), while the smallest increase (19 percent) occurred in the Philippines. However, adverse external factors caused a serious setback in exports in these countries during the 1980s. Between 1980 and 1986, the value of these countries' total exports declined, although it recovered somewhat in 1987, with Thailand performing relatively better, with exports increasing by 8 percent in 1987.

The imports of the ASEAN-4 countries also increased at a rapid pace during the 1970s. However, the imports of Indonesia and Thailand increased much less than their exports, whereas the reverse was true in the Philippines, and in Malaysia growth of imports matched that of exports. In the 1980s these countries tried to maintain their imports in the face of falling exports, but as their debts mounted they were sometimes forced to cut back. This in turn adversely affected their investment and growth.

In the cases of Indonesia and Malaysia, the trade account is a poor measure of their current account positions. This is because of the large size of payments falling under services and remittances. For example, during the period 1970–80, Indonesia's external debt outstanding increased from US$3 billion to US$21 billion, while its trade surplus increased from US$0.1 billion to US$11 billion. The external debt outstanding of the ASEAN-4 countries taken together increased from US$6 billion in 1970 to US$52 billion in 1980. These countries borrowed heavily during the 1980s when their exports suffered a setback. As a result, their total external debt rose sharply to about US$106 billion by the end of 1986.

## South Asia

The South Asian countries are the poorest in Asia and have also registered the slowest economic growth (table A.2). In the 1970s real GDP increased by some 2 percent, 3 percent, and 5 percent per year in Nepal, India, and Sri Lanka, respectively—rates marginally below those of the 1960s. Bangladesh and Pakistan showed real GDP growth of 6 percent and 7 percent, respectively, over the same period. South Asian agricultural production in the 1970s barely kept pace with population growth, while industrial production increased by less than 5 percent per year. Per capita income increase has been relatively low and poverty remains widespread.

In the 1980s, South Asia has performed much better, with annual growth increasing during the period 1980–86 in all the countries except Bangladesh. Excellent performance of the agricultural sector is the major factor responsible for this improvement. For reasons discussed later, the industrial sector also performed better. However, the service sector showed the highest growth rate in practically all of the South Asian countries. In 1987, severe drought in several countries and floods in Bangladesh caused a major setback in South Asian economic growth.

The structure of production has changed rather slowly in most South Asian countries (table A.4). Agriculture continues to dominate the economies of Bangladesh, Burma, and Nepal. The share of agriculture has fallen significantly in Pakistan, India, and Sri Lanka. It is worth noting, however, that except for Sri Lanka the decline in the share of agriculture resulted largely from an increase in the share of the service sector rather than in that of the industrial sector.

Although its share in total GDP has fallen, agriculture is by far the largest source of employment in all South Asian countries, with its share ranging from 43.5 percent in Sri Lanka to nearly 70 percent in India (table 1.1). While the amount of employment provided by the industrial sector has remained relatively small, the amount provided by the service sector has grown steadily, with the latter becoming an important source of employment in all South Asian countries.

Until recently, trade promotion was not assigned high priority by the South Asian countries. Despite this, their overall exports increased at a fairly high annual rate during the 1970s. As table A.8 shows, the most rapid growth in exports was achieved by Pakistan (21 percent), while the lowest occurred in Nepal (7 percent). Imports, however, increased faster than exports. Half of this increase was accounted for by oil, while a large part of the balance consisted of manufactured goods and fertilizers. From 1980 to 1986 exports increased at an annual rate of between 1 percent and 10 percent, while imports showed virtually no growth (table A.9).

Because of the widening trade deficit in the earlier period, the net inflow of external resources into South Asian countries increased rapidly from US$1.4 billion in 1970 to US$6.1 billion in 1980. Thereafter, these inflows declined steadily but started to increase again in 1985; the year 1986 was the first year in which the net inflow exceeded the level attained in 1980. The total external debt of the South Asian countries increased from US$12 billion in 1970 to US$37 billion in 1980, and to US$63 billion in 1986. India accounted for more than half this debt. Since most of it was, at least until recently, on highly concessional terms, the debt-service burden of these countries has remained manageable (table A.14). The only exception is Burma, where the debt-service burden has reached 55 percent. This is due less to the size of its external debt than to falling exports caused by domestic capacity constraints and to the low prices of that country's principal exports.

## China

Despite political upheavals, the Chinese economy continued to grow at a satisfactory annual rate of 4 percent from 1960 to 1970. Growth in agricultural output of 2 percent barely kept pace with the increase in population during this period. Industrial production increased by 12.7 percent a year in real terms, with heavy industry increasing by 15.7 percent. However, the industrial sector was plagued by imbalances, bottlenecks, and shortages.

The results of the economic reforms launched in 1979 have gone beyond expectations. From 1980 to 1986, annual growth in GDP was almost 8 percent, and in 1987 real GDP growth exceeded 9 percent. While agricultural production grew by about 7 percent per year, industrial production increased by 11 percent. Within the industrial sector, the share of light industry steadily increased at the expense of heavy industry.

China's economy has undergone substantial structural transformation in recent years. The share of agriculture declined from 35 percent in 1970 to 31 percent by 1986, whereas that of the industrial sector increased from 41 percent to 46 percent during the same period (table A.4). The share of the services sector, which is relatively less developed than in other countries, declined from 24 percent in 1970 to 23 percent in 1986. Agriculture, however, still provides nearly two-thirds of total employment in China (table 1.1). It is also worth noting that while the share of the services sector in total GDP has declined, its share in total employment has increased. Industry still accounts for the smallest share of the labor force in China.

China's merchandise exports grew by 23 percent per year from 1970 to 1980. Growth has been particularly large since 1978, when the country began its open-door policy. Exports have increased from US$1.6 billion in 1970 to US$31.4 billion in 1986 (tables A.11a and A.11b). Crude oil and other raw materials now constitute about half of total exports. Light manufactures, including textiles, have also shown a substantial increase since 1978. Until 1984, imports nearly equaled exports but increased rapidly thereafter, so that the trade deficit increased sharply from US$1.1 billion in 1984 to US$15.2 billion in 1985 and US$12.0 billion in 1986 (table A.7). The government therefore adopted drastic measures to limit imports. These measures were quite successful and the trade deficit plummeted to US$3.7 billion in 1987.

China had virtually no external debt until 1978, and up to 1984 its annual borrowings were quite modest. Since then it has contracted large amounts of external debt through both official and commercial sources. By the end of 1986 its external debt had increased to US$22.0 billion. China has also encouraged direct foreign investment, most of it through joint ventures. During the period 1980–85, such investment amounted to US$3.4 billion, nearly two-thirds of which was from Hong Kong. China's debt-service burden remains small, and the government has adopted a cautious policy regarding future external borrowing.

## External Factors Affecting Development

The major external factors that have affected economic performance include (1) the international trading environment, (2) the two oil shocks, (3) technological change, (4) commodity prices, and (5) currency realignments. Apart from influencing each other at the international level, each of these factors directly or indirectly affects many macroeconomic variables in Asia itself. Hence it is difficult to measure separately their impact on these different variables in various countries.

The international trading environment has been a major factor shaping the export demand for commodities. This environment has been affected by the growth and structural transformation occurring in the industrialized countries and the trade policies pursued by them. Real growth in the countries belonging to the Organisation for Economic Co-operation and Development (OECD) averaged 3.4 percent per year during the period 1970–79 and fell to 2.1 percent during the period 1980–87. Accompanying this change was a major structural shift within the industrialized countries. During the period 1970–87, the share of manufacturing output in their GDP fell from 30 percent to 23 percent. Within the manufacturing sector, output shifted away from traditional raw material-intensive subsectors toward high technology and information-based products. All of these factors have contributed to depressed export demand for primary commodities from Asia.

Following the reduction of nontariff barriers to trade in the post–Second World War period, industrialized countries reduced tariffs on manufactured goods to negligible levels through successive rounds of multilateral trade negotiations. By the early 1970s, the world's trading environment was freer than at any time since the early 1900s (Hughes 1987).

High OECD growth rates accompanied by trade liberalization in the 1960s and early 1970s opened up markets for both primary and manufactured goods from Asia. The NICs responded by rapidly increasing their labor-intensive manufactured exports, while the ASEAN-4 increased their primary exports. These factors provided a major boost to both groups' economic growth during the early 1970s. Even the South Asian countries benefited from these trade policies, although to a lesser degree.

The mid-1970s and the 1980s witnessed limitations on the free movement of goods and services. Because of their slow economic growth and growing problem of unemployment, the industrialized countries began to limit the rate at which they were importing labor-intensive manufactured goods from developing countries, notably clothing, textiles, and footwear. These restrictions were tightened and extended to other items that affected the NICs as well as other countries such as India and Pakistan. The NICs nevertheless continued to account for a high proportion of total developing-country exports by diversifying, moving upmarket, and rapidly expanding into electronics, computers, machinery, and chemicals. Similar shifts in other countries occurred at a comparatively slow rate and, although these countries were less successful in achieving this restructuring, they have achieved in recent years some growth momentum.

In the 1970s, the industrialized countries also began to increase protection for their agricultural goods. The European Community (EC) imposed maximum barriers through its Common Agricultural Policy. Japan's agricultural policies have traditionally been protectionist, and the United States became increasingly protectionist as markets for agricultural products shrank. The primary exports of the ASEAN-4 were adversely affected by these policies in the industrialized countries. This caused serious problems in the ASEAN-4's balance of payments and debt service, which affected their investment and growth.

The favorable international trading environment of the 1970s was interrupted by the two oil shocks in 1973 and 1979. These led to major adjustments on the part of the non-oil-producing countries—adjustments that included restraint in consumption and investment, decreases in imports, increases in exports, changes in the production structure, and additional external financing. The pace of adjustment was rather quick during the 1970s, partly because of the relative stability of oil prices after 1974 and partly because of the rapid growth in exports achieved in the latter part of the 1970s. The high GDP growth in the industrialized countries noted above helped in this regard. Most countries increased domestic saving in order to keep dependence on external debt within manageable limits. Bangladesh, Nepal, and Sri Lanka were slow in restructuring their economies and, as a result, saving in these countries either remained stagnant or declined. In their effort to maintain growth momentum, they rapidly increased their dependence on external assistance.

The second oil shock affected non-oil-producing countries more than the first one because the increase in oil prices was far greater in absolute terms. In addition, and perhaps more importantly, the prolonged recession in the industrialized countries made it difficult to expand exports. Most borrowed heavily from official and commercial sources in the hope that the world economic environment would improve quickly and enable them to meet their growing debt-service liabilities. This hope was not realized.

The oil-exporting countries, Indonesia and Malaysia, were major beneficiaries of the increase in oil prices. Their export and tax revenues increased rapidly. This enabled them to embark on ambitious investment programs that contributed to sustained and rapid growth until 1984.

The recent fall in oil prices has benefited all non-oil-producing countries. The NICs have benefited the most because they are heavily dependent on imported energy. South Asian countries, which spend a large proportion of export earnings on oil imports, have also benefited considerably. Among the ASEAN-4 countries, the Philippines and Thailand have benefited, whereas Indonesia and Malaysia have been adversely affected. Indonesia, which depends on oil for nearly two-thirds of its exports and half of its revenues, has been severely affected.

In general, countries with diversified production structures and large ratios of domestic saving to total investment withstood the oil shocks better and responded faster to the new international environment. Korea among the NICs and India among the low-income countries illustrate this point well. The Korean case demonstrates that if accumulation of debt is accompanied by increased saving and exports, there is no cause for concern (Sachs 1981). The Indian one shows that external borrowing can be restrained by an increase in domestic saving. In contrast, the experience in Burma, the Philippines, and Sri Lanka shows that increased debt accompanied by falling saving ratios and stagnating exports can cause serious debt problems, even if the borrowing has been on highly concessional terms.

An important side effect of the two oil shocks in developed countries has been the heightened concern about the continued availability of material resources. Major studies carried out in the 1970s indicated the possibilities of scarcity emerging not merely for oil, but also for metals and several agricultural commodities. This spurred major technological change. Because of its effects on both demand and supply, technological change occurring in industrialized countries has strongly affected Asia. From the demand side, several dimensions are apparent. First, new materials have effected substitution away from traditional commodities. Plastics and fiber optics are replacing steel, copper, and aluminum. Second, high energy prices have led to a major emphasis on energy-saving technologies that have greatly reduced the demand for oil in industrialized countries. Third, demand for commodities has been reduced by material-saving technologies and by products that contain reduced amounts of primary inputs for the same quantity of final output, often with better quality. Finally, improved technologies for secondary recovery have also reduced the demand for primary output of numerous minerals and metals.

On the supply side, technological change has been the motivating force behind increases in productivity, thereby lowering costs of production. For example, world grain yields increased by 24 percent from 1975 to 1985, following a 31 percent rise during the preceding decade. The food self-sufficiency threshold achieved in some countries of South and Southeast Asia is attributable to the Green Revolution, particularly in regard to paddy and wheat. Similarly, new technology for producing palm oil has greatly increased the supply of edible oil and has contributed to sharply reduced world prices.

The two most significant technological innovations during the 1980s were microelectronics and biotechnology. Microelectronic technology consists of the development of complex, compact, and powerful integrated circuits that can be used in information processing. The technology has greatly reduced the unit cost of processing information and has therefore become technically and economically feasible for numerous subsectors of the economy and for small business units. From the point of view of the developing countries, the major export industries likely to be affected by microelectronic technology are the electronics industry itself and the clothing industry. Since technological progress will lead to factor intensity reversals in both of these industries, they will experience a shift from labor-intensive to capital-intensive production processes. The implication of this for the low-income countries in South and Southeast Asia is that they may incur a further loss in comparative advantage.

The recent developments in biotechnology, including genetic engineering, are important in three main areas: (1) chemical substances generated from genetically engineered organisms, (2) genetically engineered microorganisms, and (3) genetic engineering of plants and animals (Chen 1987). Since the full-fledged impact of the biotechnological revolution will probably not occur earlier than the beginning of the twenty-first century, it is difficult to assess its full impact on developing countries. There is, however, a danger that the developed countries that have ready access to these technologies will be able to produce agricultural commodities at low prices, thereby affecting the income of the agrarian economies of Asia and of other regions.

Since the beginning of this century the prices of primary commodities have shown a steady decline relative to the prices of manufactured goods (Grilli and Yan 1988). The buoyancy brought about by the high growth rates in the OECD countries was reflected in nonoil primary commodity prices during the first half of the 1970s. Following the first oil shock, nonoil primary commodity prices peaked in 1977. These developments helped the primary-commodity-exporting countries of South Asia and the ASEAN-4 to mitigate the impact of high oil prices on their balance-of-payments positions. However, slower growth rates in developed countries, low population growth, changes in consumer taste, and technological change emphasizing techniques for saving raw materials depressed the demand for primary products during the

1980s. The real prices of many primary products began falling in 1981, and the situation in this regard became precarious by 1985. By mid-1986, real commodity prices had reached their lowest level in this century (Kohli and Ali 1986). While real prices rose slightly in 1987, the outlook for a significant recovery in the medium term is not favorable. The severe decline in prices has not noticeably stimulated demand, nor has it caused a reduction in supply. Furthermore, despite excess capacity in most of the primary commodity subsectors, additional capacity is still coming on-stream. This problem is aggravated by the fact that the EC countries and the United States are generating large surpluses of several commodities because of heavy subsidies provided to farmers. As already pointed out, the share of primary inputs in the production process is declining, thereby delinking growth in the industrialized countries from commodity markets (Drucker 1986).

The sharp declines in commodity prices during the 1980s seriously affected the foreign exchange earnings of the commodity-exporting countries of South and Southeast Asia. They also aggravated debt-service problems and forced many countries to curtail investment drastically. Since commodity prices are projected to remain depressed, major structural adjustment will be needed by countries desiring to achieve satisfactory growth rates without encountering balance-of-payments difficulties. The situation is particularly difficult in the ASEAN-4 countries and several South Asian countries. The NICs have benefited from low commodity prices, and they are likely to benefit even more in the years to come.

The first oil shock was preceded by the breakdown of fixed exchange rates in 1973. The era of floating exchange rates has been marked by turbulence. The U.S. dollar depreciated from 1970 to 1980, appreciated sharply from 1981 to 1985, and collapsed in 1986 and 1987. From the point of view of demand for Asian exports, the high U.S. growth rate of GDP and U.S. dollar appreciation during the period 1983–85 worked in favor of the commodity-exporting countries but had the opposite effect on exporters of manufactured goods. In 1986 and 1987, the effects of the slowdown in the U.S. economy and the depreciation of the dollar on manufactured exports from Asia was more than offset by the appreciation of major non-U.S. currencies. This illustrates the difficulties associated with using a cause-and-effect relationship to describe the responses of Asian developing countries to changes in a single external factor. Despite this, it is pertinent to highlight some of the implications of this sharp appreciation. It also may be noted that most Asian currencies have remained stable relative to the U.S. dollar. While Indonesia's currency has in fact depreciated against it, the currencies of Korea, Singapore, and Taiwan have appreciated moderately but have depreciated relative to other major currencies.

The appreciation of the Japanese yen and other currencies that led to the depreciation of real trade-weighted exchange rates has benefited Asia. The competitiveness of the NICs, which export a range of low- to high-technology goods, has greatly increased during the past two years (Lee et al. 1986). Bangladesh, India, and Pakistan, which export manufactured goods, have also gained from these changes because of the greater competitiveness of their labor-intensive and low-technology manufactured exports. However, the ASEAN-4, as well as Nepal and Sri Lanka, whose exports are predominantly primary goods, have been disadvantaged by the appreciation of the yen because their marginal gains have been offset by higher-cost imports. Thailand is an exception because of its diversified structure of production and exports.

As the competitiveness of Asian developing countries' exports vis-à-vis Japanese exports improves as a result of the appreciation of the yen, it becomes increasingly difficult for Japanese producers to expand exports. Therefore, many Japanese investors are investing abroad. The pressure to relocate is particularly strong on Japanese producers engaged in labor-intensive and low value-added products. It should be noted, however, that direct foreign investment (DFI) levels are not determined by production cost alone. Considerations such as the host country's political stability and absorptive capacity and its policies toward DFI also play an important role. Although there has been an upsurge in Japanese direct foreign investment in the NICs and the ASEAN-4 during 1986 and 1987, it is too early to assess the full impact of the appreciation of the yen on Japanese investment abroad (table A.16).

Finally, the impact of a stronger yen on external debt needs to be evaluated. Appreciation of the yen increases the cost (in terms of domestic goods) of servicing yen-denominated debt. It also increases the external debt outstanding denominated in dollars. The appreciation of other currencies has a similar impact. The extent of the impact depends largely on the currency composition of external debt. While most debt is dollar-denominated, the currency composition of external debt among Asian developing countries does vary. About a quarter of Indonesia's and Thailand's public long-term debt, and more than 15 percent of the public long-term debt of Bangladesh, Malaysia, and the

Philippines, is denominated in yen. As far as external debt is concerned, these countries were the major losers in the recent currency realignments.

It appears that on balance the NICs and some South Asian countries benefited from the appreciation of the yen and other currencies because the positive impact on their exports was greater than the negative impact on their debt-service burdens. The position of the ASEAN-4 is less clear. However, if large amounts of Japanese direct investment occurs in these countries, as appears likely, it could have a long-term positive influence on their trade and growth.

## Internal Factors in Development

Differences in growth rates in various countries at a similar stage of development suggest that domestic policies are critical in determining the pace and pattern of economic growth. At the end of the Second World War, most Asian countries were quite poor and differences in the levels of their per capita incomes were quite small. Yet because of differences in domestic policies, some of these countries are now among the most dynamic in the world, while others remain very poor.

The development strategies pursued have varied widely. China, India, and other countries in South Asia adopted what has been termed an "inward-looking" development strategy. This assigns a major role to the public sector in development planning, the justification for this being "market failure." The rationale for such intervention in these countries was the superior coordinating ability of the state. The development of heavy industry was emphasized because it was considered basic to the growth of the industrial sector, which was assigned the highest priority. A pessimistic view was taken of the possibilities for promoting exports and for transforming domestic saving into capital goods through trade.

In sharp contrast, the NICs adopted an "outward-looking" development strategy. Since these countries have limited raw material resources and domestic markets, an export-oriented strategy has been the most appropriate one for them to follow. It is worth noting that while these countries pursued a strategy of export-led growth, strict controls were imposed on imports, and the role of the state was very important in investment and in directing domestic production. It is only recently (and partly because of pressure from the United States) that these countries, especially Korea and Taiwan, have begun to relax restrictions on imports.

The inward-looking development strategy has come under heavy criticism in recent years. This is partly because of the excellent performance of the NICs, which have pursued outward-looking development strategies, and partly because of the inefficiencies in production that have occurred in countries that pursued inward-looking strategies. In practically all countries, state intervention in pricing, production, and investment is on the decline. While this is particularly true in the NICs and the ASEAN-4, some progress has also been made in China and in South Asia. Trade promotion is receiving attention in all countries, not merely as a means of avoiding bottlenecks in domestic production, but also for achieving greater self-reliance in economic growth.

In the 1960s almost all governments played a major role in total investment and in sectoral allocation of resources. In Bangladesh, Pakistan, and Sri Lanka many private sector enterprises were nationalized. In other countries the governments assumed a major role on the grounds that the private sector was either incapable of or not interested in setting up industries that they considered of national importance. Even in countries such as Korea, Malaysia, and Indonesia, the public sector continued to play a large role in many sectors of the economy. In the past decade, there has been a significant reduction in the role of the public sector in investment, especially in the industrial sector. In some countries the changes took place fairly early, while in others they were late in coming. This was primarily because, with some notable exceptions, public sector enterprises in all countries had performed poorly and had in fact become a major burden on the exchequer.

In countries such as Thailand the government greatly reduced its involvement in the manufacturing sector in the early 1970s, while Bangladesh and Pakistan denationalized a large number of companies in the late 1970s and early 1980s. It is worth noting that in the NICs, whose performance in terms of overall growth has been outstanding for nearly three decades, the role of the public sector is the smallest. Excellent performance of the private industrial sector has been largely responsible for the rapid development in these countries. On the other hand, the public sector enterprises in the South Asian countries that have absorbed nearly half of total investment have performed poorly. This fact explains much of their unsatisfactory record in terms of domestic saving and overall growth.

In the South Asian countries all development expenditures are now financed by borrowed funds, whereas in the ASEAN-4 countries government saving is shrinking steadily (Kohli 1987). Unless loss-making enterprises in the public sector are either closed down or transferred to the private sector, this situation is likely to get worse. Shortages of resources are also forcing these governments to reduce the involvement of the public sector in total investment, especially in the industrial sector.

Just as the role of the private sector in total investment needs to be expanded, the performance of public sector enterprises needs to be improved. This issue is receiving growing attention not only in the mixed economies of South and Southeast Asia, but also in the socialist economies such as China and Burma. Various measures are under consideration or are being implemented to achieve this objective. They include allotting greater responsibility and autonomy to enterprises in determining output mix, labor and price policies, appointment of private entrepreneurs to run enterprises, and leasing of public enterprises to the private sector. While there are some noticeable improvements in efficiency resulting from these new policies, much more needs to be done to raise the efficiency and productivity of the public sector enterprises in most countries.

More recently, there has been a strong tendency to privatize public sector enterprises, particularly those that are incurring losses. This is especially true in the ASEAN-4 countries. Many of the South Asian countries have also declared their intention to privatize such enterprises, although progress in this direction has been slow. This is not to suggest that the government has no role to play in promoting industrial development. The experience of the NICs has shown that the government has an important role in providing an environment congenial to private investment, as well as proper fiscal incentives, labor laws, and credit policies. Further, an adequate workforce and infrastructure should be made available for producing and transporting goods. Clearly, investment in such public goods is most properly made by the government.

Price controls have been used by many countries, including Korea and Thailand, to varying degrees for several decades. They have generally been associated with rationing controlled commodities. Their main objective has been to ensure the availability of scarce essential commodities to the poorer segments of society and to contain inflationary pressures. Their use has been most extensive in the South Asian countries where some price controls are still in force today. While the objectives of price controls are laudable, rarely are price controls successful in achieving them. Artificially low prices of goods and services have led to reduced profits, poor maintenance, and curtailed output, thereby aggravating supply problems. They have also led to hoarding, black marketeering, and quality decline, hurting the very people they are intended to protect. Low prices of agricultural outputs and inputs also tend to lead to subsidies for the producers, which in turn impose a burden on the national budget.

In recent years price controls, because of problems associated with implementing them effectively, and because of the economic cost involved, have been abolished or drastically reduced in most Asian developing countries. The NICs have practically no price controls in force now; prices are determined entirely by the market. Price controls have also been greatly reduced in the ASEAN-4, although some subsidy on fertilizers still remains in a small number of countries. In the South Asian countries, price controls on most manufactured goods have been abolished. As a result, the output of erstwhile controlled commodities has expanded. While the scale of price controls on food and fertilizer has been reduced, they still impose a heavy burden on the national budget in most South Asian countries. There is an urgent need to examine the possibility of reducing these subsidies so that greater resources can be made available for development.

Trade and exchange rate policies have had an important bearing on Asian growth. Rapid expansion of trade helps countries increase domestic output. It also provides foreign exchange for importing capital goods and raw materials, which are necessary for expanding domestic production. At first, most countries adopted protectionist policies to achieve rapid industrial and economic growth (except Hong Kong and Singapore). Over the years this has significantly changed.

The resource-poor NICs were the first to recognize the importance of liberal trade policies in ensuring efficiency and productivity. Timely adjustments in their exchange rates also kept their rapidly growing industries competitive in the international market. Korea and Taiwan, however, pursued dualistic policies. While all possible measures, including an assured and duty-free supply of raw materials and concessional interest rates on loans, were taken by these countries to promote exports, the domestic market was kept relatively protected from imports (Rhee 1985). In recent years, however, because of external pressure and rapidly expanding trade surpluses, these countries have begun to liberalize imports.

In the South and Southeast Asian countries, such developments have been gradual. An important change has been the replacement of quantitative controls with tariffs. As part of their agreement with the IMF, some of the countries also reduced import duties and simplified their tariff structures so as to make their industrial production more efficient and competitive. Unfortunately, these reforms were generally introduced at a time when world prices of primary commodities were falling rapidly. As a result, the reforms did not achieve the intended objective and the reform process was itself slowed down. Greater success has been achieved in promoting exports through provision of incentives. These incentives include drawbacks of export or excise duties, export credit, and establishment of quality control standards. However, high import duties in many countries still make the domestic market more attractive than the export market. The quality of these export products remains generally low, and there have been no incentives to improve it. For this reason many industries have not kept up with technological advances abroad, resulting in the decrease of their total exports in recent years. A more vigorous effort at expanding exports will be necessary in the future if the Asian countries are to sustain the pace of development without risking external debt problems.

Devaluation of domestic currency generally improves a country's trade balance by making domestic products more competitive with imports and making domestic products cheaper in the international market. However, analysis of real effective exchange rates shows that, during the 1970s and early 1980s, the exchange rates of a majority of large countries in Asia appreciated relative to their major trading partners (Lee 1987), the exceptions being Indonesia and Pakistan. It is only in recent years that other countries—Malaysia, Korea, and Thailand—have depreciated their currencies in the wake of slow export growth. The impact of this depreciation is evident in the growth of their exports and smaller current account deficits.

Generally, Asian countries that have high domestic saving rates are also the ones that have been able to achieve high economic growth. The NICs' record in mobilizing domestic resources has been impressive (table A.5). This has also been true of the ASEAN-4, although during the 1980s their saving rates fell because of low commodity prices. The poor growth performance of the South Asian countries is due largely to their low domestic saving rates. This has also made these countries

ace, which potentially could lead
though external factors do influ-
factors are of crucial importance
of individual countries. In most
significantly contribute to overall
vestment is generally quite large.
ncipal source of domestic saving.
is are of primary importance, and
g have a major role to play in the
ies.

 be the primary factor in mobiliz-
t financial deepening and positive
ence on the overall saving perfor-
Asian Development Bank (1985) has
nd increased access to deposit-tak-
g directly, even though this effect is
ments in financial intermediation
cy with which investible funds are

An estimate of the level of financial deepening and real interest rates is provided in table 1.2. Financial deepening is defined here as the ratio of M2 (currency and all bank deposits) to GDP. With some exceptions, countries with high domestic saving rates have more developed financial systems. The main exceptions are Korea, which shows a relatively low level of financial deepening, and Pakistan, which shows a comparatively developed financial sector relative to its domestic saving.

Although financial deepening has taken place in most of the countries, there is still considerable scope for improving the efficiency of their financial sectors and for promoting financial development, especially in rural areas. Excessive bureaucratic controls on the allocation of funds, as well as low-interest loans granted to preferred sectors (including government borrowing), reduce the efficiency of resource use and breed corruption. Thus, there is growing pressure for liberalization of the financial sector in Asian developing countries.

While some countries have to a great extent liberalized their financial sectors, others still have a long way to go. The need is particularly urgent in South Asia, where household saving is generally low. Rural saving could be greatly expanded if deposit-taking institutions that cater to local conditions and needs are established. It is not so much the

**Table 1.2**
**Selected Financial Indicators for Asian Countries, 1970–86 (%)**

| Country | M2[a]/GDP 1970–79 | M2[a]/GDP 1980–86 | Real Deposit Rate[b] 1970–79 | Real Deposit Rate[b] 1980–86 | Inflation Rate[c] 1970–79 | Inflation Rate[c] 1980–86 |
|---|---|---|---|---|---|---|
| **NICs** | | | | | | |
| Hong Kong | 81.0 | 118.2 | −2.1[d] | −0.3 | 7.9 | 9.2 |
| Korea | 32.7 | 36.4 | 0.4 | 3.3 | 15.2 | 9.7 |
| Singapore | 61.6 | 70.4 | 0.8 | 1.2 | 5.9 | 6.7 |
| Taiwan | 55.5 | 89.0 | 2.0 | 3.7 | 9.5 | 5.7 |
| **ASEAN–4** | | | | | | |
| Indonesia | 14.9 | 20.5 | −0.1 | 1.9 | 17.3 | 10.4 |
| Malaysia | 41.8 | 60.5 | 1.4 | 4.5 | 5.5 | 4.4 |
| Philippines | 19.9 | 21.9 | −3.6 | −3.1 | 14.6 | 18.0 |
| Thailand | 35.3 | 48.5 | 0.1 | 5.7 | 8.0 | 6.6 |
| **South Asia** | | | | | | |
| Bangladesh | 17.7[e] | 24.5 | −11.6[d] | 1.2 | 19.7 | 12.0 |
| Burma | 23.8 | 31.6 | — | — | 10.9 | 4.7 |
| India | 30.6 | 43.5 | −0.0 | −1.4 | 7.4 | 9.5 |
| Nepal | 15.8 | 27.5 | 2.9 | 1.0 | 7.8 | 11.4 |
| Pakistan | 41.9 | 41.0 | −3.3 | 1.3[f] | 12.0 | 7.4 |
| Sri Lanka | 23.7 | 30.8 | 1.3 | 3.8 | 6.9 | 13.6 |
| **Other Asia** | | | | | | |
| China | 27.6[g] | 45.8 | — | 0.4[h] | 0.5 | 5.1 |

Dashed cells indicate not applicable.
a. Broad measure of money consisting of currency and demand deposits, plus time, savings, and foreign deposits of residents.
b. $([100 + r] / [100 + P]) - 1$, where r is nominal 12-month deposit rate and P is inflation rate.
c. Percent change in consumer price index.
d. 1972–79.
e. 1974–79.
f. 1980–83.
g. 1977–79.
h. 1983–85.
SOURCES: Asian Development Bank, *Key Indicators of Developing Member Countries of ADB*, July 1987; International Monetary Fund, *International Financial Statistics Yearbook 1987*; World Bank, *World Tables 1987*; country sources.

cost of capital but the availability of credit with a minimum of red tape and delay that is crucial to encouraging rural borrowers. Depositors should also be assured of the safety of their deposits and be given a reasonable rate of return on them.

The wide variance in saving rates in Asian countries cannot be fully explained by the differences in the financial and monetary policies pursued by these countries. Thus a thorough analysis of the various economic factors affecting saving performance is required if we are to understand these differences. The impact of other factors such as the saving habits of households, political stability, and social and cultural factors in promoting saving also needs to be examined.

In recent years there has been a growing recognition of the importance of human resource development and technological capability in achieving sustained economic growth. As long as agriculture was the main source of economic growth, such factors were not considered to be of great importance. However, with the expanding role of the industrial sector, their importance is being recognized. It is now well accepted that the economic miracle of Japan and the NICs is to a large extent the result of a well-educated, dedicated, and motivated labor force and capable management that greatly add to the level of labor productivity in these countries.

In many countries in South and Southeast Asia, projects are delayed and cost overruns occur because of shortages of skilled labor and management deficiencies. The low quality of production and maintenance of existing assets can also be explained by the poor quality of the labor force. Low productivity of labor has been an important factor in the slow rate of economic growth relative to the level of investment in most South and Southeast Asian countries. To ensure sustained growth, these countries must modernize their educational systems and upgrade their social overhead capital and institutions. In the NICs, the literacy rate was as high as 65 percent some thirty years ago. This is much higher than today's literacy rates in most South and some Southeast Asian countries. India, which is reported to have the world's third largest technically qualified labor force, has a literacy rate of only 36 percent. The literacy rates in Bangladesh and Pakistan are even lower at 26 percent and 24 percent, respectively.

Human resource development is also vital in achieving scientific and technological progress, which is the basis of sustained growth in a rapidly changing world. The great success achieved by many developing countries in food production during the past two decades is primarily a result of quick adoption, adaptation, and diffusion of technology generated by international research institutions. However, as the countries' economic base shifts from agrarian to industrial, technological development becomes more important.

Outside the NICs, investment in technological development has been minimal. Advance in technology has been assigned a low priority, and there is no unified planning procedure for technology in most Asian developing countries. Technological goals are not incorporated into the design, formulation, appraisal monitoring, and evaluation of projects. Equally important is the fact that while scarce resources are spent in countries like India and Pakistan on institutions that do research and development (R & D), there has been very limited success in commercializing the technology produced by them. The major weaknesses of these institutions are: (1) lack of links with productive and knowledge sectors, (2) lack of links with the various R & D institutions engaged in similar activities, (3) modeling of organization and operation after government departments, and (4) greater emphasis on research (producing papers) than on development. Consequently, most R & D efforts by these countries have proven to be inappropriate or unproductive (Kohli and Ali 1986).

In order to sustain long-term industrial development, the Asian developing countries must define their technological plans, policies and priorities, create an environment conducive to the development of science and technology, and devote adequate resources to R & D in the areas selected for emphasis. The infrastructure necessary for the development, production, and diffusion of technology must also be identified and provided.

The most immediate constraint on technological development is a shortage of qualified people. Technological development requires a large base of highly qualified scientists and engineers, and an even larger base of technical staff. This would require major changes in the education system in many countries.

## Looking Ahead

The future development of Asia will depend greatly on the performance of the developed world. Most medium-term forecasts for the world economy indicate that production and trade in the industrialized world will grow at a slow pace—slower than during the past two decades. In the industrialized countries, consumer tastes are shifting from low-technology to high-technology products, and from resource-intensive to knowledge-intensive goods and services. These changes, together with demographic factors, have caused demand for and prices of primary commodities to slacken. The trend is likely to continue and may even accelerate in the developed world. Asia will thus have to change its production structure to cope with these developments.

The recent large current account surpluses of Japan and the NICs have been attributed to the massive annual trade deficits of the United States, which increased from US$36 billion in 1980 to US$170 billion in 1986. Such large deficits cannot continue for long. The NICs will either have to increase their imports from the United States or greatly reduce the growth in their exports to the United States. The latter appears more likely because of the slower growth in GDP anticipated in the United States. The projected slower growth in the EC will also adversely affect exports from the Asian developing countries.

In view of the projected developments in the world economy, it will be difficult for the NICs to maintain their recent high growth rates as exporters. Increased wages and pressure to revalue their currencies and to open up their markets will also affect their exports. The NICs are likely to respond to these changes by diversifying their products and markets and moving upmarket into higher value-added and more technology-intensive industries. Their success will, however, greatly depend on their capacity to keep up with changing technologies. At the same time, the NICs may have to adopt a more balanced growth strategy in which increasing the income of both the rural and the urban labor force will receive as much attention as export promotion efforts. In general, the NICs are likely to achieve a fairly high growth rate, but below that achieved in the 1970s or during the mid-1980s.

Since the prospects for commodity prices are not very promising, the ASEAN-4 will have to reduce their dependence on the export of these goods. These countries have already recognized this and have embarked on structural adjustment programs aimed at improving overall economic efficiency and diversifying their economies. Prospects for the export of light manufactured goods are bright and should improve further with the market-oriented trade and domestic liberalization policies now being introduced and expanded. Even better prospects should be in store if these countries can continue to attract DFI and thereby expedite the transfer of modern technology and management systems. In general, the ASEAN-4 are expected to achieve a higher growth rate than in the recent past but below that attained in the 1970s.

The performance of the agricultural sector will continue to be a major factor in the overall growth of South Asian countries. Apart from continuing their efforts at increasing food production to meet their expanding needs, they will have to diversify their agricultural sector to provide employment and income to their growing rural populations. At the same time, industrial production will have to be substantially increased. The success of these structural changes will depend on the availability of human and capital resources and on a policy environment that calls for greatly increased domestic resource mobilization efforts, expansion of education and training facilities, and other measures for enhancing the productivity of resources. For instance, the improved performance of public sector enterprises and a policy environment conducive to private sector development will be important for increasing productivity. If these policies and programs are adopted, South Asian countries should be able to sustain the GDP growth rate already achieved by them during the 1980s.

In China, economic reforms under way in the late 1980s should enable the country to maintain the rapid growth achieved since 1979, because the productivity improvements achieved in the rural economy are now spreading to the urban areas. However, large investments will be required to improve the quality and competitiveness of China's products in the world market. With these improvements, China should be able to continue to expand its exports. China will also provide a growing market for the high-technology equipment and machinery that will be required for modernizing its industry and socioeconomic infrastructure.

In summary, developing Asia will continue to experience healthy growth in the years to come, and the differences in growth among country groups are likely to narrow. The national policies regarding economic development and trade promotion in Asia are also likely to converge. Because of the growing shortage of budgetary resources and the poor performance of public sector enterprises, the role of the public sector in direct investment is likely to decline in South and Southeast Asian countries, and that of the private sector is likely to increase. Their governments will, however, continue to play an important role in providing economic and social infrastructure and in creating a policy environment conducive to investment. With regard to trade, a more balanced approach with a distinct outward orientation is likely to emerge. Slower growth in the industrial countries will require the NICs to adopt a strategy under which export promotion and national welfare are given equal attention. At the same time, the heavily indebted ASEAN-4 countries and the inward-looking South Asian countries will have to increase exports to finance their rising import requirements and to meet debt-service obligations. Success in this regard will depend crucially on the flexibility with which domestic policies are pursued.

# 2

*Edmar L. Bacha*

# Economic Trends in Latin America

This chapter might have been about Latin America's economic growth. For the most part, however, Latin America has not grown since the beginning of the 1980s. Moreover, its short-term economic prospects do not suggest that the end of economic stagnation is in sight. What follows is thus a study more of the stagnation than of the growth of Latin America. It reviews the postwar economic record of the region, comparing both the industrialized countries and other major regions with the middle-income developing economies of the Asia-Pacific region and Southern Europe. The debt crisis, external shocks, and domestic adjustments are briefly discussed. Some of the structural maladies of the Latin American economies, which seem to underlie both their lackluster economic performance as well as their lethargic response to the recent debt crisis, are discussed as well. The chapter concludes with a brief discussion of the changes in economic policies and institutions that seem to be needed to prevent stagnation from becoming a permanent feature of the Latin American economic landscape.

## The Postwar Economic Record

As table 2.1 shows, when compared with that of other middle-income developing economies, Latin America's economic development since the Second World War has not been very satisfactory. First, although national saving rates have traditionally been relatively high in Latin America, marginal saving increased much faster in the Asia-Pacific region. Second, incremental capital-output ratios, although somewhat lower than in Southern Europe, have been much higher in Latin America than in Asia. In spite of the relative abundance of natural resources

Table 2.1
**Comparative Macroeconomic Record for Latin America and Other Regions: Selected Variables and Years, 1950–85 (%)**

**Average National Saving Ratios[a]**

| Region[b] | 1960 | 1970 | 1981 |
|---|---|---|---|
| Latin America & the Caribbean | 19.4 | 20.4 | 19.5 |
| Southern Europe | 18.6 | 20.6 | 18.8 |
| Asia-Pacific | 10.3 | 18.0 | 25.7 |
| Industrial Market Economies | 23.2 | 25.0 | 22.0 |

**Incremental Capital-Output Ratios[c]**

| Region[b] | 1960–65 | 1965–70 | 1970–81 |
|---|---|---|---|
| Latin America & the Caribbean | 3.6 | 3.2 | 3.6 |
| Southern Europe | 3.7 | 3.5 | 5.4 |
| Asia-Pacific | 2.4 | 2.4 | 3.2 |
| Industrial Market Economies | 4.2 | 5.2 | 7.9 |

**Export and Manufacturing Ratios**

| Region[b] | Share of Manufacturing in GDP at Factor Costs, Excluding Services<br>1981 | Share of Manufactures in Total Merchandise Exports<br>1980 | Share of Exports of Goods and NFS in GDP at Market Prices<br>1980 |
|---|---|---|---|
| Latin America & the Caribbean | 43.9 | 22.2 | 16.9 |
| Southern Europe | 50.5 | 65.3 | 22.0 |
| Asia-Pacific | 47.2 | 47.0 | 47.2 |
| Industrial Market Economies | 53.8 | 73.6 | 19.8 |

*Continued on following page*

**Table 2.1 Continued**

**Comparative GDP Growth Rates**
(average annual real growth rates in percent)

| Region[b] | 1950–65 | | 1965–81 | | 1981–85 | |
|---|---|---|---|---|---|---|
| | Total | Per capita | Total | Per capita | Total | Per capita |
| Latin America & the Caribbean | 4.9 | 1.9 | 5.5 | 2.9 | 1.4 | −0.8 |
| Southern Europe | 6.2 | 4.4 | 5.6 | 3.9 | 2.5 | 1.3 |
| Asia-Pacific | 5.4 | 2.8 | 8.0 | 5.6 | 4.8 | 2.7 |
| Industrial Market Economies | 4.6 | 3.3 | 3.6 | 2.8 | 2.8 | 2.2 |

a. Gross national savings (excluding net current transfers from abroad), expressed as a percentage of gross national product at current market prices.
b. The following are the countries included in each region:
*Latin America and the Caribbean*: Antigua and Barbuda, Argentina, Bahamas, Barbados, Belize, Bermuda, Bolivia, Brazil, Ecuador, El Salvador, French Guiana, Grenada, Guadeloupe, Guatemala, Guyana, Haiti, Honduras, Jamaica, Martinique, Mexico, Netherlands Antilles, Nicaragua, Panama, Paraguay, Peru, Puerto Rico, St. Christopher & Nevis, St. Lucia, St. Vincent & the Grenadines, Suriname, Trinidad and Tobago, Uruguay, Venezuela, and Virgin Islands (U.S.).
*Southern Europe*: Cyprus, Gibraltar, Greece, Israel, Malta, Portugal, Turkey, and Yugoslavia.
*Asia and the Pacific*: American Samoa, Fiji, French Polynesia, Guam, Hong Kong, Indonesia, Kampuchea, Kiribati, North Korea, Laos, Macao, Malaysia, Mongolia, New Caledonia, Papua New Guinea, Philippines, Singapore, Solomon Islands, Thailand, Tonga, Territory of the Pacific Islands, Vanuatu, Vietnam, and Western Samoa.
*Industrial Market Economies*: Australia, Austria, Belgium, Canada, Denmark, Finland, France, Germany, Iceland, Ireland, Italy, Japan, Luxembourg, Netherlands, New Zealand, Norway, Spain, Sweden, Switzerland, United Kingdom, and the United States.
c. Calculated as the sum of the gross domestic fixed investment from the first year of the period to the year preceding the ending year, divided by the change in GDP over the period (both at constant prices). Since the total of fixed investment prior to 1970 is not available for Latin American countries, gross domestic investment was used for the periods 1960–65 and 1965–70.
SOURCE: World Bank, *World Tables*, 3d ed. (1983), and private communication.

in Latin America, the GDP growth rate is much lower there than in the Asia-Pacific region at the same level of investment. Third, exports continue to be excessively concentrated in a small number of primary products despite the high level of industrialization on the continent. In fact, although by the early 1980s manufacturing was already responsible for 43.9 percent of GDP excluding services, its share in total merchandise exports was only 22.2 percent. Import substitution failed to develop into export-oriented industrialization as markedly as in other middle-income developing economies. For example, the share of manufacturing in GDP in Asia and the Pacific was not much higher than that of Latin America but the share of manufactures in merchandise exports in Asia and the Pacific was more than twice as large as that in Latin America (47 percent). In Southern Europe, the share of manufacturing in GDP was 50.5 percent, and its share in merchandise exports was 65.3 percent. It is the inward orientation of Latin American industry, rather than the degree of industrialization or the overall degree of openness, that strongly contrasts with the experience of Southern Europe and the industrial market economies. The consequence of this inward orientation of industry has been to make the share of total exports in Latin America's GDP the lowest of the four groups of countries (table 2.1).

Furthermore, income distribution has remained uneven, especially in countries with a deeply rooted colonial tradition based in part on the subjugation of indigenous cultures or the importation of slave labor, as in Peru, Brazil, or Mexico. The contrast with other developing countries can readily be seen. Household income shares of the poorest 40 percent in the 15 percent range are the rule in Asia and Southern Europe but the exception in Latin America (table A.17). What is exceptional in the former two regions—household income shares of the poorest 40 percent in the 15 percent range—is the rule in Latin America. The trickle-down approach has failed to work in the region as well as it seems to have elsewhere. Finally, inflation rates in Latin America have traditionally been among the highest in the world (International Monetary Fund 1988). Although the tolerance for inflation may vary across regions, price instability denotes a major malfunction of Latin America's economic system.

In spite of these pitfalls, in terms of per capita income growth, Latin America's economic performance from the end of the Second World War to the early 1980s was adequate in both absolute and relative terms. In 1981 per capita incomes in the region were twice as high as in 1950 (World Bank 1983). Moreover, since 1965, despite a much higher rate of population growth, Latin America managed (though barely) to start closing the gap separating the region from the industrial market economies, although always failing to keep pace with the high rates of expansion of the two other regions with middle-income developing economies—Asia and Southern Europe (table 2.1).

## Debt and Stagflation

After the onset of the debt crisis in 1982, adequate GDP growth rates, which had been the redeeming factor in Latin America's economic development record, evaporated into thin air. Latin American countries not only stopped growing in absolute terms but also started losing ground both to other middle-income developing economies and to industrial market economies (table 2.1). Meanwhile, inflation climbed to three-digit levels. An entire decade of growth had been lost. Today, the prospect of secular stagnation looms large on the economic horizon of most countries in the region.

Latin America's debt crisis exploded in August 1982. In the oil-importing countries of the region, the need to adjust was offset by the oil price hike of 1979 and the subsequent reaction of the OECD countries (Bianchi et al. 1987). Most of these countries assumed the crisis to be cyclical and borrowed heavily to finance their accumulating current account deficits. Some, especially those in the Southern Cone, borrowed heavily in order to expand imports and so help lower inflation, thus exacerbating overvalued exchange rates.

The oil exporters, believing forecasts of increasing energy prices in the future, also borrowed heavily. In just two years, in 1980 and 1981, the region's external debt rose by approximately US$100 billion to nearly US$290 billion, most of which was financed by commercial banks. In 1982, this unstable state of affairs culminated in the prolonging of the recession in the OECD and the Mexican moratorium on debt repayment. Adjustment became essential in all countries.

Stagflation was the consequence of Latin America's adjustment to the debt crisis. This involved two sets of external shocks: financial strangulation and deterioration in the terms of trade. The financial strangulation resulted from the sharp curtailment of foreign finance at a time when interest payments were increasing substantially. This forced Latin America to abruptly reduce its current account deficit and start generating a substantial transfer of real resources abroad, as measured by the region's trade surplus (including nonfactor services). The

**Table 2.2**
**Impact of the Net Transfer of Financial Resources for Latin America, 1979–86[a]**

|       | Net Capital Inflows | Net Factor Services | Transfer of Financial Resources from Abroad | |
|-------|---------------------|---------------------|----------------------------|-----------------------|
|       | Billions of US $ | Billions of US $ | Billions of US $ | As a Percentage of GDP |
| 1979  | 29.1  | −13.6 | 15.5  | 3.4  |
| 1980  | 29.7  | −18.2 | 11.5  | 2.2  |
| 1981  | 37.6  | −27.2 | 10.4  | 1.8  |
| 1982  | 20.4  | −38.8 | −18.4 | −3.0 |
| 1983  | 3.0   | −34.4 | −31.4 | −5.1 |
| 1984  | 9.3   | −36.3 | −27.0 | −4.1 |
| 1985  | 3.3   | −34.8 | −31.5 | −4.5 |
| 1986  | 8.7   | −30.5 | −21.8 | −2.9 |

a. The transfer of financial resources from abroad is equal to the difference between net capital inflows and net factor services.
SOURCE: United Nations, Economic Commission for Latin America, *Balance Preliminar de la Economía Latinoamericana 1987*, table 15, p. 23; except for the GDP figures, which are as in note b of table 2.4.

burden of this transfer was magnified by the external terms of trade simultaneously turning significantly against the region's primary product exports, which meant that a higher volume of exports became necessary to generate the same trade surplus. As table 2.2 shows, the impact of the net transfer of financial resources—that is, the difference between net capital inflows and net factor services—had a positive value of 2.5 percent of Latin America's GDP in the period 1979–81. It then became negative in 1982, reaching an average value of –4.6 percent from 1983 to 1985. This decline in GDP was worsened by the concomitant deterioration of Latin America's terms of trade, which negatively affected GDP in the period 1981–86 by an additional 1.8 percent (table 2.3). These shocks were absorbed by the economies almost entirely through a contraction of real investment rates.

Table 2.4 illustrates the consequence of the external strangulation process. This table shows the behavior in the period 1979–86 of the ratio of investment to GDP and of its sources of financing, namely, the net transfer from outside Latin America and internal saving. The net transfer is equal to foreign saving (that is, to the current account deficit) minus net factor services going abroad.[1] Internal saving is equal to the difference between GDP and consumption. As the table indicates, from

**Table 2.3**
**Impact of Deterioration in the Terms of Trade for Latin America, 1980–86**

| | Merchandise Exports at Constant 1980 Dollar Prices (Billions of US $) | Terms of Trade (1980 = 1.0) | Purchasing Power of Exports[a] (PPE) (Billions of US $) | Difference between PPE and Exports at Constant 1980 U.S. Dollar Prices | |
|---|---|---|---|---|---|
| | | | | Billions of US $ | As Percentage of GDP in 1980 Prices |
| 1980 | 89.1 | 1.000 | 89.1 | — | — |
| 1981 | 95.9 | .940 | 90.1 | −5.8 | −1.1 |
| 1982 | 87.4 | .852 | 74.5 | −12.9 | −2.5 |
| 1983 | 87.5 | .856 | 74.9 | −12.6 | −2.5 |
| 1984 | 97.7 | .930 | 90.9 | −6.8 | −1.2 |
| 1985 | 92.0 | .910 | 83.7 | −8.3 | −1.5 |
| 1986 | 78.3 | .840 | 65.8 | −12.5 | −2.2 |

Dashed cells indicate not applicable.
a. The purchasing power of exports is equal to the product of the constant dollar value of exports and the terms of trade.
SOURCES: United Nations, Economic Commission for Latin America, *Balance Preliminar de la Economía Latinoamericana 1987*, tables 12 and 15, pp. 20, 23; A. Bianchi, R. Devlin, and J. Ramos, "The Adjustment Process in Latin America, 1981–86." Paper presented at the Symposium on Growth-Oriented Adjustment Programs, Washington, D.C., February 25–27, 1987, table 2; except for the GDP in 1980 dollars, the sources from which are as in note b of table 2.4, with the following values in billions of U.S. dollars: 1980 ($524.5), 1981 ($528.1), 1982 ($521.8), 1983 ($508.2), 1984 ($527.6), 1985 ($545.4), 1986 ($565.4).

Table 2.4
Financing of Capital Formation for Latin America, 1979–86 (as % of GDP)

| | Gross Capital Formation[a] (1) | Foreign Savings[b] (2) | Factor Services (3) | Net Transfer from Abroad[c] (4) | Internal Savings[d] (5) |
|---|---|---|---|---|---|
| 1979 | 23.4 | 4.7 | −2.4 | 2.3 | 21.1 |
| 1980 | 23.3 | 5.8 | −3.0 | 2.8 | 20.5 |
| 1981 | 23.2 | 7.4 | −4.2 | 3.2 | 20.0 |
| 1982 | 20.5 | 7.0 | −5.7 | 1.3 | 19.2 |
| 1983 | 17.4 | 1.8 | −5.3 | −3.5 | 20.9 |
| 1984 | 17.4 | 0.4 | −5.3 | −4.9 | 22.3 |
| 1985 | 17.4 | 0.6 | −4.6 | −4.0 | 21.4 |
| 1986 | 18.8 | 2.3 | −3.9 | −1.6 | 20.4 |

a. Gross capital formation is as in IMF, *World Economic Outlook* (1987), table A7, p. 46, and represents arithmetic averages of country ratios, weighted by the average U.S. dollar value of GDP over the preceding three years.
b. Foreign saving is equal to the current account balance, and factor services are equal to the net investment income as it appears in U.S. dollar terms in IMF, *World Economic Outlook* (1987), table A36, p. 79. The U.S. dollar value of Latin American GDP was calculated as follows: the basis is an estimate of the GDP value for 1984 in IDB (1986), table 3, p. 408; the other numbers were constructed by applying the U.S. GDP price deflator (IMF, *World Economic Outlook*, 1987) to the real product series in the United Nations ECLA (1987). The estimated series for Latin American GDP (in billions of U.S. dollars) is as follows: 1979 ($453.0), 1980 ($524.7), 1981 ($578.8), 1982 ($608.5), 1983 ($614.9), 1984 ($662.3), 1985 ($706.8), 1986 ($751.9).
c. The values for net transfers from abroad were obtained as a residual from the identity: (4) = (3) + (2).
d. The values for internal saving were obtained as a residual from the identity: (5) = (1) − (4).
SOURCES: Inter-American Development Bank, *Economics and Economic Progress in Latin America, 1986 Report*; International Monetary Fund (IMF), *World Economic Outlook*, October 1987; United Nations, Economic Commission for Latin America (ECLA), *Balance Preliminar de la Economía Latinoamericana 1987*.

the period 1979–81 to the period 1983–85, internal saving did not rise to compensate for the sharp negative movement of the net resource transfer out of Latin America. As a consequence, investment ratios dropped sharply, from over 23 percent to close to 17 percent of GDP. In real terms, investment must have dropped severely, in view of the decline in the terms of trade. Such a decline artificially raises the nominal value of investment in comparison to nominal GDP, because of the high import component of the former.[2]

The previous discussion suggests that there was not any significant deterioration of the "internal" saving rate in Latin America during the 1980s. This is contrary to the perception of some observers. For example, it has been asserted that "this decline [of the investment ratio] reflected large decreases in the inflow of capital . . . and a fall in domestic saving ratios in most countries. . . . Domestic saving ratios declined in conjunction with the near stagnation of Latin American economies in the first half of the 1980s" (Balassa et al. 1986:97). There seems to be an error in this evaluation that stems from the adoption of an inappropriate concept of "saving" to analyze whether domestic economic behavior aggravated the impact of the external shocks. Clearly, an increase in international interest rates is an external shock and not a domestic maladjustment. If, however, output does not expand and/or consumption does not contract, this increase in dollar interest rates will be accounted for as a decline in domestic saving, as this concept is conventionally measured (that is, as the difference between GNP—which is now lower because of the higher interest outflows—and consumption). It is this peculiarity that justifies the replacement of "national" saving with "internal" saving as a more adequate concept to measure the relative importance of external shocks and domestic economic action in the financing of domestic investment. The substitution of internal saving also implies that the foreign contribution to domestic investment financing should be measured not by the current account deficit but by the eventual trade-cum-nonfactor-services deficit, also known as the net resources gap.

Deterioration in the terms of trade may also lead to a decline of the nominal saving rate, because nominal consumption tends to increase relative to GDP when import prices rise in relation to export prices.[3] For this reason an appropriate accounting framework must be able to isolate the impact of changes in the terms of trade from that of alterations in real domestic economic magnitudes. When these methodological precautions are taken, it appears that domestic actions are not responsible for aggravating the negative impact of the external shocks to the region's economies.

The region's reaction to the external shocks was entirely passive. Investment rates simply shrank, through both direct contraction of government capital formation and the crowding out of private investment (table 2.4). This contraction in demand provided the opportunity to implement other demand-switching measures—such as import controls and real exchange-rate devaluations—in order to be effective in expanding trade surpluses. Adjustment through recession rather than through demand switching was widespread in the region, particularly in the period 1981–83 in countries that were more severely affected by the external shocks or that, because of their failure to shore up investment after the first oil shock, lacked the necessary structural flexibility to expand exports or substitute imports. In view of the severity of the external shocks, temporary declines in output and employment were unavoidable.

## Economic Maladjustments

The Latin American pattern of adjustment to the external shocks was not conducive to sustaining economic growth in the face of external adversity. In contrast to the experience of other medium-income developing countries, the Latin American middle-income developing countries did not succeed in expanding their capacity to invest through increases in either productivity or national saving. Moreover, although financial strangulation was by and large a consequence of foreign economic actions, capital flight contributed to the problem in some Latin American countries. This was especially true for Argentina, Mexico, and Venezuela, which until 1983 had allowed disequilibrium in exchange rates and domestic interest rates while maintaining free convertibility in the capital account. In contrast, Brazil and Colombia, which combined the adoption of more nearly balanced exchange rates and domestic interest rates with strict outward capital controls, were by and large successful in avoiding significant capital flight.

Both the comparative record of Latin America's economic development in the post–Second World War period and its lethargic reaction to the external shocks of the 1980s are clear indications of the deeply rooted weaknesses of the region's economic system. A. Bianchi and his colleagues (1987) have identified four features of the region's economies that magnified the impact of the external shocks and limited the speed and capacity of response (table 2.5). The first is the high level of external debt. In Latin America, the debt-led strategies of the 1970s raised the debt/export ratio from 1.4 in 1970 to 2.3 in 1979. Korea, in contrast, had a ratio of 1.0. The second is the high proportion of Latin American debt at floating interest rates (66 percent). In contrast, the proportion for Asia in general was 12 percent and for Korea, 33 percent. The third is the low level of exports relative to GDP. Latin American exports averaged 13 percent of GDP in 1979, as opposed to 38 percent for Korea. The fourth is the very high dependence of the region on the export of primary commodities. Some 75 percent of Latin American exports consisted of relatively few natural resource-intensive commodities. This contrasted with Korea, where 90 percent of exports consisted of manufactured products, with far more responsive supply and demand schedules. The authors conclude that, as interest rates shot up and capital inflows collapsed, manufactured exports could not possibly have expanded as fast as in Korea. Adjustment, then, could not have been expansionary.

**Table 2.5**
**Selected Latin American and Asian Countries:**
**Indices of Financial Vulnerability and Trade Flexibility in 1980–81 (%)**

| | Financial Vulnerability | | | Trade Flexibility | |
|---|---|---|---|---|---|
| | Percent of Debt at Float- ing Rates | Interest Payments/ Exports | Exports/GDP | Exports/ Tradables[a] | Basic Commodity Exports/ Total Exports[b] |
| Latin America | 64.5 | 28.0 | 13 | 27 | 76 |
| Argentina | 58.3 | 15.1 | 7 | 15 | 79 |
| Brazil | 64.3 | 28.3 | 9 | 19 | 60 |
| Colombia | 39.2[c] | 16.3 | 15 | 26 | 76 |
| Mexico | 73.0 | 19.0 | 14 | 30 | 61 |
| Peru | 28.0[c] | 19.8 | 21 | 40 | 84 |
| Venezuela | 81.4[c] | 10.4 | 32 | 62 | 98 |
| Asia | | | | | |
| Korea | 33.3 | 6.2 | 38 | 67 | 10 |
| Taiwan | — | < 5.0 | 52 | — | 14 |

a. Agriculture, mining, and manufacturing.
b. Fuels, minerals, metals, and agricultural commodities.
c. 1980–82.
SOURCE: Adapted from table 5 of Bianchi et al. 1987 (see sources of table 2.3 above).

The debt crisis has revealed other structural rigidities of Latin America's economies. Latin American governments contracted most of their external debt either directly or through their state enterprises. Moreover, when the debt crisis erupted, under pressure of external creditors and private domestic debtors, the governments nationalized a good part of the external debt originally contracted by the local private sector. Nearly all medium- and long-term Latin American debts are now the responsibility of the region's governments. Thus financial strangulation provoked not only a balance-of-payments crisis but also, and perhaps more importantly, a major fiscal crisis.

Under these circumstances, a domestic transfer should have been made from the private to the public sector to offset the sharp and sudden increase in the transfer of resources out of the country. In principle, the resources could have come from additional taxes, contraction of other government expenditures, the printing of more money, or additional public sector borrowing in the domestic capital market.

Generally, Latin American governments failed to raise additional taxes or to contract their consumption expenditures. Adjustment was accomplished by reducing public sector investment—in both infrastructure and social services—and by borrowing more heavily either from the banking sector or from local capital markets. Additional domestic government borrowing tended to crowd private sector investment out, thus completing the stagflationary pattern of Latin America's adjustment to the debt crisis. The problems caused by the awkwardness of public sector adjustment were compounded by the negative impact of the widespread indexation mechanisms that developed in Latin America as a means of maintaining approximate parity of relative prices in the face of chronic inflation. It was such automatic and retrospective indexation mechanisms—applying to wages, exchange rates, public sector tariffs and prices, government-controlled prices in the private sector, and interest rates—that allowed countries like Brazil to maintain relatively high rates of economic growth despite extremely high rates of inflation.

The existence of such rigid indexation mechanisms, especially when Latin American economies were hit by the external shocks, tended to contribute to the substantial acceleration of inflation rates. The situation was further exacerbated by Latin American countries, having to devalue their currencies to compensate for these shocks. A simple model helps to understand why.

Let prices be formed on the basis of a fixed markup over primary costs, which consists of labor costs and imported input costs:

$$P = M(W + EP^*) \tag{2.1}$$

where $P$ is the final output price; $M$ is 1 plus the fixed markup rate; $W$ is the wage rate; $E$, the exchange rate; and $P^*$ the foreign input price in foreign currency. The labor and material input coefficients are normalized at unity. Lower-case letters represent the rate of change of the variable in the period. Then, the following expression obtains from equation 2.1 for the rate of inflation:

$$p = aw + (1 - a)(e + p^*) \tag{2.2}$$

where $a$ is the labor share in primary costs. Assume that wage changes are indexed to the change of output prices in the previous period, $p_{-1}$. This is also happening with the exchange rate, except that it may change by more, reflecting a maximum devaluation. The rates of change of wages and of the exchange rate are then given by, respectively,

$$w = p_{-1} \tag{2.3}$$

and

$$e = p_{-1} + u \tag{2.4}$$

where $u$ reflects a maximum devaluation in a given time period. After simplification, substitution of equations 2.3 and 2.4 into equation 2.2 leads to:

$$p = p_{-1} + (1 - a)(p^* + u) \tag{2.5}$$

This shows that an external price shock or a maximum devaluation leads to an acceleration of the inflation rate proportionally to the share of imported inputs in primary costs—and not only to a jump in the price level, as may be the case in nonindexed economies. Obviously this acceleration of inflation would have to be validated by a quickening of monetary expansion, which may be expected in view of the budgetary difficulties of the central government caused (as previously described) by the external shocks.[4]

## Conclusion

The previous section reviewed a number of Latin American economies' structural problems. These problems help to explain both the unsatisfactory economic performance of the region in the postwar period and the stagflationary phases experienced since the beginning of the 1980s. Three groups of interrelated factors have been identified: (1) a high level of public sector external debt contracted at floating interest rates; (2) a low level of industrial exports, coupled with high dependence on a handful of primary commodities; and (3) a lack of flexibility in the public sector and the rigid indexation mechanisms. A fourth component, the extreme degree of concentration of income and wealth, should be added. An inward orientation, an inoperative public sector, and a high concentration of land ownership and higher educational levels seem to be important factors in explaining the region's economic maladjustments, as revealed in its high incremental capital-output ratios. Debt and inflation, which were the escape valves in the 1970s, became the major problems in the 1980s. It is not clear whether the region will be able to recover from its present calamitous state without a major international debt-relief initiative, but clearly the region's economic problems run deeper than its external debt. A. Bianchi and his colleagues (1987) point out that growing out of the debt problem would require a structural transformation in two senses: a growth strategy would have to be oriented outward and be based largely on domestic efforts to raise saving and productivity levels. Public sector reform—the privatization of public enterprises, an administrative overhaul, tax simplification and universalization, and a modernization of the state's regulatory framework—would be essential in this process. Indeed, broad consensus on the needed structural changes seems to be taking shape in Latin America. There is greater agreement about the importance of a less inward orientation and a shift toward more export-led growth, of increased national saving, of a more focused distributive effort, of improved productivity and efficiency, and of the necessity of a more coherent and stable macroeconomic policy.

Agreement on such general principles is an important first step, even though the means to achieve them are not very visible in the region. For, as Fishlow (1985) points out, despite signs of convergence in theoretical approaches, the strategy chosen for policy implementation will ultimately depend on political considerations rather than economic consistency. Policymaking, in turn, as observed by E. Amadeo and T. Banuri (1987), should be seen not as the autonomous actions of an omnipotent state, but rather as the constrained decisions of one actor among many, all of them operating in a situation of conflict and tension. The nature and intensity of the social divisiveness and polarity visible from the historical record have traditionally constrained the autonomy of governments to pursue desired macroeconomic objectives.

Now that inflation and debt are no longer solutions to these internal social conflicts, Latin American countries—with their high levels of political tension and long history of political mobilization and organization along functional lines—are faced with the major challenge of reorganizing their economies and pulling themselves out of their current trend toward secular stagnation. Effective policy changes may require new institutions that are capable of coping with social conflict in a more productive manner than in the past. For example, Amadeo and Banuri (1987) suggest that labor conflicts and wage rigidities could be dealt with by adapting the social corporatist model of Northern Europe to Latin American conditions, rather than by following the "weak labor" model of East Asia favored by Bela Balassa and his colleagues (1986).

Perhaps comfort can be taken in J. M. Keynes's dictum that today's politicians are slaves of the thoughts of some defunct economist. Perhaps progress will accelerate fast enough to ensure that the needed institutional and policy changes will be effected before all hope is lost.

# Part Two

# External Economic Policies

# 3

*Edward K. Y. Chen*

# Trade Policy in Asia

In the last two decades, the economic growth of the Asia-Pacific region, which encompasses the western Pacific Basin from Korea in the north to Indonesia in the south, has been most impressive by any standards. This chapter focuses on the "Asia-10 countries," namely, Japan, China, Hong Kong, South Korea, Singapore, Taiwan, the Philippines, Malaysia, Thailand, and Indonesia, which by and large have had faster economic growth than the rest of the world. In the 1950s and 1960s, Japan surprised the world with economic growth of 10 percent a year and more. In the 1960s and 1970s, the Asian NICs—Hong Kong, Singapore, Taiwan, and Korea—demonstrated that they could achieve similar or even greater success. And recently, China has been growing at an average rate close to 10 percent (table A.2). The ASEAN-4—Thailand, the Philippines, Indonesia, and Malaysia—have increased their growth rates more recently (although the Philippines started industrialization earlier than any of the four NICs), but their potential should not be underestimated; for example, if its recent growth trends can be sustained, Thailand seems poised to become Asia's fifth NIC or its fifth "little dragon."

Can the experience of economic growth in these Asia-Pacific countries become an example for other developing countries? The answer depends on the level of generalization. If we confined ourselves to the observation of what has happened concomitantly with the rapid growth in income, we could generalize that the rapid economic growth of the Asia-Pacific countries is based on export-oriented industrialization, specifically the export of light, labor-intensive products. Countries or groups of countries that have higher growth rates in manufactured exports also enjoy higher rates of growth in GDP. Of course, this association of economic growth with manufactured export growth is not definite proof of export-led economic growth in the sense that the causal direction runs from the growth of manufactured exports to the growth of income (Lewis 1980; Riedel 1984). Yet on the basis of some econometric and time-series causality analyses, there is evidence that export is the engine of economic growth (Chen 1980; Rana 1985). Among the Asia-10 countries, the most spectacular export-led growth based on labor-intensive manufactures is found in the Asian NICs. This chapter concentrates on the experience of the NICs and discusses the economic policy and other noneconomic, institutional aspects that led to their economic miracle. The implications of the Asian NIC model for other developing countries in the region is also explored. First, is the NIC model in theory transferable to other developing countries? Second, even if it is theoretically transferable, would it in practice be possible, considering that the world market for manufactured exports is limited? Before answering these questions, let us examine the Asian experience of export-led industrialization and the factors contributing to its success.

## Export-Oriented Industrialization

Developmental strategies for industrialization can be broadly divided into import substitution and export orientation, strategies that are not mutually exclusive. Import substitution can further be divided into two stages. During the first, "easy" stage, nondurable consumer goods are produced, and during the second, "difficult" stage, consumer durables, intermediate goods, and capital goods are produced. The first stage of import substitution (IS1) is easy because production is roughly in line with the prevailing comparative advantage. The second stage of import substitution (IS2) becomes difficult because of rapidly increasing costs precipitated by limited economies of scale, dependence on foreign resources and expertise, and development of monopolistic controls. Import substitution is associated with a package of policies that aim at protecting the infant industries and discriminating against exports. Such policies include overvalued exchange rates, multiple exchange-rate systems, import controls, high tariffs, and quantitative restrictions on imports. These measures discriminate against exports because they force exporters to face import prices that are above the world level for the inputs they want.

Export orientation can also be divided into a first stage of exporting manufactures that are more labor-intensive (EO1) and a second stage of exporting products that are more capital- and technology-intensive (EO2). There is also a stage in which import substitution of capital and intermediate products (secondary import substitution) occurs simultaneously with export orientation. Sectors providing financial, technical, and other professional services may grow concomitantly. This "EO2 complex" stage may take place after EO1 or some time after EO2 has begun.

Thus four possible stages of development may be proposed: IS1, IS2, EO1, and EO2/EO2 complex. Generally, countries pass through the various stages in this order. Latin American countries went from IS1 to IS2 for some time before switching to EO1, during which high growth rates were experienced. But it seems that they went from EO1 to EO2 so readily and extensively that they got into trouble. The Asian NICs did not go through IS2. Hong Kong did not even pass through IS1, and in Singapore the IS1 stage was very short. Both Korea and Taiwan moved into EO1 when the stage of easy import substitution was over. As early as the beginning of the 1970s, both countries began to diversify into capital-intensive and technology-intensive industries and therefore in some ways went into the stage of EO2/EO2 complex. They have been more cautious than Latin American countries. Thus, despite some setbacks in some of their heavier industries, particularly the energy-intensive ones, Korea and Taiwan have managed to succeed in establishing some capital- and technology-intensive industries and in upgrading many of their existing light industries. Hong Kong and Singapore began to move into EO2 after the late 1970s. Indeed, the common problems facing all NICs presently and in the near future are related to the economic transformation from EO1 to EO2, and this transformation may be more intriguing than that from IS1 to EO1.

## The NICs' Economic Policy Changes

In the process of industrialization, Hong Kong was the only country that did not go through an import-substitution stage before developing an export orientation. The beginning of industrialization in Hong Kong resulted from historical factors that included the communist takeover in China and the Korean War (Chen 1984). The change of regime in China reduced entrepôt trade and caused massive flows of capital, labor, and entrepreneurship from China into Hong Kong. The Korean War resulted in a United Nations embargo of China, which further reduced Hong Kong's volume of entrepôt trade. Thus, Hong Kong had to industrialize for its survival and it took advantage of the inflow of production factors for industries.

Under a typical colonial administration, it was not expected that the government would play an important role in directing the transformation of the economy. Fortunately, because of laziness or the laissez-faire attitude of the government, no measures were taken to protect the newly established firms and industries, and hence no biases against exports developed. Under these circumstances, Hong Kong could fully exploit its comparative advantage for export-oriented industrialization from the beginning. Given the small size of the domestic market, the lack of resources, and the possibility of obtaining imported inputs at world prices, entrepreneurs certainly would choose export orientation to maximize their earnings.

Although Singapore is smaller than Hong Kong in size and population, it underwent a brief period of import substitution (Lee 1973; P. Chen 1983). With the development of self-government in 1959, Singapore attempted to promote industrialization through active government programs. From 1960 to 1963, protective tariffs and quantitative import restrictions were introduced. At that time, the hope of establishing a common market with Malaysia was an important reason for Singapore to pursue import-substitution policies and for two years after Singapore's independence, from 1965 to 1967, more import duties and restrictions were introduced. However, the common market never came into being and Singapore was then forced to adopt an export-oriented development strategy. In the Economic Expansion Incentives Act of 1967, the tax rate on profits was reduced from 40 percent to 4 percent. At the same time there were other tax concessions related to expenditure on research and development and on capital equipment.

Although tariffs on some imports remained, the incidence of import quotas was gradually reduced.

In Korea and Taiwan, the switch from import substitution to export orientation required a reform in exchange-rate policy in addition to import liberalization and export incentives. The policy changes in Korea took place in 1960 and 1961 under the Park Chung Hee government (Brown 1973; Frank 1975; Hansan and Rao 1979; Lau 1986). It was believed (1) that the easy stage of import substitution had been completed and that it would be difficult to turn to a higher stage of import substitution; and (2) that under these circumstances, the balance-of-payments problem could be solved only by export promotion. To promote exports, first, the won was devalued in 1961 (from 62.5 won to 130 won per U.S. dollar) and again in 1964 (from 130 won to 256 won per U.S. dollar); second, measures to liberalize import restrictions were taken, especially after the devaluation in 1964; and third, various export incentives were introduced. These included tariff and tax concessions on imports of raw materials by exporting firms, accelerated depreciation, and various export credit subsidies. An interesting form of export incentive was the assignment of export targets to industrial associations, firms, and regions. When export targets were not met, measures were taken to rectify the situation, ranging from threats of sanctions to provision of additional incentives and government actions to remove bottlenecks.

Rigorous import-substitution policies were pursued by the Taiwanese government during the period 1951–57. Strict import controls were imposed in 1951 and were accompanied by a multiple-exchange-rate system. Import substitution was generally a success during this period, leading to the doubling of manufacturing production. By 1958, however, easy import substitution came to an end, and the manufacturing sector was faced with many problems, including falling prices and runaway competition. A series of policies switching to export orientation were adopted from 1958 to 1960 (Hsing 1971; Ho 1978; Li and Yu 1982; Kuo 1983; Lau 1986). They were preceded by the 1955 Rebate of Taxes on Export Products Regulations, which provided for the rebate of import duty, defense surtax, and commodity tax for exporting products. Like any package of policies aiming at export promotion, the measures taken by the Taiwanese government included reforms in exchange-rate systems, import liberalization, and export incentives. First, the multiple-exchange-rate system was gradually collapsed into a single-rate system, and the exchange rate applicable to the bulk of imports to and exports by private enterprises was devalued to around NT$40 per U.S. dollar. Second, the government gradually liberalized and finally abolished the commodity import quota system. Import controls were also liberalized. In 1961, domestic manufacturers seeking protection had to show that they were capable of satisfying domestic demand and that their prices did not exceed the prices of comparable imports by more than 25 percent. In 1964, this was reduced to 15 percent, in 1968 to 10 percent, and in 1973 to 5 percent. The reduction in tariffs was reflected by the decline of the ratio of net customs revenues to total imports from 42 percent in 1955 to 28 percent in 1960, 22 percent in 1965, 18 percent in 1970, and 14 percent in 1976 (Lee and Liang 1982:315). Third, the provision of export incentives included the setting up of three export-processing zones in Kaohsiung, Nantze, and Taichung; cheap loans for exports; further tax concessions for some export products; and export insurance and promotion by government organizations.

## Import Substitution versus Export Orientation

The experiences of the NICs indicate that only under export-oriented industrialization can sustained, rapid economic growth be achieved. Under import substitution, any success is short-lived. An important question, then, is why export orientation is a better policy. If one goes by the traditional static trade theory, the gain from international trade will only lead to a once-and-for-all increase in income as a result of improvement in resource reallocation. In contrast, the infant industry argument hinges on the dynamic effects of a learning process that will lead to higher economic growth. Similarly, the superiority of export orientation has to be explained on the basis of dynamic effects. Anne Krueger (1981) gives the following explanations. First, export promotion is a better policy because it involves incentives rather than controls, and because measures can be applied more generally across the board. Whereas import-substitution policies discriminate against exports and create market distortion, many export-promotion policies give similar incentives to production for domestic and export markets. Also, whereas import controls are usually highly selective, export incentives usually do not differentiate much between individual export commodities. Second, it is easier to detect the effectiveness of export-promotion policies because export performance can be observed easily and the policy mistakes of export promotion corrected more quickly. Third, export promotion gives industries the opportunity to enlarge their markets and achieve greater economies of scale. Fourth, export-oriented development forces industries to compete in the international market and achieve greater X-efficiency (Balassa 1981).

These explanations are not the complete story. To explain the generation of sustained growth under export orientation, we need a virtuous-circle hypothesis. It has been shown that the export sector usually has a high rate of profits and a higher propensity to save (Chen 1977, 1979; Maizels 1968). This can perhaps be explained by Krueger's analysis of how exporting firms achieve greater economies of scale and X-efficiency. In the Asian NICs, the rapid growth of exports was accompanied by a high rate of capital formation. Foreign capital (aid, loan, or investment) was crucial to the development of the NICs at certain stages. But in all cases, the level of domestic saving rapidly increased as exports grew. It seems that a two-way relationship exists between saving and investment on the one hand and export growth on the other, giving rise to a virtuous circle of development.

We can also explain the superiority of export orientation over import substitution by the two-gap models of Hollis Chenery and L. J. Taylor (1968). These models, it may be said at the risk of oversimplification, assert that export growth will generate foreign exchange earnings to overcome the foreign-resources constraint, which for developing countries is more binding than the domestic-resources constraint. It implies that export growth will enable a developing country to import capital, intermediate goods, and technology for growth in productivity and therefore income. It has been shown by a simple simultaneous-equation model that these hypothesized relationships did exist in the NICs (Chen 1976, 1980). Thus, inasmuch as the availability of foreign resources is a binding constraint, export orientation is a better policy than import substitution. The gain from trade in this case is dynamic in the sense that export growth will initiate an interactive process of capital accumulation and technological progress.

Even if export orientation is a better policy, one might still ask whether the stage of import substitution is necessary as a precondition for export orientation. It seems economists increasingly believe that import substitution is not really necessary (Scott 1977; Myint 1982). This is an issue difficult to generalize; it depends on the initial conditions of the country and the types of industries developed. It is certainly difficult to conceive that manufactured products can be produced immediately at world-competitive prices without some previous industrial base. Even if one can cite examples of industries that can penetrate world markets successfully without first producing for the home market (the garment and electronics industries), their products could not have been manufactured at competitive prices without the industrial base and infrastructure created by the manufacture of other products under import substitution. In Hong Kong and Singapore, an infrastructure favorable to export-oriented industrialization was built during the entrepôt stage of economic development. Also, Hong Kong and Singapore are special cases because industrialization was to a large extent triggered by the inflow of entrepreneurs from Shanghai to Hong Kong and from developed countries to Singapore. A stage of import substitution for the breeding of indigenous entrepreneurship could therefore be avoided. Thus Hong Kong did not undergo an import-substitution stage, and Singapore could have done so, if it had so chosen.

## Factors Supporting Export-Oriented Industrialization

Even if export orientation is in theory a better strategy, there is no assurance that a country adopting this strategy will experience rapid economic growth. A complicated set of economic, political, and cultural factors seems to have been important in assuring the success of export-oriented industrialization. It did not take long for neoclassical economists to assert that the economic success of the NICs demonstrates a great victory of neoclassical economics, which emphasizes automatic adjustments and free market forces. It is true that the adoption of an export-oriented industrialization strategy implies "getting the prices right" so that they can be competitive in the world market.[1] But it is not true that this can be achieved through automatic adjustments. The role of the government has been important in correct pricing, in setting objectives, and in implementing policies. For example, monopolies have to be destroyed, labor and capital market imperfections have to be removed, overvaluation of exchange rates has to be corrected, trade restrictions have to be reduced, and incentives for exporting have to be established. Thus what is important is a kind of neoclassical interventionism rather than the invisible hand of the classical school. But the experience of the NICs does lend strong support to the classical and neoclassical conviction that competition is better than protection, and therefore export-oriented industrialization is better than import substitution. It is certainly no easy task, however, for a developing country to

adopt export-oriented industrialization at the early stage of development. The role of the government is important, as is, above all, the response of the people to government policies. If successful economic
development were as simple a matter as export orientation and "getting the prices right," there would be very few low-income countries
left today. Besides economic factors, there is growing belief that noneconomic elements have also contributed to the economic success of the
NICs.

The cultural factor would of course come to mind. But the cultural
commonality of the NICs is the Confucian culture, which for decades
has been regarded as an inhibiting rather than moving force for economic development. One would have to challenge an academic giant,
Max Weber ([1905] 1930), if one attempted to associate the economic
success of the NICs with Confucianism. The futurologist Herman Kahn
(1979) was the first scholar who had the courage to explicitly attribute
the economic success of East Asia to Confucian ethics. This was soon
echoed by Roderick MacFarquhar (1980) and further developed by
Peter Berger (1983). Philosophers, notably Tu Wei-ming (1984), and historians like Yu Ying-shih, have had further insights into the Confucianism explanation of economic success in East Asia. Berger circumvents
Weber's hypothesis by arguing that the old imperial or state Confucianism has evolved gradually because of changing political, economic, and
social circumstances into a new form of vulgar or secular Confucianism
that is much more conducive to economic development and the rise of
modern capitalism. Essentially, the culturalist school has emphasized
the following aspects of Confucianism: (1) work ethic and self-discipline, (2) hierarchy and obedience, (3) respect for scholarship, (4) family
cohesiveness, (5) thriftiness, and (6) flexibility and adaptability.

The adaptability of entrepreneurs within a Confucian culture can
be related to Confucianism's world outlook and characteristic dimension of rationalization (figure 3.1). Confucianism evaluates the world
through affirmation and uses adaptation to the world in the pursuit
of the highest good. The method of Confucian rationalization is cog-
nition. On the other hand, Christianity evaluates the world through
abnegation and uses mastery of the world in the pursuit of the highest good. The method of Christian rationalization is ethics. Most recently, political scientists have participated actively in analyzing the
economic success of the four NICs from the perspective of their own
discipline. The beginning of this trend can be traced to a paper by
Chalmers Johnson (1985) of the University of California at Berkeley.

**Figure 3.1**
**Contents of Religious World View**

| Methods for Pursuit of Highest Good / Evaluation of the World | Active | Passive | Dimension of Rationalization |
|---|---|---|---|
| World Abnegation | Mastery of the World: e.g., Christianity | Flight from the World: e.g., Hinduism | Ethical |
| World Affirmation | Adaptation to the World: e.g., Confucianism | Theoretical Grasp of the World: e.g., Greek Philosophy | Cognitive |

Johnson attempts to establish a link between political institutions and economic development. This subject of the relation between economics and politics is of course not new, but its application to East Asia and Johnson's conclusion that an autocratic government is conducive to economic development are most interesting. It is argued that a development-oriented autocratic "hard" state is necessary for economic development because it provides a stable environment for investment and a machinery for the effective implementation of policies.

Besides these systematic economic, cultural, and political theorizations about the economic success of the NICs, there are also other, less formal explanations that emphasize preconditions (i.e., the Japanese occupation in Taiwan and Korea or the British presence in Hong Kong and Singapore), geographic location, country size, and natural resources endowment. While these factors might be of some significance, the case for any of them playing a dominant role can largely be refuted on the basis of historical, empirical, and theoretical analysis.

## An Eclectic Model of Development in the NICs

The economic, cultural, and political explanations discussed above suffer from two weaknesses. First, each theory is a partial explanation in the sense that it does not give due consideration to other factors or even if it does, it makes no attempt to show the interactions between them. Second, each theory is supposed to be universally true and applicable to all types and stages of economic development. For example, if Confucianism is conducive to economic development, it does not matter to these authors whether economic development occurs because of import-substitution or export-oriented industrialization.

A model that does not suffer from these two weaknesses may be presented. It is an integrated, or eclectic, model that shows the importance of economic and noneconomic factors and how these factors are interrelated. More importantly, it is argued that the "takeoff" and the most rapid economic growth of the NICs occurred during EO1 (i.e., export-oriented industrialization on the basis of labor-intensive manufactured exports). Any development model explaining the economic success of the NICs should be confined to the EO1 stage, and an attempt to overgeneralize will invariably encounter serious difficulties.

**The EO1 stage.** The starting point of such an eclectic model is in the EO1 stage. The most important factors of production are entrepreneurship and labor. Of course, capital is necessary for any production to take place. But it is relatively less important because the scale of production is generally medium or small in the EO1 stage. The technology used is standardized, and production is not land-intensive because factories can be housed in multistory industrial buildings. The characteristics of EO1 are (1) export of labor-intensive manufactured products based on realizing existing comparative advantage; (2) demand-determined export growth, in the sense that exports react passively to what the markets want; and (3) continuous export growth sustained by the rapid adaptations of entrepreneurs that result in rapid product diversification. Essentially, the success of EO1 depends on the supply of a class of flexible and adaptable entrepreneurs, the supply of a class of skilled and docile labor, and an adequate supply of capital and standardized technology.

The structure of the model is illustrated by figure 3.2 and can be explained in terms of how the interplay of economic and noneconomic factors facilitates the entrepreneurship, labor, and capital that are essential for the success of EO1.

*Entrepreneurship.* An autocratic government provides a stable political environment and a set of consistent economic policies for

## Figure 3.2
## Model of a NIC in Southeast Asia under the EO1 Stage of Industrial Development

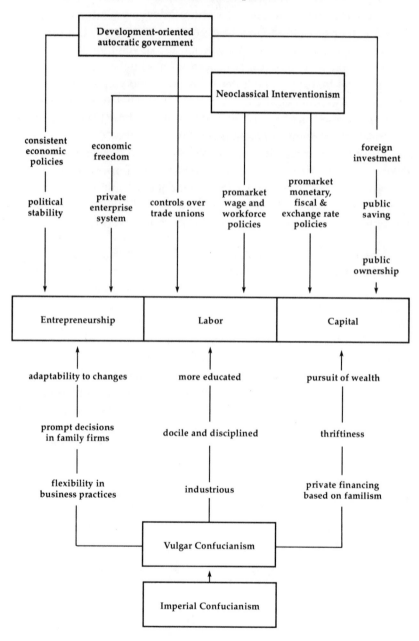

entrepreneurs. Neoclassical interventionism provides a framework of economic freedom and a private enterprise system. Vulgarized Confucianism gives rise to a class of entrepreneurs who are flexible and adaptable. The existence of family firms enables prompt decisions to be made. Informal (very often verbal) contractual agreements facilitate flexibility and confidentiality in business transactions.

*Labor.* An autocratic government can effectively keep trade unions under control so that wage increases will not be out of line with increases in labor productivity. Neoclassical interventionism provides a set of policies to ensure that the labor market is working under competitive conditions and that no unrealistic minimum wage laws are legislated. Confucian values, such as self-discipline, obedience, commitment to work and family, old-age protection dependent on family ties, and so on, give rise to an industrious, docile, and productive labor force. Moreover, the labor force in Confucian societies has displayed higher educational attainment than that in other societies in the developing world. Higher educational standards generally result in greater productivity and adaptability.

*Capital.* An autocratic government is in a better position to mobilize public savings through schemes such as a central provident fund and to take up public ownership in activities where large capital investment is required. An autocratic government is also in a better position to promote foreign investment by giving concessions to foreign investors because of the absence of strong opposition parties. Neoclassical interventionism provides a set of monetary, fiscal, and exchange-rate policies that are conducive to domestic saving and capital accumulation. In a Confucian society, thriftiness is a virtue. Moreover, in a society where an autocratic government prevails, the pursuit of political excellence is replaced by the pursuit of greater wealth and business excellence. The sense of family also facilitates the private means of financing investment through pooling resources; such a means is already adequate for the establishment of small- and medium-sized firms.

**The EO2/EO2 complex stage.** The specific cultural and political institutions, in conjunction with the appropriate economic policies that minimize factor-price and exchange-rate distortions, have produced in the NICs an adequate supply of capital; a plentiful supply of productive, docile labor; and an available class of adaptable, flexible, and resourceful entrepreneurs. As a result, a most favorable environment has been created for EO1, or the first stage of export-oriented industrialization, in which mainly labor-intensive products are produced and production is largely determined by the extent and type of demand prevailing in overseas markets. Will the NICs be able to achieve similar or greater success in the next stage of development—the EO2/EO2 complex stage? Let us first examine the differences between EO1 and EO2/EO2 complex, as given in table 3.1.

In the new stage of development, a different type of neoclassical interventionism is necessary for an economy to acquire dynamic comparative advantage. Also, a different caliber of entrepreneurs is needed to face the problems imposed by a type of economic growth that is based on the supplier's ability to direct the market. The new class of entrepreneurs must be able not only to adapt but also to create and transform. Technological creation and transformation and highly trained and educated workforce will become essential for the second stage of export-oriented industrialization. If all these generalizations are true, one can no longer have as much optimism about the economic future of the NICs. Confucianism may be too soft a cultural system to effect such a transformation. The autocratic political institution may be too closed a system to formulate and implement policies for the emergence of a complex industrial structure.

But this is a static analysis. The whole world is constantly changing, and the NICs have been dynamic and resilient. We anticipate that

### Table 3.1
### Stages of Industrial Growth: EO1 versus EO2/EO2 Complex

| EO1 | EO2/EO2 Complex |
|---|---|
| Export of labor-intensive light manufactured products based on existing comparative advantage | Export of capital-, technology-, and knowledge-intensive light and heavy manufactured products based on the acquisition of dynamic comparative advantage. |
| Growth is largely demand-determined | Growth is substantially supply-determined |
| Growth sustained by rapid *adaptations* (products and techniques) | Growth sustained by rapid *transformations* (industries and technology) |
| Tourism and personal services are of some importance | Rising importance of the service sector, especially financial services |
| Capital goods and intermediate products mainly imported | Some degree of secondary import substitution |

political institutions will change and cultural systems will undergo evolutionary processes when an economy moves toward a higher stage of development. The political democratization and economic liberalization movements in Korea and Taiwan are part of this process. If Confucianism has already evolved once from the imperial to the vulgar, there is reason to believe it will undergo another evolution to cope with the changing needs of a higher level of export-oriented growth. Thus, from a dynamic point of view, there is no reason to believe that the rapid economic growth of the NICs cannot be sustained in the future.

## A "Flying Geese" Pattern

The success of export-oriented industrialization depends crucially on the availability of world markets for manufactured products. Since the early stage of their industrialization, the NICs have accounted for a fast-increasing share of world trade in manufactures. A wave of new protectionism consisting mainly of nontariff barriers has been established in the developed countries, which are the major markets for developing countries' manufactured exports. How have the NICs been able to maintain their rapid economic growth in the past two decades? And even if the NICs themselves can survive, can the NIC model be transferred to the other developing countries in the Asia-Pacific region so that the entire region can engage in export-oriented industrialization and not be subject to a zero-sum game?

The experience of the Asia-Pacific region seems to suggest that, as far as the competition for markets is concerned, it is possible for the entire region to engage in export-oriented industrialization and at the same time achieve rapid economic growth. The reason is simple. There has been a high degree of sophisticated subregional division of labor developed in the region in the course of economic growth. One can of course also ask whether Confucianism and a development-oriented autocratic state are absolutely necessary for export-oriented industrialization to work. It is difficult for political institutions and almost impossible for cultural systems to be transferred. One should perhaps take the view that countries without the cultural and political environment of NICs would find it much more difficult to succeed in EOI. But there are always alternative means to the same end. The presence of NIC communities and foreign direct investment might be a close substitute for the inheritance of a Confucian culture; an efficient and effective democratic government might be a close substitute for a hard-line state. Moreover, most developing countries are today embarking on an export orientation-cum-import substitution rather than a pure EO1 strategy.

According to William Cline (1982), there is a possible limitation to the spread of export-oriented industrialization from the NICs to other developing countries because of the fallacy of composition. This means that while export-oriented industrialization may work well if pursued by a limited number of countries, it may break down if a large majority of developing countries seek to pursue it at the same time. There is certainly an element of truth in this argument, considering that the capacity of Western markets to absorb manufactured imports has been decreasing and that protectionism has been rising. But we should also agree with Gustav Ranis (1985) that all developing countries do not reach the same stage of economic development and produce the same types of industrial products. Even within the NICs, a high degree of industrial and product differentiation exists. Also, we must not neglect the importance of markets in the developing countries. With China adopting its Open Door policy, the potential of the China market, for example, should never be underestimated.

Thus it may be safe to conclude that even if a majority of the Asia-Pacific developing countries adopt the strategy of export-oriented industrialization, these countries will still be able to achieve rapid growth at the same time because of the possibility of complementarity in the process of such industrial growth. Most importantly, such complementarity is not necessarily the result of deliberate regional economic cooperation but may simply proceed from the different stages of economic development existing in different countries and the changing comparative advantages in countries over time.

The idea of different stages of economic development in this region can best be explained in the framework of the so-called flying geese hypothesis. In terms of today's situation, we can envision the pattern of flying geese shown in figure 3.3. The leader of the flying geese is undoubtedly Japan, followed by the NICs. Of the ASEAN-4, Malaysia and Thailand have not only a higher per capita income level than the Philippines and Indonesia, but also a much better economic and political infrastructure for industrialization. China is not a goose but some other huge bird flying side by side with the geese. China has the potential of complementing and competing with the

**Figure 3.3**
**"Flying Geese" Pattern of Asian Industrial Development**

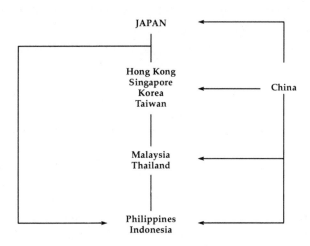

various layers of the flying geese at various levels of industrial production. In some areas, China is competing or potentially could compete with Japan and the NICs. On the other hand, China is also producing downstream labor-intensive products in competition with the ASEAN-4.

In the terminology of Chenery and Taylor (1968), industries can be classified into early-stage industries (e.g., food, textiles, and leather goods), middle-stage industries (e.g., chemicals and petroleum refining), and late-stage industries (e.g., clothing, consumer durables, capital, and intermediate goods). Now we can add a fourth stage, high-tech industries, which would encompass industries associated with information technology, biotechnology, and material science. If we use the presentation of F. C. Lo and B. N. Song (1986), the flying geese pattern can be depicted as in table 3.2. In contrast to Lo and Song, however, I think that China is presently in the early, middle, and late stages (rather than in an early-to-middle stage) and will be in a late-to-high-tech stage (rather than a late stage) in the year 2000. I also think that Korea and Taiwan are now ahead of Hong Kong and Singapore in technological capability. My view, then, is different from Lo and Song's, regarding the stage of development of the NICs in 1986 and 2000. In any case, we can see that the developing countries in this region are in different stages of industrial development. Even for countries in the same

Table 3.2
Current and Projected Stages of Industrial Growth in
Asia-Pacific Countries, 1986–2000

| | Stages | |
|---|---|---|
| Country | 1986 | 2000 |
| Indonesia | Early to middle | Middle to late |
| Philippines | Middle | Late |
| China | Early, middle, and late | Late to high-tech |
| Thailand | Middle | Late to high-tech |
| Malaysia | Middle to late | Late to high-tech |
| Hong Kong | Late | Late to high-tech |
| Korea | Late to high-tech | High-tech |
| Taiwan | Late to high-tech | High-tech |
| Singapore | Late to high-tech | High-tech |
| Japan | High-tech | High-tech |

SOURCE: Adapted from F.C. Lo and B.N. Song, "Industrial Restructuring of the East and Southeast Asian Economies," paper presented at the Conference on the Asia-Pacific Economy Towards the Year 2000, Beijing, November 1986.

stage of development, specialization is normally possible, so that complementarity can be achieved.

## The Semiconductor Examples

A subregional division of labor exists in all the major industries in the Asia-Pacific region. A good example is the manufacture of semiconductors, which comprises four distinct phases of production: (1) design and mask making, (2) wafer fabrication, (3) assembly, and (4) final testing. What is significant is that each stage requires different levels of skill and different factor intensities. The design and mask-making stage requires relatively high-level design and production engineers. The wafer fabrication stage is capital-intensive and requires a high standard of precision and product quality control. The assembly stage, involving mostly bonding, is highly labor-intensive. The final testing stage requires skilled labor and considerable investment in the acquisition of equipment.

To take advantage of the lower wage rates (even after consideration of productivity) in developing countries, U.S. semiconductor manufacturers began moving the assembly stage of production to Asia at a very early stage. In the case of consumer electronics, Hong Kong was the first place where offshore semiconductor assembly plants were set up. Fairchild Semiconductor Corp. established the first plant there in 1962. Wafers were shipped to Hong Kong, and the assembled products were sent back to the United States for final testing. The small size of the semiconductor chips makes their transportation cost very low; therefore, it is profitable to assemble semiconductors in offshore plants in low-wage countries. Offshore assembly was also encouraged by the U.S. Tariffs Schedule, sections 806.30 and 807.00, under which imports of assembled goods are taxed only on the value added to the goods at offshore plants.

In 1964, Fairchild and Motorola Inc. invested in Korea. Many American semiconductor manufacturers set up assembly plants in Taiwan between 1967 and 1969. In 1968 and 1969, National Semiconductor Corp., Texas Instruments Inc., and Fairchild opened facilities in Singapore. In the early 1970s, numerous facilities were built in the ASEAN-4 (Davis and Hatano 1985). By 1974, there were eight U.S.-owned offshore assembly plants in Hong Kong, nine in Korea, three in Taiwan, nine in Singapore, eleven in Malaysia, and six in the rest of Asia. Japanese and European semiconductor manufacturers did not exactly follow the American strategy. Even though Japanese firms operated facilities in Korea, Taiwan, and Malaysia, and European firms operated facilities in Malaysia and Singapore, offshore production of U.S. firms was larger by far.[2] For example, in 1981 Japanese producers imported semiconductors valued at approximately US$129 million from offshore assembly locations (US$62 million from Korea, US$37 million from Taiwan, and US$30 million from Malaysia). In 1980, European firms imported US$530 million from offshore plants (of which US$162 million was from Malaysia and US$156 million from Singapore). On the other hand, in 1980 the United States imported US$2.3 billion from offshore assembly plants in Asia. Japanese semiconductor firms responded by automating the assembly process and improving technology and design. In the early 1980s, Japanese firms also invested substantially in the United States and Europe in anticipation of protectionist measures they expected would be imposed on the export of electronic components from Japan. In Asia, and especially in the NICs, indigenous firms have been established to assemble semiconductors and compete with foreign multinational firms. These entrepreneurs are most often engineers and technicians who have gained experience from working for foreign companies. But, more importantly, an integrated semiconductor industry has been developed in the NICs. For a long time, foreign firms engaged only in assembly work in the host countries. There were few backward and forward linkages. It was only in the final testing that some U.S. firms had set up offshore test facilities in the Asia-Pacific region. In the past few years, Hong Kong and Singapore have emerged as regional centers of testing for the international semiconductor industry. Fairchild, Motorola Inc., and Teledyne Inc. have established specialized test facilities in Hong Kong, while Advanced Micro Devices and National Semiconductor have set up similar specialized facilities in Singapore (Scott 1985).

Since the early 1980s, efforts have been made in the NICs to integrate backward assembly with wafer fabrication by setting up indigenous or joint-venture firms. In Hong Kong, three fabrication plants were set up from 1981 to 1982 and one more recently. Two of these plants have a Chinese connection in the sense that they are joint ventures between Hong Kong and China. In the past few years, Hong Kong has been facing political uncertainty over the scheduled change in sovereignty in 1997. (The Sino-British Joint Declaration over the Future of Hong Kong was announced in September 1984. This agreement has given short-term stability to Hong Kong, but the longer-term future is highly uncertain, as nobody knows whether the agreement will be honored or for how long.) Therefore, there has been a lack of long-term investment committed by the local people. Capital invested by China should be able to fill some of the gaps. But, more fundamentally, Hong Kong lacks the kind of government support for research and development and personnel training that is found in the other NICs.

In Korea, the government took a keen interest in the development of an integrated semiconductor industry. In 1982, the Semiconductor Industry Promotion Plan was announced. A new, 2000-acre electronics industrial park was set up in Gumi, southeast of Seoul. The government also created the Korean Institute of Electronics Technology (KIET). By 1985 there were four fabrication plants in Korea, all of them major Korean corporate enterprises with the capability and willingness to invest heavily in research and development on a long-term basis. They have been acquiring technology through licensing, subcontracting, and joint-venture relationships.

Taiwan's fabrication industry stems from direct foreign investment by the United States in offshore plants. Unlike Korea, once started, the local fabrication industry in Taiwan was concentrated in many medium- and small-sized firms. The Hsinchu Industrial Park was established in 1980, and from the very beginning attracted a few Taiwan-U.S. joint ventures engaged in the production of semiconductors. Above all, the government-supported Electronics and Research Service Organization (ERSO) fabricates wafers at Hsinchu. As early as 1977, in fact, ERSO started making digital watch chips with technology licensed from RCA Corp. ERSO then set up United Microelectronics Corp. in 1979 as a quasi-public company owned by three government-controlled banks and five private companies. This company began production at Hsinchu in 1982 and is now doing well.

Singapore was an assembly and testing center for semiconductors for many years, relying mainly on the investment of transnational corporations. The Singapore government was keen to develop an integrated semiconductor industry, but its attempts were largely in vain. Finally, in the early 1980s, Italy's SGS-Ates agreed to set up a fabrication facility in Singapore and later a design center to design chips for the regional market.

Generally, in the past few years, a pattern of subregional specialization in the semiconductor industry in the Asia-Pacific region has emerged (Scott 1985; Henderson 1986). The NICs have integrated the industry backward to wafer fabrication and design and forward to final testing. Increasingly, they have concentrated their efforts in the latter direction. This is to be expected in view of their changing comparative advantage. Capital is not scarce in these economies, and there is a supply of highly trained technical personnel whose salary levels are still below those in developed countries. As long as one is satisfied with a one- to two-year time lag in technology, one can easily acquire the technology in the open market through licenses, patents, or foreign equity shares. The assembly of semiconductors has increasingly been taken up by the ASEAN-4, especially the Philippines and Malaysia. Thus, in the development of the semiconductor industry in this region, the flying geese hypothesis finds very strong support. Japan takes the lead in the development of the industry. The NICs first engage in assembly and upon graduation pass on this work to the next tier of economies, the ASEAN-4. Today, direct foreign investment in electronics in the ASEAN-4 is not confined to that from the United States, Japan, and Europe. The NICs, especially Hong Kong, invest considerably in assembly facilities in the ASEAN-4. Meanwhile, the NICs take after Japan in engaging in the design and fabrication of wafers, and Japan focuses on innovations in design and production technology.

## Conclusion

This chapter has described the experience of export-oriented industrialization in Asia with special reference to the four Asian NICs. It is argued that while export orientation is a better strategy than import substitution, the realization of rapid growth under export-oriented industrialization is not an easy matter. First, promarket economic policies aimed at eliminating market distortions must be implemented. But some noneconomic factors are probably equally important in ensuring the success of stage 1 in the development of export-oriented industrialization (EO1). Specific political institutions (a strong development-oriented state) and cultural values (Confucianism) are seemingly relevant in this connection. An eclectic model has been developed to explain the success of the NICs under EO1. It is further argued that a high degree of sophisticated subregional division of labor analogous to a flying geese pattern helps explain not only sustained growth in the NICs but also the spread of rapid economic growth to other developing countries in the Asia-Pacific region.

# Trade Policy in Latin America

The nineteenth century German economist Friedrich List ([1841] 1955) said nations can and should adapt their economic policies to the circumstances of their stage of development. He argued that countries will grow out of barbarism as they trade freely with more advanced nations, develop their agriculture, and stimulate industry, fishing, shipping, and foreign trade, possibly by imposing restrictions. When the nations have achieved a degree of wealth and power, farmers, manufacturers, and traders can be encouraged to consolidate their dominant position so that free exchange and free competition can be reinstated in their own markets and abroad.

List's relativism counters the inflexibility of the theories of Adam Smith's disciples, who argued in favor of free trade without considering the specific economic or institutional situations of particular countries. For example, List was concerned about the position of Germany in relation to England and France, and argued that if Germany wished to develop its own industry, it would have to impose some restrictions on the entry of goods from those two countries. He held the same view in the case of the United States, although the United States had a natural barrier, namely, the high cost of transport involved in trading over long distances overseas.

Since then, the debate on the benefits of free trade and free markets versus the need to protect and defend local production and stimulate infant industry has continued in more sophisticated forms. Those countries that were the first to defend one or the other position have modified their own commercial policies over time, in response not only to fluctuations in the world economy but also to changes in their own competitive status. The wisdom of List's relativism must be viewed from the perspective of the individual country. The principle of regulating commercial policy in accordance with the level of economic development, so that trade becomes the main vehicle of development, is particularly relevant in the closing years of this century. Except for countries that have neither a large enough market nor the natural resources, all countries, whether already industrialized or in the process of becoming so, have been through these stages of protectionism and inward-looking development. It is only as they develop their productive capacities that they have moved toward trade liberalization, and this movement has usually been slow.

## Liberalization and Protectionism

In what is known today as the industrialized world, substantial progress has been made in lowering tariffs and eliminating barriers, especially since the 1960s through the Kennedy and Tokyo rounds of multilateral negotiations. Those advances toward trade liberalization occurred in the context of an unprecedented postwar prosperity. However, the process has not been uniform across countries or products, and this has created imbalances in trade relations that have significantly affected developing countries. Bela Balassa (1984) suggests that tariff reductions made by industrialized countries have been less for manufactured imports from developing countries. So the tariffs developing countries face are higher than the average tariff level (9 percent versus 7 percent in the United States, 7 percent versus 6 percent in the European Community (EC), and 7 percent versus 5 percent in Japan). Further, higher tariffs are more common for imports coming from developing countries than for manufactured imports on average. For instance, in the United States, tariffs of over 10 percent are applied to 20 percent of the imports from developing countries but to only 9 percent of total manufactured imports. Comparative figures for the EC are 12 and 6 percent, and for Japan, 18 and 13 percent. Other nontariff restrictions have been applied to the exports of developing countries, and these have affected particularly the middle-income countries.

Restrictions come in all forms and disguises, from voluntary limitations on exports and market-stabilizing agreements to the open use of quotas and quantitative limitations. Voluntary limitations are achieved by invoking antidumping principles or demands of compensation rights. These often serve as mechanisms for volume and price restrictions. And it is no secret that the industrialized countries have used their power and leverage to impose a set of bilateral reciprocal conditions. A 1987 report by the Economic Commission for Latin America and the Caribbean (ECLAC) (1987b) concludes that this kind of agreement is usually applied to products that developing countries have a great interest in exporting, such as textiles, clothing, steel, and shipbuilding.

Trade restrictions tend to become more severe during recessions or during periods of slow economic growth in the industrialized world. Economists have debated at length whether a reduction in the pace of growth of developing countries' manufactured exports can be attributed to a drop in the rate of economic growth of industrialized countries or rather to the implementation of protectionist measures (Balassa 1984). Evidently, in times of crisis nontariff restrictions tend to increase, and no one can say for certain whether developing countries' manufactured exports fall as a result of a decrease in demand or of a higher level of protection in the developed markets. A detailed analysis should also include the orientation of macroeconomic policies adopted by developing countries during such times. Whatever the answer, it is interesting to note that the period in which the developing countries' manufactured exports increased at the fastest rate, from 1973 to 1980, was in fact a period in which the industrialized countries grew relatively slowly, at an average rate of 2.8 percent versus 4.7 percent between 1965 and 1973 (World Bank 1987).

What does seem to be a fairly constant feature of international trade is the very high level of protectionism exercised by industrialized countries on behalf of their agricultural sectors. Much has been written to illustrate the different kinds of instruments used by those countries to protect their agriculture and the high costs involved (World Bank 1986). This protectionism applies not only to agricultural farm products but also to products with a higher value added. A World Bank study (1986) concludes that for many agricultural products—including fish, vegetables and prepared fruit, edible oils, and elaborate products of coffee, cacao, rubber, and leather—the highest tariffs are reinforced by a wide range of nontariff barriers. The greater the degree of elaboration, that is, the more labor and capital services involved in production, the more barriers goods from developing countries face in international markets (World Bank 1986).

Industrialized countries have strongly resisted dismantling protectionist policies and subsidies favoring their agricultural sectors—areas where developing countries often enjoy clear comparative advantage. Domestic politics have often prevailed over economic logic. While these distortions continue in the market for agricultural products, it is difficult to say that the benefits of trade liberalization and of a growing interdependence between countries are being fairly and equitably shared. This kind of protection of agriculture in the industrialized countries is a contributing factor in the recession cycles in developing countries and leads the governments of developing countries to adopt costly policies designed to support or subsidize their own agricultural sectors. Such policies increase the inability of developing countries to implement counter-cyclical measures when their terms of trade deteriorate, or to generate surpluses that could be transferred toward their own industrialization efforts (Economic Commission for Latin America and the Caribbean 1987a).

Of course, along with the external factors of economic crisis, there are basic internal factors such as domestic macroeconomic policies, and there is a risk that emphasis on the former will lead to neglect of the latter. Protectionism is likely to stay with us for a long time and can be abandoned only gradually; meanwhile, other kinds of solutions must be sought, and it may be that the experiences of Asia will be most relevant for Latin America.

## Economic Cycles and the Stability of Policy

Many observers have searched for explanations of the rapid economic advances of some Asian countries and their success in consolidating export-led economies. At the same time, observers have tried to explain why progress in Latin America has been limited. A look at the main differences in the economic environments of the two regions may shed light on the phenomenon better—not simply the reasons for their unequal development but also the lessons Latin America can learn from the Asian experience.[1] Two closely related factors may be of special importance: the problem of economic cycles and the lack of stability in macroeconomic policy.

Most Latin American economies have been highly dependent on exports of primary products, both agricultural and mineral. It can also be said that most of these economies are rich in natural resources, unlike Japan, Korea, and Taiwan, which are net importers of raw materials. As exporters of primary products, Latin American countries are in an ambivalent position. They have usually been able to import manufactured products and technology to ensure the maintenance of minimum living standards, especially among the middle and upper classes, without needing to significantly diversify efforts in the development of other activities such as industry. But the fluctuations of prices for primary products have contributed to an unbalanced macroeconomic  policy and prevented any political commitment to long-term economic objectives.

The unfavorable evolution in the terms of trade for primary products compared to manufactured goods may have had less importance than has been supposed, and discussion of it does not have much value for the actual design of economic policy. There is no conclusive evidence of the negative effects of such long-term trends on the economies of exporting countries. For instance, a recent study covering the period 1900–86 shows that distinctions deserve to be made between the various types of primary products (Grilli and Yang 1988). Mineral and nonedible agricultural products show a constant drop in prices when compared to foodstuffs. The fall in the price of foodstuffs is due to the declining price of food products such as cereals and rice. The rise in the prices of tropical beverages (including coffee, cocoa, and tea), also included with foodstuffs, was not able to offset the decrease. What is interesting is that the developing countries are the only exporters of tropical beverages, but many of them are net importers of foodstuffs; therefore, they might have been able to benefit from the price changes. It is true that the prices of metals and mineral products did tend to fall in comparison to manufactured products between 1900 and 1986, but a more detailed examination offers a slightly different picture. The strong downward movement from 1900 to 1941 was offset by a mild upward trend from 1942 to 1986. The trend of the last forty years, particularly up to the 1970s, should have brought important gains in the purchasing power of exporting countries, if the significant increases in productivity achieved in the exploitation of their natural resources since the Second World War are taken into account.

In sum, it is important to be cautious about statements concerning the relationship between the evolution of the developing countries' purchasing power and their terms of trade. Although there has been a constant decline in those terms, it has been less steep and less uniform (depending on the products and the time period concerned) than was initially supposed. Certainly anyone studying the effect of the decline on the earnings of exporting countries must take into account the benefits of the increase in the volume of exports that has occurred in the postwar period. On the other hand, the negative effect on production of such decline may have been mitigated by increases in productivity, at least to some degree.

The factor that may have had more impact on the development process is the short- and medium-term fluctuation of the terms of trade, and its effect on the external sectors of the economies concerned and on the orientation of economic policies. Table 4.1 shows how the terms of trade changed between 1970 and 1986 for the major countries in Latin America. During the 1970s, there was a clear trend toward improvement, but in the 1980s there has been a significant trend in the opposite direction (International Monetary Fund 1987). Abrupt short-term changes can be observed in all countries annually. Price cycles in primary export products have been one of the determining factors in the implicit or explicit specification of the economic development model of Latin American countries. Whenever the terms of trade have improved, currencies have become overvalued, and imports have been liberalized, exchange controls weakened, and fiscal policy relaxed both in spending levels and in relation to tax revenue. Whenever the terms of trade have deteriorated, policy has often gone in the other direction: major devaluations have taken place, export incentives have increased, strong import restrictions have been implemented, exchange controls have been used, and in some cases, fiscal policy has been tightened. External capital flows have made the upward or downward movements in these cycles more pronounced.[2]

With respect to the instability of macroeconomic policy, fluctuations in the terms of trade and frequent changes in direction of economic policy have combined to create an adverse climate for activities, such as those related to manufactured exports, that require a long-term planning horizon. The various economic indicators have behaved erratically because of changes in the external sector and the lack of a consistent economic policy. Four indicators of economic policy, two related to the external sector and two to domestic policy, may be considered. Table 4.2 shows the evolution of the effective real rate of exchange and a liberalization index (measured by the relationship of

Table 4.1

Major Latin American Countries' Terms-of-Trade Index,
1970–86 (1980 = 100)

| | 1970 | 1971 | 1972 | 1973 | 1974 | 1975 | 1976 | 1977 | 1978 | 1979 | 1980 | 1981 | 1982 | 1983 | 1984 | 1985 | 1986 |
|---|---|---|---|---|---|---|---|---|---|---|---|---|---|---|---|---|---|
| **LAIA[a] countries** | | | | | | | | | | | | | | | | | |
| Argentina | 60.1 | 57.6 | 60.9 | 79.5 | 94.2 | 85.1 | 89.6 | 94.6 | 89.9 | 95.7 | 100.0 | 93.9 | 85.2 | 86.0 | 90.8 | 86.4 | 78.8 |
| Brazil | 90.1 | 98.7 | 109.4 | 128.0 | 112.8 | 98.3 | 93.1 | 90.0 | 90.6 | 100.2 | 100.0 | 96.3 | 84.9 | 80.7 | 96.0 | 84.1 | 77.4 |
| Chile | 131.6 | 117.0 | 124.7 | 145.4 | 121.9 | 117.0 | 132.8 | 151.5 | 131.8 | 121.1 | 100.0 | 85.0 | 79.8 | 77.7 | 85.2 | 82.2 | 101.0 |
| Colombia | 178.8 | 130.6 | 123.6 | 158.5 | 155.6 | 86.4 | 94.7 | 83.9 | 96.4 | 96.9 | 100.0 | 87.4 | 75.3 | 82.1 | 76.4 | 70.5 | 77.4 |
| Ecuador | 84.0 | 72.5 | 80.7 | 85.2 | 82.1 | 68.0 | 93.6 | 144.6 | 125.2 | 104.1 | 100.0 | 84.8 | 86.6 | 93.1 | 98.6 | 94.7 | 111.3 |
| Mexico | 68.8 | 75.4 | 75.8 | 90.7 | 87.2 | 77.5 | 71.0 | 66.3 | 76.2 | 82.3 | 100.0 | 100.9 | 86.6 | 91.4 | 84.6 | 80.0 | 57.1 |
| Peru | 108.9 | 98.7 | 92.0 | 109.6 | 122.8 | 88.4 | 86.3 | 85.6 | 72.0 | 91.7 | 100.0 | 88.5 | 79.6 | 94.8 | 91.1 | 86.3 | 74.7 |
| Venezuela | 22.7 | 21.9 | 20.3 | 30.7 | 64.3 | 63.2 | 66.3 | 67.4 | 59.3 | 77.0 | 100.0 | 102.7 | 94.4 | 100.9 | 112.2 | 110.3 | 60.0 |

a. Latin American Integration Association, formerly Latin American Free Trade Area (LAFTA).
SOURCES: Economic Commission for Latin America and the Caribbean; Inter-American Development Bank.

Table 4.2

Major Latin American Countries' Real Effective Exchange Rate and Liberalization Index[a], 1971–86 (1976–78 = 100)

| | 1971 | 1972 | 1973 | 1974 | 1975 | 1976 | 1977 | 1978 | 1979 | 1980 | 1981 | 1982 | 1983 | 1984 | 1985 | 1986 |
|---|---|---|---|---|---|---|---|---|---|---|---|---|---|---|---|---|
| **Real Effective Exchange Rate** | | | | | | | | | | | | | | | | |
| Argentina | 92.1 | 105.2 | 98.6 | 87.2 | 118.9 | 90.3 | 110.2 | 99.4 | 75.7 | 67.5 | 75.6 | 115.2 | 103.6 | 95.7 | 129.4 | 106.9 |
| Brazil | 92.0 | 95.6 | 103.9 | 103.0 | 103.3 | 98.6 | 97.9 | 103.5 | 114.9 | 127.6 | 103.8 | 98.3 | 115.7 | 109.2 | 109.6 | 101.3 |
| Chile | 67.3 | 51.1 | 44.3 | 86.7 | 113.2 | 99.4 | 92.7 | 107.8 | 98.5 | 83.8 | 75.3 | 83.9 | 90.5 | 91.4 | 103.8 | 106.2 |
| Colombia | 112.6 | 114.1 | 115.8 | 109.7 | 112.6 | 106.8 | 96.1 | 97.1 | 94.7 | 95.9 | 88.9 | 81.1 | 83.8 | 89.5 | 115.0 | 124.3 |
| Mexico | 91.9 | 94.9 | 95.4 | 92.1 | 90.4 | 93.9 | 105.2 | 10.9 | 96.7 | 89.0 | 80.1 | 115.0 | 121.0 | 100.3 | 98.0 | 144.5 |
| Peru | 74.5 | 75.7 | 83.0 | 82.5 | 74.6 | 79.8 | 94.4 | 125.9 | 124.1 | 114.0 | 96.5 | 92.4 | 100.3 | 101.1 | 121.0 | 94.6 |
| Venezuela | 98.2 | 99.5 | 106.7 | 109.3 | 104.6 | 101.2 | 98.1 | 100.7 | 104.2 | 98.6 | 89.5 | 81.8 | 76.6 | 106.7 | 96.3 | 95.5 |
| **Liberalization Index** | | | | | | | | | | | | | | | | |
| Argentina | 7.4 | 5.1 | 3.6 | 4.1 | 10.9 | 6.4 | 9.2 | 7.5 | 8.1 | 8.5 | 9.3 | 11.4 | 9.0 | 7.8 | 7.9 | 7.5 |
| Brazil | 8.5 | 9.2 | 9.9 | 14.3 | 11.6 | 9.6 | 8.3 | 8.2 | 9.7 | 11.6 | 10.2 | 9.2 | 9.5 | 8.4 | 7.7 | 6.0 |
| Chile | 11.6 | 11.1 | 15.9 | 21.4 | 28.4 | 20.1 | 21.5 | 23.5 | 25.2 | 25.5 | 25.3 | 20.6 | 20.5 | 23.9 | 24.5 | 25.4 |
| Colombia | 26.4 | 14.1 | 13.7 | 16.7 | 15.3 | 14.9 | 14.0 | 14.6 | 14.0 | 16.3 | 16.5 | 17.2 | 14.9 | 13.9 | 14.9 | 15.0 |
| Mexico | 8.7 | 8.9 | 9.5 | 10.6 | 9.6 | 9.3 | 9.4 | 11.0 | 12.4 | 13.8 | 14.0 | 11.8 | 8.9 | 9.4 | 10.4 | 11.9 |
| Peru | 14.9 | 14.5 | 16.0 | 21.1 | 22.3 | 19.2 | 21.4 | 19.3 | 18.1 | 22.6 | 24.3 | 23.7 | 22.8 | 17.6 | 19.4 | 18.2 |
| Venezuela | 19.3 | 20.7 | 19.8 | 19.2 | 25.8 | 29.9 | 36.2 | 38.5 | 29.3 | 25.5 | 25.7 | 28.9 | 13.4 | 19.9 | 19.4 | 21.9 |

a. Imports of goods and nonfactor services as a proportion of GNP.
SOURCES: Inter-American Development Bank, International Monetary Fund, *International Financial Statistics*, various issues.

imports to GNP). The instability of these two indices, which are fundamental to exports and to import substitution, is evident. With the exception of Brazil (and Venezuela, where the bolívar has been persistently overvalued in terms of exports other than oil), all governments have sent erratic messages to their exporters. Fluctuations in effective real rates of exchange have been much greater in the Latin American nations than in countries that have successfully implemented export strategies. For example, the coefficient of variation of exchange rates for Brazil and Mexico between 1979 and 1984 was double that of Korea, which was the country showing the greatest variation of all Asian NICs (Balassa and Williamson 1987). The same fluctuations occurred with the liberalization index.

What reasons may explain such increases and decreases in import levels over short periods? A large part of the answer may lie in the variability of nonessential spending levels, composed of such items as arms purchases, capital-intensive public-investment projects, and consumer goods imports. When foreign exchange or external loans have been available, they have been used to a great extent in activities that do not enhance the exchange-earning capacity of the economy.

With respect to internal policy, the money supply (M1) and fiscal deficits of the entire public sector as related to GNP also indicate a high degree of instability, reflecting the fluctuations in the external sector as well as internal imbalances principally caused by the public sector. The lack of discipline in fiscal policy, which has been a constant feature of Latin American economies, may deserve special emphasis. It is true that an important part of public revenue originates in the external sector, mainly from taxation on imports and on exports of primary goods. The short- and medium-term fluctuations of the external sector imply unavoidable variations in revenue that, when negative, are never offset by a reduction in expenditure. The inflexibility of public spending is a well-established fact not only in terms of current expenditure but also in terms of investment programs.[3]

The instability of macroeconomic policy has increased uncertainty about the future and created an atmosphere in which speculative activities become attractive to entrepreneurs. The fluctuations in investment and inflation demonstrate again the unfavorable climate for long-term planning in both the private and the public sectors. The most serious aspect of this is the existence of a vicious circle of instability that can be broken only by shock tactics directed not at the symptoms of the crisis, as has been recently the case in Latin America, but at the structural causes that produce them. Nevertheless, in democratic regimes where governments change every four or five years and in the midst of unpredictable fluctuations in the external sector, the political viability of implementing rapid and profound adjustment processes and the practical viability of maintaining the same economic model for decades seem to be, even in the best of cases, remote.

## Export-Oriented Industrialization

Without a stable macroeconomic framework to support long-term policies aimed at the expansion and diversification of exports, Latin America has not been able to match the developmental performance of the East Asian and Southeast Asian countries. The concentration of exports by products confirms the hypothesis that Latin America has been left behind in its efforts at diversification. The top ten export products made up less than 60 percent of total exports in Germany, the United States, and the United Kingdom, and 74 percent of total exports in Japan. In contrast, export concentration ratios in the Latin American countries (with the exception of Argentina and Brazil) exceeded 80 percent; for Venezuela and Chile, in fact, they exceeded 90 percent. Underdevelopment has been characterized by dependence on only a few sources of exchange revenue, and this dependence has often contributed to preventing the successful implementation of long-term macroeconomic strategies.

With the exception of Brazil, which has recorded high real rates of growth in manufactured exports, other countries do not display the dynamism that would allow us to say that their industrialization process is export-oriented. In the absence of an export-oriented industrialization process, the performance of the industrial sector has in most cases been dictated by the ups and downs of internal demand. With the variability of internal demand, industrial performance on a year-by-year basis has also been erratic. In Latin America, the annual rate of industrial sector growth ranged from 5 to 6 percent in the 1980s. In comparison, export-oriented countries have experienced a self-sustaining and dynamic industrialization process, despite the inevitable oscillations of international trade in recent decades.

Much has been said explaining the dynamism of an export-oriented industrialization process. One reason for this dynamism is that growing and stable foreign exchange earnings ensure the capacity to import the intermediate and capital goods required for additional increases in production. The certainty that growth and expansion in demand will not be interrupted by a balance-of-payments crisis stimulates productive investment (Balassa and Williamson 1987). Further, orientation toward external markets allows for greater economies of scale, fuller utilization of production capacity, and the profitable introduction of technical innovations.

But there is perhaps one aspect that has not been made sufficiently clear: comparative advantage does not necessarily run counter to the industrialization process in developing countries as had been initially thought by some Latin American economists. There is a lesson to be learned from recent economic history: despite the efforts of governments to retain their comparative advantage by employing protectionist measures, they have achieved only limited success in industrial development. It is interesting to note that protectionism has worked best in agriculture.[4] A number of developing countries have managed to break into international markets with manufactured goods, upsetting key areas of industrial production in advanced economies. Also, given the acceleration of technological change and the growing surge of new products, hopefully the process of displacement of comparative advantage will also accelerate, and the protectionist efforts of governments will continue to lose ground even in the most closed economies.

It is also interesting that countries that have based their industrialization process on exports have dramatically reduced their relative dependence on imports of manufactured goods. This can be measured in a number of ways. One indicator is the relationship between the value of manufactured exports and the value of manufactured imports, as estimated in table 4.3. The data show that in the period 1970–84 only Brazil was able to achieve a level of industrial self-sufficiency comparable to that of the newly industrialized Asian countries, since in most industrialized countries the self-sufficiency index is greater than one. In most Latin American countries, however, the industrial sector does not make any net positive contribution to the balance of payments.

## Conclusion

The lack of continuity in Latin American economic policy might also be due to the frequent absence of a minimum level of social cohesion and to a wide range of social and political conflicts. As noted by Miguel

Table 4.3
Major Latin American Countries' Index of Industrial Self-sufficiency,[a]
1970–84, Selected Years

|  | 1970 | 1975 | 1980 | 1981 | 1982 | 1983 | 1984 |
|---|---|---|---|---|---|---|---|
| LAIA[b] countries | 0.28 | 0.23 | 0.33 | 0.30 | 0.36 | 0.69 | 0.72 |
| Argentina | 0.19 | 0.27 | 0.24 | 0.26 | 0.48 | 0.39 | 0.42 |
| Brazil | 0.18 | 0.25 | 0.65 | 0.93 | 0.91 | 1.50 | 2.24 |
| Chile | 1.48 | 1.33 | 0.91 | 0.87 | 0.91 | 1.34 | 0.91 |
| Colombia | 0.09 | 0.25 | 0.23 | 0.21 | 0.19 | 0.15 | 0.17 |
| Mexico | 0.23 | 0.22 | 0.16 | 0.11 | 0.18 | 0.81 | 0.66 |
| Peru | 0.70 | 0.21 | 0.72 | 0.28 | 0.48 | 0.48 | 0.61 |
| Venezuela | 0.02 | 0.02 | 0.07 | 0.07 | 0.06 | 0.13 | 0.19 |

a. Ratio of manufactures exports to manufactures imports. Industrial goods are those included in sections 5–9 of SITC classification, based on CEPAL data.
b. Latin American Integration Association, formerly Latin American Free Trade Area (LAFTA).
SOURCES: Economic Commission for Latin America and the Caribbean; Inter-American Development Bank.

Urrutia (1987), social cohesion and the absence of violence are prerequisites for accelerated economic growth in economic systems where investment is mainly in the hands of the private sector. The social problems derived from an unequal distribution of income and the absence of solid and legitimate political institutions hinder the creation of the stability necessary to achieve sustained rates of saving and investment.

Some observers have emphasized the apparent relationship between a country's political system and its levels of saving and investment. Centralized political systems may have the advantage because, in order to break the vicious circle of underdevelopment and transfer resources for the industrialization process, they can more effectively implement forced saving schemes and measures to push down consumption levels. It could be argued that Western European countries in the nineteenth century, Russia during the first half of this century, and some Asian countries more recently, have had governments in which political power has been highly centralized. In more open systems, with the existence of trade unions and the active participation of a wide variety of social and economic interests, it is not easy to implement policies that sacrifice today's consumption for tomorrow's growth. It can also be argued that the political system should change side by side with economic development and that in an export-oriented industrialized economy it is almost impossible to retain a rigid and closed political system.

Recently, because of the U.S. trade deficit, there has been increasing pressure on countries such as Japan, Taiwan, and Korea to increase their own levels of consumption and to reduce their external current account surpluses. Part of this imbalance is due to their internal policies, in which macroeconomic policy is completely subordinated to the objectives of increasing exports and accumulating international reserves. In this context, voluntary and forced saving schemes have been used, and consumption and imports have been restricted as much as possible. These policies, directed at the conquest of international markets but also at the protection of home markets, have been consistently applied for several decades and have undoubtedly produced results in economic development. For instance, even though countries such as Taiwan and Korea have restricted labor union activities, increases in productivity in these countries have led to wage levels that are presently higher than in Latin American countries where the unions have been much more active (Balassa and Williamson 1987).

Latin America's dilemma is clear. Its political systems have become increasingly more open, but in the process, conditions have been created for instability in macroeconomic management. The result is an unfavorable climate for saving and long-term investment. As Balassa and his colleagues have shown (1986: ch. 3), given the high external indebtedness and the foreseeable evolution of international capital markets, without high internal rates of saving and investment it would be impossible to sustain economic growth and to advance in the diversification of exports. In this respect, it would seem of the utmost importance for Latin American governments to behave maturely. It is always possible to blame external factors for the results of internal mismanagement. But this is ultimately self-defeating, since the solutions to the problems must always come from within, particularly from the macroeconomic policies that are adopted by governments.

Three basic elements may be expected of a maturely designed macroeconomic policy in Latin America. First, at the minimum there needs to be a consensus on the direction of the development process, so that continuity and stability in policy are achieved regardless of changes in government. Second, policymakers need to accept that sustained economic growth requires a major effort toward increasing internal saving and introducing fiscal discipline. Inflationary financing has created more problems than solutions, especially because productive investment is discouraged and undesirable consequences in income distribution are created. Third, as most Latin American countries are at an intermediate stage of economic development, internal demand cannot be the main or only source of growth; exports must also be used as a driving force for growth and industrialization.

The most important lesson for Latin America to draw from the Asian experience may be the need for continuity and stability in economic policy. The Asian NICs have directed policy at export promotion with a selective and gradual import-substitution process. There has been much discussion about the overprotection of domestic markets in countries that have succeeded as exporters. Their excessive current account surpluses and high accumulation of international reserves, which are the result of restrictive import policies, have produced significant imbalances and distortions in international trade.

In Latin America, the massive use of external credit within inward-looking economic models has led to a recession that has not been seen since the 1930s. Perhaps due to the cycles generated by an overdependence on natural resources or the lack of political consensus on the direction of the development process, these countries have not been able to meet the challenge posed by the recent fall in their terms of trade or by the closing of international capital markets since 1982. Repeated crises in their balance of payments have only worsened the problems arising from their economic instability and the lack of confidence in their future. As Antonio J. Urdinola (1987:67) has remarked:

> Latin America's greatest failure has been its inability to overcome the macroeconomic instability that its own wealth of natural resources has brought about. . . . Variations in real exchange rates, in commercial, fiscal, and financial policy, all closely related to the ups and downs in the prices of primary products, have prevented Latin America from being able to undertake a successful import-substitution process alongside an aggressive export promotion drive, as Japan, Korea, and Taiwan have managed to do.

We still know comparatively little about the relationship between short-term stabilization policy and long-term growth policy (Khan 1987). Nonetheless, an export-oriented development model requires continuous effort and a clear message to manufacturers that a long-term policy favorable to their export activities is here to stay. Given that a stable macroeconomic climate is a precondition for success in promoting and diversifying exports, Latin America needs a political consensus to ensure long-term policy continuity despite changes in government. Otherwise, how will these countries mitigate and absorb negative fluctuations in their terms of trade in the midst of a balance-of-payments crisis that has been caused by excessive external indebtedness and lack of access to fresh resources in international capital markets?

Recent experience suggests that most Latin American countries have been unable to implement a clear macroeconomic policy. The destabilizing forces of excessive external indebtedness and the recent decline in their terms of trade have increased the uncertainties surrounding future government policies. Overwhelmed by such negative external factors, Latin American countries do not have any other alternative but to face the hard reality of an increasing need for the adoption and implementation of a stable, outward-oriented macroeconomic policy.

# 5

*Youngil Lim*

# Comparing Brazil and Korea

Brazil and Korea have been strong performers in recent industrial growth and are likely to continue to be so. But Brazil, since the 1981–83 recession, has been experiencing extraordinary difficulties with external debt servicing and inflation. Korea, in contrast, has been faring rather well. According to estimates made by the United Nations Industrial Development Organization (UNIDO), from 1980 to 1987 Brazil had a 2.1 percent average annual growth of manufacturing value added compared to 13.1 percent for Korea. The question that arises is, What happened in each country? Both are highly indebted, with relatively sophisticated industrial bases. And in both countries, governments have intervened to control credit allocation in investment and imports. Why and how has Korea continued to increase exports of manufactured goods, service its debt, and grow quickly with little inflation, whereas Brazil has experienced a well-publicized debt-service moratorium, rapid inflation, and faltering growth?

These questions have often been answered in terms of differences in macroeconomic management (Sachs 1985; Lin 1988; Aghevli and Márquez-Ruarte 1985). But that is only one side of the story. Rarely has a supply-side comparative examination been conducted, that is, an examination of the competitiveness of industry itself in each country, based on differences in industrial organization, incentive structure, policy on competition, and industrial restructuring. Also, the widely held impression that Korea's success owes mainly to the adoption of a free-market philosophy and an export-led growth strategy has been seriously questioned (Luedde-Neurath 1986).

This chapter attempts to answer some of those questions by comparing relevant information from existing studies. It will examine differences between the two countries in export promotion incentives and import-substitution policies, that is, in policies with respect to external competition. It will go on to compare features of internal competition from industrial organization theory, including concentration, sources of profit making, the role of state enterprises, and direct foreign investment (DFI).

## Export-Promotion Incentives

Korean industry, it has been widely believed, grew rapidly, above all because its export-led strategy was based on the theory of the free market, whereas in Brazil the government intervened in the market and followed an import-substitution strategy under a high level of protection (Balassa 1978). There is some validity to this view, but it is not the whole story. In fact, the Korean government has been implementing a scheme of import substitution concealed under the more visible export promotion strategy. The government has intricately mixed both strategies so that exporters are not subject to the antiexport biases that import substitution under protection brings. The significant difference between Korea and Brazil seems to be that in Korea intervention is used to promote the competitiveness of industry, with an incentive system based on automatic rules of export-performance criteria, whereas in Brazil there is less emphasis placed on international competitiveness.

The Korean government early on adopted a policy of nurturing infant industries under protection. It encouraged competition in international markets by providing information on what to produce and where to sell, by subsidizing credit, and by providing transportation rebates, tax and tariff exemptions, accelerated depreciation, wastage allowances, and so on (a total of thirty-eight schemes during the 1960s and 1970s) to compensate for the negative effects of protection on exports (Hong 1979; Lim 1981). By 1982 virtually all the subsidy measures had been discontinued, except for credit allocation.

True, an exporter can still find "contrived free-market conditions," that is, he can import raw materials, intermediate products, machines, and parts at world market prices, borrow money at a below-market rate for investment and export financing, and hire inexpensive labor at a fraction of the wage rate in industrialized countries (a major export destination). If the laborers learn their skills quickly to produce output of acceptable quality in the world market, then the contrived free-market environment provides a powerful incentive for entrepreneurs to take risks, that is, to invest, produce, and sell abroad.

However, the incentive benefits are provided on the basis of a rather strict export-performance criterion applicable to all exporters without sectoral discrimination. The letter of credit from abroad provides an objective, easily identifiable criterion for evaluating a firm's export performance. Exporters are graded and ranked annually and rewarded with incentive bounties according to the sum of the letters of credit received. This criterion tends to make the cost of cheating high because the record of customs clearances enables easy cross-checking. At the same time, the cost of evaluating the performance of exporters is low, since only the letter of credit entitles a firm to apply for each of the incentive benefits—a simple procedure to minimize rent-seeking activities. The most powerful features of the system are the exporter's automatic access to bank credit at a below-market rate of interest and entitlement to use foreign exchange, normally unavailable to non-exporters (including consumers). Nonexporters have to pay a curb market rate of interest that is two or three times higher than the official rate and black market foreign exchange rates, unless their output is designated by the government as national priority goods (such as machinery, steel, electronics, oil refining, or petrochemicals) that need to be nurtured like those from an infant industry.

In contrast, the Brazilian incentive system appears to be more discretionary and selective. For instance, in the BEFIEX program, a key incentive scheme for exporters, only 19.6 percent of manufactured exports received incentive benefits in 1980.[1] Note that this benefited only one hundred firms. In Korea in January 1980, 2,708 exporting firms claimed incentive benefits (*Joong-Ang Daily News* [1980]1981). The BEFIEX benefit seems concentrated in a few selected sectors. For instance, in 1980, metal products, machinery, and transport equipment accounted for 83.0 percent of the export commitment under the BEFIEX program and for 70.8 percent of net foreign exchange earnings (table 5.1). Transport equipment alone made up 49.2 percent and 36.2 percent of the export commitment and net foreign exchange earnings, respectively. It is conspicuous that the smaller the net foreign exchange

**Table 5.1**
**Brazilian Export Incentives: BEFIEX Sectoral Programs, 1980**
**(US $ billions)**

| Sector | Export Commitment | | Net Earnings of Foreign Exchange | | col.(3)/col.( 1) Percent |
|---|---|---|---|---|---|
| | Amount[a] (1) | Share (%) (2) | Amount (3) | Share (%) (4) | |
| Food | 0.39 | 1.5 | 0.32 | 3.0 | 82.1 |
| Chemicals | 0.40 | 1.6 | 0.16 | 1.5 | 40.0 |
| Wood Products | 0.20 | 0.8 | 0.17 | 1.6 | 85.0 |
| Paper and Pulp | 1.26 | 5.0 | 0.86 | 8.1 | 68.3 |
| Textiles, Garments | 1.66 | 6.6 | 1.33 | 12.5 | 80.1 |
| Footwear | 0.17 | 0.7 | 0.14 | 1.3 | 82.1 |
| Metals | 5.93 | 23.5 | 2.33 | 22.0 | 39.3 |
| Machinery | 2.59 | 10.3 | 1.34 | 12.6 | 51.7 |
| Transport Equipment | 12.39 | 49.2 | 3.85 | 36.2 | 31.1 |
| Other | 0.19 | 0.8 | 0.13 | 1.2 | 68.4 |
| **Total** | 25.18 | 100.0 | 10.62 | 100.0 | 42.2 |

a. Total export commitments during the contract period at the end of 1980.
SOURCE: Beneficio Fiscaio a Programas Especiais de Exportacao (BEFIEX), *Annual Report 1980.*

earnings ratio, the greater the BEFIEX commitment. Furthermore, the amount of tax credit received on export by the transport equipment industry was more than four times the amount of export profits in 1979 (World Bank 1983). Brazil appears to have subsidized more import-intensive exports. In Korea the foreign exchange earnings ratio is less concentrated in specific sectors.

Furthermore, exemption and reduction of taxes and import duties in Brazil (the most prevalent industrial incentives among twenty-four schemes) were used not only for export promotion but—more heavily—for import substitution. According to a World Bank estimate, about 70 percent of the total exemptions (or reductions) of tariff duties and other taxes were made to support industrial production for domestic sales and only 30 percent to reduce discrimination against exports.[2] Thus the Brazilian incentive system appears to have been less of an enticement to export production than the Korean system. This effect shows up in the export shares in each subsector of manufacturing.

Let us look at the pattern of sectoral shares in manufacturing exports for the two economies (tables 5.2 and 5.3). The average manufacturing

**Table 5.2**
**Export-Output Ratio by Industry for Korea,[a] 1971 and 1980 (%)**

|  | 1971[b] | 1980[b] |
|---|---|---|
| **Light Industries** | 19 | 29 |
| Food, Beverages, and Tobacco | 2 | 8 |
| Textiles | 26 | 38 |
| Apparel | 46 | 74 |
| Leather Products | 23 | 42 |
| Footwear | 51 | 63 |
| Wood Products | 41 | 33 |
| Rubber Products | 28 | 38 |
| Miscellaneous Products of Petroleum | 0 | 2 |
| Plastic Products | 4 | 10 |
| Printing and Publishing | 1 | 7 |
| Professional and Scientific Equipment | 11 | 62 |
| Miscellaneous Products | 61 | 64 |
| **Heavy Industries** | 9 | 19 |
| Paper Products | 1 | 6 |
| Industrial Chemicals | 7 | 11 |
| Other Chemical Products | 1 | 2 |
| Petroleum Products | 3 | 1 |
| Nonmetallic Mineral Products | 5 | 15 |
| Iron and Steel Products | 16 | 21 |
| Nonferrous Metal Products | 16 | 13 |
| Fabricated Metal Products | 10 | 45 |
| General Machinery | 15 | 17 |
| Electrical Machinery | 25 | 33 |
| Transport Equipment | 4 | 46 |
| **Total Manufacturing** | 15 | 24 |

a. Export data in SITC have been reclassified by KSIC and converted at the average exchange rate of each year.
b. Each year is represented by the three-year average around it.
SOURCE: Soogil Young, "Import Liberalization," Korea Development Institute Working Paper no. 8613, December 1986.

export-output ratio for Korea, which grew from 15 percent to 24 percent between 1971 and 1980, is higher than Brazil's, which grew from 5.7 percent to 9.1 percent between 1970 and 1979. For Korea, a high and increasing share has been recorded in transport equipment, fabricated metal products, footwear, and professional scientific equipment, while the share of wood and rubber products has declined. This appears to reflect the paucity of natural resources and the gains in human skill.

### Table 5.3
### Export-Output Ratio by Manufacturing
### Subsector for Brazil, 1970 and 1979 (%)

|                          | 1970 | 1979 |
|--------------------------|------|------|
| Nonmetallic Minerals     | 0.8  | 1.8  |
| Metallurgy               | 3.2  | 3.7  |
| Machinery                | 3.6  | 14.2 |
| Electrical Equipment     | 1.4  | 4.4  |
| Transport Equipment      | 0.7  | 9.9  |
| Lumber and Wood          | 4.2  | 8.9  |
| Furniture                | 0.3  | 0.8  |
| Paper                    | 0.9  | 7.7  |
| Rubber                   | 0.9  | 3.4  |
| Leather                  | 13.5 | 21.3 |
| Chemicals                | 5.7  | 11.4 |
| Pharmaceutical Products  | 0.8  | 2.5  |
| Perfumery                | 0.2  | 1.1  |
| Plastics                 | 0.1  | 0.8  |
| Textiles                 | 7.4  | 6.5  |
| Apparel and Footwear     | 1.0  | 7.4  |
| Food                     | 13.3 | 16.9 |
| Beverages                | 0.3  | 1.8  |
| Tobacco                  | 11.5 | 22.1 |
| Printing and Publishing  | 0.3  | 0.6  |
| Miscellaneous            | 2.2  | 7.7  |
| **Total**                | 5.7  | 9.1  |

SOURCE: World Bank, *Brazil: Industrial Policies and Manufactured Exports*, 1983, p. 38.

In Brazil, a double-digit share has been recorded in leather, food, and tobacco products. This reflects Brazil's natural resource endowment. Machinery, transport equipment, chemicals, and miscellaneous manufactures display a rapidly increasing share because the industrialization policy favors heavy industry.

## Import-Substitution Policies

Looking at Brazil's import-total supply ratio (table 5.4) one finds a general tendency toward import substitution in the heavy industry subsectors such as general machinery, fabricated metal products, nonferrous metal products, iron and steel, and industrial chemicals. An

### Table 5.4
### Ratio of Manufactured Imports to Total Supply for Brazil, 1970 and 1979 (%)

|  | 1970 | 1979 |
|---|---|---|
| Nonmetallic Minerals | 2.7 | 2.4 |
| Metallurgy | 10.0 | 4.6 |
| Machinery | 28.4 | 19.5 |
| Electrical Equipment | 18.8 | 14.1 |
| Transport Equipment | 7.8 | 3.6 |
| Lumber and Wood | 0.4 | 1.0 |
| Furniture | 0.1 | 0.1 |
| Paper | 8.6 | 4.9 |
| Rubber | 2.9 | 4.4 |
| Leather | 0.5 | 2.6 |
| Chemicals | 15.6 | 11.8 |
| Pharmaceutical Products | 6.0 | 8.1 |
| Perfumery | 2.2 | 1.2 |
| Plastics | 0.5 | 0.3 |
| Textiles | 0.6 | 0.6 |
| Apparel and Footwear | 0.8 | 0.3 |
| Food Products | 0.9 | 5.1 |
| Beverages | 4.5 | 1.3 |
| Tobacco | 0.0 | 0.1 |
| Printing and Publishing | 2.3 | 2.0 |
| Miscellaneous | 21.7 | 21.1 |
| **Total** | 8.0 | 6.8 |

SOURCE: World Bank, *Brazil: Industrial Policies and Manufactured Exports*, 1983, p. 35.

interesting phenomenon occurs in Korean transport equipment: both the export-output ratio (table 5.2) and the import-total supply ratio (table 5.5) increase. One would assume that this is due to intraindustry trade, although it may reflect the aggregation problem (as when distinctly different products such as ships and cars are grouped together). However, this similarity between the two ratios conceals the contrasting strategies the two countries have in raising competitiveness.

The available evidence suggests that Brazilian industrialization took place under heavier protection than that of Korea. For example, the average tariff rate for all industries in Brazil in 1980 was more than triple that of Korea in 1978 (Luedde-Neurath 1986; World Bank 1983). The available estimates of effective protection also confirm the general impression that Brazilian manufacturing has been more heavily protected than its Korean counterpart. In 1978 the effective

Table 5.5
Ratio of Manufactured Imports to Total Supply for Korea,
1971 and 1980 (%)[a]

| | 1971[b] | 1980[b] |
|---|---|---|
| **Light Industries** | 13 | 14 |
| Food, Beverages, and Tobacco | 14 | 13 |
| Textiles | 20 | 17 |
| Apparel | 1 | 1 |
| Leather Products | 25 | 49 |
| Footwear | 0 | 0 |
| Wood Products | 2 | 4 |
| Rubber Products | 3 | 4 |
| Miscellaneous Petroleum Products | 1 | 3 |
| Plastic Products | 3 | 2 |
| Printing and Publishing | 4 | 4 |
| Professional and Scientific Equipment | 44 | 59 |
| Miscellaneous Products | 15 | 25 |
| **Heavy Industries** | 34 | 25 |
| Paper Products | 18 | 21 |
| Industrial Chemicals | 45 | 29 |
| Other Chemical Products | 10 | 13 |
| Petroleum Products | 4 | 7 |
| Nonmetallic Mineral Products | 5 | 6 |
| Iron and Steel Products | 43 | 19 |
| Nonferrous Metal Products | 44 | 33 |
| Fabricated Metal Products | 33 | 27 |
| General Machinery | 77 | 56 |
| Electrical Machinery | 39 | 29 |
| Transport Equipment | 38 | 45 |
| **Total Manufacturing** | 23 | 21 |

a. Import data in SITC have been reclassified by KSIC and converted at the average exchange rate of each year.
b. Each year is represented by the three-year average around it.
SOURCE: Korea Development Institute, KDI Trade Tapes.

rate of protection for total manufactures in Korea was 30.6 percent, while the corresponding rate in Brazil from 1980 to 1981 was 43.6 percent (Nam 1981).

A more important aspect of these countries' differences over import policy appears to be their use of import liberalization as a tool to expose domestic industry to international competition, thereby strengthening the competitiveness of domestic production. The

Korean government has been pursuing a long-term goal of gradual import liberalization, for which it has used several policy tools, such as reduction of the tariff rate, import licensing, and import surveillance. Since the mid-1960s, the average tariff rate has been gradually reduced from 40 percent until in 1984 it stood at 21.9 percent, although the rate

**Table 5.6**
**Import Licensing Liberalization Ratio (ILLR)[a] by Industry for Korea, 1977, 1980, and 1984**

|  | Total Imported Items in 1977 | ILLR (percent) | | |
|---|---|---|---|---|
|  |  | 1977 | 1980 | 1984 |
| Food, Beverages, and Tobacco | 191 | 49 | 45 | 61 |
| Textiles | 227 | 40 | 70 | 90 |
| Apparel | 75 | 21 | 42 | 91 |
| Leather Products | 32 | 66 | 87 | 100 |
| Footwear | 9 | 44 | 100 | 100 |
| Wood Products | 50 | 72 | 82 | 100 |
| Rubber Products | 26 | 39 | 92 | 92 |
| Miscellaneous Petroleum Products | 12 | 92 | 100 | 100 |
| Plastic Products | 14 | 0 | 93 | 100 |
| Printing and Publishing | 17 | 82 | 88 | 94 |
| Professional and Scientific Equipment | 72 | 57 | 60 | 75 |
| Miscellaneous Products | 62 | 34 | 54 | 70 |
| Paper Products | 42 | 45 | 88 | 93 |
| Industrial Chemicals | 305 | 48 | 77 | 84 |
| Other Chemical Products | 107 | 87 | 96 | 98 |
| Petroleum Products | 17 | 94 | 100 | 100 |
| Nonmetallic Mineral Products | 99 | 58 | 86 | 91 |
| Iron and Steel Products | 92 | 57 | 76 | 84 |
| Nonferrous Metal Products | 76 | 82 | 90 | 89 |
| Fabricated Metal Products | 82 | 61 | 85 | 95 |
| General Machinery | 278 | 49 | 54 | 70 |
| Electrical Machinery | 137 | 20 | 29 | 56 |
| Transport Equipment | 81 | 32 | 31 | 46 |
| **Total Manufacturing** | 2,093 | 50 | 67 | 80 |

a. The number of the automatic import-approval items relative to the total number of them actually imported. Commodities have been counted in terms of Korea's tariff lines.
SOURCE: Soogil Young, "Import Liberalization and Industrial Adjustment in Korea," Korea Development Institute Working Paper no. 8613, December 1986.

for finished products was higher than that for intermediate products or raw materials (Young 1986).

Licensing requirements for imports have also been gradually reduced since the mid-1970s. The trend is reflected in the number of product items placed on the automatic approval list announced annually as a proportion of items at the four-digit level of the Customs Cooperation Council Nomenclature (CCCN). Table 5.6 presents this ratio broken down by twenty-three product subcategories in manufacturing only. Every year new product items are added to this list; the choice is based on whether a specific product item has become competitive enough to be able to meet foreign competition. Also, preannouncement of specific items warns the relevant producers to prepare themselves. However, if there is a sign that the producers may falter because of the import competition, then the product is placed on the import surveillance list. The authority monitors carefully whether imports are hurting the industrial subsector, and if necessary, the product is pulled from the list of automatic approval for import.

Compared to the Korean policy to reduce tariff rates and liberalize import licensing, Brazil's policy since 1980 has been to stiffen import restrictions. It does so partly through establishing a financial operations tax on most imports and partly through a number of administrative barriers that often reject import licenses outright. In recent years, the balance-of-payments crisis has intensified the need to restrict imports.

## Internal Competition

**Concentration ratios.** On the average the eight largest Brazilian firms made up 59.1 percent of total sales in their respective sectors in 1977, whereas the thirty largest Korean ones made up 34.1 percent in the same year. The sectoral breakdown also shows a generally higher concentration ratio in Brazil than in Korea.[3] For example, of all the producers of transport equipment the eight largest firms in Brazil made up 83 percent of total sales, whereas in Korea the thirty largest firms in this sector represented only 55 percent of total sales. A higher concentration ratio in Brazil was also found in the manufacture of machinery, paper products, printing and publishing, beverages, and chemicals, to name just a few (Baer 1987; Lee 1980). A higher concentration is also observed in heavy industries such as transport equipment, petroleum refining, and chemicals for both countries. The higher concentration in Brazil seems to be related to the involvement of large state enterprises and multinational companies as compared to that of Brazilian-owned private enterprises. In Brazil, the average net assets of state enterprises were more than twenty-five times those of privately owned firms, whereas those of multinational firms were more than twice as large. As a group, state enterprises and multinational firms appear to be involved heavily in almost all subsectors of manufacturing.

In Korea, multinational companies have a much smaller share in industrial activities. The foreign affiliates in Korea employed 9.5 percent of the manufacturing labor and produced 19.3 percent of the manufacturing output in 1978 (UN Centre on Transnational Corporations et al. 1987). In 1977, foreign affiliates in Brazil employed 23 percent of the manufacturing labor and produced 32 percent of the manufacturing output. A study conducted in 1976 revealed high correlations between structural market-power indicators of U.S. multinational corporations in Brazil and their profits after taxes (Conner 1976). But, in general, foreign firms in Brazil, compared to their local counterparts, are reported to be greater exporters with higher labor productivity and greater capital and skill intensity (Willmore 1986). From 1972 to 1976 profit repatriations from DFI were recorded as 0.4 percent of exports for Korea and 6.5 percent for Brazil (World Bank [1978] 1986).

In 1979 in Brazil, among the publicly owned enterprises in manufacturing alone, the federal government operated 56 enterprises, state governments, 33, and municipal governments, 3. In addition, it has been reported that in 1982, 46 public enterprises contributed 70 percent of the manufactured output value (Economist Intelligence Unit 1986; Lloyd's Bank 1986).[4] In Korea, 98 public enterprises contributed 10.6 percent of the nonagricultural GDP in 1977, and within the manufacturing sector the Korean public enterprises shared 14.9 percent of output in the period 1974–77 (Il 1979; Floyd et al. 1984). It is well known that state enterprises normally earn a lower rate of profit than nonstate ones, a situation that reflects the general empire-building tendency of the state enterprises. In 1982 in Korea, for instance, the operating profit to business capital recorded was 3.7 percent for government-invested enterprises and 10.1 percent for all industries (Song 1986b). Unfortunately, comparable information is not available for Brazil, a problem that reportedly stems from secrecy or even refusal by some state enterprises to submit financial data to the Ministry of Planning (Baer et al. 1977). The Brazilian state of affairs contrasts with that of the Korean public enterprises, which since March 1984 have been subjected to a performance evaluation system to improve management efficiency. Under the performance bonus system, "the operating profit has been continuously improving; it increased 50 percent in 1984 and 20 percent in 1985. Cost-saving effort was recognized especially in the inventory management. Unnecessary large stock of inventory was penalized by the appropriate criteria" (Song 1986a).

Table 5.7
Performance of Manufacturing Subsectors in Brazil and Korea, 1979 (%)

| | Asset Turnover Ratio[a] | | Net Profit on Asset[b] (%) | | Net Profit on Sale[b] (%) | | Growth Rates of MVA[c] (%) | |
|---|---|---|---|---|---|---|---|---|
| | Brazil | Korea | Brazil | Korea | Brazil | Korea | Brazil | Korea |
| Nonmetallic Minerals | 0.70 | 0.99 | 8.5 | 2.9 | 12.2 | 2.9 | -6.1 | 8.6 |
| Metallurgy | 0.68 | 0.78 | 0.7 | 2.0 | 1.0 | 2.5 | 20.0 | 31.0 |
| Machinery | 0.93 | 0.89 | 3.3 | 1.8 | 3.6 | 2.0 | 7.4 | 0.0 |
| Electrical Equipment | 1.12 | 1.30 | 10.4 | 3.2 | 9.3 | 2.5 | 7.2 | 18.2 |
| Transport Equipment | 1.08 | 0.87 | 4.3 | -0.8 | 4.0 | -0.9 | 6.7 | 15.3 |
| Wood Products | 0.83 | 1.59 | 10.5 | -0.6 | 12.7 | -0.4 | 0.0 | -7.1 |
| Furniture | 1.43 | 1.75 | 9.4 | 4.7 | 6.6 | 2.7 | 8.2 | 14.6 |
| Paper | 0.71 | 1.33 | 5.1 | 2.0 | 7.1 | 1.5 | 13.9 | 12.2 |
| Leather Products | 1.44 | 1.56 | 12.6 | -4.1 | 8.7 | -2.6 | 4.4 | -17.1 |
| Chemicals | 0.79 | .97 | 5.7 | 3.4 | 7.2 | 3.5 | 29.0 | 11.5 |
| Pharmaceuticals | 1.17 | 1.47 | 0.1 | 10.5 | 0.1 | 7.1 | na | na |
| Perfumes and Soap | 1.66 | 1.21 | 7.1 | 5.3 | 4.3 | 4.4 | 14.6 | 18.7 |
| Plastics | 1.23 | 1.47 | 13.1 | 4.7 | 10.6 | 3.2 | 8.2 | -7.9 |
| Textiles | 0.98 | 1.09 | 9.9 | 0.3 | 10.2 | 0.3 | 8.1 | 12.4 |
| Clothing | 1.36[d] | 2.45 | 13.8[d] | 0.5 | 10.1[d] | 0.2 | 4.7 | -3.9 |
| Footwear | — | 1.42 | — | -1.4 | — | -1.0 | 4.4 | -32.7 |
| Processed Food | 1.36 | 1.62 | 8.0 | 3.1 | 5.8 | 1.9 | -1.1 | 23.5 |
| Beverages | 0.75 | 1.21 | 8.4 | 5.1 | 11.3 | 4.2 | 4.3 | 18.0 |
| Tobacco | 1.02 | na | 12.3 | na | 12.0 | na | 7.2 | 4.6 |
| Printing and Publishing | 1.36 | 1.54 | 8.4 | 5.2 | 6.2 | 3.4 | -6.5 | 13.8 |
| Miscellaneous | 1.17 | 1.79 | 10.2 | -1.4 | 8.8 | -0.8 | 6.7 | -3.0 |
| **Total Manufacturing** | 0.95 | 1.24 | 5.9 | 1.9 | 6.2 | 1.5 | 7.2 | 10.7 |

na = Not available.
Dashed cells indicate not applicable.
a. Total value of sales over total assets.
b. Net profit refers to profit net of taxes.
c. Manufacturing value added, in 1980 prices.
d. Includes footwear.
SOURCES: Korea, Bank of Korea, *Financial Statement Analysis for 1979*; United Nations Industrial Development Organization (UNIDO), data bank; World Bank, *Brazil: Industrial Policy and Manufactured Exports*, 1983.

**Public enterprises.** Table 5.7 suggests that there is greater market competition in Korea than in Brazil. In general, the asset turnover ratio and growth rate of output are greater in Korea than in Brazil, while the profit ratio on assets or on sales is smaller. This is so with only a few exceptions such as machinery, transport equipment, and perfumes. The evidence can be interpreted to mean that Korean firms produce and sell on thinner profit margins than Brazilian ones. In other words, one country works harder than the other, although it is hazardous to judge on data for only one year. In Brazil, the dominant position of large-scale public enterprises has created in recent years special financing problems under an inflationary condition. The generally accepted role of public enterprises in Brazil is to provide steady output and employment opportunities when private enterprises are not willing to do so while not raising the price of output ahead of general inflation. But the controlled price of the output under an inflationary condition means that the government must intervene to cover the losses incurred by public enterprises.[5]

The Brazilian government has been subsidizing losing enterprises through budget deficits that are financed by increases in the money supply by the central bank. The system has been maintained with money creation (so-called high-powered money). It should be added that the state enterprises have also borrowed heavily from abroad, thereby raising the need for further financing for "monetary correction," which includes an exchange-rate correction on foreign debt. Because of state enterprises, government borrowing increased from 3.0 percent of GDP in 1980 to 8.8 percent of GDP in 1983 (World Bank 1985). This further accelerated the general inflation level. An indexation system for all contracts has further exacerbated such vicious circles. The inflationary situation hardly provides a favorable business climate in the short run for industrial enterprises (particularly the public enterprises) to invest, produce, and export.

In the long run, the prevalence of large-scale public and multinational enterprises, coupled with a high rate of protection, raises the question of whether the concentrated and protected industry will make "monopoly profit." The issue of efficient resource allocation is involved here. A systematic analysis of the issue, however, requires detailed data on a sufficiently large sample of industrial enterprises. Unfortunately, such data are not available for Brazil. But they are for Korea. A profit-function analysis of the Korean data therefore follows.

## Analytical Framework for Sources of Profits

The method adopted here to test sources of profitability borrows essentially from a study conducted by Richard E. Caves and Masu Uekusa (1976).[6] However, my regression equations include some additional variables deemed relevant because of policies and institutions specific to different economies. By quantifying the sources of profitability, efficiency implications can be inferred. It would have been desirable to apply the method to long-term series data in addition to cross-section data, but data availability limits my regression analysis to the cross-section data for a few years. The results reported should therefore be regarded as tentative, exploratory, and preliminary.

**Variables.** The following equation is regressed with variables explained below:

$$NAP = f(GRS, RFC, NWA, TOA, ADV, ERP, CNR, EXS, SIZ)$$

where

$NAP$ = Net [of taxes] Profits over Total Assets

$GRS$ = Growth Rate of Sales

$RFC$ = Rate of Financial Costs [interest payments and discounts] over Total Liabilities

$NWA$ = Net Worth over Total Assets

$TOA$ = Turnover Ratio of Total Assets

$ADV$ = Advertising Expenditures over Total Sales

$ERP$ = Effective Rate of Protection [tariff]

$CNR$ = Concentration Ratio

$EXS$ = Exports over Sales

$SIZ$ = Size of Enterprise [assets per firm]

This specification of the explanatory variables differs from the one that Caves and Uekusa (1976) adopted for their study of Japan. Their explanatory variables included only the (1) concentration ratio, (2) advertising outlay over total sales, (3) growth rate of sales, (4) exports over total sales, and (5) fixed costs plus wages over total costs. In this study, all of these are included except the last. In including this variable, they argued:

> The practice of permanent employment and the prevalence of high debt-equity ratios contribute to fixed costs and thereby increase the risk to which large enterprises are exposed. They should raise reported profits because they increase the risk exposure of equity capital and thus presumably raise the risk premium demanded by those who supply it [1976:93].

In Korea, by contrast, the practice of permanent employment or company loyalty does not exist; if anything, scouting personnel from other enterprises is a form of competition for pursuing profit or maximizing wealth. Even in Japan, it is reported that only large enterprises practice permanent employment, and the practice covers only one-third of the total labor force. The reasons for including the other variables follow.

**Growth rate of sales (GRS).** The first variable, growth rate of sales, is included in the regression to remove any "windfall" from a specific industry's profits. Growth rate of sales differs from industry to industry as does an industry's ability to adjust output capacity. To the extent that the adjustment involves substantial lags, an unexpected increase in sales would bring windfall profits, especially in the short run (as in a one-year period). Caves and Uekusa (1976:74, 92) caution, however, that growth rate of sales could "pick up too many influences to allow a clear interpretation," especially if data are long-run averages for individual enterprises.

**Rate of financial costs over total liabilities (RFC).** The rate of financial costs refers to the ratio of total interest paid (including discounts) over total debts (short-term plus long-term debts). As such, the ratio expresses an average rate of interest. It has been alleged that the pressure of interest burdens an enterprise, especially a financially weak one that has little collateral to offer (presumably because it is smaller). Some evidence has also been cited indicating that smaller enterprises rely on high-cost sources of loans, including the curb market, more than larger enterprises. This variable may pick up such vulnerability, particularly when the money supply is tight; therefore, a negative correlation is expected. This is included in our analysis because the view is widely held among business people and news media. It is also possible that borrowing from the high-cost source may be motivated by profitable opportunities previously unforeseen. Hence, if these opportunities are captured by borrowing, even from the high-cost source, it is possible to show a positive correlation.

**Net worth over total assets (NWA).** This ratio measures the extent of the enterprise's own capital, including retained earnings, as a proportion of total assets. Hence, the lower the proportion of net worth, the higher the assets financed by loans from the banking system and other loan markets (often called indirect financing). Much of the net worth is owned by either the entrepreneurs themselves or their family members, as the securities market is not yet well developed, especially by the standards of Western economies. In other words, the shareholders are not diffused among the citizens at large, and hence the consequences of risk taking are not passed on to general shareholders. What Harvey Leibenstein's X-efficiency theory calls the "effort-responsibility-consequences" connection is kept within the appropriate decision-making unit. He argues that if these consequences are not kept within that unit, irresponsibility increases the costs of production and decreases the profitability of enterprises—with important consequences for development (Leibenstein 1978).

The above hypothesis contrasts with the views held for industrialized countries. Caves and Uekusa (1976) argue in effect that the larger the ratio of net worth to total assets, the smaller the risk exposure. Hence, under these conditions, they claim smaller profits. It seems just the opposite, especially for Korea.

**Turnover ratio of total assets (TOA).** This variable measures total sales over total assets, indicating how many times the total assets are used per year for production and sales. The variable is used to test whether and to what extent "stretching capital" adds to profits. Thus it has often been recommended that work shifts be increased so that scarce capital in less developed countries can be economized. When this is done, as noted by Gustav Ranis,

> this meant that the average workweek per machine was two to three times that encountered in the country of origin, and since physical depreciation is much less important than economic obsolescence, using a machine twice as intensively does not wear it out twice as fast. (1973:398)

He further reports that capital stretching is common in East Asian economies to judge from the micro-level observation that he conducted.[7] Perusal of the sample data indicated a wide variation in the capital-turnover ratio (or the sales-to-assets ratio) among industries and among different sizes of enterprises. This variable is supposed to pick up this effect on profitability and is expected to have a positive correlation.

**Advertising expenditures over total sales (ADV).** Advertising functions as a means for disseminating information about the product and for product differentiation (real or imagined), which thereby increases entry barriers. Although it is not always clear which of these augments the profit, conventionally the latter is thought to be the more relevant item the variable is supposed to represent. Conceptually, however, the function of information dissemination can be said to increase awareness of competing products especially where ignorance is prevalent, as in developing economies, and hence advertising can be a market-perfecting activity. In contrast, product differentiation by advertising in developed countries can be a barrier-creating activity. Nevertheless, since operationally it is impossible to distinguish the two different effects of advertising, we include the variable as an independent one and not as a proxy for entry barrier, as in some existing studies.

**Effective rate of protection (ERP).** Developing countries often utilize protection from international competition with a high tariff as a means of industrialization. Korea is no exception in spite of its outward-looking policies. The effective rate (or value-added rate) of protection could be as high as 400 percent for certain industries at the four-digit level of industrial classification. Hence, the degree to which they are effectively protected could be a source of differential profit rates among different industries. To the extent that this variable is significant, resources could be misallocated in a static sense, although a dynamic efficiency effect could be positive if a protected industry is truly an infant industry made viable under such protection. However, the analysis of dynamic effects is beyond the scope of this exercise.

**Concentration ratio (CNR).** This is a conventional variable (proportion of output by the three largest enterprises) used to test the effect of market power on the profit rate (and resource misallocation due to the monopolistic rent that results). However, Caves and Uekusa (1976) warn that this variable could be insignificant in a rapidly industrializing economy.

> We suggest reasons why periods of very fast macroeconomic growth should translate themselves into microeconomic imbalances. When it appears profitable at the margin to expand production in practically every industry, an industry's profit rate may depend primarily on how fast it can enlarge its capacity. In industries that face long planning and construction delays in expanding capacity, substantial short-term windfalls may accrue even if the industry is potentially competitive enough that they will be eliminated in the long run. Industries adjusting quickly will reap smaller windfalls, even if concentration is high enough to keep profits above the competitive norm in the long run. Thus concentration may fail to register a significant influence on profits in periods of explosive growth, unless we take account of differences in short-run constraints on the expansion of industries' outputs. And interindustry differences in growth should be a more potent determinant of profit rates in periods when growth is on average very rapid than when it is normal, because windfalls then bulk larger in the interindustry variance of profits.

In this connection, it should be noted that Korea has enjoyed rather rapid growth. We could therefore expect an insignificant effect of concentration in profit making.

**Exports over sales (EXS).** Ordinarily, in a free-enterprise system the distinction of sales between the domestic market and overseas markets should not arise. However, the export-led growth policy indirectly introduced subsidies for exporters, subsidies that included low-interest loans, reduced taxes, rebates on public utilities, and tariff-free imports of raw materials. Under the policy, exporters would equate marginal costs and marginal benefits, including policy-contrived marginal gains. The latter would add to the profitability of an exporter over nonexport enterprises. This variable, then, is included to pick up the effect of such incentives for exports on profits, prompting us to expect a positive coefficient.

**Size of enterprise (SIZ).** The size variable represents an entry barrier due to the extent of scale economies in various senses. A large firm can do anything that a small firm can, but not vice versa. For instance, large borrowers can command lower interest rates due to lower risk to the lender, bargaining power, ability to discriminate against small firms, or even the various government policies favoring large firms. An empirical question arises then as to whether the rationale of scale economies is borne out by high profitability.

## Regression on the Korean Data

The equation is regressed on two sets of data. The first one deals with the interindustry variation of profits for sixty-eight industry classifications in manufacturing. The second deals with profit variation among establishments of different sizes (measured by number of workers) in fifty-three subgroups of small- and medium-scale enterprises. The first set of data comes from the Bank of Korea's *Financial Statements Analysis* (1976, 1977, 1978), which is based on a sample of 938 manufacturing enterprises selling 100 million won (W) of output or more. The sample is random but stratified by industry classification, by export orientation, and by establishment size (thus excluding many small-scale enterprises). The second set of data comes from *Jungso Kiup Siltae Chosa Bogo 1977* (Report on the survey of current status for medium and small enterprises 1977), published by the Medium Industry Bank in December 1978. The data are compiled from a stratified random sample of 1,946 small- and medium-scale enterprises (defined as those employing fewer than 300 workers or owning assets of less than $500 million). Apparently, some of the data on enterprises in the middle range overlap between these two sources; however, the former excludes small-scale enterprises (employing fewer than twenty workers), and the latter excludes large-scale enterprises (employing 300 workers or more).

The results of the regression are presented in table 5.8. These years can be considered as normal boom years, with the country having recovered by 1974 and 1975 from the effects of the oil shock. Gross national product increased by 11.5, 10.5, and 12.5 percent for 1976, 1977, and 1978, respectively, while the wholesale price index rose by 12.1, 9.2, and 11.7 percent. All other developmental indicators showed no abnormal situation that might prompt a special interpretation of the regression result.

The regression indicates that the variable of growth rate of sales (GRS) has a positive sign with a high statistical significance at the 1 percent level of confidence except for the 1976 interindustry data. The estimate of the same coefficient for the 1977 Medium Industry Bank's data shows no significance. Thus some windfall profits appear to

## Table 5.8
### Regression of Net Profit over Total Assets Using Various Data Sources, 1976–78

| Variable | Coefficient | t-ratio | Standardized Coefficient | Elasticity at Means |
|---|---|---|---|---|
| **Bank of Korea, 1976** | | | | |
| GRS | 0.014 | 0.837 | 0.077 | 0.127 |
| RFC | −0.196 | −0.956 | −0.103 | −0.390 |
| NWA | 0.208 | 6.296 | 0.561 | 1.185 |
| TOA | 2.442 | 3.216 | 0.294 | 0.811 |
| ADV | 0.489 | 1.690 | 0.186 | 0.101 |
| ERP | 0.426 | 3.068 | 0.301 | 0.114 |
| CNR | −0.156 | −0.463 | −0.041 | −0.026 |
| EXS | −0.004 | −0.059 | −0.005 | −0.002 |
| SIZ | 0.000 | 0.367 | 0.035 | 0.021 |
| *Intercept* | −3.940 | −1.657 | | |
| $R^2$ 0.503 | | d.f. 58 | | |
| **Bank of Korea, 1977** | | | | |
| GRS | 0.056 | 3.287 | 0.336 | 0.562 |
| RFC | 0.209 | 0.764 | 0.095 | 0.439 |
| NWA | 0.108 | 2.381 | 0.250 | 0.639 |
| TOA | 2.032 | 2.003 | 0.221 | 0.733 |
| ADV | 1.002 | 2.383 | 0.286 | 0.224 |
| ERP | 0.271 | 1.578 | 0.167 | 0.076 |
| CNR | −1.975 | −0.722 | −0.084 | −0.290 |
| EXS | 0.115 | 0.922 | 0.972 | 0.050 |
| SIZ | −0.000 | −0.034 | −0.419 | −0.003 |
| *Intercept* | −5.732 | −1.612 | | |
| $R^2$ 0.318 | | d.f. 58 | | |
| **Bank of Korea, 1978** | | | | |
| GRS | 0.045 | 2.911 | 0.252 | 0.487 |
| RFC | −0.405 | −2.205 | −0.220 | −0.911 |
| NWA | 0.227 | 6.389 | 0.548 | 1.332 |
| TOA | −0.116 | −0.126 | −0.014 | −0.047 |
| ADV | 0.997 | 3.495 | 0.315 | 0.234 |
| ERP | 0.277 | 2.223 | 0.189 | 0.081 |
| CNR | 2.025 | 1.063 | 0.095 | 0.314 |
| EXS | −0.093 | −0.545 | −0.047 | −0.023 |
| SIZ | −0.000 | −1.461 | −0.157 | −0.129 |
| *Intercept* | −1.285 | −0.422 | | |
| $R^2$ 0.540 | | d.f. 58 | | |

*Continued on following page*

## Table 5.8 Continued

| Variable | Coefficient | t-ratio | Standardized Coefficient | Elasticity at Means |
|---|---|---|---|---|
| **Bank of Korea, Pooled 1976, 1977, and 1978** | | | | |
| GRS | 0.043 | 4.586 | 0.248 | 0.432 |
| RFC | −0.103 | −0.855 | −0.052 | −0.218 |
| NWA | 0.173 | 7.927 | 0.427 | 1.008 |
| TOA | 1.658 | 3.310 | 0.195 | 0.605 |
| ADV | 0.853 | 4.560 | 0.277 | 0.189 |
| ERP | 0.342 | 4.111 | 0.227 | 0.096 |
| CNR | −0.196 | −0.544 | −0.029 | −0.031 |
| EXS | 0.047 | 0.842 | 0.046 | 0.019 |
| SIZ | −0.000 | −0.000 | −0.029 | −0.019 |
| *Intercept* | −4.316 | −2.739 | | |
| | $R^2$ 0.427 | d.f. 194 | | |
| **Medium Industry, 1977** | | | | |
| GRS | 0.006 | 1.252 | 0.124 | 0.061 |
| RFC | 0.123 | 0.893 | 0.097 | 0.135 |
| NWA | 0.128 | 4.440 | 0.883 | 0.922 |
| TOA | 2.650 | 2.484 | 0.292 | 0.592 |
| EXS | 0.030 | 1.793 | 0.215 | 0.088 |
| NOF | 0.018 | 2.517 | 0.287 | 0.111 |
| SIZ | 0.001 | 0.201 | 0.032 | 0.016 |
| *Intercept* | −6.071 | −1.931 | | |
| | $R^2$ 0.584 | d.f. 46 | | |

0.000 means a negligible number. See the text for the notation of variables.
A scatter diagram of the residuals indicates no heteroscedasticity. A perusal of simple correlation matrix for all the variables suggests no multicolinearity.
Similar regression exercises for profit rates before tax yield a slightly better fit than presented in this table in terms of R-squares and t-ratios.
The estimate of ERP for 1978 in a study conducted by the Federation of Korean Industries was adjusted to ensure compatibility with the Bank of Korea's interindustry data classification.

have been making industries more profitable because of the high-growth phase of the economy and its attendant demand for some industries' output. However, it seems that medium- and small-scale enterprises were not able to capture many sales opportunities during this period.

The rate of financial costs over total liabilities (RFC) is not statistically significant enough to influence profit rates in any systematic manner except in interindustry data for 1978. For that year, a negative correlation was found, suggesting that higher financial costs meant a lower profit rate. But the variable is not robust despite the widely held view that high financial costs, especially on loans from curb markets, threaten bankruptcy for many enterprises.

The ratio of net worth over total assets (NWA) shows a positive coefficient and is very significant and robust among all the variables for all the years, for interindustry data, and for the 1977 medium-scale industry data. The X-efficiency hypothesis appears to be amply supported by these findings. The hypothesis is that the larger the net worth (private ownership) relative to total assets, the greater the entrepreneurial efforts, thus making enterprises more profitable.

The turnover ratio of total assets (TOA) shows a significant positive coefficient for all years except for the interindustry data in 1978. The possibility of using capital more intensively to increase the rate of return is enhanced among different industries and different firm sizes within an industry. Witness that the data for 1977 for medium-scale industries are quite significant at the 2 percent significance level. Along with net worth over total assets, the capital-turnover ratio as a measure of entrepreneurial effort proved quite significant.

Advertising expenditures over total sales (ADV) appear to be an important determinant of profits for all the interindustry data except 1976. It is statistically significant at the 1 percent level for 1978, the 2 percent level for 1977, and the 1 percent level for a pooled regression of all three years. It would have been interesting to have estimated the coefficient for the Medium Industry Bank's data on establishment size, but advertising information is not available. As we have seen, whether advertising is a barrier or a market perfecter is a matter of interpretation, especially for a developing country.

The effective rate of protection (ERP) also appears to be a source of profit making. The variable is significant at the 1 percent level of significance for 1976 and for the 1976–78 pooled data, and at the 5 percent level for 1978, but is not significant for 1977. This seems to support the view that the protected domestic market is more profitable than the subsidized exports. (See the variable exports over sales [EXS] below.)

The concentration ratio (CNR) is insignificant for all the years tested, contradicting both theoretical expectations and a widely held view. Caves and Uekusa's explanation for the Japanese case appears to apply to the Korean case as well: during a period of explosive growth, concentration would fail to significantly influence profits, and windfalls through the high rate of sales would dominate over concentration.

Exports over sales (EXS) do not explain the variation in profit rates at all, contradicting our expectation of a positive coefficient. This appears to support the allegation that Korean enterprises do export in order to receive government subsidies, although exporting per se might be unprofitable. The observed price for exports, which is lower than the price for domestic sales, corroborates the findings here.

The size of enterprise (SIZ) shows no significance in explaining the variation of interindustry profit rates. An explanation for this finding might be similar to that offered for the insignificance of the concentration variable. In a rapidly growing economy, potential entry barriers would be offset by the high rate of sales. Market opportunities could be captured by entrepreneurs regardless of firm size. This finding suggests that the Korean emphasis on large-scale enterprises, based on the rationale of scale economies, might have been overemphasized.

The number of firms (NOF) applied only to the Medium Industry Bank's data and is not available for the Bank of Korea's interindustry data. The number of firms in each observation (by size of employees and by industry) is a variable reflecting the degree of competition in that industry. It is hypothesized that the larger the number of firms in each category, the greater the degree of competition; and the greater the competition, the more the firm will have to make its profits by being efficient, since it must survive with little access to bank loans. The regression shows a positive coefficient, significant at the 2 percent level of confidence.

Overall, these regressions offer little support for profit making through subsidized export activities, concentration-caused monopoly rent, and scale economies (entry barriers). The variable of the export-sales ratio bears little statistical significance in spite of the policy measures that provide hordes of incentives to export. Some argue that exporting to the world market enables firms to exploit economies of scale; hence, the efficiency and profitability of exporting firms should have been one of Korea's main sources of growth.[8] However, our findings fail to support this view. Indeed, as some critics have pointed out, enterprises might export to receive incentive benefits such as subsidized bank credits that are often used for domestic speculation, including the purchase of land, because funds are fungible in use. More lucrative business is to be found in the tariff-protected domestic market than in the export market, in which a business must compete with more efficient foreign producers. This view seems borne out by the statistical significance (*t*-value) of the variable representing the effective rate of protection. Though quantitatively not overwhelming, some market distortions and consequent inefficiency in a static sense should be recognized here.

## Conclusion

The evidence examined suggests that during the 1970s and 1980s, both Brazil and Korea have resorted to export promotion concurrently with import-substitution strategies to industrialize. But the Korean strategy, apparently, has been to manipulate export subsidies and import controls in order to enhance industry competitiveness with international markets in mind. Brazil's policy seems to have placed less emphasis on export promotion than on import substitution. Performance criteria for assistance from the Brazilian government appear to be less stringently defined by policymakers and less stringently perceived by industrial actors, including state enterprises, than those in Korea. The advantages of export-led growth could be many. But with or without export subsidies, exporters must produce goods acceptable to foreign buyers in both quality and price. Competition in overseas markets tends to force the exporters to cut costs and be more efficiency-conscious than producers of import-substitution goods under protection. Although the Brazilian experience is yet to be analyzed comparatively, existing Korean evidence appears to support the hypothesis. For instance, M. Nishimizu and S. Robinson (1984) have shown that much of the total-factor productivity growth in Korea (which shows a faster pace than in Japan) has been highly correlated with export growth and negatively correlated with import-substitution growth. The result, however, does not establish the causal relationship between strong competitiveness and export growth. Whether strong competitiveness enabled exports to grow fast or export activities made industry more efficient is unclear. It could most likely be a two-way street.

Evidence also suggests that internal competition may be less severe in Brazil than in Korea, although establishing this would require more data and analysis. Brazilian firms appear to earn a higher profit rate (over assets and sales) with a lower turnover ratio of assets than Korean firms. The dominant large-scale state enterprise sector in Brazil has acquired state subsidies to cover its losses, proportionately to loss making. In Korea, the dominant jaebols (business conglomerates) compete fiercely in domestic markets as well as overseas and are comparable to the Japanese *zaibatsu*. Evidence indicates that the monopoly element has failed to provide an important source of profit making in Korea.[9] Jaebols, however, have also been competing in the adoption of new technology (the details are yet to be analyzed) and in developing new products that are new to Korean industry but not necessarily to the world market. The competition has created a fast-growing demand for engineers and scientists. In general, the growth in the number of scientists and engineers appears higher in Korea than in Brazil (Westphal et al. 1985).

The evidence for the two countries presented here leads to a tentative conclusion that the international competitiveness of industry (however defined) may be higher in Korea than in Brazil. This seems to explain in part the continuous and faster growth in export earnings that enables Korea to fully service its debt and grow quickly, even through the 1980–83 world recession. The tentative conclusion should be further analyzed if we are to understand the situation more fully. Desirable items for such an agenda would include (depending on data availability) the following: (1) a comparative total-factor productivity (TFP) analysis comparable to that of Nishimizu and Robinson (1984) to measure the sources of TFP, particularly between exports and import substitution in Brazil; (2) a comparative TFP analysis between large-scale industry and small- and medium-scale industry; (3) a comparative test of the resource allocation theory comparable to that of Caves and Uekusa (1976); and (4) comparative case studies of each socioeconomic regime on how the conflicts of interest groups are resolved.[10]

# Part Three

# Regional Cooperation and Integration

# 6

*John Wong*

# The ASEAN Model of Regional Cooperation

Developing countries have never experienced an easy journey in their endeavors toward regional economic cooperation. Apart from structural rigidities, which are inimical to genuine economic integration, these economies are generally oriented toward industrialized countries and have a low degree of economic complementarity with one another. There is also a lack of political will to subordinate individual national interests to common regional goals. Not surprisingly, then, the past three decades have witnessed a high failure rate for regional experiments. In Latin America and East Africa, for instance, many of the prominent regional groupings that were launched in the 1960s and 1970s with great fanfare have in recent years broken up, become defunct, or simply faded away.[1]

Of all these groups, the Association of Southeast Asian Nations (ASEAN) stands out as exceptional. ASEAN came into being with the signing of the Bangkok Declaration in 1967 by Indonesia, Malaysia, the Philippines, Singapore, and Thailand (the small, newly independent state of Brunei joined as the sixth member in 1984). It celebrated its twentieth anniversary at its third summit meeting, which took place in Manila in December 1987. It has been no small achievement for ASEAN to have surmounted its enormous initial political and economic obstacles to survive twenty trying years. Its continuing existence is in itself a testimony to this success. ASEAN has emerged as one of the few highly visible regional groupings among developing countries today, and one that carries considerable political weight in the international arena.

This chapter first outlines the main features of economic cooperation in ASEAN. It then reviews ASEAN's progress, together with a discussion of its problems and constraints. Finally, it attempts to highlight some unique aspects of ASEAN's regional cooperation experience and see if they could hold any useful lessons for other developing countries.

## Regional Cooperation: The Great Experiment

ASEAN encountered a number of obstacles as it embarked on its venture. First, the timing was bad. In 1967 the war in Vietnam still raged unabated, and there was a real possibility that it would spill over into Thailand. Singapore had been independent for only two years. Indonesia's confrontation with Malaysia had just ended the previous year, and the Philippines had not yet formally settled its dispute with Malaysia over Sabah. The failure of previous attempts at regionalism in Southeast Asia was still fresh in the memories of the governments involved.[2]

ASEAN is the most heterogeneous of regional groups in terms of history, culture, language, religion, and ethnicity. Great diversity also exists among the member countries in physical area, population size, and stage of economic development. Indonesia is by far the largest country in the region, but its economic development lags behind the others. At the other end of the spectrum is the small city-state of Singapore, the most industrialized country in Southeast Asia with the highest per capita income. (Brunei, which does have a higher per capita income, was not an independent state until January 1984.) Because of its diversity, the region has not developed any strong, historically rooted regional movement comparable to Pan Americanism.

In view of these kinds of obstacles, ASEAN had to begin in a modest way. The Bangkok Declaration was a brief document, calling broadly for regional cooperation in various areas but containing no grand design for such supernational objectives as the formation of a political alliance or an economic community. There was no blueprint for achieving its regional cooperation objectives, and the declaration provided almost no institutional structure. No formal ASEAN charter existed; nor was there an ASEAN secretariat until one was established in Jakarta some nine years later. This simple framework for ASEAN cooperation stands in sharp contrast to other regional schemes, which are often accompanied by lofty aims complete with ambitious targets, comprehensive programs for economic cooperation, and an elaborate regional bureaucracy. ASEAN had none of these. However, as ASEAN continued, more favorable preconditions for regional cooperation began to unfold.

The ASEAN countries are among the world's fastest-growing economies, chalking up 5 to 10 percent growth in real gross domestic product (GDP) over most of the period 1960–86 (table A.2). Except for Singapore, the ASEAN countries are endowed with a large natural resource base, and the continuing export of such primary commodities as natural rubber, tin, palm oil, coconut products, rice, sugar, and petroleum and natural gas has provided the main engine of growth for their economies.[3] This rapid economic growth has increased the propensity for more serious economic cooperation endeavors, especially since the ASEAN economies have generally followed open and outward-looking development strategies and have been better positioned to interact with each other through greater regional economic cooperation.

The modest beginnings have worked to ASEAN's advantage. ASEAN's process of economic cooperation was highly unstructured and open-ended in its early phase. As such, it differed from other regional schemes that followed an aggressive approach to regional cooperation, establishing clear-cut targets for cooperation within a specified time frame, such as the formation of a common market. In fact, ASEAN officials have consciously avoided the term *economic integration*. In this way, cooperation has never been forced upon the member countries before a sense of community could be created. Consequently, ASEAN led little more than a symbolic existence in its early years and made virtually no progress toward any form of substantive cooperation beyond laying down the framework in which the five member governments would periodically consult with one another. It was only after 1975, when Vietnam and Cambodia came under communist rule, that the wheels of ASEAN cooperation began to turn. Political crises in Indochina stiffened the will of ASEAN leaders to approach regional cooperation more seriously and prompted the member governments to activate the ASEAN apparatus. The first ASEAN summit conference was convened in Bali in February 1976. It led to the signing of the

Declaration of ASEAN Concord, which contained more explicit guidelines for concrete economic cooperation activities.[4]

The Bali Summit provided the ASEAN regional economic cooperation framework with much-needed substance in the form of action plans. Shortly after the Bali Summit, the ASEAN Secretariat was established in Jakarta and charged with the responsibility of coordinating all levels of regional activities. The secretariat works through a series of committees, which in turn are served by a host of subcommittees, expert groups, ad hoc working groups, and other subsidiaries. The highest policy-making body is the ASEAN Ministerial Meeting, which meets at infrequent intervals. This relatively simple organizational chart belies the often cumbersome decision-making process, which is the result of ASEAN's peculiar "consensus mechanism."

The consensus requirement is perhaps the single most important feature of the ASEAN process. The ASEAN leaders have always attached considerable significance to the notion of ASEAN solidarity. This is more than political rhetoric, and when translated into policy, it requires all major decisions to be made by consensus. Consensus was at first considered indispensable for the continuing survival of a group characterized by such enormous political, economic, and social diversity. In practice, consensus implies reciprocity and in its basic form simply means that no member country should demand from others what it itself cannot offer. Applied to the process of regional cooperation, the requirement for consensus is apt to lead to lengthy negotiations and repeated consultations. It becomes an intense political exercise, with all parties balancing their pros and cons. This consensus-building process, not surprisingly, has contributed to the relative lack of implementation of ASEAN projects to date.

On the other hand, the consensus mechanism has had some important benefits. It helps improve the difficult problem of distributive gains associated with almost all regional cooperation programs by ensuring that no member need be upset by the final arrangements or suffer unduly from an uneven distribution of benefits and costs. In certain cases, the consensus mechanism actually assists the implementation of a regional cooperation program. In reaching a consensus, the parties concerned would normally have settled their differences at the working committee level, thereby easing the way for subsequent acceptance of a particular program at higher levels. In short, the value placed on consensus is simply ASEAN's special way of building commercial diplomacy into the main technique of regional cooperation. It has not made progress any easier, but it has safeguarded it against breakdown. No member has resigned from ASEAN in protest.

Another notable feature of ASEAN's basic strategy for economic cooperation is its open-minded attitude toward extraregional economic elements, particularly foreign investments. Economic cooperation arrangements in developing countries often represent an attempt to achieve a higher degree of regional self-reliance and to devise measures to restrict the activities of foreign enterprises. The idea is to prevent transnational corporations (TNCs) from taking undue advantage of the enlarged regional market as well as to protect the infant industries created by regional cooperation. In contrast, ASEAN took a more realistic approach to this issue for two main reasons: its leaders were fully aware that their economies, being open and outward-looking in nature, could not possibly disengage themselves from interaction with the world economy; and ASEAN took the view that foreign investment could make a positive contribution to the envisaged regional economy. Hence, ASEAN policymakers have been pragmatic enough not to exclude foreign economic interests from participating in regional cooperation processes. In fact, some ASEAN projects specifically have provisions allowing them to utilize foreign economic elements in the form of capital and technology.

The ability of ASEAN to survive as a regional scheme owes a great deal to its unique strategy of cooperation, as manifested in its flexible structure and open-ended approach, in its liberal treatment of foreign economic elements, and in its consensus-based decision-making process. This strategy is both the strength and the weakness of ASEAN's approach to regional economic cooperation. An open-ended approach does not carry an overriding sense of urgency to succeed. Perhaps because of that, ASEAN has not achieved sufficient momentum for a breakthrough in its regional cooperation endeavors.

## Current Progress

ASEAN economic cooperation is proceeding on a wide front, with activities related to food, energy, transportation, telecommunications, agriculture, forestry, finance, and tourism. There is an ASEAN Food Security Reserve, an ASEAN Emergency Petroleum Sharing Scheme, an ASEAN Money Swapping Arrangement, and so on. Taken as a whole, these various ASEAN activities and events will in the long run contribute to the cause of ASEAN economic cooperation. However, these activities, piecemeal in nature, have often been introduced in an ad hoc manner and accepted merely as a political gesture. They are of peripheral significance to the main framework of regional cooperation. What is significant for increasing the level of economic integration of the member countries is the activities in the formal area of cooperation involving trade and industry, activities that are to be systematically carried out within the ASEAN institutional structure.

The existing mechanism of ASEAN economic cooperation as it has evolved from the Bali Summit is made up of three basic components: (1) Preferential Trading Arrangements (PTAs), (2) ASEAN Industrial Projects (AIPs), and (3) ASEAN Industrial Complementation (AIC). The first concerns the crucial area of trade liberalization; the second and third deal with industrial cooperation. All three bear close resemblance to the concepts originally recommended by the United Nations Study Team in 1970.[5]

## Trade Liberalization

The trade structure of ASEAN is typically biased toward the industrial countries of the West and Japan, which annually absorb some 60 percent of its total trade (tables A.11b and A.12b). This leaves relatively little room for the growth of intra-ASEAN trade. As shown in table 6.1, intra-ASEAN trade accounted for about 13 percent of ASEAN's total trade in the early 1970s and inched up to around 15 percent in the late 1970s, until it peaked at 20.5 percent in 1983. In volume terms, intra-ASEAN trade has grown from US$4 billion in 1973 to US$31 billion in 1983. It thus appears that in both absolute and percentage terms, the level of intraregional trade achieved by ASEAN is higher than that of many other regional groupings, including the Latin American Integration Association (LAIA)—formerly the Latin American Free Trade Association (LAFTA)—and the Andean Pact countries.

However, such a relatively high level of intra-ASEAN trade is more apparent than real. Most intra-ASEAN trade still consists of traditional flows, such as Thailand's rice to the food-deficient members, Malaysian and Indonesian primary commodities to Singapore for reexport, and so on. Thus an increase in the international price of an ASEAN primary commodity would be enough to raise the level of intra-ASEAN trade. Indeed, the high level of intra-ASEAN trade registered in 1983 was

**Table 6.1**
**Intra-ASEAN Trade, 1973–85**

| | ASEAN Exports to ASEAN | | ASEAN Imports from ASEAN | | ASEAN Total | |
|---|---|---|---|---|---|---|
| | US $ millions | Percent of Total | US $ millions | Percent of Total | US $ millions | Percent of Total |
| 1973 | 1,906 | 14.2 | 2,019 | 13.5 | 3,925 | 13.9 |
| 1974 | 2,775 | 12.1 | 2,998 | 12.5 | 5,773 | 12.3 |
| 1975 | 2,837 | 13.5 | 2,991 | 12.2 | 5,828 | 12.8 |
| 1976 | 3,404 | 12.8 | 3,906 | 14.2 | 7,310 | 13.5 |
| 1977 | 4,067 | 12.8 | 4,750 | 14.9 | 8,817 | 13.8 |
| 1978 | 4,801 | 13.2 | 5,433 | 14.1 | 10,294 | 13.6 |
| 1979 | 7,153 | 14.2 | 8,100 | 16.2 | 15,253 | 15.2 |
| 1980 | 9,788 | 14.3 | 11,120 | 16.4 | 20,907 | 15.3 |
| 1981 | 10,739 | 15.2 | 11,884 | 15.8 | 22,624 | 15.5 |
| 1982 | 13,541 | 19.8 | 15,179 | 19.1 | 28,720 | 19.4 |
| 1983 | 14,561 | 20.8 | 16,493 | 20.3 | 31,053 | 20.5 |
| 1984 | 12,573 | 16.6 | 14,294 | 18.4 | 26,867 | 17.5 |
| 1985 | 9,895 | 14.6 | 11,181 | 17.0 | 21,076 | 15.8 |

SOURCE: IMF, *Direction of Trade Statistics* (relevant years).

caused mainly by the oil price hike in 1982, just as the sharp decline of intra-ASEAN trade to 15.8 percent in 1985 was caused by the fall in oil prices after 1983. Thus efforts are still needed by ASEAN to reorient its trade toward a greater regional focus.

At the Bali Summit in 1976, the member governments committed themselves to trade liberalization as a long-term objective to be achieved within the framework of ASEAN PTAs. The PTA process would follow a flexible and open-ended approach, with no specific goals such as a free trade area or a targeted level of trade liberalization within any specific time frame. PTAs, which merely provide a mechanism by which intra-ASEAN trade can be liberalized at a pace acceptable to all members, operate through five schemes: exchange of tariff preferences, long-term quantity contracts for basic commodities, trade financed at lower interest rates, preferential government procurement, and liberalization of nontariff measures. Of these, the exchange of tariff preferences, or tariff reductions, is by far the most important mechanism and is carried out through both voluntary and across-the-board reductions.

Initially, tariff reductions were negotiated on a product-by-product basis, with member countries voluntarily extending a 10 percent margin of preference (later raised to 20 to 25 percent) to a number of commodities in a progressive manner. However, it soon became clear that such a system did not work well, as member countries tended to offer articles with very low trade content or even irrelevant items that were neither manufactured nor traded in the region (including even snow plows).[6]

In April 1980, the ASEAN economic ministers agreed to seek more wide-ranging, across-the-board tariff cuts, initially for items with an import value below US$50,000. The ceiling was progressively raised to US$10 million by 1982. In May 1984, tariff reductions were extended to all goods traded subject to the national exclusion list for "sensitive items." Furthermore, to qualify, the commodity items had to have high local value added of up to 50 percent.

Up to 1986, the total number of commodity items exchanged under the PTA scheme stood at 18,933; roughly half were covered by the across-the-board approach. But tariff reductions were negotiated on the basis of the Brussels Tariff Nomenclature at the seven-digit commodity level. Because of this high degree of disaggregation into minutely defined commodity groups (under the Brussels Tariff Nomenclature a box of matches, for instance, can be split into different commodity items according to the number of sticks, and pigs' bristles and hogs' bristles are different commodities), the number of commodities covered by PTA is not impressive. Consequently, the real impact of PTAs on intra-ASEAN trade expansion remains limited and is estimated to be within the range of 0.06 percent to 5.20 percent.[7]

Furthermore, despite many years of efforts to liberalize trade, there has been no significant change in the intra-ASEAN trade structure. As previously noted, intra-ASEAN trade is still dominated by primary commodities. With the exception of the Philippines (whose trade relations with the other ASEAN countries have been the weakest) and Singapore (which is the most industrialized member of ASEAN), the exports of one ASEAN country to another have basically been composed of primary commodities (table 6.2). In 1976, manufactured products occupied a very small proportion in the export structure of intra-ASEAN trade: only 7 percent for Indonesia, 21 percent for Malaysia, and 15 percent for Thailand. By 1984, shares for manufactured exports had increased to 29 percent, 24 percent, and 37 percent, respectively, but this was due more to the industrialization progress of the ASEAN economies than to efforts at trade liberalization.

Nor has there been any significant shift in the direction of intra-ASEAN trade. In 1985, as the region's entrepôt trade center, Singapore

**Table 6.2**
**Commodity Structure of Intra-ASEAN Exports, 1976 and 1984**
**(% of total exports to ASEAN)**

| SITC Code | Commodity | Indonesia 1976 | Indonesia 1984 | Malaysia 1976 | Malaysia 1984 | Philippines 1976 | Philippines 1984 | Singapore 1976 | Singapore 1984 | Thailand 1976 | Thailand 1984 |
|---|---|---|---|---|---|---|---|---|---|---|---|
| 0 | Food and Live Animals | 5.5 | 4.3 | 10.5 | 5.4 | 23.4 | 7.8 | 7.8 | 3.8 | 70.8 | 48.7 |
| 1 | Beverage and Tobacco | 0.0 | 0.1 | 0.8 | 0.3 | 0.1 | 0.1 | 0.7 | 0.3 | 0.1 | 0.4 |
| 2 | Crude Materials | 42.1 | 13.4 | 36.2 | 8.8 | 0.6 | 0.8 | 3.5 | 1.7 | 13.4 | 11.6 |
| 3 | Mineral Fuels | 45.2 | 47.4 | 25.0 | 47.1 | 12.9 | 0.8 | 34.6 | 44.4 | 0.1 | 0.1 |
| 4 | Animal Oils | 0.2 | 1.4 | 6.2 | 14.4 | 10.8 | 1.2 | 0.3 | 0.4 | 0.1 | 1.0 |
| 5–8 | Total Manufactured Goods | 6.9 | 29.4 | 20.6 | 24.1 | 47.2 | 20.0 | 53.1 | 49.4 | 15.3 | 37.2 |
| 9 | Others | 0.2 | 4.1 | 0.7 | 0.2 | 5.0 | 69.3 | 0.7 | 2.0 | 0.2 | 1.0 |
| | **Total**[a] | 100 | 100 | 100 | 100 | 100 | 100 | 100 | 100 | 100 | 100 |
| | Total Exports to ASEAN: (millions of U.S. dollars) | 758 | 2,487 | 1,176 | 4,397 | 69 | 353 | 1,850 | 6,326 | 507 | 1,005 |

a. Totals may not sum due to rounding.
SOURCE: Naya, "Toward the Establishment of an ASEAN Trade Area." Report prepared for the ASEAN Secretariat and the Committee on Trade and Tourism, 20 March 1987.

still occupied the pivotal position by handling half of all regional trade. Prior to the formation of ASEAN, most of the regional trade was concentrated in the triangle made up of Indonesia, Malaysia, and Singapore. In 1985 this sector still accounted for 84 percent of total intra-ASEAN trade for exports and 86 percent for imports (International Monetary Fund [IMF] 1987).

Before the Manila Summit in December 1987, a number of ASEAN experts representing different organizations put forth various proposals and new concepts for more effective intra-ASEAN cooperation in trade. Of note are the proposals made by Hans Christoph Rieger of the Institute of Southeast Asian Studies in Singapore, Seiji Naya of the East-West Center in Hawaii, and the Group of Fourteen at the Institute of Strategic and International Studies in Malaysia.

Rieger proposed the establishment of a customs union comprising Indonesia, Malaysia, the Philippines, and Thailand, coupled with a free trade area for all goods of ASEAN origin, so as to provide linkages with Singapore and Brunei (Rieger 1987). In a plan that was less radical but more comprehensive, Naya suggested an ASEAN Trade Area with, among other things, a set goal of putting 80 to 90 percent of ASEAN's total trade under the PTA scheme by the year 2000. This was to be implemented through scheduled tariff reduction at some 10 percent a year (Naya 1987). The main thrust of the Group of Fourteen's recommendation for an ASEAN Market Liberalization Initiative was based on according a minimum 50 percent margin of preference (MOP) on all nonagricultural products within the framework of a six-minus-$x$ principle (Institute of Strategy and International Studies 1987). According to this principle, all of the ASEAN members may participate, and any member may choose not to participate in the scheme.

A number of proposals were made to improve the PTA scheme over the next five years, including reduction of the exclusion lists of individual member countries to not more than 10 percent of the number of traded items; deepening of MOP to 50 percent of intra-ASEAN trade value; reduction of the ASEAN content requirement in the rules of origin from 50 percent to 35 percent during a five-year period; and agreement to an immediate freeze on nontariff barriers.

The proposals were accepted by the six heads of state at the Manila Summit. It was decided that the progress of the improved PTA system should be reviewed on an annual basis at subsequent meetings over the next five years. Though the Manila Summit did not bring about any breakthroughs, such as a clear move to a free trade area, the existing PTA scheme, now deeper and broader, was expected to generate more intra-ASEAN trade in a gradual manner.

## Industrial Cooperation

Industrial cooperation plays a significant role in the long-term economic integration process of a regional grouping. Liberalization of trade through various PTA arrangements by itself does little to create more intraregional trade. It may be likened to a demand-side approach that in the short run will not operate to alter radically the structure or orientation of intraregional trade. To be effective, trade liberalization must be backed up by appropriate supply-side measures, such as greater industrial cooperation within the region, that will operate to expand the regional economy within the grouping.

Clearly, intraregional trade will grow only in response to the expansion of the regional economy. In the case of ASEAN, the regional economy is still small due to the lack of complementarity among the ASEAN economies. Except for Singapore, the ASEAN countries are resource-based economies, producing a more or less similar range of primary commodities for export to the industrial countries outside the region. This competitive feature of the ASEAN economies (except Singapore) limits the growth potential of intra-ASEAN trade in primary commodities, with two important exceptions: the flow of petroleum products from one energy-exporting member (Indonesia) to the other energy-deficient members; and the flow of rice from one food-surplus member (Thailand) to the food-deficient members. It is clear that only manufactured exports will provide a dynamic source for the long-term growth of intra-ASEAN trade, and industrial cooperation creates the supply-side condition necessary for the growth of trade in manufactures.

Industrial cooperation, then, will provide the impetus needed for ASEAN's continuing industrial growth. All the ASEAN countries have made a determined effort to push ahead with industrialization. The manufacturing sector of ASEAN has been growing rapidly over the years at rates generally higher than overall GDP growth rates; and the share of manufactured exports in ASEAN's total exports is also rising. Such trends are likely to continue. At the same time, the manufacturing industries are faced with a number of constraints. The most obvious is that the domestic markets of the member countries—even Indonesia's, which is small because of limited purchasing power—are too small to permit efficient operation of a wide range of manufacturing industries. Industrial cooperation could provide an opportunity for old industries to expand and new ones to be set up to take advantage of a regionally based division of labor and specialization.

The manufacturing sectors in most ASEAN countries are in the process of making the critical transition from import substitution to export expansion. In the short run, industrial cooperation makes it possible for member countries to pool their domestic markets and thus provides a convenient arrangement for the extension of the import-substitution phase. Here, of course, lies a real danger: member countries may seek to maximize the short-term gains of industrial cooperation by extending their industrialization process into the second stage of import substitution (IS2), with the problems described in chapter 3 of this volume. Yet the dynamic impact of the enlarged regional market cannot be ignored. Some uneconomical small firms may now be able to expand output and reduce their costs while others, after being subjected to the shock of competition within a larger regional market, may become more efficient.

At the center of ASEAN's current efforts toward industrial cooperation are its two basic schemes, the AIPs and the AICs. In June 1981 a simplified version of AIC called the ASEAN Industrial Joint Venture (AIJV) was introduced. The AIP scheme sought to establish new, large-scale, government-initiated industrial projects via comprehensive packages, whereas the AIC program was designed to promote greater complementarity among existing industries in the region, mainly through private initiative. The AIJV scheme, in turn, represented an innovative move toward industrial complementation on the part of ASEAN by modifying the complex AIC approach into a simpler, more easily implemented package. It was felt that governments were better equipped to handle large projects involving heavy capital outlays, but that the private sector, on account of its extensive commercial linkages, would be in a better position to initiate and promote relatively smaller AIC projects. Both schemes, if successfully implemented, could further advance the overall economic objectives of the member countries in terms of creating employment, utilizing local raw materials, and saving on foreign exchange.

In March 1976, the ASEAN economic ministers designated the first AIP package, which included urea projects for Indonesia and Malaysia, a diesel engine project for Singapore, a superphosphate project for the Philippines, and a soda ash project for Thailand. Each of these industrial projects was expected to cost US$250 to US$300 million, with the host country taking up 60 percent of the total equity and the remaining 40 percent being equally shared among the other member countries. Such a "package-deal" approach seemed to make considerable economic sense, since industries, if established via regional cooperation, could become economically viable by virtue of the resultant larger regional market. Apparently because of this rationale, a second package of AIPs was also identified a year later for prefeasibility study at the Second ASEAN Summit—the Kuala Lumpur Summit—in 1977. This included the manufacture of heavy-duty rubber tires for Indonesia, metal-working machine tools for Malaysia, newsprint and electrolytic tin plate for the Philippines, and television picture tubes for Singapore, as well as potash mining and fisheries projects for Thailand.

In retrospect, ASEAN leaders seem to have misjudged the difficulty of implementing the AIPs, the progress of which has been woefully slow. It has taken seven years for Indonesia to get its urea project off the ground and eight years for the Malaysian AIP to get up to speed. The current status of the AIP scheme is indeed dismal. By

May 1986, Indonesia's urea project in Aceh was producing only 53,000 tonnes of ammonia, mainly for domestic consumption. In September 1985, Malaysia's urea plant began production; by May 1986, it had turned out 126,000 tonnes of ammonia. Both projects have been losing money, due in part to the world slump in fertilizer prices. Both the Philippines and Singapore have withdrawn from their original AIP projects. The Philippines selected copper fabrication as a substitute, but to date there has been no commercial bidder for this project. Singapore's replacement was a project for the development of a hepatitis B vaccine, approved in May 1984; it is still in the process of finalizing the technology. Thailand has taken many years just to complete a feasibility study on the soda ash project and is now considering a new one to replace it.

Industrial complementation in ASEAN means simple horizontal specialization in production; member countries specialize in producing different components or parts for a single product. Following the approval of the first AIP package, steps were taken to formulate the basic guidelines for industrial complementation in ASEAN. Because of the difficulties later faced by the AIP program, the focus of ASEAN's industrial cooperation efforts shifted to industrial complementation activities, and the Basic Agreement on ASEAN Industrial Complementation was signed in October 1980. It specified that an AIC package must be participated in by at least four of the five member countries. Another key provision of the agreement entrusted the ASEAN Chambers of Commerce and Industry with the crucial task of identifying appropriate products or industries for inclusion in an AIC package. The ASEAN Chambers of Commerce and Industry is supposed to act as an official spokesperson for the private sector; for the purpose of industrial complementation, it becomes the recognized channel of communication between the private sector and governments. In this way, it is hoped that participation of the ASEAN Chambers of Commerce and Industry in the region's industrial complementation scheme will supply the private sector's much-needed initiative and flexibility—characteristics that the AIP program, dominated as it is by bureaucrats, has been lacking.

The institutional machinery for the operation of the AIC program has proved to be complicated. The process of bringing about an industrial complementation project is a complex interaction between the ASEAN Chambers of Commerce and Industry and the ASEAN governments. Proposals for industrial complementation are first initiated by "national industry clubs" and then submitted to "regional industry clubs." The regional industry clubs then forward the proposals to the Working Group on Industrial Complementation of the ASEAN Chambers of Commerce and Industry. The secretary-general of the ASEAN Chambers of Commerce and Industry transmits the AIC proposals to the chair of the Committee on Industry, Minerals, and Energy (COIME), which is the ASEAN government committee mainly responsible for the accreditation of AIC projects. Since each layer requires extensive consultation, discussion, and approvals, the process tends to be time-consuming, especially for new products, which also require a great deal of basic data and information. Some thirty AIC proposals have thus far been submitted to various regional industrial clubs for consideration, but only two packages (involving automobile parts and components) have gone through the whole exercise and been formally approved by the ASEAN Chambers of Commerce and Industry. Of these, only one has been considered workable and thus accepted.

This first AIC package was not yet fully implemented at the end of 1985, and trade under this scheme totaled just over US$1 million. The cost of pushing the package through has probably exceeded the benefits to be derived from it. Given the complex institutional mechanism that accompanies an AIC package and the disparate industrial structures of the ASEAN economies, it would take a major effort to launch an AIC package that would be economically significant and at the same time workable and acceptable to the member countries. Thus many of the problems inherent in the AIC process have become transparent.

It was with a view to accelerating progress in industrial complementation that the innovative new concept of the AIJV was introduced. One distinguishing feature of the AIJVs is that they can proceed even with only two private sector partners from ASEAN, and in fact not all the participants need to be from ASEAN provided that the ASEAN national component is at least 51 percent. This makes it much easier to formulate a project because the chance of mismatching among member countries is reduced. Furthermore, AIJVs can be launched on a smaller scale with less capital investment and therefore less risk.

At the implementation level, AIJVs also have greater flexibility than the conventional AIC projects because AIJVs can be approved individually by the relevant ASEAN economic ministers, as long as they are likely to yield benefits to the participatory countries at no unacceptable costs to the other members. In addition, AIJV investors are free to locate their operations in any of the participatory countries.

Tariff preferences granted in the AIC scheme must be in accordance with the ASEAN Preferential Trading arrangements, that is, on a most-favored-nation basis for all member countries, but tariff preferences on AIJV products apply only to the member countries involved for a four-year period, during which nonparticipating countries waive their PTA rights. Approved AIJV products initially were given a 50 percent tariff preference, but this level was increased to 75 percent in August 1986. In short, AIJVs not only can bypass the cumbersome institutional machinery required for a normal AIC package, but also can enjoy some added incentives.

At the thirteenth COIME meeting in January 1981, three potential AIJV projects—a magnesium clinker plant, a minitractor plant, and a security paper mill—were identified and recommended for pre-feasibility study. In May 1984, at the Sixteenth ASEAN Economic Ministers' Meeting, a list of twenty-one proposed AIJVs, mostly for the manufacture of motorcycle and automobile parts, was considered. At the Eighteenth ASEAN Economic Ministers' Meeting in August 1986, two more AIJV projects were approved, bringing the number of them to five. They include (1) security paper plants in Malaysia and Brunei; (2) potash, feldspar, and quartz mining in Thailand and Indonesia; (3 slaughtered meat plants in Thailand and the Philippines; (4) automatic lamps manufacture in Malaysia and the Philippines; and (5) electrical motorcycle parts manufacture in Malaysia and Thailand. The ASEAN economic ministers also agreed to deepen the MOP on all AIJV products from 50 percent to 75 percent. At the Nineteenth ASEAN Economic Ministers' Meeting in Singapore in July 1987, a proposal to raise the 49 percent equity limit on non-ASEAN investors was considered, so as to allow more AIJVs to work with transnational corporations (TNCs).

Finally, at the Manila Summit in December 1987, the ASEAN heads of government agreed on some broad measures to promote intra-ASEAN investment as a means of accelerating industrial cooperation. Specifically for the AIJV scheme, the proposal for liberalizing equity participation from 49 percent to 60 percent was approved, and the MOP was increased from a minimum of 75 percent to a minimum of 90 percent. Procedures for the setting up of AIJVs were also simplified.

Thus the AIJV scheme, now commonly regarded as the most promising of the whole array of industrial cooperation programs, is stealing the limelight from the AIC process. Thanks to its flexibility of implementation and its ability to utilize non-ASEAN capital and technology, the AIJV has become an attractive solution to the ASEAN impasse on industrial cooperation. However, it should be kept in mind that AIJVs are by their very nature still not a complete substitute for the lack of progress in a normal AIC package. It will require a number of AIJVs to have a significant impact on the industrial complementation process.

## Some Lessons

More than a decade after the Bali Summit, ASEAN's achievements in the major area of regional economic cooperation have been uneven and modest. Its trade liberalization program, which lacks sufficient breadth and depth, is still ineffective in terms of restructuring ASEAN's trade pattern and shifting it toward a greater regional focus, even though some nineteen thousand commodity items are now on the official list of tariff preferences. Results of industrial cooperation as embodied in the AIP and AIC programs are even more disappointing, and only a number of small joint ventures under the AIJV scheme are actually moving ahead. Is the lack of conspicuous success in ASEAN's economic cooperation endeavors tantamount to a failure for ASEAN itself, as in the case of other ill-fated Third World regional groupings?

A proper evaluation of ASEAN's progress toward regional cooperation must be made by placing it in the context of the historical circumstances under which ASEAN has evolved—that is, the geopolitical forces that have shaped it and the chronic problems that are inherent in the economic structures of the member countries. It is also not appropriate to pass judgment on ASEAN's present pace of progress without taking into account its own stated time frame. The ASEAN leaders have all along stressed that economic cooperation is to be realized as a long-term goal, and fluctuation of events in the short run is considered irrelevant to these long-term objectives. As long as the ASEAN institutional apparatus is kept in existence, the option of cooperation is open and the process continues. In any case, it does not cost much to maintain the ASEAN machinery; the ASEAN Secretariat in Jakarta is inexpensive to run compared to many huge international bureaucracies. Hence there is quite a favorable cost-benefit ratio for ASEAN members.

Furthermore, ASEAN is already reaping remarkable benefits from its extraregional cooperation activities. Over the years it has been successful in developing a unified perception of the many regional and international economic issues, such as protectionism, that affect it as a group. ASEAN has also developed a framework for regular dialogues with Australia and New Zealand, Canada, the EC, Japan, and the United States in order to improve bilateral relations. In this way, it has learned to yield some considerable external leverage in order to secure a better deal for its common interests. Gains from external cooperation can serve to increase ASEAN's internal cohesiveness. They can also provide the needed incentive for the group to maintain its operational momentum despite sluggish progress and even despite setbacks in its intraregional cooperation programs.

Ultimately, the effectiveness of ASEAN as a regional economic grouping will depend on breakthroughs in its formal areas of cooperation covering the trade and industry sectors. It is here that ASEAN's past experiences in economic cooperation will be instructive both for ASEAN itself and for other regional groupings among developing countries. It is not possible in this context to go into all the major causes and circumstances that have led to the underperformance of ASEAN's economic cooperation programs. Many of the underlying causes are well known and have been extensively discussed by ASEAN scholars and officials elsewhere. Here, ASEAN's past problems in economic cooperation will be examined in terms of two "gaps": one expectation, the other implementation.

**The expectation gap.** The underperformance of ASEAN's existing programs can be attributed to the existence of what may be called an expectation gap. Because of structural and policy obstacles, there has been a difference between what the existing economic cooperation programs were expected to achieve and what was actually attainable. Both the trade liberalization and the industrial cooperation programs were established to build some measure of regional economic integration. Yet neither has made much progress even though both may be theoretically sound. Apparently these programs could not overcome the structural and policy constraints.

The basic structural constraint on ASEAN's economic cooperation efforts is obvious. ASEAN is one of the world's few regional groupings that is characterized by vast disparities in the economies of its member countries in terms of size, structure, orientation, resource base, and stages of economic development. Some member countries in ASEAN do not even enjoy physical contiguity with each other. The differences in their economic structures and orientations, as well as in their levels of economic development, are particularly unfavorable to efforts at regional economic cooperation. The less-developed members in the group are usually more inward-looking in their overall economic orientation, since they are generally preoccupied with such domestic economic and social development problems as poverty, unemployment, and inequality of income. These countries cannot depend on external economic cooperation programs to cope with these problems, at least at the initial stage; rather, they need to devise appropriate domestic policies. The governments of the less-developed members are also reluctant to fully commit themselves to regional economic activities, which are perceived as invariably operating in favor of the more-developed members. Ironically, the more-developed members (which are generally outward-looking and are supposed to capture more gains from the various regional cooperation programs in the short run) may not necessarily accord high priority to a particular regional cooperation program either. This is because regional economic cooperation in developing countries can sometimes lead to serious trade diversion, which adversely affects the economically more-efficient members.

To tackle the problem of unequal distribution of gains, some regional groupings—the Andean Pact countries, for instance—have devised special treatment for the less-developed members in the group.[8] However, ASEAN has no such provisions. The issue of distributive gains is instead dealt with indirectly, under the consensus mechanism of decision making. It is tacitly assumed that in reaching a consensus, no member country should take undue advantage of the others, and none should feel it is being exploited. Admittedly, this is an inefficient way of dealing with the equity issue, as in actual practice members tend to stall the decision-making process whenever they think their national interests are at stake. This leads to delay in the implementation of regional cooperation programs. In addition, ASEAN has introduced the five-minus-one principle, which allows for negotiations excluding one country if that country prefers to be excluded. It has rarely been applied, however, because of the strong preference for the prevailing consensus principle. Neither of these principles seeks to address the equity issue in a direct and efficient manner; it ultimately requires some kind of redistributive arrangements. The main problem in ASEAN is that its least-developed member is Indonesia, which happens to be the largest country, whereas the more-developed members like Brunei or Singapore happen to be disproportionately small. Small members are inherently limited in their capacity to satisfy the needs of large members in any redistributive exercise.

Along with these structural constraints, there are a number of self-imposed policy barriers that the ASEAN governments have chosen to erect against their regional cooperative programs. From the start, ASEAN has consciously avoided the term "integration"; all its regional activities are officially referred to as "cooperation," which is by definition a lower level of regional activity. Some ASEAN governments have expressly stated their reluctance to participate in any substantial market-sharing arrangement as opposed to types of cooperation that involve pooling resources. This not only rules out any direct moves toward a free trade area or a common market, but also sets a natural upper limit on virtually all trade and industrial cooperation activities. As a result, the actual progress of ASEAN economic cooperation has fallen short of common expectations.

**The implementation gap.** A survey of ASEAN's regional cooperation experience would reveal that some of the programs have had good potential for regional economic integration and yet have failed to achieve anything substantial. This points to the difference between what is achievable and what has actually been achieved, or what may be called the implementation gap. Apart from the structural and policy constraints previously discussed, the various regional economic cooperation programs have underperformed because of a number of technical and administrative problems that have arisen in the process of implementation.

To begin with, the AIP would have had greater success if the projects had been selected more carefully and sufficient technical preparation had been carried out beforehand. The first AIP package was hastily adopted after the Bali Summit without careful deliberation or a feasibility study. Sound preparatory work would have revealed the numerous practical problems inherent in Thailand's soda ash project, as well as the duplication in Indonesia of the designated diesel engine project for Singapore. Singapore had to withdraw hastily from the diesel engine project, and Thailand took years to complete its feasibility study on the soda ash project, only to abandon it later.

Proper technical preparation not only would have avoided the political embarrassment caused by the scrapping of some AIP projects but also could have reduced the many difficulties encountered at the implementation stage. To set up any new industry, a host of basic industry-specific problems pertaining to optimal location, infrastructural support, raw materials supply, labor availability, and pricing and market arrangements first have to be sorted out. It has been argued that if all these details had been dealt with at the beginning by the ASEAN leaders—who from the outset stressed that final approval would be given only to projects that were economically viable—the whole AIP package might not have been launched at all. There are many industries in the ASEAN region that could not be competitive at world market prices even if all the national markets in the region were fully integrated. None of the present AIP projects would have passed such a stringent market test. This inability to compete in world markets in many industries despite full regional integration also explains why it is so difficult for regional groupings to come up with a viable package of industries to achieve regional integration—a package that would yield optimum resource allocation on a regional basis and yet satisfy the various national objectives of the individual members. If tradeoffs must be made between economics and politics or between efficiency and equity for the sake of fostering the larger cause of regionalism, these decisions would best be made at the highest level by the political leadership. Such a procedure would be preferable by far to letting indecisive bureaucrats chip away at the problems in their endless rounds of meetings.

This leads to the second aspect of administrative constraint, which involves the critical role to be played by ASEAN's bureaucrats. It has been the practice of ASEAN political leaders to concern themselves only with the broad principles of the regional programs while leaving implementation to officials of the individual governments. These bureaucrats, though technocratically competent, tend to be overly cautious and averse to taking risks—unlike the business leaders, who have a keen sense of the market and are capable of perceiving prospective gains in the longer run. In the business world, successful new enterprises are normally launched on the basis of entrepreneurial decisions, but seldom in a bureaucratic way. Nor can bureaucrats match politicians in their ability to develop a vision and make bold decisions on larger issues and for the longer term. Not surprisingly, most ASEAN projects have been stymied in the implementation process as the bureaucrats struggle to balance the minutest costs and benefits and jealously safeguard national interests. Such a defensive approach is hardly conducive to the innovative decision making that is required to initiate a major regional project.

The bureaucratic decision-making process is intertwined with complicated institutional arrangements covering the operation of all the regional cooperation programs. Although the ASEAN Secretariat, which functions only as a coordinating body, has not yet developed into an unwieldy structure, it is already accompanied by a web of working committees, expert groups, ad hoc working groups, and other subsidiaries. The complicated institutional structure, when coupled with the bureaucratic decision-making processes, has combined to cause delays in the implementation of regional programs.

## Conclusion

Regional economic cooperation in ASEAN, as in many other regional groupings of developing countries, is destined to be a long, laborious process. In a microeconomic sense, ASEAN's existing economic cooperation programs could considerably enhance their operational effectiveness and improve their performance standards if some of the administrative and technical constraints were removed and the key problems were properly addressed. However, the chances of substantial progress still depend critically on those of a more favorable macroeconomic environment, which in turn depend on the continuing economic growth and development of ASEAN. In the final analysis, economic development remains the most effective technique of achieving regional economic cooperation.

7

*A. R. Bhuyan*

# Beginnings of Cooperation in South Asia

The South Asian Association for Regional Cooperation (SAARC) adopted its charter at the Dhaka Summit on 8 December 1985. This was followed by summits in Bangalore in November 1986 and Kathmandu in November 1987. The countries included in SAARC are Bangladesh, Bhutan, India, Maldives, Nepal, Pakistan, and Sri Lanka. Less than a decade ago the idea of regional cooperation in South Asia was viewed with suspicion, and mistrust loomed large in bilateral relations between the major South Asian countries. With such a beginning, even the mere statement of a goal of fostering regional cooperation is an achievement. This chapter examines some of the major problems and policy options confronting the South Asian countries with respect to regional cooperation.[1]

## Objectives of SAARC

The stated objectives of SAARC are to promote the welfare and quality of life of the people of South Asia; to promote economic growth, cultural development, collective self-reliance, mutual trust and appreciation of one another's problems, and collaboration in various identified fields; to strengthen cooperation in international forums on matters of common interest; and to cooperate with other international and regional organizations with similar aims and purposes. Actual cooperation has so far been restricted to nonpolitical, noncontroversial issues. Under the provisions of the charter (Article X), bilateral and contentious issues have been excluded from SAARC's agenda. Moreover, all decisions must be made on the basis of unanimity, thus giving the smallest member the power of veto.

Adhering to these principles, SAARC has identified eleven areas in which it seeks to achieve its broad objectives: agriculture; rural development; telecommunications; meteorology; health and population activities; postal services; transportation; science and technology; arts, culture, and sports; women in development; and the prevention of drug trafficking and drug abuse. Six new problem areas—including terrorism, the rights of children, and tourism—were identified during the second summit. Other subjects of importance for the long-term development of the region have been excluded from consideration, such as trade, industry, finance, and energy. It would be unwise to permanently rule these out of the agenda of SAARC's activities just because they are controversial. Cooperation in certain areas such as industrial trade and investment is a sensitive subject. It may indeed generate controversies because of the wide variations in size and development of the member economies and the difficulties that may arise in harmonizing national economic policies with a regional free trade perspective. However, although disagreements are not uncommon in regional groupings, efforts at integration must continue. By its very nature, promoting regional cooperation is not an easy task. But economic cooperation is believed to offer opportunities for alleviating the many economic problems the countries of South Asia face.

## Trade Issues

The list of activities on SAARC's agenda is impressive, but political sensitivities within the region have at least initially placed emphasis on confidence-building measures. Building self-reliance among the South Asian countries is a major objective of SAARC, and the question arises whether or not this is possible without active collaboration in trade, industry, finance, investment, and related areas. The Bangalore Declaration of the Heads of State of Government expressly recognized that building collective self-reliance would necessitate greater exchange of ideas, experience, technology, and goods and services on the basis of mutual benefit between the countries. Yet trade has been omitted from the agenda for cooperation, and not even a first step has been taken in this area so far.

South Asian countries have in recent years become increasingly dependent upon the industrial countries for both exports and imports (tables A.11b and A.12b). In 1986, the industrialized countries absorbed between 40 and 61 percent of each SAARC country's exports and supplied 42 to 64 percent of their imports. Imports from the developed industrial countries consist mainly of manufactured goods. Industrial countries are also the largest buyers of the manufactured exports of all South Asian countries. As shown in table 7.1, intraregional trade among SAARC members is minimal and has been on the decline in recent years, with exports falling from 5.1 percent of the total in 1979 to 3.6 percent in 1985, and imports decreasing from 3 percent to 1.9 percent of the total during the same period. With the exception of Bhutan, Nepal, and Maldives, intraregional trade accounted for less than 10 percent of both total exports and imports in 1985.

The traditional argument for expanding trade is well known: the benefits of economic cooperation will remain small unless the static and dynamic gains that result from trade expansion are fully exploited. The adoption of measures for liberalization and expansion of trade among SAARC countries appears necessary and expedient. However, cooperation in this area would require several difficult decisions. Straightforward liberalization of trade by dismantling all trade barriers could benefit the larger countries more than the smaller ones. Freeing of trade in such a situation might result in relationships of dominance and dependence between strong and weak partners.

The apprehension is that unrestricted trade would give India and, to some extent, Pakistan a greater advantage because of their size and levels of industrial development. The smaller and weaker countries with fragile industrial structures may fear that in a regional free-trade regime, intragroup competition would result in dislocation of their infant industries or reductions in their level of production. While the grounds for these fears may be more apparent than real and may not withstand empirical scrutiny, trade liberalization should be designed so that the smaller and relatively less-developed partners in the region are able to enter into a pattern of relationships that is mutually beneficial and provides a firm basis for collective self-reliance.

**Table 7.1**
**Intraregional Exports and Imports of South Asian Countries,**
**1979 and 1985 (% of total world exports and imports)**

| | Year | World (US $ millions) | Region | Bangla-desh | India | Maldives | Nepal | Pakistan | Sri Lanka |
|---|---|---|---|---|---|---|---|---|---|
| | | | | | Percentage of World Total | | | | |
| **Export from** | | | | | | | | | |
| Bangladesh | 1979 | 656 | 7.9 | | 1.8 | — | — | 5.7 | 0.3 |
| | 1985 | 999 | 7.7 | | 3.0 | — | 0.5 | 4.2 | — |
| India | 1979 | 7,679 | 4.0 | 1.3 | | — | 1.0 | — | 1.6 |
| | 1985 | 9,882 | 2.2 | 0.6 | | — | 0.8 | 0.1 | 0.7 |
| Maldives | 1979 | 7 | 21.4 | — | — | | — | 8.6 | 12.8 |
| | 1985 | 24 | 17.1 | — | — | | — | — | 17.1 |
| Nepal | 1979 | 68 | 41.3 | 11.6 | 25.4 | — | | 4.1 | — |
| | 1985 | 136 | 33.2 | — | 28.9 | — | | 1.3 | 2.9 |
| Pakistan | 1979 | 2,056 | 6.2 | 2.3 | 1.8 | — | — | | 2.0 |
| | 1985 | 2,738 | 5.3 | 2.4 | 1.4 | — | — | | 1.5 |
| Sri Lanka | 1979 | 978 | 6.3 | 0.4 | 1.3 | 0.1 | — | 4.5 | |
| | 1985 | 1,265 | 4.2 | 1.1 | 0.5 | 0.4 | — | 2.2 | |
| South Asia[a] | 1979 | 11,444 | 5.1 | | | | | | |
| | 1985 | 14,984 | 3.6 | | | | | | |
| **Import to** | | | | | | | | | |
| Bangladesh | 1979 | 1,928 | 3.8 | | 2.1 | — | 0.5 | 1.1 | 0.1 |
| | 1985 | 2,697 | 3.6 | | 2.3 | — | — | 1.3 | — |
| India | 1979 | 9,899 | 0.7 | — | | — | 0.2 | 0.3 | 0.1 |
| | 1985 | 17,640 | 0.7 | 0.2 | | — | 0.2 | 0.2 | — |
| Maldives | 1979 | 12 | 38.3 | — | 20.8 | — | | 6.7 | 10.8 |
| | 1985 | 71 | 9.1 | 0.1 | 0.6 | — | | 0.4 | 8.0 |
| Nepal | 1979 | 163 | 52.1 | — | 52.0 | — | | 0.1 | — |
| | 1985 | 286 | 32.2 | 2.0 | 30.2 | — | | — | — |
| Pakistan | 1979 | 4,061 | 2.8 | 0.9 | 0.7 | — | — | | 1.2 |
| | 1985 | 5,889 | 1.6 | 0.8 | 0.3 | — | — | | 0.5 |
| Sri Lanka | 1979 | 1,449 | 12.7 | 0.1 | 10.3 | — | — | 2.2 | |
| | 1985 | 1,832 | 6.4 | — | 4.1 | 0.2 | 0.2 | 1.8 | |
| South Asia[a] | 1979 | 17,512 | 3.0 | | | | | | |
| | 1985 | 28,415 | 1.9 | | | | | | |

Dashed cells indicate trade nil or negligible.
a. Excluding Bhutan for which complete data are not available.
SOURCE: International Monetary Fund (1986), *Direction of Trade Statistics, Yearbook, 1986.*

Polarization of benefits has resulted in considerable dissatisfaction in many integration schemes, such as the East African Community, the Latin American Free Trade Association (LAFTA), and the Central American Common Market (CACM). SAARC has the advantage of drawing on the lessons of these integration schemes and can thus adopt appropriate precautionary measures to guard against bitterness in mutual relations and ensure a smooth and continued existence.

Total elimination of trade barriers does not appear feasible in South Asia. The experience of Latin America and the Association of Southeast Asian Nations (ASEAN) should be instructive in this regard. For example, although the "pure-trade approach" to economic integration achieved some success at the initial stages of LAFTA, negotiations for liberalization of intraregional trade eventually stagnated because of disagreements over the timing and extent of tariff reduction proposals. Negotiations for tariff reductions for traditional products posed no serious difficulty in LAFTA. However, because proposals for intraregional trade liberalization required the incorporation of nontraditional products, the members were reluctant to expose their products to intraregional competition. In fact, the practical impact of trade liberalization on LAFTA's intraregional trade expansion was small, as indicated by the fact that imports subject to the LAFTA Agreement in 1979 constituted no more than 6 percent of the region's total imports. The experience of ASEAN, which adopted the across-the-board approach to trade liberalization, has been similar. An Asian Development Bank (ADB) study indicates that the six years of ASEAN tariff-cutting negotiations resulted merely in the proliferation of the number of items accorded preferential tariffs (about 11,000 as of March 1983) rather than in actual expansion of intra-ASEAN trade (Akrasanee 1984). It has also been reported that trade liberalization in ASEAN has affected only 2 percent of the region's intraregional trade (Kappagoda 1987).

A somewhat different approach—as adopted by the Latin American Integration Association (LAIA), which replaced LAFTA—could be envisaged for SAARC, providing for negotiation of multilateral trade agreements based on initial bilateral agreements. Instead of across-the-board tariff cuts, LAIA proposes an economic preference area made up of regional tariff preferences and partial agreements on trade promotion. These partial agreements concerning bilateral tariff reductions could be multilateralized through a negotiated process. This approach could facilitate mutual trade liberalization between countries sharing some common interest and also create an environment conducive to regional cooperation in other areas (Inter-American Development Bank [IADB] 1984).

It should not be difficult to design a mechanism of trade expansion acceptable to all countries of the South Asian region. To allay fears that the subcontinental size of the Indian economy and its multisectoral character might tilt the advantages of trade in its favor, free trade within the region could begin with a selected number of items, such as those appearing in the bilateral negotiations that have already taken place between these countries. For example, bilateral agreements between India, on the one hand, and Pakistan, Bangladesh, Nepal, and Sri Lanka, on the other, contain lists of various products such as coal, minerals, cotton, and silk textiles for mutual trade. Trade between these countries could start with these mutually accepted products, which would enable them to procure these goods within the region and thus promote the building of regional collective self-reliance (Adiseshiah 1987). Intraregional trade flows benefit all countries, large and small. The import requirements of different countries could be made known to one another so that production could be expanded to meet each other's needs.

## Industrialization Issues

Industrialization is a central element in development policy. Limited national markets handicap the creation of optimum industrial capacities, and regional cooperation for expansion of markets via the reduction of trade barriers becomes indispensable to pursuing the goal of collective self-reliance. The growth effects that accrue from economies of scale, external economies, specialization, and increased economic efficiency associated with enlarged markets have provided the basis for economic integration in Latin America and Southeast Asia. This can apply to the South Asian region as well (Waqif 1987). In fact, industry is the most dynamic sector in the major economies of the region. Although it has been excluded from SAARC's agenda for cooperation, the desired structural transformation of these economies can hardly be brought about without meaningful regional cooperation in this sector.

In order to promote national and collective self-reliance and ensure equitable distribution of opportunities and benefits among various countries, adoption of a policy of balanced regional industrialization through agreed-upon specialization will be necessary. This would entail allocating particular industries to particular countries where they best fit. This allocation of industries would be based on actual or potential comparative advantage in the different countries, determined by taking into account their resource endowments, location, and available physical and infrastructural facilities. Joint industrial programming as adopted by the Andean Pact for the promotion of balanced and harmonious development in that subregion can serve as a model for this type of planning.

The objectives of the Andean Pact program are greater expansion, specialization, and diversification of industrial production; maximum utilization of the subregion's resources; increased productivity and effective utilization of production factors; rational utilization of economies of scale; and equitable distribution of the benefits of integration. A principal mechanism of the Andean industrial policy is the sectoral industrial development program, which locates industrial plants in member countries. The allocation of such plants can be exclusive or may be shared between two or more countries. Products of the regional industries allocated to member countries receive a margin of preference for intra-area trade and are provided with adequate protection through an external tariff.

A parallel of the sectoral industrial program of the Andean Pact can be found in the ASEAN Industrial Projects (AIPs), whereby priority industries are assigned to each member country in accordance with comparative advantage. A great merit of this is that as a member country concentrates on an assigned industry or industries, specialization is developed, and economies of scale, with their cost-reducing benefits, are realized. Wasteful parallelism in the growth of industrial activities in different countries is avoided, ensuring the intercountry distribution of industrial projects and thus achieving equitable distribution of income and employment in the region.

Creation of a regional industrial structure is, however, bound to encounter certain problems, at least in the initial stage. Attempts in that direction in ASEAN and the Andean Pact led to polarization of benefits, which resulted in considerable dissatisfaction with many of the existing integration schemes. Conflicts with national priorities inevitably arose, as partners were confronted with deciding the location and distribution of investments so as to avoid discrimination. Neither ASEAN nor the Andean Pact countries have found a solution to this dilemma so far. Therefore, a set of flawless instruments must be devised to rectify the disadvantages of polarization that may arise as a result of investment decisions in the region (Zehender 1987). This issue must be carefully examined by SAARC.

Joint-venture collaboration in various sectors offers a good opportunity for promotion of industries and diversification of the production

structures of individual South Asian countries. Studies could be undertaken to identify various fields in which joint ventures might be profit-
ably undertaken. Currently, a number of joint-venture projects are
under way between India and Sri Lanka, Nepal, and Bhutan. Similar
opportunities exist for other countries. Some examples of joint ventures
in the region include fertilizer industries based on natural gas in Pakistan and Bangladesh; paper and newsprint industries using the huge
forest resources of the eastern Indian state of Assam and of Bangladesh;
and a tire-producing unit in Sri Lanka.

Expansion of trade and industry in the region will require cooperation in other spheres as well, including freer intraregional travel and
more frequent exchange of industrial managers; cooperation in research and exchanges of market information; development of satisfactory regional transportation, communication, and information-sharing
systems; facilities providing easy availability of investment and credit
funds (for example, regional financial institutions and development
banks); and payment and clearing mechanisms to settle intraregional
trade imbalances. Attempts are under way to promote functional cooperation in some of these areas, but a great deal more needs to be done.

## Agricultural and Rural Development

Agricultural and rural development are two key areas for cooperation
among SAARC countries. Agriculture in the region is beset with the
problem of low productivity and is frequently subject to such natural
disasters as droughts and floods. In Bangladesh and the other densely
populated countries where there is no scope for expansion of arable
land, only increased productivity and expanded production that arise
from intensive cultivation through the application of improved inputs,
can provide a lasting solution. The inclusion of meteorology in the
SAARC agenda for cooperation and the creation of the SAARC Mete-
orological Research Centre might play a meaningful role in mitigating
the effects of natural calamities. Regional cooperation for agricultural
development will require collective research aimed at finding ways to
tackle these perennial problems and at developing regional programs
in, for example, afforestation, promotion of new technology, and the
genetic engineering of new seeds. The agricultural program adopted
by the Economic Community of West African States (ECOWAS) provides for technical cooperation in a number of specific activities, such

as combating hunger, distributing more productive varieties of seeds through extension services, financing genetic research programs, setting up community production and processing units, and organizing a storage system for foodstuffs and other important products (UNCTAD 1982–83). This program could provide a model for SAARC as it develops its own strategies.

A related issue is the acute food shortages faced by some countries in the region. Ensuring food security within each country as well as within the region as a whole should be a high priority. Regional efforts to accomplish this have a greater chance of success, since the costs of autonomous national policies are likely to be much higher than each country's share of costs in a regional solution (Zehender 1984). Approval by the SAARC Council of Ministers in its third session (June 1987) of a South Asian Food Security Reserve modeled after the ASEAN Food Security Reserve Agreement was a move in the right direction (UNCTAD 1982–83).

## Infrastructure Development

Development of regional infrastructure is another avenue for cooperation. It is covered by the three agreed-upon areas on SAARC's agenda: transportation, telecommunications, and postal services. Cooperation in these sectors is essential for promoting trade, industry, tourism, and overall resource development in the region. The development of roads, waterways, ports, air links, and telecommunications and postal systems in the South Asian countries deserves priority attention. Some specific suggestions in this regard include the establishment of regional transportation networks such as the Asian Highway Project and the Trans-Asian Railway Project; the development of inland waterways, with special provision for transit facilities for landlocked countries; the establishment of a regional shipping line with multimodal transport including containerization, as well as regional shipbuilding and repairing facilities; the development of regional air linkages combining the resources of different national airlines and building regional facilities for training and aircraft maintenance; and greater cooperation in telecommunications and postal systems through standardization of rates and equipment. In the telecommunications and transport sectors, regional arrangements and institutions are already under consideration by SAARC. This process must be accelerated, since cooperation in these fields and intensification of linkages will yield immediate benefits to current economic plans and exchanges between peoples and organizations in all these countries.

## Development of Water and Energy

Cooperation in development of water resources and energy is vital but has not yet been considered by SAARC. Regional initiative is needed to exploit the vast potential for harnessing the huge water resources of the Himalayas for the agricultural and energy development of the countries directly involved. In Nepal alone, the hydropower potential is estimated at about 83,000 megawatts, of which less than .01 percent has been utilized so far (Agarwal 1984). Full utilization of this potential will require regional cooperation and possibly sizable external assistance. A coordinated policy regarding river control, regulation of water flows, and water resource development could be instrumental in exploiting the Himalayan waters for energy development, irrigation, flood control, and inland navigation in the countries of the subcontinent, particularly, Nepal, India, and Bangladesh.

## Scientific and Technical Cooperation

The main objective of SAARC's cooperation in science and technology should be to make available appropriate technology commensurate with the factor endowments and skills prevailing in the region. As in other developing regions, the South Asian countries have long been dependent on technologies that are often inappropriate for local needs. The scientific and research organizations of major South Asian countries have commendable records of research in such areas as industry, agriculture, medicine, plant genetics, water resource management, and biotechnology. These institutions could combine their resources and research and development efforts to solve the complex problems of economic development and to improve the quality of life of the region's peoples.

## Expansion of Health and Population Activities

All SAARC members have experienced high population growth and have had varying degrees of success with population control programs. Regional efforts through exchanges of information and sharing of common experiences may be effective in reducing population growth. On matters of health development in general, sharing expertise and knowledge on a regional basis would be beneficial and might generate regional research and action programs. The relatively well-endowed partners could provide technical assistance in the form of trained personnel to their less-developed partners, open training facilities in specialized fields to the region's doctors, and devise projects for the cooperative supply of pharmaceutical products.

## Education and Other Areas

Education does not come under the specific agreed-upon areas of cooperation in SAARC, although there is much the countries in the region can do in this area by themselves. For example, the individual governments of these countries and SAARC itself could institute educational scholarships and fellowship programs through the establishment of a SAARC Educational Fund to facilitate exchange of scholars and researchers between the universities and research institutions of these countries. As a first step in that direction, the Council of Ministers in its June 1987 meeting decided to create SAARC chairs, fellowships, and scholarships that would commence from the academic year 1988.

Cultural exchanges and sports are other noncontroversial areas that can reinforce the concept of cooperation in the region. An institutional framework for holding periodic sports events and games is already in place in the form of the South Asian Federation. South Asian cultural centers could also be established in all member countries to exchange books, newspapers, and other publications as a means of learning about each other. The radio and television networks of these countries could also be effective in fostering greater interaction and awareness among the cultures of the region. A beginning has already been made with the launching of the program of SAARC audiovisual exchanges at the Kathmandu Summit on 2 November 1987.

The status of women and the problem of drug trafficking and drug abuse are other issues for which SAARC is committed to creating a regional framework for cooperation. The rights of children and combating terrorism are other subjects now being contemplated at the highest official level for inclusion in SAARC's agenda. All of these are social questions of great concern to the public—ones that official government attitudes may not necessarily address and translate into concrete actions (Gonsalves 1987). However, these issues offer voluntary organizations useful opportunities to come together to deliberate on the problems confronting the region.

## SAARC and International Negotiations

SAARC mandates cooperation in international negotiations, with a goal of arriving at a common position on major international issues such as the North-South dialogue. By joining with countries of other developing regions in various multilateral forums such as the World Bank, the IMF, United Nations Conference on Trade and Development (UNCTAD), and the Uruguay Round of General Agreement on Tariffs and Trade (GATT), SAARC can project a unified viewpoint on such multilateral issues as trade, aid, and development and thereby achieve better results.

Because of their divergent economic and geopolitical interests and perceptions, the SAARC countries have so far been unable to arrive at a common position on the North-South dialogue or in the GATT negotiations. Even in matters of South-South negotiations, such as on the Generalized System of Tariff Preferences (GSTP), the SAARC countries have moved in different directions (Adiseshiah 1987). A common stand will not only solidify the spirit of SAARC but also strengthen their bargaining position with the industrialized countries. The most recent illustration of how lack of unanimity can damage common interests is the signing of the latest Multifibre Agreement (MFA) in August 1986, in which the South Asian countries were forced to accept unfair bilateral arrangements on textile exports to the United States and the EC. A united stand might have produced a different result.

SAARC could also take joint action on matters of mutual concern, such as commodity issues involving the setting up of export-stabilization agreements within the framework of UNCTAD's integrated program of commodities. The establishment of an international tea association modeled after the existing International Jute Agreement is a case in point.

The experience of ASEAN offers lessons in matters of cooperation on international issues. ASEAN has carried on dialogues with major trading partners, United Nations bodies, and major trading blocs. It also has adopted joint actions concerning liberalization and improvement of the IMF compensatory financing scheme on items of interest to ASEAN countries including natural rubber, timber products, vegetable oils, tin, copper, sugar, and hard fibers. The dialogues ASEAN has pursued with its most formidable trading partners and with world bodies indicate the effectiveness of common approaches to issues, particularly in trade and industry. ASEAN has also gained respect and international recognition by this means.

## Conclusion

It was not expected that SAARC would make any swift or dramatic progress. The member governments wanted to adopt a cautious, step-by-step approach, and at the initial stage they restricted the scope of cooperation to some mutually accepted noncontroversial areas. In their anxiety to ensure progress they emphasized confidence-building measures and activities. The complex and contentious issues of trade, industry, and other areas of economic cooperation were excluded from consideration at the beginning, possibly to be taken up at a more propitious time.

For regional cooperation to be meaningful and effective, and for the professed SAARC objective of attaining collective self-reliance to be realized, cooperation should be extended to include such areas as trade, industry, monetary cooperation, and energy. Efforts must be accompanied by appropriate safeguards to protect the weaker partners. With the affirmation of commitment at the highest political level, SAARC can be expected to grow stronger and bring prosperity to the peoples of the South Asian region.

# Economic Integration in Latin America

Economic integration agreements have been under way in Latin America since the late 1950s. These agreements have most commonly been seen as mechanisms for improving and continuing import-substituting industrialization under expanded frontiers. Two factors behind this growing political interest in economic cooperation have been a sense of fatigue with import substitution within the small national boundaries and the progress achieved in industrialization, which implies the need to develop activities intensive in economies of scale. At present there are four formal integration agreements that include the large majority of countries in the region and over 95 percent of its population, gross domestic product (GDP), and trade flows.[1]

The first formal steps were taken in 1958 and 1960 by the countries forming the Central American Common Market (CACM), including Costa Rica, El Salvador, Guatemala, Honduras, and Nicaragua. In 1960 the Latin American Free Trade Association (LAFTA) was formed by Argentina, Bolivia, Brazil, Chile, Colombia, Ecuador, Mexico, Paraguay, Peru, Uruguay, and Venezuela; in 1980 LAFTA was converted into the Latin American Integration Association (LAIA). Subsequently, the Caribbean countries formed the Caribbean Free Trade Area (CARIFTA). Later, a more ambitious agreement led to the replacement of CARIFTA by the Caribbean Community (CARICOM), which embraces Barbados,

Guyana, Jamaica, Trinidad-Tobago, and nine other smaller states.[2] In 1981 seven of the latter members (with a total population of 600,000) created the Organization of East Caribbean States within CARICOM. Finally, a cooperative effort that began in 1969 led to the formation of the Andean Common Market (ANCOM). With the resignation of Chile in 1976, ANCOM consisted of Bolivia, Colombia, Ecuador, Peru, and Venezuela. In 1987, ANCOM became a more flexible regional grouping.

Over the course of the past two-and-a-half decades, the process of economic integration has suffered numerous setbacks. Frequent, abrupt political changes have been a deterrent to economic cooperation. During the 1960s, LAFTA was disrupted by military coups in Argentina and Brazil. Progress was then generated by middle-of-the-road democratic governments in the Andean countries. In the 1970s, military coups created obstacles for ANCOM, especially with the resignation of Chile in 1976 as a result of the 1973 coup.

Economic events have also hampered progress. In the early 1960s, the need to enlarge the markets for import substitution became apparent and led to the creation of LAFTA, CACM, and subsequently ANCOM. Economic events in the 1970s and 1980s, however, helped to reduce the desire for integration and later contributed to actual regression in that area. The so-called Dutch disease also contributed to the trend against integration in these nations.[3] After 1973 the substantial increase in the price of oil weakened industrialization efforts and export expansion in countries like Ecuador, Mexico, and Venezuela. The abundance of foreign exchange made it difficult for these countries to export nonoil products. Since voluntary integration requires the consensus of all partners, it was not enough that the need for integration had increased in some of the oil-importing nations. Additionally, in the second half of the 1970s easy access to bank loans weakened efforts to earn foreign currency through exports to regional partners. And in the 1980s, the debt crisis, a recessionary framework, and the proliferation of import restrictions and retaliatory practices within Latin America adversely affected intraregional trade.

In spite of this, the interrelationships among the Latin American countries have expanded substantially since the 1950s. Intraregional trade, especially in manufactured goods, and financing have been positively influenced and encouraged by cooperative arrangements, mostly within the formal integration agreements. In brief, notwithstanding the notorious shortcomings in relation to expectations, significant progress has been made throughout the period, although the countries among and within each agreement remain very heterogeneous in nature.

The first section discusses some of the most relevant features of LAFTA, the largest grouping in the region. The next section concentrates on the Andean Pact. Despite the difficulties it experienced, the Andean Pact became the most comprehensive process of economic integration in the region. The chapter closes with an account of events in the 1980s and a summary appraisal.

## The Evolution of LAFTA: From Montevideo I to Montevideo II

**The beginning of LAFTA.** By the 1950s, the goal of establishing a Latin American Common Market began to receive a substantial amount of attention. The idea was supported by several political and intellectual groups, and the United Nations Economic Commission for Latin America (ECLA) provided the corresponding technical background (Wionczek 1969). Throughout the 1950s, the project took shape and eventually resulted in the formation of LAFTA and the CACM.

The more ambitious plans envisioned grouping the entire region into one common market. On the other hand, the specific trade problems faced by the southern countries of the region underlined the need for some sort of multilateral trade agreement. During the postwar years, several of the Latin American countries already had bilateral trade agreements similar to those prevailing in other areas of the world. The agreements included inconvertible trade balances that reached large relative levels. One main underlying purpose at the outset of the integrative endeavors was to achieve a combination of trade preferences and multilateralization of balances.

During the 1950s several national trade and foreign exchange reforms tended to eliminate or lessen the impact of the bilateral agreements. The consequence was a fall in the share of intra-Latin American trade in the region's total trade from over 11 percent in the period 1953–55 to 6 percent in 1961. Thus, the reestablishment of previous trade flows on a more efficient and stable basis became one of the main purposes of economic integration.

The efforts culminated in 1960 with the signing by seven Latin American countries of the Montevideo Treaty, which gave rise to LAFTA.

Subsequently, Colombia and Ecuador joined LAFTA in 1961, Venezuela in 1966, and Bolivia in 1967. LAFTA then included ten South American countries as well as Mexico. In 1960 these eleven nations comprised 90 percent of the population in Latin America, 95 percent of the region's GDP, and 92 percent of its exports.

**Commercial policy in the early years.** The goal of the Montevideo Treaty was the creation of a Latin American common market. However, its provisions only considered the elimination of tariffs and other restrictions on most reciprocal trade within a period of twelve years (1962–73), according to the general rules regulating economic integration agreements among members of the General Agreement on Tariffs and Trade (GATT).

The two main instruments established to liberalize reciprocal trade were the National and Common Lists. National Lists included preferences being granted by each country to all other partners. The internal tariffs were to be reduced for reciprocal trade an average of 8 percent a year and the commodities benefiting from preferences were to be defined in annual negotiations. The Common List included products on which all countries agreed to eliminate all trade restrictions. After the first 3-year period of the treaty it was to include at least 25 percent of reciprocal trade, and after 6, 9, and 12 years, 50 percent, 75 percent, and almost all trade was to be included. The treaty did not include formal regulations designed to establish a common external tariff, nor did it include adequate measures to achieve an equitable distribution of the benefits of integration and the harmonization of economic policies.[4]

During the first three annual negotiation rounds, LAFTA showed progress toward the elimination of barriers to reciprocal trade. Most of the preferences covered products for which trade had taken place within previous bilateral agreements. Thus an important result of the process was to consolidate and broaden traditional areas of reciprocal trade. By 1964, the goal of moving toward trade liberalization had been achieved, with respect to both the National Lists and the first step of the Common List. By the mid-1960s, the share of reciprocal trade to total trade of the region increased to levels that were similar to those that had existed a decade before. However, progress in annual negotiations stalled thereafter, and no agreement was reached on the second step of the Common List in 1967, primarily because of the shortcomings of the Montevideo Treaty and the lack of political willingness on the part of several member countries to accelerate the integration process.

Partner countries at intermediate levels of development attempted to rekindle the process by attacking some of the main shortcomings. Thus, in 1964, they succeeded in gaining approval for a resolution calling for the harmonization of trade policies and movement toward a common external tariff pari passu with the liberalization of reciprocal trade. The most significant innovation in the resolution was a chapter calling for a regional industrial policy that would include the joint programmed allocation of investment. This was intended to address the distributive imbalances feared by the less-developed and medium-developed member countries.

Subsequently, the Declaration of the Presidents of America adopted in Punta del Este in 1967 proposed the start of the implementation of a common market to be achieved in no more than fifteen years from 1970. The one article of the declaration that had significance for the near term was the leeway granted for the creation of subregional groupings within LAFTA. This implied the acceptance by the larger LAFTA members of the decision of Andean countries to implement a more comprehensive scheme, as delineated in the Bogota Declaration of 1966.

Finally, the persistent stagnation of trade negotiations led to the signing of the Protocol of Caracas in 1968, which modified the Montevideo Treaty. The period prescribed to liberalize reciprocal trade was extended until 1980. Neither the resolution of 1964 nor the Protocol of Caracas was implemented, yet LAFTA continued to survive and a few additional tariff preferences were granted in the subsequent annual negotiation rounds.

**LAFTA's survival after 1965.** Since 1965 the number of concessions made in the National Lists has been below expectations except in the period 1968–69, when the entry of Bolivia and Venezuela brought an increase of the number of concessions agreed to at the corresponding annual negotiation rounds. In the periods 1962–64 and 1968–69, 74 percent and 13 percent, respectively, of all concessions agreed to in the National Lists for the period 1962–79 were granted. Only 2 percent were agreed to after 1970 (Vacchino 1981; United Nations ECLA 1984).

After 1965, progress was made in the form of financial arrangements and the so-called Complementarity Agreements. The financial arrangement known as the Agreement on Multilateral Settlements and Reciprocal Credit was promoted by the central banks. Its purpose was to foster direct relationships among Latin American commercial banks rather than relationships through financial intermediaries in developed nations. This would improve the credit availability for reciprocal trade to countries with balance-of-payments problems and those countries that were trying to "save" international reserves. The agreement included all LAFTA countries and the Dominican Republic. Initially, two-thirds of reciprocal trade was to be settled under the multilateral payment system. The ratio subsequently rose significantly and exceeded 80 percent of reciprocal trade in 1980 (LAFTA 1983). Within a settlement period (now fixed at four months), the central banks of the surplus countries grant credits (up to given amounts) to deficit countries. At the end of each four-month period, debtor countries settle their balances in convertible currency. One important result of this system has been the growing interconnection among local banks and the encouragement of reciprocal trade that credit availability tends to bring about.

The Complementarity Agreements specify that two or more member countries could agree to liberalize trade of a specific group of commodities and establish other mechanisms fostering reciprocal trade. The preferences granted within an agreement were to be extended solely to countries participating in that specific agreement.[5] In practice, the agreements were arrived at in sectoral meetings with the active participation of private entrepreneurs.

The Complementarity Agreements were set up mainly in sectors in which output was diversified within the firms and where intrafirm specialization was possible. Frequently, agreements were achieved among subsidiaries of foreign enterprises, which could easily design a pattern of specialization and make use of tariff preferences because of the availability of the corresponding marketing channels. In fact, transnational corporations (TNCs) were heavily represented in the sectoral meetings leading to the agreements. Most of these TNCs had subsidiaries in more than one country (Tironi 1976). Thus representatives of the same TNC were in a position to bargain from within the national delegations of the subsidiaries' host countries.

After 1964 most of the limited additional liberalization that took place was implemented via Complementarity Agreements. By 1970 there were eighteen Complementarity Agreements in force, all covering manufactured goods.[6] However, they included few countries—mostly the three larger nations—and covered very specifically defined goods. Since the mid-1980s it has become increasingly difficult to reach agreements: either competing domestic firms have been excluded from expected benefits or governments have been reluctant to grant the tariff preferences demanded.

**The performance of reciprocal trade.** As previously stated, reciprocal trade declined in the 1950s. However, with the inception of LAFTA it began to climb. During the first half of the 1960s about 90 percent of the reciprocal trade benefited from tariff preferences agreed to in LAFTA.

Overall reciprocal exports continued to exhibit a slight upward trend after 1964, as shown in table 8.1. By the late 1960s, it continued to grow for each country, except for Peru and Venezuela, despite the small weight of new trade preferences granted in later years. Furthermore, the margin of preferences was reduced by member countries that made unilateral tariff reductions.[7] In several cases, tariffs to third-party countries ended up being lower than the rate agreed to by the LAFTA countries. According to some estimates, the weighted-average tariff preference protecting reciprocal trade rose from 18 to 36 percent from 1963 to 1966, and then fell to 22 percent in 1969 (Instituto para la Integración de América Latina [INTAL] 1974). But actual tariff preferences continued to be reduced in the 1970s, as did the share of trade under LAFTA preferences.

One factor that sharply reduced the efficacy of preferences was the broad coverage of tariff exemptions in force in member countries. An estimate for 1980, covering eight members of LAFTA and two other Latin American countries, indicated that 47 percent of imports were subject to the general national tariff; 5 percent benefited from tariff preferences negotiated in LAFTA, ANCOM, or CACM; and 48 percent were exempted from tariffs (INTAL 1986). The latter reduced the significance of negotiated preferences. Exemptions included imports by public firms, which thus weakly contributed to generating demand for domestic and regional output of manufactures.

The continued increase in reciprocal trade after 1964 can be explained by four variables. First, by 1965 almost two-thirds of the preferences already granted were not yet being used. Utilization increased gradually as marketing channels were established, product designs adjusted, production bottlenecks removed, and information on trade opportunities made available. Second, the rate of utilization of preferences was affected by the development of financial agreements put into operation in 1966. Third, trade not having direct preferences in the National Lists tended to benefit from the improvement of information

**Table 8.1**
**Intra-LAFTA and Total Exports by Country,**
**(annual averages for selected periods, 1962–86, US $ millions)**

| | 1962–64 | | | 1968–70 | | | 1979–81 | | | 1984–86 | | |
|---|---|---|---|---|---|---|---|---|---|---|---|---|
| | Total Exports | Intra-LAFTA Exports | Intra-LAFTA Exports/ Total Exports (%) | Total Exports | Intra-LAFTA Exports | Intra-LAFTA Exports/ Total Exports (%) | Total Exports | Intra-LAFTA Exports | Intra-LAFTA Exports/ Total Exports (%) | Total Exports | Intra-LAFTA Exports | Intra-LAFTA Exports/ Total Exports (%) |
| Argentina | 1,330 | 196 | 14.7 | 1,584 | 356 | 22.5 | 8,332 | 1,865 | 22.4 | 7,757 | 1,378 | 17.8 |
| Bolivia | 92 | 3 | 3.3 | 199 | 17 | 8.5 | 958 | 334 | 34.9 | 652 | 356 | 54.7 |
| Brazil | 1,350 | 99 | 7.3 | 2,310 | 250 | 10.8 | 19,374 | 3,382 | 17.5 | 25,012 | 2,516 | 10.1 |
| Colombia | 486 | 9 | 1.9 | 633 | 57 | 9.0 | 3,420 | 592 | 17.3 | 4,268 | 447 | 10.5 |
| Chile | 567 | 50 | 8.8 | 1,088 | 119 | 10.9 | 4,164 | 951 | 22.8 | 3,872 | 581 | 15.0 |
| Ecuador | 125 | 8 | 6.4 | 183 | 16 | 8.7 | 2,231 | 359 | 16.1 | 2,487 | 102 | 4.1 |
| Mexico | 835 | 33 | 4.0 | 1,141 | 81 | 7.1 | 14,611 | 711 | 4.9 | 21,244 | 711 | 3.3 |
| Paraguay | 41 | 12 | 29.3 | 54 | 20 | 37.0 | 299 | 130 | 43.5 | 291 | 125 | 43.1 |
| Peru | 583 | 58 | 9.9 | 907 | 58 | 6.4 | 3,337 | 552 | 16.5 | 2,663 | 265 | 10.0 |
| Uruguay | 166 | 13 | 7.8 | 204 | 26 | 12.7 | 1,021 | 352 | 34.5 | 937 | 293 | 31.2 |
| Venezuela | 2,678 | 143 | 5.3 | 3,135 | 157 | 5.0 | 17,573 | 1,241 | 7.1 | 13,549 | 778 | 5.7 |
| Total[a] | 8,253 | 624 | 7.6 | 11,438 | 1,157 | 10.1 | 75,321 | 10,470 | 13.9 | 82,732 | 7,553 | 9.1 |
| Non-oil-exporting countries | 3,940 | 379 | 9.6 | 5,873 | 828 | 14.1 | 36,610 | 7,272 | 19.9 | 42,137 | 5,340 | 12.7 |

a. Deviations from stated totals due to rounding.
SOURCE: Instituto para la Integración de América Latina (INTAL), *El Proceso de Integración en América Latina*, 1975, 1981, 1983, 1984, and 1986 issues (Buenos Aires: INTAL).

networks, as well as from the newly developed marketing and financial channels. In fact, trade not favored by tariff preferences in LAFTA rose faster in the 1970s, increasing from only one-fifth to roughly one-half of reciprocal trade. Fourth, the Andean Pact had a positive influence on the growth of reciprocal trade of its member countries. Although it began from a low base, the reciprocal trade of the Andean countries expanded faster than that for other LAFTA members during the 1970s.

Throughout the period under study, the share of exports of manufactured goods increased notably for the region as a whole; in fact, it rose from 3 percent in 1960 to 17 percent of total exports in 1980. That trend was particularly strong with respect to exports from Argentina and Brazil (and to a lesser degree from Mexico, where the share of oil increased in the 1970s). Exports of manufactures to the world as a whole also increased, but the share of manufactured goods sold in the region increased even faster for the period 1960–1980, climbing from 13 to 43 percent of reciprocal exports.[8]

The case of Brazil was particularly noteworthy. In 1980, 80 percent of its exports to LAFTA were comprised of manufactures. This was more than double the high ratio of manufactures in total Brazilian exports (37 percent). On the other hand, in the early 1980s, exports of Brazil's manufactures to Latin America were five times as large as its imports of manufactures. Argentina had a more balanced trade of manufactures in the 1970s, which in more recent years have also turned into a large surplus for Brazil. It must be noted, however, that Brazil is a more "closed" economy than the LAFTA average. By 1980, total exports of goods represented only 8 percent of GDP in Brazil but 15 percent in the rest of LAFTA.

More disaggregated data provide useful insights into the export performance of Latin American countries. As shown in table 8.2, exports of basic foodstuffs and raw materials (excluding fuels) fell from 41 percent to 26 percent of reciprocal exports between 1965 and 1979, while manufactures rose from 27 percent to 51 percent.[9] The share of basic foodstuffs and raw materials decreased despite an almost doubling in real terms. Extraregional exports also exhibited a similar pattern, but with less intensity: the share of manufactures rose from 12 percent to 17 percent, growing 8.2 percent annually in real terms (IADB 1984). In some manufacturing sectors the pattern differs and extraregional exports rose faster. This was especially true for machinery and transport equipment, for which by 1965 exports were being made

166

## Table 8.2
### Composition of Intra- and Extra-regional Exports by Product Group for Latin America, 1965, 1970, 1975, and 1979 (US$ millions)

| Groups | Intra-regional exports 1965 US$ millions | 1965 Percent | 1970 US$ millions | 1970 Percent | 1975 US$ millions | 1975 Percent | 1979 US$ millions | 1979 Percent | Extra-regional exports 1965 US$ millions | 1965 Percent | 1970 US$ millions | 1970 Percent | 1975 US$ millions | 1975 Percent | 1979 US$ millions | 1979 Percent |
|---|---|---|---|---|---|---|---|---|---|---|---|---|---|---|---|---|
| **Basic Foodstuffs and Raw Materials** | 521.2 | 41.4 | 700.2 | 34.8 | 1,576.9 | 25.4 | 2,897.8 | 26.2 | 5,210.5 | 59.5 | 7,290.1 | 58.3 | 15,363.4 | 50.5 | 26,120.3 | 47.3 |
| Food and Live Animals | 341.1 | 27.1 | 447.1 | 22.2 | 1,099.3 | 17.7 | 1,992.5 | 18.0 | 3,537.8 | 40.4 | 5,079.9 | 40.6 | 10,291.0 | 33.8 | 18,237.5 | 33.0 |
| Beverages and Tobacco | 4.1 | 0.3 | 11.2 | 0.6 | 32.7 | 0.5 | 54.3 | 0.5 | 49.9 | 0.6 | 76.5 | 0.6 | 343.1 | 1.1 | 587.6 | 1.1 |
| Crude Animals, Inedible | 153.3 | 12.2 | 208.8 | 10.4 | 373.8 | 6.0 | 610.1 | 5.5 | 1,474.5 | 16.8 | 1,936.5 | 15.5 | 4,368.4 | 14.4 | 6,342.4 | 11.5 |
| Animal and Vegetable Oils and Fats | 22.7 | 1.8 | 33.1 | 1.6 | 71.1 | 1.1 | 240.9 | 2.2 | 148.3 | 1.7 | 197.2 | 1.6 | 360.9 | 1.2 | 952.8 | 1.7 |
| **Fuels and Minerals Fuels** | 397.9 | 31.6 | 474.5 | 23.6 | 1,849.7 | 29.8 | 2,525.6 | 22.8 | 2,465.0 | 28.1 | 2,991.6 | 23.9 | 9,930.3 | 32.7 | 19,506.3 | 35.3 |
| **Manufactured Products** | 335.7 | 26.6 | 820.3 | 40.8 | 2,750.3 | 44.3 | 5,613.8 | 50.7 | 1,070.8 | 12.2 | 2,201.9 | 17.6 | 4,943.7 | 16.3 | 9,384.4 | 17.0 |
| Chemical Elements and Compounds | 70.1 | 5.6 | 147.6 | 7.3 | 508.2 | 8.2 | 970.8 | 8.8 | 123.9 | 1.4 | 189.1 | 1.5 | 858.7 | 2.8 | 1,290.3 | 2.3 |
| Manufactured Goods (by material) | 167.6 | 13.3 | 386.0 | 19.2 | 997.8 | 16.1 | 2,015.0 | 18.2 | 905.1 | 10.3 | 1,741.1 | 13.9 | 2,690.7 | 8.8 | 4,680.9 | 8.5 |
| Machinery and Transport Equipment | 52.1 | 4.1 | 176.8 | 8.8 | 909.6 | 14.6 | 1,817.6 | 16.4 | 22.1 | 0.3 | 173.9 | 1.4 | 820.7 | 2.7 | 2,134.2 | 3.9 |
| Miscellaneous Manufactured Articles | 45.9 | 3.6 | 109.9 | 5.5 | 334.7 | 5.4 | 810.4 | 7.3 | 19.7 | 0.2 | 97.8 | 0.8 | 573.6 | 1.9 | 1,279.0 | 2.3 |
| **Other Products** | 5.1 | 0.4 | 15.1 | 0.8 | 32.6 | 0.5 | 33.0 | 0.3 | 13.5 | 0.2 | 24.3 | 0.2 | 166.7 | 0.5 | 240.7 | 0.4 |
| **TOTAL** | 1,259.9 | 100.0 | 2,010.1 | 100.0 | 6,209.5 | 100.0 | 11,070.2 | 100.0 | 8,759.8 | 100.0 | 12,507.9 | 100.0 | 30,404.1 | 100.0 | 55,251.7 | 100.0 |

SOURCE: United Nations, international trade tapes processed by Inter-American Development Bank.

primarily to the region. As these "industries matured [they] began to export to the rest of the world" (IADB 1984: 98).

Thus the market provided by LAFTA for the increased production of manufactures, especially of Argentina and Brazil, constituted significant support. The contribution of LAFTA markets was particularly strong for exports with larger value added that were faced with restricted access to world markets. However, from the perspective of producers, price signals were unstable and markets were not integrated. In fact, countries could reduce the preferences they had granted by cutting their external tariffs at any time. On the other hand, importers were granted preferences for given products to all partners, which created competition in the importer nation. However, any given supplier did not gain preferences in all partner markets but in only one or a few nations because of the nature of negotiations. Liberalization was multilateral from the perspective of demanders, but tended to be bilateral for suppliers.

In summary, LAFTA made a positive contribution to the expansion of reciprocal trade, despite the fact that the provisions of the Montevideo Treaty and the Protocol of Caracas were not fulfilled. In particular, it provided a broader market for manufactured exports and for the utilization and expansion of installed capacity in some sectors.

**The main shortcomings of the agreement.** The shortcomings of the original treaty were not solved as the obstacles to progress became stronger. Countries pressing for a more comprehensive scheme saw three main problems in the performance of LAFTA. First, advances were for the most part made only when one country was interested in gaining access to partner markets and when there was no opposition from sectors in that country who felt threatened by such initiatives. Liberalization based on commodity-by-commodity negotiation at the request of interested parties rendered the process self-exhaustible.

Second, when LAFTA offered opportunities for the creation of new industries, the allocation was left completely to market forces. Such an approach might be appropriate among countries enjoying both advanced and similar levels of development and having stable trade policies. But that was not the case in the developing economic environment of Latin America, where substantial differences among member countries were the rule. Relatively higher levels of development were present in Argentina, Brazil, and Mexico. Consequently, medium- and small-sized countries feared that, without a change in the framework provided by LAFTA, further liberalization would leave some countries primarily limited to the production of raw materials while others specialized in manufactures. The latter was thought to contribute more to self-sustained growth because of the greater role in manufacturing activities of technological progress, economies of scale, more dynamic demand, stronger linkages to other domestic activities, and the assumption that comparative advantage could be gained. Additionally, commodities tended to have low tariff preferences, while manufactures tended to benefit with large preferences. This influenced the distribution of the subsidies implicit in tariff preferences.

The third major limitation of LAFTA was the absence of a harmonical economic policy. All that was regulated under LAFTA was the liberalization of segments of reciprocal trade, without the harmonization of external tariffs, exchange rates, and other important policies. Thus, the profile of effective preferences could experience sharp and unexpected changes. One problem that became evident as the integrating project was being implemented was related to the distribution of costs and benefits with foreign enterprises. The bargaining position of foreign enterprises is improved if internal barriers to trade are removed without domestic policies being brought into harmony. Thus there is a profit-creation effect in favor of foreign enterprise within the customs union (Tironi 1981). Several countries feared that the acceleration of the integration process within the prevailing framework would tend to concentrate its benefits in the economies of the most-developed members and in the TNCs more than in Latin American national firms. Market comparative advantages could be distorted by the incentives granted to TNCs by host countries.

The period agreed upon for the implementation of a free trade zone, which had been extended from 1973 to 1980 by the Protocol of Caracas, ended long before the fulfillment of its targets. In 1980 a new treaty, Montevideo II, gave life to the Latin American Integration Association (LAIA).

## The Cartagena Agreement

The Andean Pact was formed with the signing of the Cartagena Agreement in 1969 by Bolivia, Chile, Colombia, Ecuador, and Peru. It progressed significantly until 1973, the year in which it was signed by Venezuela. First there was the need to revise various agreements and proposals in order to take Venezula's entrance into account. A long discussion followed. It ended with the withdrawal of Chile in October 1976, mostly as a consequence of the inconsistency between the nature of the Andean Pact and the extreme global monetarism of the economic experiment imposed on Chile after the coup of 1973. After the withdrawal of Chile the process moved slowly, and in the mid-1980s the situation was critical.

The Andean Pact included middle-of-the-road, reformist, and moderately nationalistic governments. But during the 1970s various coups and the spread of monetarism contributed to a relaxation of "Latino-Americanist feelings" and encouraged the search for an open, or nonselective, integration with the markets of industrialized nations.

The Andean countries' integration agreement arose out of the experience gained in LAFTA. It was the product of a growing awareness among these countries that an intensive process of economic integration could remove some of the major obstacles to development while affirming national sovereignty. The Andean Pact was consistent with continued participation in LAFTA, according to regulations agreed to in 1968, which accepted the creation of subregional agreements. Within LAFTA the Andean countries functioned as one economic unit in their negotiations with other LAFTA and GATT members in such matters as tariff preferences, trade agreements, and the renegotiation of preferences with the other members of LAIA according to Montevideo II.

Within the Andean group, there is heterogeneity among partners with respect to levels of overall and industrial development and size of the domestic market. Nonetheless, the heterogeneity is much less than that within LAFTA: by 1980 the ratio of GDP between the larger and smaller partners in the Andean group was 18.9 as compared to 58.0 in LAFTA. In terms of population, the divergence within the Andean group was even smaller, 4.6 as compared to 41.7 in LAFTA.

The most important features of the Cartagena Agreement are (1) an institutional setup that was equipped with executive power; (2) a scheduled program for liberalizing reciprocal trade and gradually establishing a common external tariff; (3) a system designed to achieve an equitable distribution of the benefits of integration, whose principal instruments were sectoral programs for industrial development (the system also allowed for several forms of tariff preferences for Bolivia and Ecuador, the two countries of least relative development); and (4) the harmonization of economic policies beginning with direct foreign investment (DFI).

**The process of integrating goods markets.** The Cartagena Agreement established a selective program for the elimination of internal tariffs among the Andean countries. Included in this program are four main categories of commodities, each having different liberalization mechanisms. From the outset, tariffs were suppressed on commodities not being produced and on products making up the first step of the Common List of LAFTA; thus an expanded market was instantaneously provided for potential investment in those sectors. Approximately 30 percent of the customs schedule was reserved for Sectoral Programs for Industrial Development (SPID); each program was to establish its own process of liberalization. The trade barriers on the remaining goods—about two-thirds of the customs schedule—have gradually been reduced since 1971. Among these items, where there was production in national markets, each country was authorized to postpone the start of liberalization for about 5 percent of the items of the customs universe.

In accordance with a program of gradual automatic liberalization, about 3,000 items or groups of commodities (out of 5,000) were subject in 1979 to a maximum internal ad valorem tariff of 32 percent and an average rate of 14 percent—that is, less than one-third the tariff rates prevailing in 1969.[10] The Cartagena Agreement had established that internal tariffs were to be reduced by 10 percent annually until they were eliminated in 1981, but this date was repeatedly postponed (Aninat et al. 1984). In spite of delays, a significant margin of preference (MOP) was at work by 1981 in favor of reciprocal trade among Colombia, Peru, and Venezuela, as shown in table 8.3, while Bolivia and Ecuador were granting light margins.

Exports from Bolivia and Ecuador benefit from special preferences because of their status as less-developed partners. In the gradual

Table 8.3
Tariff Preferences in Andean Reciprocal Trade, 1981 (% of CIF prices)

|  | Average External Tariff (1) | Average Internal Tariff (2) |
|---|---|---|
| Bolivia | 20.4 | 18.8 |
| Colombia | 32.6 | 17.4 |
| Ecuador | 32.1 | 28.7 |
| Peru | 34.6 | 18.5 |
| Venezuela | 31.0 | 22.0 |

SOURCE: A. Aninat, R. Ffrench-Davis, and P. Leiva, "La Integración Andina en el Nuevo Escenario de los Años Ochenta," in Apuentes *CIEPLAN* no. 62 (Oct.), 1984. Based on data of the Board of the Cartagena Agreement (JUNAC).

program of liberalization, commodities produced by Bolivia and Ecuador were allowed duty-free into the markets of other member countries by 1974. Ecuador was able to make significant use of these special MOPs, while for the less-developed Bolivia the benefits from the MOP have been very limited.

The progressive removal of barriers is one crucial factor explaining the rapid increase in reciprocal trade. The removal of barriers encouraged commercial contacts among Andean countries that were infrequent before the Cartagena Agreement despite the improvement brought by LAFTA. Reciprocal knowledge of supply and demand and the opening of marketing channels also increased trade in commodities that had not benefited from formal MOPs. As a consequence, the low levels of trade prevailing when the Cartagena Agreement was signed rose to 13 percent of the total trade of the Andean countries by 1982, a fourfold increase in the share of reciprocal trade.

As expected, a large share of the increase was concentrated in manufactured products, which account for 84 percent of the increase in reciprocal exports between 1970 and 1982. By 1982 intra-Andean exports of manufactures were 29 percent of total manufactured exports. Exports of these products to third countries also grew quickly (25 percent per year in current U.S. dollars), but not by as much as the 39 percent to Andean markets. Importantly, "manufactured" exports to the rest of the world were more intensive in raw materials with a low value added. The Andean countries made use of their domestic markets to foster nontraditional exports that had high value added and poor access to markets in industrialized nations.

The Andean import policy was to be expressed in a Common External Tariff (CET) schedule covering the universe of tradable products.[11] A "minimum common external tariff" was implemented gradually between 1971 and 1976. According to this instrument, the countries could not charge lower duties than the agreed-upon rates to imports from outside the region, but they were allowed to maintain higher rates. Subsequently, the countries were to have modified their tariff schedule yearly until common rates were reached among all members in 1981. Deadlines related to the CET schedule also have been repeatedly postponed. However, a minimum CET was revised downward, approved in October 1976, and is now in force.

The levels and structure of the CET were based on three general criteria designed to foster productive activities that are labor-intensive, contribute to technological development, or are infant industries. The criteria were combined in a pioneer application of effective protection to the setting of a desired or target tariff schedule (Junta del Acuerdo de Cartagena [JUNAC] 1981).

Progress was also made in other areas supporting trade. A common customs nomenclature was established and the Andean Investment Corporation (Corporación Andina de Fomento) was created. Furthermore, the Andean Reserve Fund (Fondo Andino de Reservas) began to operate in 1978. Its purpose was to support temporary balance-of-payments problems of member countries, to improve the investment of the central banks' reserves, and to serve as an avenue for the harmonization of exchange rate policies and financial relations with third countries.

**Regional investment planning.** SPIDs were considered to be the main direct instruments for industrial planning and equitable distribution of the benefits of integration among member countries. Because of their economic and technological importance and the economies of scale involved in their production, one-third of total tradable items was earmarked for eventual inclusion in subregional investment planning. The SPIDs prescribed that groups of new industrial activities with technological linkages be assigned to a particular country. A similar process was to take place with all product families in each sector reserved for an SPID. The designated country was given the right to produce the assigned product family and was guaranteed a market free of import restrictions and tariffs in the other countries. The assigned country was to decide which specific items within each product family would be produced and the timing of such production. Partner countries agreed not to promote the development of similar activities for a certain number of years, to liberalize imports of production originating only in the designated country, and to apply a duty equal to the CET against other nations. The CET, which was approved simultaneously with the allocation of activities, set the maximum surcharge over international prices the exporting country could impose. Such an approach was intended to establish a complementary relationship between market and planning.

The first SPID was approved in 1972. It included an important segment of the metallurgical-mechanical sector (about one-third of the demand estimated for 1980). The program encompassed chiefly machine tools, mining equipment, electrical equipment, and instruments. Production of these goods is relatively labor-intensive and allows the development of expertise that can be disseminated to the rest of the economy.

Items reserved for the program comprised several other sectors. The most outstanding, and at the same time controversial, were the petrochemical and automotive sectors.[12] After long and hard negotiations, the petrochemical program was approved in August 1975 and revised slightly in 1978. This second SPID required a sizable capital investment, had an extremely high capital-output ratio, and would provide negligible employment, mainly to technicians and highly qualified professionals.

Finally, in 1977 the SPID for the automotive industry was approved. If the program, which included the allocation of categories of vehicles and of main components, had been implemented, it would have brought about a reduction in the number of vehicle models assembled and specialization in the components produced. However, partly because of the lack of agreement between the Andean group and the TNCs engaged in the sector, the program was not implemented.

Implementation of the SPIDs has been very limited. But this outcome, rather than being related to the shortcomings of the programs themselves, was strongly influenced by the trends in economic policies being enforced in member countries. The excessive availability of foreign funds during the 1970s weakened efforts to promote further industrialization and fostered integration to world markets rather than to regional markets. This factor also caused more intensive activity in the financial dimension at the expense of other national economic activities.

What remained in trade relations, therefore, were the tariff preferences and the development of trade and financial channels, which encouraged a significant increase in reciprocal trade in manufactures up to the early 1980s.

**Policies toward foreign investment.** When liberalization of reciprocal trade within an integration process is not accompanied by coordinated industrial and foreign investment policies, integration can weaken the position of the developing country vis-à-vis TNCs. As mentioned above, the gamut of options open to foreign enterprises is expanded with economic integration, because by investing in any one country a TNC has access to the markets of all the other member countries. This is strengthened by the fact that TNCs were already established in several countries of the region.

Various research projects conducted during the 1960s brought to light the unequal distribution of benefits and costs between transnational enterprises and the host countries. The limited or heterogeneous contributions they were making to capital formation, technological progress, development of administrative skills and exports were exposed (Lahera and Sánchez 1985; Tironi 1981; Vaitsos 1974; White 1986). There were indications that a liberal policy toward foreign capital turned out to be most attractive to investments with short payback periods. This was partly a consequence of the investors' perception that overly favorable conditions carried the risk of being modified after a short time. On the other hand, the perception of stability appeared to be a good inducement to investment ventures with more positive effects. This consideration led ANCOM to the establishment of what were assumed to be strict but stable regulations.

Thus, uniform standards for the treatment of foreign investment were approved during the first months of the Andean Pact's existence. The agreement, known as Decision 24, established a common set of rules as the minimum restrictions to be applied by each government to foreign capital. The rules allowed for differentiated treatment of activities closely linked to integration as distinguished from other activities. Foreign investors in the first group of activities would not receive more favorable treatment than the norm, whereas each country had the option of making use of clauses of exception for other activities.

Some of the fundamental aspects of Decision 24 were that (1) it was stable because of its multinational character, that is, it could be modified only with the agreement of all member countries; (2) the policy was selective in that each new foreign investment required the explicit authorization of a national body responsible for the regulation of investment; (3) it regulated the use of domestic credit by foreign investors, and limited the clauses frequently introduced by foreign investors to restrict exports bearing foreign brands and royalties; and (4) automatic reinvestment of profits and purchase of shares in domestic enterprises were required to pass through the same selection process as the initial investment.[13]

The agreement established norms for gradually transferring ownership of the foreign firms into domestic hands. Three categories of firms were defined according to the composition of their capital: national, mixed, and foreign. National firms were those with more than 80 percent of Andean capital; mixed firms were those with an Andean capital share between 51 and 80 percent.[14] The remainder were foreign enterprises. Decision 24 stipulated that foreign enterprises should gradually be transformed into mixed enterprises, generally within fifteen years. Foreign firms that did not commit to a timetable with domestic authorities for conversion into mixed enterprises would not benefit from tariff preferences within the Andean market. Enforcement of this provision was left to the host country. Clearly, this was not a rule against foreign investment, but an attempt to capture for host countries the potential benefits of the common market.

In the period 1974–84, forty-five agreements of transformation were signed in Colombia. By 1984, eight firms had already achieved a share of at least 51 percent of national capital, thirty-one had operated within the schedule of transformation, and eleven were behind schedule (Lahera 1986). One factor that made compliance with the transformation rule more difficult was the debt crisis that emerged in the early 1980s. The financial situation of firms worsened, and foreign currency, which was needed to divest, became more scarce, leading to a reduced interest in taking over shares of foreign firms.

There was strong opposition to Decision 24 by some foreign investors and business associations. However, there was no significant withdrawal of investment. New activities were developed, agreements defining the conversion of foreign firms into mixed enterprises were signed, and in general the countries organized or improved institutions to regulate direct foreign investment (DFI) and developed some capacity to negotiate with foreign investors and owners of technology. Nonetheless, member countries gradually weakened their control pari passu with a general trend of market liberalization (Lahera and Sánchez 1985–86).

## Integration and Crisis in the 1980s

The three significant events during the 1980s were the drastic fall in reciprocal trade in all integration agreements within Latin America, the replacement of LAFTA by LAIA, and the bilateral agreement between Argentina and Brazil.

In the early 1980s, reciprocal exports suffered a sharp drop of 35 percent below the 1981 peak. In general, total and reciprocal exports had been rising until 1981, with the exception of the Southern Cone countries and Peru, where exports had started receding earlier. This was in part due to the financial and terms-of-trade shocks experienced by the region.

Total exports also fell, although moderately, and as a consequence, the share of reciprocal exports returned to the low levels prevailing in the mid-1960s.[15] The main force behind the drop in reciprocal exports was the downward trend in overall imports throughout the region. Recessive domestic adjustments led to a general reduction of imports. In addition, all countries reintroduced varied restrictions, even on imports originating in partner nations. Large exchange-rate devaluations also discouraged imports. Since there were simultaneous devaluations in most Latin American countries, the comparative costs among them did not change much. However, these costs did change notably vis-à-vis the industrial nations. Therefore, the volume of exports to the rest of the world tended to rise.

Total exports of manufactures (under the UNCTAD definition) performed better than other Latin American exports in the period 1980–85, rising to 23 percent of total exports (IADB and INTAL 1987a). Terms of trade moved in favor of manufactures, and the combination of depressed domestic demand and devalued exchange rates contributed to increase manufactured exports. The change in the destination of these exports is noteworthy. In nominal terms, sales to the rest of the world rose 66 percent from 1980 to 1985, while they fell 38 percent within Latin America.

The conclusion that can be reached is that the region did not manage to use reciprocal trade as a compensatory anticyclical mechanism. Each country tried to reduce imports from all sources, which negatively affected its partners. However, with the same availability of foreign currency the debtor nations could have been successful in maintaining reciprocal imports, which would have meant larger reciprocal exports. As a consequence, total exports and overall output, particularly in manufacturing, could have performed better.[16]

In 1980, LAFTA was replaced by a new agreement called LAIA, with the signing of Montevideo II. This new treaty had a flexible framework without specific targets. It was not directed toward starting a new advanced stage but was designed simply to preserve the economic cooperation that had survived up to 1980 in an unfavorable political environment for integration.

The main achievement during the first five years of Montevideo II has been the renegotiation of the import preferences available in 1980. They comprise both the National and Common Lists, the preferences for less-developed partners (called the Historical Patrimony), and the Complementarity Agreements. The preferences in the lists were negotiated on a bilateral basis, with the exception of the Andean countries, which acted as a group. Preferences were negotiated as percentages of national tariffs, which is an improvement over the heterogeneous base of preferences in LAFTA.

Complementarity agreements were replaced by trade agreements (*acuerdos comerciales de alcance parcial*) covering 25 sectors. Again, bilateralism was the rule. Half the agreements include only 2 countries, and only one covered 8 of the 11 country members. Only 23 items, representing 59 percent of the trade recorded, were captured under the trade agreements. However, the stability of the agreements must be stressed, with 21 agreements lasting between 13 and 23 years. The dominance of bilateralism is apparent. In 1984, of the US$2.2 billion of intraregional imports covered under tariff preferences, 84 percent was negotiated bilaterally.

The payments system of LAFTA continued to be active and improved in 1982. Reciprocal trade covered under the system fell substantially, roughly parallel with total reciprocal trade. As a consequence, the share covered by the system declined to around 80 percent. The increase in reciprocal credit lines to US$2.8 billion within the four-month period of payments was a significant support to reciprocal trade (INTAL, *El Proceso de Integración de América Latina* 1985–86).

There are two new features in LAIA that must be mentioned. One is the authorization of deals with non-LAIA nations. Accordingly, Mexico has signed bilateral accords that include tariff and nontariff preferences with Costa Rica, Cuba, Nicaragua, and Panama. Argentina, Colombia, and Venezuela have done the same with the Central American countries. The other feature is the regional tariff preference (PAR), implemented in 1984. Member countries agreed on a PAR ranging from 2 percent to 10 percent of the external tariffs (plus the equivalent of other import restrictions). The lower rate applies to the imports of Bolivia, Ecuador, and Paraguay from Argentina, Brazil, and Mexico; and the 10 percent applies to the reciprocal trade of the latter three. Because of lists of exceptions and tariff franchises, the effective PAR is negligible, with an average price preference in the 0.2-1.2 percent range. Thus, it has rightly been termed "symbolic" (INTAL, *El Proceso de Integración de América Latina* 1985–86: 228).

After a sharp increase in intraregional trade in the 1970s, ANCOM displayed some trade dynamism until 1982 but collapsed in 1983 with a 56 percent fall in nonoil exports. A mild recovery still left 1986 nonoil reciprocal exports 42 percent below those of 1982. The program of liberalization continued, with Colombia and Peru reducing internal tariffs to zero, but other restrictions were increased. Given the lack of accomplishments and in order to save the achievements made in ANCOM, the secretariat proposed a series of reforms reducing the targets agreed upon in 1969 and drastically relaxing the balance of market and planning originally sought. Only 13 percent of the customs items were left in SPIDs, and the investment assignments were relaxed or suppressed (Salgado 1987). The exceptions were few and were in favor of Bolivia and Ecuador. These agreements may also be bilateral, as in LAIA, thus weakening multilateralism.

There was, however, one significant move: a recently established *peso andino* is being used within the payments chamber of LAIA. The peso andino is a six-month promissory note tied to the LIBOR rate (plus a small spread) issued by the Andean Reserve Fund (FAR) and is delivered to the five central banks members. The notes were first used in 1985 to settle imbalances among Andean countries in the ALADI payments chamber.

**The Argentina-Brazil accord.** In July 1986 the presidents of the two more-industrialized nations of South America (Argentina and Brazil) signed a statement of cooperation and integration that called for a gradual process open to other democratic countries in Latin America. In December 1986 they ratified their political will to assure the success of the Economic Integration and Cooperation Program and signed sixteen protocols on issues as varied as the renegotiation of preferences, binational firms, an investment fund, biotechnology, economic research, and nuclear cooperation.

The agreement that attracted the most attention was Protocol No. 1 on Capital Goods, which takes the form of an Economic Complementation Agreement of LAIA. It was designed to regulate production, trade, and technological development in capital goods (INTAL 1987).

The target of Protocol No. 1 is to form a customs union covering half of total capital goods (including seven sectors of the LAIA nomenclature). It established rising goals of reciprocal trade each year, with an annual maximum imbalance between the two countries no larger than 10 percent of their trade. Capital goods will benefit from tariff preferences and, in the case of imports by the public sector, in public auctions

the supply of the partner would receive half of the 30 percent preference available to domestic producers.

## Conclusion

For over two-and-a-half decades, there have been formal efforts by
Latin American countries to achieve economic integration. The first
such attempts (LAFTA and CACM) were successful for a number of
years. However, progress eventually stagnated. In both cases, the
schemes adopted at the start seemed to have exhausted their capacity
to continue the process of economic integration. Neither organization
included a comprehensive system directed toward a balanced distribution of the benefits and costs of integration.

In LAFTA, the achievements were especially limited. It was a less
comprehensive scheme than that of CACM, and the distributive problem was greater because of the greater heterogeneity of its members.
However, trade did expand and the scheme allowed some specialization in production and a higher rate of utilization of installed capacity
in countries that had advanced in their industrialization with an inward approach during the 1940s and 1950s.

The design of the more recent Cartagena Agreement benefited
from the experience gained by the Andean countries with their participation in LAFTA. The terms of the agreement took shape through the
successive proposals of the Junta and decisions of the commission and
through the general implementation of the agreement and its protocols. Achievements included liberalization of reciprocal trade; the establishment of a minimum CET in its two steps covering the period
1972–76 and 1977 onward, respectively; the establishment of norms for
common treatment of foreign investment; the basis for an Andean technological policy and several Andean Programs of Technological Development; a development program for the metallurgical-mechanical
sector; and the FAR and Court of Justice. With all its shortcomings and
downswings and the difficulties in incorporating broader sectors, the
process moved ahead throughout the first decade of the existence of
ANCOM.

Notwithstanding the progress achieved by the Andean Pact, economic integration of the Latin American countries suffered serious setbacks in the 1980s. Already approved decisions were being loosely
implemented, and many other important decisions awaited approval

and implementation. Most important of all were the many common decisions that were already adopted but not fully implemented.

It is not uncommon for integration schemes in the economic history of Latin American countries to have unfulfilled goals. An analysis of national policies during the period under review shows numerous failures and shortcomings. Additionally, the many political changes taking place within each member country were a source of strain for the integration schemes.

# Part Four

# Relations between Regions

## 9

*Atsushi Murakami*

# Japan and the United States: Roles in Asian Development

The world now faces serious international economic disequilibrium. Since 1985 the U.S. economy has been suffering from its current account deficit externally and its fiscal deficit internally and has fallen to the position of a net debtor. On the other hand, Japan has recorded a huge surplus in its current account during these years and is the largest creditor in the world. This disequilibrium is primarily due to the economics of the Reagan administration, which emphasized tax reduction, expecting it to result in increases in saving, investment, productivity, economic growth, and fiscal revenue. However, contrary to this optimistic expectation, the United States has increased consumption rather than saving, which has led to the expansion of the fiscal deficit. Because of the strong dollar, maintained until the agreement between the G-5 nations (United States, Japan, Britain, West Germany, and France) in September 1985, U.S. exports until that year were handicapped and imports were encouraged. A number of American firms shifted their production to countries other than the United States, further reducing the nation's export capacity. Thus a domestic consumption boom was coupled with a rapid increase in imports. These twin deficits were offset by an influx of foreign capital. Undoubtedly, the most important task for President Bush is to cut government expenditures, raise tax revenues, restrain domestic consumption, and strengthen export potential.

Japan cannot entirely escape from responsibility for the international economic disequilibrium. Throughout the process of postwar economic recovery and development, it has pursued an economic philosophy that emphasizes production and exports. As a result, the so-called fullest production system has been constructed. Substantial import restrictions have been retained, covering a variety of agricultural, marine, and dairy products. Almost all types of manufactured goods, ranging from labor-intensive light manufactures to capital-intensive heavy industrial products and chemicals, have been produced in Japan and exported abroad.

In the years prior to 1985, Japan achieved economic growth that was mainly based on external demand encouraged by the low value of the yen. This would appear to explain the accumulation of the nation's current account surplus to historic levels. Thus Japan faces the task of changing its policies in the direction of emphasizing consumption and imports and of altering its "fullest production system" to fully implement the principle of international division of labor. Japan has been proceeding in this direction in recent years by opening its markets and expanding internal demand. This process has particularly been accelerated by the rapid increase in the value of the yen since 1985. Japan is now in the midst of an economic structural adjustment.

With this as background, this chapter analyzes the economic relations of the United States and Japan with the Asian developing countries. Developing Asia includes the Asian NICs except Taiwan (Hong Kong, Korea, and Singapore), the ASEAN-4 (Indonesia, Malaysia, the Philippines, and Thailand), and other Asian countries that mainly consist of the South Asian countries and China. Export flows from both the United States and Japan to Asia are discussed. The significant role of Japan as a main supplier of inputs (machinery and equipment) necessary for economic development in the Asian developing countries is emphasized. Import flows from Asia to the two developed countries are examined.[1] Highlighted is the crucially important role of the United States in providing a large market for the exports of the Asian countries. In spite of its tremendous efforts in recent years, the role of Japan has still been limited in this respect. Capital outflow from the United States and Japan in the form of official development assistance (ODA) and direct foreign investment (DFI) is considered. After reviewing the general tendencies of the flow, Japanese DFI in Thailand is examined as a case study on recent Japanese initiatives in Asia. Finally, the expected role of Japan in the context of its industrial adjustment and of the radically changing environments in the dynamic Asian economies is analyzed.

## Role of Supplier of Essential Inputs for Asia

Exports from Japan to the Asian developing countries, from 1982 to 1986, accounted for 25 to 27 percent of Japanese total exports. Thus Asia has been an important export market for Japan. The Asian developing countries have absorbed huge amounts of Japanese products. Incidentally, the U.S. share of total Japanese exports exceeded Asia's and showed a tendency to increase during these years. This demonstrates the widening Japanese trade surplus with the United States, which is resulting in increasing economic friction between the two countries.

The commodity composition of Japanese exports to Asia has been concentrated in manufactured goods (SITC 5–8) in general, and machinery and transport equipment (SITC 7) in particular. The former account for 94 to 95 percent of total exports, while the latter make up nearly half of the total. (It is noteworthy that in these years the share of machinery and transport equipment has been on the increase, rising from 46.1 percent in 1982 to 51.9 percent in 1986.) If these inputs had not been available from Japan, the Asian developing countries would not have experienced satisfactory rates of economic growth.

Although relevant data are not presented here, Japan must have been one of the main suppliers of essential inputs for the individual Asian developing countries. For example, it is widely recognized that as exports of final manufactured products from Korea to the world market expanded, Korea in turn increased its imports of various materials, intermediate products, and parts from Japan. Thus an unfavorable balance of trade between the two countries resulted. This also holds true for the relations of Japan with other Asian countries (Taiwan, Hong Kong, Singapore, the Philippines, Thailand, and China, among others). Only Indonesia and Malaysia have had favorable trade balances with Japan because of their high exports of raw materials, including oil. But even for these two countries, supply of manufactures from Japan—mainly machinery and equipment—seems to be indispensable for their industrial development. The trade balance between Japan and Asia as a whole favored Japan from 1982 to 1986, as can be seen in the U.N. *Commodity Trade Statistics* for those years.

Furthermore, the Japanese trade surplus has shown an upward trend year by year.

The value of U.S. exports to Asia has remained nearly constant in the past five years and has been smaller than that of Japan. Japanese exports were greater by 32.2 percent in 1982, 47.6 percent in 1983, 55.6 percent in 1984, 70.7 percent in 1985, and 87.8 percent in 1986, while the share of U.S. total exports to Asia ranged from 13 to 14 percent throughout this period. Thus it can be asserted that U.S. exports to Asian developing countries are not as significant for the United States or for Asia as are those from Japan.

The commodity composition of U.S. exports to Asia is more diversified than that of Japan. Exports of food (SITC 0) and crude materials (SITC 2) constitute a considerable portion of U.S. exports. The proportion of manufacturing exports (SITC 5–8) to total exports ranges from 65 to 73 percent, and the proportion of machinery and transport equipment (SITC 7) remains at 35 to 46 percent, with both these proportions clearly increasing each year over the period. The significance of the United States as a supplier of essential inputs to Asian developing countries is undeniable, but its role has been rather limited in comparison with Japan's. As previously mentioned, it is now crucially important for the United States to expand its exports in order to reduce the current account deficit. The Asian market—not only Japan, but also developing Asia—is expected to be an important one for U.S. exports. Because of the appreciation of the NICs' currencies against the U.S. dollar, the opening of markets by these countries, and the strengthening of U.S. competitiveness, total U.S. exports to the Asian NICs showed a tremendous increase in 1987 and in the early months of 1988.

## Role of Absorbers of Asian Products

U.S. imports from Asian developing countries for the five-year period 1982–86 accounted for 15 to 18 percent of total imports. Moreover, the value of U.S. imports from Asia has been larger than Japanese imports from Asia throughout the period and has increased each year, while Japanese imports have remained nearly constant. The main reason for this seems to have been the stagnation in the price of primary commodities, which account for a larger proportion of Japanese imports from this region. U.S. imports from Asia exceeded those of Japan in absolute terms by 7.8 percent in 1982, 39.8 percent in 1983, 56.2 percent in 1984, 66.2 percent in 1985, and 95.3 percent in 1986.

U.S. imports from Asia have largely consisted of manufactured goods. Approximately 80 to 90 percent of U.S. imports are manufactures. Among them, the share of miscellaneous manufactured goods (SITC 8) has been predominant. The share of manufactures increased rapidly from 76.8 percent in 1982 to 87.1 percent in 1986 in these five years.

The upsurge of domestic consumption in the United States and the rising trend in imports are blamed for the twin deficits. Because of these trends, the United States has played an important role as an absorber of Asian manufactured products. Without the United States as the absorber it is difficult to imagine the industrial development of Asia. The United States has recorded balance-of-trade deficits in the period in question. The U.S. trade deficit with Japan is well known and is one of the key factors explaining the economic friction between the two countries. The trade balance between the United States and developing Asia has also been unfavorable to the former. The U.S. trade deficit in relation to Asia was equivalent to 23.8 percent of the total U.S. deficit in 1982. The corresponding figures for 1983, 1984, 1985, and 1986 were 26.4, 23.9, 22.1, and 22.8 percent respectively. Because of these deficits the U.S. government has put pressure on the Asian NICs to appreciate their currencies against the U.S. dollar and has declared the graduation of the NICs from the Generalized System of Preferences (GSP) after 1 January 1989. It is understandable that the United States is concerned about the rapidly increasing levels of imports from Asia, particularly from the Asian NICs. Again, however, the role the United States has performed so far in providing a market for Asian developing countries and in promoting their economic success must be appreciated.

On the other hand, the Japanese contribution in this respect has been rather poor. Japan has absorbed 26 to 28 percent of total imports from Asian developing countries in the period 1982–86. These shares are greater than the percentage shares of imports from the United States, demonstrating that Asia is an essential import market for Japan too. They are also larger than the Asian share in U.S. imports. However, as pointed out earlier, the value of Japanese imports from Asia has been smaller than that of U.S. imports from Asia over the period.

The overwhelming proportion of Japanese imports from this region have been composed of primary commodities (SITC 0–4) in general, and mineral fuels (SITC 3) in particular. Mineral fuels, largely imported from Indonesia, alone accounted for 54.2 percent of Japanese imports from the region in 1982. Though this share shows a decreasing trend, it was still 34.6 percent in 1986. In contrast with the United States, Japanese imports of manufactures from Asia have been limited. It should be noted that the Japanese share of manufactured goods as a proportion of imports has been expanding steadily, from less than 20 percent in 1982 to more than 30 percent in 1986. Nevertheless, the level is small and the rate of increase slow. In this sense Japan has not played a major role as an absorber of Asian-made manufactures.

Japan has been the largest supplier of necessary inputs for Asia, but the United States has provided the market for its goods. This sort of asymmetrical division of labor between two developed countries cannot continue. Under strong pressure to rectify the twin deficits, the United States will be forced to restrict consumption and imports. Thus it is commonly argued that Japan will need to take up the slack by increasing consumer imports. In this respect, prospects are optimistic.

Since September 1985, Japan has been transforming its economic structure in the direction of more consumption and imports. The price mechanism operating in the era of the strong yen has promoted this transformation. First, the strong yen encourages imports. Second, a number of Japanese firms—especially small ones in the comparatively disadvantaged sectors—have turned to the Asian NICs, the ASEAN-4, and other developing countries for survival. The main goal of these countries is to export their products to the Japanese market. The non-price-competitive power of the Asian developing countries has admittedly been improved in terms of quality, design, and delivery. The attitude of Japanese consumers toward Asian-made goods has become more favorable in a short span of time. The income effect generated from the expansion of domestic demand, that is, the increase in government expenditures on public works, is likely to be favorable for imports. Japan is now prepared to execute its responsibility as an absorber in Asia. Not only have Japanese imports from the Asian developing countries increased in recent months, but also imports of manufactured goods in particular have increased dramatically (*Nihon Keizai Shinbun*, 30 January, 7 and 26 February, and 20 March 1988). Moreover, the rate of penetration of imports—for example, of photo film, calculators, black-and-white televisions, radio cassettes, cameras, and cotton fabrics—in the Japanese market showed a rising tendency (*Nihon Keizai Shinbun*, 30 March 1988).

# Role of Suppliers of Capital

**Official development assistance (ODA).** Until very recently, the United States has been the largest provider of ODA to the developing world. In spite of the prevailing opinion that the United States has tired of providing external assistance, the share of U.S. ODA in total development assistance showed an increasing trend in the early 1980s. However, the ratio of U.S. ODA to U.S. GNP is low and there is no sign of any improvement. Moreover, the share allocated to Asian developing countries has been small—11.6 percent in 1982 and 10.5 percent in 1984.

Prior to 1988, Japan was the second largest source of ODA after the United States. However, the ratio of ODA-to-GNP has remained constant at around 0.3 percent. Partly due to the efforts of the Japanese government and partly due to the appreciation of the yen, Japanese ODA is expected to increase rapidly in the latter half of the 1980s and surpass U.S. ODA.[2] The greatest share of Japanese ODA has gone to Asian developing countries, although the share of Asia overall has declined from more than 70 percent in 1980 to nearly 65 percent in 1986. As a result, Asia has received larger amounts of ODA from Japan than from the United States. The major sector to which Japanese ODA has been directed is public works, but it is also committed to a variety of fields, ranging from industrial activities to health and education. It is expected that Japan will continue to contribute to the economic development of Asia.

Much criticism has recently been directed toward Japanese ODA. It is said that its ratio of ODA-to-GNP is low, as previously mentioned. Critics add that the grant element in economic assistance projects and the ratio of grants to total Japanese ODA are also low. In addition, conditions of the loans are more restrictive and the proportion of technical assistance small. Much assistance, too, is tied to procurement from Japan (although this condition may be overstated). In view of these criticisms, it is crucial for Japan not only to increase the amount of its ODA but also to improve its content and conditions. It is widely argued in Asia that repayment of loans from Japan has become difficult because of the appreciation of the yen. This is another reason why Japan should mitigate the conditions of its offers of ODA. It might also be possible for Japan to consider importing Asian goods denominated in yen.

Japan now has plans to recycle its huge balance-of-trade surplus to developing countries in various forms up to a value of US$20 billion. Perhaps the largest proportion could be disbursed to the developing world, including Asia, in the form of increased ODA.

**Direct foreign investment (DFI).** Available data on U.S. DFI in Asia are fragmented. However, some characteristics of DFI in Asia are revealed in materials published by the Japan External Trade Organization's *White Papers on Foreign Direct Investment of the World and Japan* (JETRO).

The stock of U.S. foreign investment in the world at the end of 1980 was US$215.4 billion and reached the level of US$259.9 billion by the end of 1986. The United States has been the largest investor in the world, but the rate of increase in its investment has been rather stagnant. In fact, the share of the United States in total world investment has shown a decreasing trend. It was 48.6 percent of total world flows in the period from 1971 to 1979, but only 19.2 percent in the period from 1980 to 1985. During the latter years, new investors, such as the United Kingdom, West Germany, Canada, and Japan, have emerged and have steadily increased their contributions.

However, the investment position of the United States in developing Asia has shown a clear upward trend, increasing by 90.8 percent from 1980 to 1986. The U.S. investment position in Asian developing countries in manufacturing industries was nearly US$2.6 billion at the end of 1980, but increased to US$3.5 billion by the end of 1985, an increase of 37.9 percent. Among the manufacturing firms, investment in electrical and electronics industries was heaviest with a 2.1-fold increase in investment stock, from US$710 million at the end of 1980 to nearly US$1.5 billion at the end of 1985. The main recipients of U.S. investment in these fields were Singapore, Malaysia, and Taiwan. In other fields, Hong Kong is becoming a main target of U.S. investment, which is also aiming at the larger market in China.

One of the important features of U.S. investment in Asia is its focus on offshore production. Of the products manufactured by all U.S. subsidiaries overseas, 65.5 percent were directed to the local market, 10.5 percent were brought back to the United States, and 24 percent were exported to third-party countries. Output of U.S. subsidiaries in Asia, on the other hand, was largely directed to export markets; for them, according to a report of the U.S. Department of Commerce in 1982, the corresponding figures were 41.3 percent, 22.6 percent, and

36.1 percent, respectively. Exports were even more important in the electrical and electronics industries invested in by the United States, where the figures were 12.2 percent, 65.2 percent, and 22.6 percent respectively. Of the electrical and electronics products manufactured in Singapore, 76.8 percent were brought back to the United States. The corresponding figures for Malaysia and Taiwan were 74.5 and 76.5 percent, respectively.

In sum, the stock of U.S. investment in Asian developing countries has shown an increasing trend in the 1980s toward the electrical and electronics industries in spite of general stagnation in its total investment. In addition, the output from Asia of those companies was largely exported to the United States. The balance-of-trade deficits of the United States with Asia would seem to have been due to such behavior by U.S. investors.

Japanese DFI has expanded rapidly in the 1980s. The outflow in fiscal year 1986, which was equivalent to US$22.3 billion, was nearly three times the amount in fiscal year 1982 (table A.16). The cumulative amount since 1951, when Japan reopened its foreign investment activities after the Second World War, amounted to nearly US$106 billion as of 31 March 1987. However, overseas investment in Asian developing countries has not shown any substantial increase. The share of Asian developing countries has declined from 22.7 percent in fiscal year 1983 to 10.4 percent in fiscal year 1986. This means that the largest proportion of Japanese foreign investment has been directed toward developed countries in North America and Europe with the purpose of mitigating serious trade friction between Japan and other developed countries, especially the United States.

The flow of Japanese foreign investment to Asia by industry on the basis of the cumulative amount as of the end of fiscal year 1986 was nearly US$22 billion, or 20.6 percent of total outflows. As table 9.1 shows, investment in manufacturing industries accounted for 38.2 percent of the total; investment in resource development, mainly mining, for 31.2 percent; and the share of investment in commerce and service industries for 29.1 percent. As the specialization coefficient (column $B/A$ in table 9.1) clearly indicates, investment for resource development and in manufacturing industries—particularly textiles and other miscellaneous goods—has been prominent. On the other hand, the specialization coefficient of investment in commerce, finance and insurance, in transportation, and in real estate was low. Japanese investment in manufacturing industries has been aimed primarily at

### Table 9.1
### Japanese DFI by Industry
### (according to the accumulated sum at 31 March 1987)

| Industry | World | | Asia | | Coefficient Specialization (B/A) x (100) |
|---|---|---|---|---|---|
| | US $ millions | Percent of Total (A) | US $ millions | Percent of Total (B) | |
| Food | 1,218 | 1.1 | 284 | 1.3 | 118.2 |
| Textiles | 2,146 | 2.0 | 1,203 | 5.5 | 275.0 |
| Lumber and Pulp | 1,178 | 1.1 | 200 | 0.9 | 81.8 |
| Chemicals | 4,337 | 4.1 | 1,339 | 6.1 | 148.8 |
| Ferrous and Nonferrous Metals | 5,518 | 5.2 | 1,758 | 8.1 | 155.8 |
| Machinery | 2,597 | 2.5 | 675 | 3.1 | 124.0 |
| Electric Machinery | 4,734 | 4.5 | 1,095 | 5.0 | 111.1 |
| Transport Equipment | 4,201 | 4.0 | 822 | 3.8 | 95.0 |
| Others | 2,276 | 2.1 | 946 | 4.3 | 204.8 |
| *Manufactures Subtotal* | 28,206 | 26.6 | 8,321 | 38.2 | 143.6 |
| Agriculture and Forest | 795 | 0.8 | 247 | 1.1 | 137.5 |
| Fish and Marine | 494 | 0.5 | 108 | 0.5 | 100.0 |
| Mining | 12,424 | 11.7 | 6,438 | 29.5 | 252.1 |
| *Resource Development Subtotal* | 13,713 | 12.9 | 6,793 | 31.2 | 241.9 |
| Construction | 1,047 | 1.0 | 238 | 1.1 | 110.0 |
| Commerce | 14,538 | 13.7 | 1,270 | 5.8 | 42.3 |
| Finance and Insurance | 18,099 | 17.1 | 1,069 | 4.9 | 28.7 |
| Service | 6,246 | 5.9 | 2,489 | 11.4 | 193.2 |
| Transportation | 7,826 | 7.4 | 253 | 1.2 | 16.2 |
| Real Estate Business | 6,531 | 6.2 | 404 | 1.9 | 30.6 |
| Others | 6,285 | 5.9 | 627 | 2.9 | 49.2 |
| *Commerce and Service Subtotal* | 60,572 | 57.2 | 6,350 | 29.1 | 50.9 |
| Branch | 2,884 | 2.7 | 289 | 1.3 | 48.1 |
| Acquisition of Real Estate | 595 | 0.6 | 37 | 0.2 | 33.3 |
| *Other Subtotal* | 3,479 | 3.3 | 326 | 1.5 | 45.5 |
| **TOTAL** | 105,970 | 100.0 | 21,790 | 100.0 | 100.0 |

SOURCE: Export-Import Bank of Japan, data bank.

production for the local market, as an import-substituting type of investment.

After September 1985, a number of Japanese firms rushed investment into the Asian NICs and the ASEAN countries, with the purpose of exporting Asian-made products mainly to the Japanese market. This trend accelerated in 1987 and 1988. Thus it might be said that Japanese DFI will follow the same course as that of the United States in the near future and will contribute to expanded Japanese imports from Asia.

After the readjustment of the foreign exchange rate in 1985, many Japanese firms began to shift their production activities abroad. One of the main flows of Japanese DFI has been directed toward neighboring developing Asia. Among the Asian developing countries, Thailand has been the most attractive target. According to the data published by the Thai Board of Investment, in 1987 alone, 204 Japanese firms applied for new investment in Thailand. They sought a variety of incentives, such as exemption from import duties for imported machinery and equipment and three- to eight-year holidays from business taxes. The number of investors was 3.8 times larger than it was in 1986 and amounted to 31.9 percent of the total applications by foreign firms. The planned investment by 204 firms amounted to 47.7 billion baht (one baht equals approximately US$0.04), which was 3.2 times larger than Japanese investment in 1986 and equivalent to 31.5 percent of total investment by foreign firms. Japanese investment ranked first in developing Asia in both number and value of investments. Taiwan ranked second in number of investments with 178, and the United States ranked second in terms of value of investments with 20.5 billion baht. The estimated number employed by the 204 Japanese firms was over 100,000. This trend continued in 1988. Twenty-three Japanese firms planned to move into Thailand in January 1988 with nearly 7.2 billion baht in investment. If firms that had not applied to the Board of Investment had been included, Japanese investment in Thailand would have been even larger.

Japanese DFI to Thailand appears to have one significant characteristic. According to Board of Investment data covering the period from January to July 1987, among 105 firms applying, sixty-four firms (61 percent) were export-oriented (in firms aiming to export more than 80 percent of their output, 100 percent Japanese capital is permitted), and sixty-seven firms (64 percent) were small-scale with planned investment of less than 100 million baht. The industries in which the Japanese are investing are diverse and include primary commodities, processed goods (marine products, canned food and fruits, jewelry), labor-intensive light manufactures (toys, sporting goods, wig making, garment manufacturing), machinery and parts (electrical and electronic products, precision instruments, and transport equipment), petrochemicals, department store and supermarket construction, and language school management. More than a few of these industries come from a sector in which Japan had lost international competitiveness; the firms in these industries are small firms from a comparatively disadvantaged sector of the Japanese economy that sells its products to the world as well as to Japan. This is in contrast with the capital movement from Japan to Thailand in the early 1960s, which involved large firms aiming toward import-substitution production in Thailand.

The push factor behind these capital outflows in the form of DFI is obvious. Because of the appreciating yen, the comparatively advantaged sectors of the Japanese economy have been forced to seek new areas of comparative advantage internally or move to the developing countries for survival. Thus, this capital outflow may be regarded as a part of the process of international industrial adjustment. In that case, what is the pull factor on the Thai side?

The improvement in the investment climate in Thailand has been dramatic. First, the productivity of Thai workers has increased. It is said that the level of skill of the young female Thai laborer now matches or exceeds the Japanese standard. Frequent changing of jobs is not now the common practice among laborers, who are adjusting to the Japanese style of management. Second, a new generation of entrepreneurs who studied abroad in Japan and the United States is emerging. They have not been spoiled by working in family businesses and are able to apply modern labor-management principles and quality control. Their technical standards are also higher, enabling them to be subcontractors to Japanese firms. Third, the discipline and efficiency of Thai bureaucrats, including Board of Investment staff, have been strengthened. Fourth, and most important, the middle class in Thailand has grown. Now it is possible for more of them to purchase the new houses being constructed in the suburbs of Bangkok. They constitute enough of a market to support new department stores. Finally, the infrastructure in Thailand has improved considerably. Access to airports, road transportation, telecommunications, and construction of export-processing zones have increased. These have all made the Thai business environment more favorable for foreign firms.

Thailand also has an inherent comparative advantage because of its good economic performance, social and political stability, availability of cheap labor, and the friendly nature of its people. These factors, coupled with the improved investment climate, constitute the pull factor on the Thai side and have led to the rush of investment flows into Thailand. A good investment climate is essential in order for developing countries to attract DFI on a sufficient scale. Outflow of Japanese capital will induce the potential for exports of machinery and equipment from Japan to Thailand. But many Japanese firms investing in Thailand are now motivated by the possibility of exporting Thai-made products to the Japanese market, a development often called the "boomerang effect." Indeed, the expected role of Japanese DFI in Asia is to promote the export of a variety of goods from host countries to the Japanese market, thus strengthening the role of Japan as an absorber of Asian products. Japanese investment should also encourage economic development in countries like Thailand by creating employment opportunities, developing human resources, transferring technology, and providing work for native subcontractors. Direct investment naturally entails some friction between investing and host countries. The nightmare in the early 1970s of strong anti-Japan sentiment in Thailand comes to mind. But as long as Japanese firms are export-oriented and are intermediaries connecting Thai exports with Japanese imports, it is hoped that a repetition of this can be avoided.

## Conclusion

The United States and Japan both play important roles in Asia as suppliers of necessary inputs for industrial development, as absorbers of output, and as distributors of external capital to the Asian developing countries. Japan has supplied a variety of manufactured goods, mainly machinery and equipment, to Asia, and the United States has provided the largest market for Asia's goods. Since the United States faces the task of curtailing its government expenditures and private consumption in order to rectify its serious twin deficits, Japan must assume the responsibility of being an absorber of Asian products. Japan is struggling to accomplish this through reduction of tariff and nontariff barriers and through expansion of internal demand. For the United States, it remains desirable to make every effort to increase exports to the Asian countries, including Japan.

It is essential for Asian developing countries to encourage intra-regional trade. Asia contains a variety of countries in different stages of economic development: the Asian NICs, the ASEAN countries, China, and others. There is ample space for the expansion of intra-regional trade. Each of these countries is capable of absorbing the others' goods.

Japan has become and will continue to be the largest provider of ODA in the world. Japanese ODA has been concentrated in the Asian developing countries and has focused on contributing to the establishment of firm foundations for their economic development. In the future, Japan should improve the contents and conditions of its ODA. Japanese DFI to the Asian developing countries has also been increasing. After September 1985, a number of Japanese firms rushed to invest in the Asian NICs and the ASEAN countries with the main purpose of bringing Asian products into the Japanese market. This movement and momentum is likely to strengthen Japan's role as an absorber of Asian-made manufactures.

In 1987, the Japanese government recently outlined an economic assistance program for the developing countries that integrated ODA, DFI, and increased imports to Japan (MITI 1987). This approach, together with a thorough transformation of the economic structure in Japan, can be expected to expand Japan's role in Asian development and at the same time meet the growing and urgent needs of the Asian developing countries.

## 10

*Carlos Juan Moneta*

# Latin American Economic Relations with the United States and Japan

Latin America has become less important in world trade. In 1970, the region's exports were 5.3 percent of total world trade, but by 1986 this figure had dropped to 4.1 percent (Sistema Económico Latinoamericano [SELA] 1987a). This decline in export share is evident in trade with the European Community (EC) and with the United States. Price declines in primary and energy products have reduced the value of Latin American exports. Although export volume has increased, the value of exports was equal in 1986 to the average for 1979–80. This is a cause for concern, since exports provided approximately 70 percent of the region's foreign currency between 1978 and 1981, and in 1986 amounted to 93 percent of the total income (Inter-American Development Bank [IADB] 1987). Although the region has had trade balance surpluses in recent years, these were due more to a contraction in imports than to an expansion of exports. The surpluses served to repay some of the large external debt of the Latin American countries.

Furthermore, Latin America continued to be predominantly a commodity exporter. Despite an increase in the share of manufactured exports, exports of primary products and food amounted to almost 80 percent of total exports in 1984. On the import side, primary products made up between 18 and 19 percent of total imports over the last fifteen years, while fuel imports tripled from 6 percent in 1970 to 20 percent in 1984. Despite their high share, Latin American imports of manufactured goods declined from 76 percent in 1970 to 62 percent in 1984 (SELA 1987a).

There have been changes in the relations between Latin America and the developed and developing countries. In the early 1980s, Latin American trade gradually moved away from Western developed countries and toward the developing ones. However, since the external debt crisis, Latin American trade has shifted once again to developed markets, with exports to the developed countries increasing from 64 percent of total exports in 1981 to 66 percent in 1986. At the same time, intraregional trade has decreased in importance. During this same period, the share of Latin American exports going to the developing countries (including other Latin American countries) decreased from 28 to 23 percent of total exports, and the share of imports dropped from nearly 33 to 30 percent (SELA 1987a).

## Trade Relations with the United States

U.S. exports to Latin America fell from 18 percent of total U.S. exports in 1981 to 14 percent in 1985 but increased slightly in 1986. Between 1981 and 1985, U.S. imports from Latin America fell from 16 to 14 percent of total imports. In 1986, U.S. imports from Latin America fell even further by 9 percent to US$39.5 billion, largely as a result of a reduction in hydrocarbon purchases (General Agreement on Tariffs and Trade [GATT] 1987). At the same time, U.S. imports from other developed countries and the Asian newly industrializing countries (NICs) increased significantly. The decrease in Latin American exports to the United States occurred during a sharp reduction (almost 15 percent) in the region's exports worldwide. As a result of these changes, the U.S. deficit with the region has slowly declined since 1985.

Latin American sales have been concentrated in the U.S. market. In 1982, approximately 50 percent of total Latin American sales were to the United States. Moreover, almost 90 percent of the increase in Latin American exports to the Organisation for Economic Co-operation and Development (OECD) markets was concentrated in the United States (SELA 1987b). Imports reflected a similar situation: almost 40 percent of total Latin American imports were from the United States. This concentration in the U.S. market, which is in contrast to the greater diversity in export markets that prevailed in the 1970s, places the region in a state of dependency. At the same time, there has been a significant reduction in reciprocal intra-Latin American trade.

Yet protectionist trends have continued in the United States along with coercive measures applied to medium- and small-sized Latin American countries for political reasons, such as the Nicaraguan sugar quota and the measures of retaliation against Cuba. In addition, the Caribbean economies may have been adversely affected by the adjustments made to the U.S. sugar quotas despite evaluations by the U.S. Department of Commerce and U.S. Department of State, demonstrating the benefits obtained by the Caribbean countries from the Caribbean Basin Initiative.

Among both the supporters of U.S. protectionism and those in favor of openness in U.S. policy, there is a perception that the U.S. trade imbalance is a result of an asymmetrical situation in the relative openness of the U.S. market with other countries. U.S. legislation in recent years has legitimized this perception and confronted the so-called unfair competition. Noteworthy among these proposed legislative changes are the 1984 Trade and Tariffs Act; the amendments to section 301 of the 1974 Trade Act (whereby the executive branch would be obligated, under certain circumstances, to decree for the application of trade retaliation measures); the provisions regarding reciprocity in telecommunications and intellectual property rights; the amendments to antisubsidy legislation; the amendment proposed by Representative Richard A. Gephardt of Missouri by which trade sanctions would be applied to countries that have significant trade surpluses with the United States; and H.R. 3, the Omnibus Trade Act (SELA 1987a). Special mention should be made of the 1985 Food Security Act. The act, which is aimed at recovering U.S. markets lost to EC competition through subsidized sale of cereals to the Soviet Union and possibly China, would have negative effects on Latin American agricultural exporters. Most of the legislation mentioned aims to obtain greater access to other markets and sets up obstacles for Japanese and EC imports into the United States, as well as for imports from the more successful NICs, including the Asian NICs, Brazil, and other major Latin American countries.

Prospects for greater protectionism are good. The current political discourse on trade appears to include plans for forcing a liberalization of external markets, protecting the domestic market, and restricting the benefits to countries not accepting or satisfying U.S. demands (Washington Trade Report 1987).

## Trade Relations with Japan

Latin America has also declined in importance as a trading partner with Japan. While Latin America accounted for 8 percent of total Japanese exports in 1975, the share of Japanese exports destined to the region declined to only 5 percent by 1985. This was small relative to the share of the Asian developing countries. In 1985, China had a 5.0 percent share, Korea, a 3.2 percent share, Taiwan, a 2.6 percent share, Malaysia, a 3.3 percent share, and Singapore, a 1.2 percent share (Japan Tariff Association [JTA] 1987). Two factors have contributed to the decline in the Latin American share: the sharp contraction of Latin American imports resulting from its external debt, and the significant increase in Japanese exports to the U.S. market, from 35.2 percent of total exports in 1984 to 38.5 percent in 1986 (Bradford and Moneta 1987).

Looking more closely at Japan-Latin America trade, we can see that 70 to 80 percent of Japan's exports to Latin America are destined for Mexico, Panama, Venezuela, Brazil, Chile, Peru, and Argentina. Of this group, Mexico and Brazil purchased the highest percentage (0.5 percent each) of the total Japanese exports in 1986 (JTA 1987). These imports from Japan consisted largely of machinery and transport equipment (79.5 percent), manufactured goods (11.6 percent), and miscellaneous light industrial items (5.2 percent).

Correspondingly, Japan's share of Latin American exports decreased from 7.2 to 5.3 percent between 1970 and 1984. Latin American fuel exports to Japan, following an initial increase, declined in the last decade. This decline was offset somewhat by an increase in exports of manufactured goods between 1980 and 1984. Although the increase in exports of Latin American manufactured goods is still modest, it occurred when the Latin American share of Japanese exports decreased. Imports to Japan of manufactured goods have increased relative to imports of natural resources. Nevertheless, because of Japan's need for raw materials, commodity trade in agriculture, petroleum, petroleum by-products, and mineral products continues to be very important (Bradford and Moneta 1987).

While Japan's share of Latin American exports remained relatively constant, Latin America's imports from Japan increased from 6.8

percent in 1981 to 8.4 percent in 1986 (GATT 1987). There has been a growing Latin American deficit in trade with Japan for over a decade. In 1986, Japan's exports to Latin America amounted to US$9.5 billion and its imports from the region to US$6.2 billion, thereby yielding a surplus of US$3.3 billion for Japan. This exceeded the trade balance of the previous year by almost one billion dollars. Nonetheless, the Japanese surplus fell in 1987. In that year, Japanese exports to and imports from the region are estimated to have been US$8.7 billion and US$6.4 billion, giving Japan a surplus of about US$2.4 billion—a reduction of 27.6 percent. To adequately evaluate this data, it is nevertheless necessary to apply the effects of the appreciation of the yen and the J-curve (SELA 1988).

Among the international political problems facing the Takeshita government in Japan upon its election in 1988 were its conflicts with the United States and the EC about the restructuring of the global economic system. In addition, there are pressures from the NICs and ASEAN-4 for Japan to increase its financing and open up its markets. Latin America is not included in this overall context, although the fund-recycling mechanism announced by the Nakasone government in 1987 to address the problems of external debt of developing countries will affect Latin America.

In contrast to increasing U.S. protectionism, Japan is making efforts to open up its markets. For example, Japan is establishing import promotion policies. Although these policies are targeted to its developed partners and countries in East and Southeast Asia, Japan is taking practical measures to encourage openness and deregulation and is offering technical assistance to trading partners to give them better knowledge of the Japanese market and how to compete in it. The Japan External Trade Organization (JETRO), which until recently was dedicated to promoting Japanese exports, is now promoting imports.

The principles and programs guiding the opening of the Japanese market are basically compatible with the positions existing within Latin America. The problem lies in the requirements that must be met by the Latin American countries in order to gain access to the Japanese market and in the appropriate orientation of national policies as seen from the Japanese perspective. Japanese corporations have their principal interests in trade, in optimizing their investment return, and in finding a favorable atmosphere—political and social stability, possibilities for economic development, clear and reliable rules on foreign capital, and so on. The present Latin American situation works against these conditions. In this context, Japanese financial and trade corporations are willing to support government policy provided they are offered sound and secure guaranties. Otherwise, Latin America and the Caribbean are not attractive areas for making major investments or granting substantial loans (Keizai Koho Center 1985, 1986).

Latin America's access to the Japanese market has been limited by the prevalence of certain internal protectionist pressures. But these conditions are likely to be encountered in any market. A more important factor for future expansion of trade with Japan is Latin America's lesser competitiveness as compared with the NICs'. Japan and the East and Southeast Asian countries have developed into a huge economic center that could play an important role in Latin America's indispensable process of trade diversification, a process that is now concentrated in the U.S. market. Another difficulty facing Latin America is the understandable Japanese bias toward certain countries and regions.

With the opening of Japan's markets, Latin America finds itself with a potentially huge market with which it has had very little experience. However, the opening of Japanese markets will be of little use to Latin America unless significant changes are made by Latin American countries. Without these changes, trade with Japan could remain unchanged during the next few years. On the import side, the increase in the value of the yen could harm imports of Japanese goods, especially in those product areas where prices are most elastic, such as manufactured goods. In terms of exports, prospects for obtaining significant growth in Latin American exports to Japan will not be favorable unless the range of products is widened and improved to adapt to the requirements of the Japanese market. Prospects for a significant increase in Latin American exports of petroleum and iron, which constitute the bulk of the primary resources imported by Japan from Latin America, are not bright. There are at least three reasons: Japan's diversification in its sources of hydrocarbons supply, the decrease in international prices of oil and iron, and Japan's relative trend of maintaining and reducing its mineral imports (iron imports dropped from US$3.2 billion in 1983 to US$1.8 billion in 1986). In fact, from 1983 to 1986, total imports of mineral fuels and petroleum to Japan decreased from US$58.9 billion to US$36.9 billion and from US$40.1 billion to US$19.5 billion, respectively. Meanwhile, in the same period, Japan's total imports of machinery and equipment and manufactured goods increased from US$10.4 billion to US$14.7 billion and from US$31.2 billion to US$44.0 billion, respectively (JTA 1987).

In cereals and beef, Latin America must compete with Australia and the United States. In this regard, it should be remembered that Japan is an important market for exports of U.S. foodstuffs. Agricultural trade is a sensitive topic between the United States and Japan and a source of much debate. The United States pressed for the lifting of Japan's restrictions on 12 protected agricultural products and in 1988 GATT issued a formal statement declaring the Japanese measures illegal under the rules of international trade. Subsequently, Japan partially opened up its market for some of these products. There has also been pressure for Japan to open up its market for rice, which until now, has been strictly closed to outside suppliers. Thus, although it may be possible for Latin America to increase its exports, it will be against strong competition. Latin America must make continued and regular efforts toward achieving a greater range of exportable foodstuffs and generating a demand for them.

In spite of the difficult task of competing with the Asián NICs, there are opportunities in the manufacturing sector for gradual progress because of the current Japanese policy of relocating industries overseas and expanding imports of relatively simple and intermediate industrial products from the developing countries. The manufacturing sector, which is a key sector for Latin American growth and for improving its international position, should constitute a cornerstone in Latin American strategy. Latin America should increase its share of manufacturing goods not only in the Japanese market but also in other Asian countries. To obtain results, it will be necessary to study these markets and, to this end, the following may be useful: (1) Japanese cooperation; (2) careful study of strategies used successfully by the Asian NICs to penetrate Japan; and (3) the establishment of much closer ties with the Asian NICs and ASEAN-4.

These requirements are of an operational nature and should be preceded by strategic decisions that will require intraregional agreements. Latin American countries will have to decide on an industrial strategy that is consonant with their individual capacities and options, and they will have to coordinate their external industrial policies, which need to be based on extensive knowledge of international industrial sectors and their own potential.

If an increase in trade occurs and if modifications are made in the composition of Latin American exports—which should include a larger number of exporting countries in order to break the present concentration of the Japanese market—Latin America could become a more important market for exports of Japanese technological and capital goods. As a result, the technical, financial, and trade schemes for Latin American coordination and cooperation would become more viable (Bradford and Moneta 1987).

## The External Debt and the United States

The high external debt of Latin American countries and the abrupt contraction of financial flows and DFI originating from the United States are the principal issues in Latin American-U.S. financial relations. U.S. banks account for 35 percent of Latin America's total external bank debt. However, the relative U.S. share has decreased since 1982. As a percentage of capital, the exposure by the nine major U.S. banks in Latin America declined from 197 percent in late 1982 to 121 percent in late 1986. The U.S. banking strategy shows a strong tendency toward continuing to reduce this share, which is estimated to reach from 63 to 73 percent of capital by 1990 (Morgan Guaranty Trust 1987).

The Latin American position on debt was initially conceived by the Economic Commission for Latin America and the Caribbean (ECLAC) and the Latin American Economic System (Sistema Económico Latino Americano [SELA]). These proposals were adopted in the Quito Declaration and Plan of Action by a Latin American economic conference held at the highest level in January 1984.

The United States' response is also well known. Originally proposed by private banking interests, the International Monetary Fund (IMF), and the governments of the creditor countries, the response represents nothing more than an orthodox policy of adjustment based on a perception of the debt crisis as a liquidity crisis. The failure of this policy, which has been negative for Latin American growth because of its enormous social costs and recessive adjustments, forced a change in perspective. With this change, the growth factor was theoretically incorporated into the adjustment, and insolvency, instead of liquidity, was identified as the central problem. The proposals of U.S. Treasury Secretary James Baker at a joint meeting of the IMF and the World Bank in Seoul in 1985 established the new criterion, which acknowledged the need for reactivating investments and channeling financial flows in order to resume Latin American growth. But this plan of action on the one hand laid the burden on the private sector and on multilateral financial organizations, and on the other hand required a more profound and coordinated intervention by the international financial community in the debtor countries' economic programs (SELA 1987a).

This exercise in orientation, monitoring, and control, which to a great extent was accepted by the Latin American administrations, generated strong opposition and only exacerbated the conflict between governments, the multilateral financial organizations, and the social sectors in the Latin American countries. The result was some critical political questioning; the topic of the external debt was the most important item of debate throughout Latin America. The limited results obtained by the Baker Plan, such as the renegotiation of the Mexican and Argentine programs, came at great cost to Latin America and are evidence that this strategy is not viable in providing an adequate solution to the problem of the region's external indebtedness.

More realistic proposals have been put forward in the U.S. Congress, including that of Senator Bill Bradley of New Jersey. Bradley's proposal directly links U.S. trade problems with Latin America's financial problems, pointing out how the adjustment made in Latin America has had a negative impact on the U.S. trade balance. Bradley suggests reducing the burden of the Latin American debt by reducing interest rates and condemning part of the principal. However, this proposal has little chance of being passed by Congress. Nonetheless, progress has been made in accepting the existence of a link between international trade problems, external financing, and debt, at least at the conceptual level. Although these elements are beginning to be observed in various proposals, which include certain modifications in the position of the multilateral financial organizations, they are still insufficient by any standards. Latin America runs the risk of losing a sizable portion of its real bargaining power in the face of the internal and intraregional factors (i.e., the loss of the relative importance of the external debt to U.S. banks) if it continues to be guided by the present positions of the governments in the region.

In sum, Latin America appears to be following a moderate course, but this strategy will not bring forth the desired response from developed countries. Indeed, the situation could ultimately lead to the adoption of much more radical attitudes and positions or to serious social disturbances in many countries. In an uncertain global economic context, with threats of interest rate increases and reductions in export possibilities, Latin America has limited effective options for responding to the challenge of the external debt.

## The External Debt and Japan

In May 1987, Prime Minister Nakasone announced a plan to expand internal demand, reduce the trade surpluses, increase imports, and offer substantial financial support to developing countries—support that included recycling US$30 billion to them. This new program aimed to double ODA by 1990 (instead of by 1992, as stated in the original plan), granting US$7.6 billion of assistance by 1990 (JEJ 1987a). Both the government and business sectors were very active in establishing criteria to guide their action in international cooperation and in preparing concrete proposals. As a result, the Japanese government, with the support of the business sector, stressed the promotion of financial flows toward developing countries, especially major debtors, as provided for in the emergency program. The government plans to recycle US$30 billion in new, untied funds through international cooperation institutions and multilateral development banks. The Inter-American Development Bank (IADB), the Asian Development Bank (ADB), the Export-Import Bank of Japan, and the Overseas Economic Cooperation Fund will participate through grants of soft loans in yen as well as offers to cofinance projects with Japanese banks and the World Bank.

Apparently, 67 percent of the total amount has already been committed. Among these loans, there is one of US$370 million to Argentina that will be cofinanced by the World Bank and Japan's Eximbank. Various Latin American countries (Argentina, Brazil, Ecuador, and Venezuela) have submitted investment proposals.

Traditionally, Japanese priorities have been clearly aimed at the Asian NICs and other Asian developing countries in terms of DFI and ODA. Almost 70 percent of ODA provided by Japan in recent years was concentrated in ASEAN and other Southeast Asian countries, but Latin American countries have become increasingly more important because of their problems with their external debt. In 1984, of the total Japanese capital flows (US$5.6 billion) into Latin America, only 4 percent was assigned to ODA, while the remaining 96 percent was devoted to financial cooperation with the private sector (Sociedad Latinoamericano 1986). The latter amount was composed of export credit, DFI, and especially bilateral portfolio investments, and concentrated on loans granted to Mexico and Brazil because of their external debts. This would seem to demonstrate that Japan deemed it necessary to mobilize resources in the face of the region's financial crisis, but that at the same time its export credits were being drastically reduced.

To date, the Japanese government has carefully differentiated the criteria governing its official assistance, which will undoubtedly become more generous, more flexible, and broader in the future, from the criteria applied to the external debt. In the former case, there is certainly room for negotiation on the criteria, and Latin America should make use of this without delay. The Japanese criteria applied to the external debt thus far are similar to those of international private banking and, particularly, those of U.S. banks. The feeling in Japan is that the debt should be paid, but increasingly there is the realization that there is need for a rapid restructuring of its terms. It is in this context that proposals such as a change in repayment periods, reduction of interest rates, partial conversion of the debt into assets, and provision of funds for reactivating the economy may find a place. All such proposals, however, are likely to be met with basically orthodox views.

A secondary market for external debt has also appeared. In March 1987, it was announced that a consortium of thirty Japanese banks (joint creditors of over US$40 billion, 15 percent of the regional banking debt) had formed the Japanese Banking Association, with its head office in the Cayman Islands, to operate as an intermediary in the sale of bad loans granted to the region. The consortium will acquire loans from the Japanese portfolio at a discount and resell them to potential Latin American investors. The latter may thus acquire local firms through capitalization mechanisms. This type of operation has already been carried out in Mexico.

Recommendations made by the Keidanren (Federation of Economic Organizations) regarding the recycling of funds and investment in developing countries stress the need for a mechanism that identifies promising investment projects (KKC 1987). This mechanism would prepare feasibility studies and obtain funding for the projects. The Keidanren also indicates that a possible measure to ensure adequate financial flows from the private sector would be the establishment of guaranties on such investments by the Export-Import Bank of Japan and multilateral financial organizations.

This does not mean that Latin America and the Caribbean should not expect a substantial improvement in their financial and trade relations with Japan. The data and arguments are presented to contribute to a realistic basis for adequately evaluating existing options. Latin America is embarking upon this new stage in a relatively marginal position with respect to Japan. It is from this standpoint that the possibilities for cooperation must be analyzed, and their viability should be measured in terms of magnitudes, priorities, and capacity to attract Japan rather than other areas that are competing for the same benefits. Any progress to be made with Japan, as well as with other Asian countries in the Pacific Basin, will depend on Latin America's own actions.

## Direct Foreign Investment

Between 1977 and 1985, Latin America's share of U.S. DFI decreased from 14 to 9 percent. Although U.S. DFI has tended to increase in developing countries, this has not been the case with Latin America, where it declined from 20 percent between 1976 and 1980 to 6 percent between 1981 and 1985 (SELA 1987a). The bulk of DFI flows from the world are concentrated in Argentina, Brazil, and Mexico. Japanese DFI flows account for only 30 percent of the DFI in those countries, but they account for 70 percent of the DFI in Panama, which was also the second highest recipient of U.S. DFI flows.

Latin America also accounts for a small share of Japanese DFI. In addition to the United States, Indonesia, Hong Kong, South Korea, and Singapore are among the top ten recipients of Japanese DFI. In Latin America, Panama leads with US$8.8 billion of Japanese investments, which are concentrated in shipping fleets (for the purpose of flags of convenience), offshore banking, and commercial operations. Brazil is next with US$4.6 billion, followed by Mexico with US$1.3 billion. These countries account for the bulk of the Japanese investment in the region, which reached US$20.4 billion in March 1987. In the mid-1980s, Latin America as a region was in third place with 17.5 percent of total Japanese investments, following Asia with 26.8 percent and the United States with 19.3 percent, although since 1986 the United States has risen in importance to first place (Sociedad Latinoamericana 1986; SELA 1986).

There are important differences between the sectoral distributions of Japanese and U.S. DFI. There has been a significant shift in the DFI flows originating from the United States and in Japan, with Japanese DFI increasing. Thus, DFI flows from the United States were negative from 1983 to 1985, leading to heavy decapitalization, while Japanese flows were positive. Moreover, U.S. DFI has strongly favored the industrial and financial sectors, while Japanese DFI has favored the primary transport and trade sectors.

In view of the significant share of U.S. DFI in the region, which stood at approximately 60 percent of DFI stock with 50 percent in the manufacturing sector, the United States continued to exercise considerable political and economic influence there. This was complemented by the harmonization of U.S. DFI with U.S. financial and trade policies, that is, by ties existing between conditions for external debt rescheduling included in the IMF agreements and loans from multilateral financial organizations or the Overseas Private Investment Corporation (OPIC) (Bitar 1986).

Other factors that must be taken into account are the international changes that have occurred and the new needs and strategies of transnational corporations (TNCs). Three principal variables are (1) the factors relating to the new terms for financing and the benefits to be obtained from the TNCs from the new interest rates that have promoted their direct participation in capital markets; (2) a greater concentration of TNCs in the developed countries; and (3) technological change and competitiveness with the TNCs of other countries. In this context, the more economically dynamic Asian NICs and ASEAN countries enjoy privileged standing as compared with Latin America. The TNCs are also showing concern for safeguarding intellectual property rights, as well as a preference for services and industrial production areas with high technology content over natural resource areas (Bitar 1986).

The expansion of the sphere of activities to include the global system as well as technological innovation has increased the interest of the TNCs in research and development, and in trade and management processes as opposed to the creation of single production units. Under these conditions, an important part of production falls to subcontractors, which is the situation in many developing countries, including some in Latin America.

It should not be expected that U.S. financial flows will increase to the levels of previous decades during the rest of the 1980s or 1990s. It does not seem that this situation can be changed by Latin American action, except perhaps by total acceptance of the new U.S. DFI criteria. Even so, change would depend on a great many outside factors that could substantially reduce U.S. financial flows. Therefore, if it were possible to return to the DFI levels of before the crisis (approximately US$1.5 to US$2 billion annually), they would still be relatively marginal compared to the region's net outflow of resources because of the interest and dividend payments. Consequently, it is a matter of real concern that some Latin American administrations are determined to obtain DFI at any cost. Under the present circumstances, more detailed attention should be given to the limitations and the cost-benefit ratio in long-term scenarios.

## Conclusion

The structure of trade relations between the developed countries and between the developed and developing countries has changed, resulting in the emergence of a new economic nucleus in the Pacific Basin. Foremost among the members of this new nucleus are Japan and the United States. A new quadrilateral relationship has been structured by the United States, Japan, Latin America, and the Asian NICs with the following characteristics: (1) Latin America is basically left to export energy products and raw materials to the world market and to continue to import manufactured goods, primarily from the United States and the EC; (2) trade and financial relations will increase, albeit asymmetrically, between the United States and Japan, with investment flows and trade becoming increasingly important between these two powers and the Southeast Asian countries; (3) Asian NIC and ASEAN-4 exports are increasing rapidly with a higher manufactured goods content to the Japanese and U.S. markets; (4) Latin America and Asia have exchanged places in their trading status with the United States (Latin America's share of U.S. imports dropped from 15.2 percent in 1980 to 10.7 percent in 1986, whereas Southeast Asia's share rose from 11.6 percent in 1980 to 15.2 percent in 1986); and (5) numerous competitive-cooperative agreements are being entered into by the United States and Japan, Japan and the Asian NICs, and the Asian NICs and the United States. China can be expected to participate in this in the future.

It has also been observed that Latin America has lost the degree of trade diversification it attained during the 1960s and is now once again relying to a great extent on the U.S. market. The United States continues to play a key role in Latin America's external debt problems, financial relations, and DFI. As the principal economic power the United States can influence the configuration and possibly the evolution of the global economic system. However, account should be taken of the Japanese presence in the Latin America's external debt problem, and of the possibility that Japan will become a highly significant source of financial flows and, to a lesser degree, of direct investment.

Japan and other Asian countries of the Pacific Basin are markets that until now have been relatively unexplored by Latin America; their importance is still secondary, but they have interesting possibilities. On the other hand, U.S. involvement should not be expected to be more favorable to Latin America in the years to come; instead, present tensions and conflicts will very likely persist. The current process in the Pacific Basin is expanding the ties between the developed economies and the developing Asian economies, as well as those of Australia, New Zealand, the United States, and Canada. However, Latin American participation in the Pacific Basin is still marginal, although it has increased in recent years. Consequently, only minimal trade relations currently exist between Latin America, and the Asian NICs and the ASEAN-4 countries.

In view of Latin America's dimensions and resources and the small likelihood that DFI flows will meet the region's real needs or that greater trade openness by the industrialized countries is likely, it would seem that Latin America must resort to making fuller and more thorough use of its own regional economic power. On this basis and through appropriate industrial restructuring, an increase and diversification of manufactured goods for export could be achieved, which would tend to compensate for the diminished importance of raw materials in world trade.

It would be advisable to reorganize regional efforts within this context and to coordinate national policies toward the Pacific Basin and intermediate developing countries. This effort should be accompanied with a political stance, in negotiations coordinated by Latin America, to take a much firmer attitude toward repayment of the external debt and rechannel internal development resources, since the funds needed cannot be expected to come from outside the region. It is also necessary to substantially increase the region's internal saving capacity and to coordinate new and functional criteria to this end.

With regard to Latin America's future strategy toward the United States, there is little to add to the considerable volume of studies and proposals prepared by SELA, ECLAC, and other regional and national Latin American bodies. Much research needs to be done, however, on the difficulties and obstacles to be faced in implementing some of these ideas and the reasons they do not meet with the necessary political and economic support. The region's external economic policies can be characterized, perhaps too rigorously, as policies basically aimed at helping the Latin American countries adjust and adapt to international change rather than at exploring the need for structural modifications as the root causes generating these problems.

# 11 Francisco Orrego Vicuña

# Latin American Trade with the Asia-Pacific Region

This chapter seeks to analyze some of the main trends in the interactions between Latin American countries and the Asia-Pacific region. It focuses specifically on the basic indicators of each economy, the volume of trade and its disaggregation by products, and the identification of potential trade complementarities.

The main trade flows in the Pacific Basin are made up of a dense network of intricate relations (Vicuña 1987). There are several levels of trade relations. At the first level is the large trade between the United States and Canada, and the United States and Japan, which exceeded US$112 billion and US$84 billion, respectively, in 1984. Trade between the United States and Latin America and the Caribbean is also large, totaling more than US$75 billion in 1984. On the second level are the trade relations existing between the five ASEAN countries (Indonesia, Malaysia, the Philippines, Singapore, and Thailand) and Japan (US$34 billion), and between Hong Kong and Korea and the United States (US$29 billion). The third level of trade relations corresponds to flows under US$25 billion and includes trade relations of a different scope, the most important being those between the five ASEAN countries and the United States (US$24 billion), Hong Kong and Korea and Japan (US$19 billion), Australia and New Zealand and Japan (US$13 billion), and Latin America and Japan (US$13 billion).

The main trade concentration is in the North Pacific between the United States and Japan (which exceeds US$90 billion) and between these two countries and the regions more directly linked to each of them—the United States and Latin America, for instance, or Japan and the ASEAN countries. A deviation from the traditional trade pattern is the diagonal-type relations between the ASEAN countries and the United States; between Hong Kong and Korea and the United States; or increasingly, between Latin America and Japan. This seems to indicate that trade interconnections in the Asia-Pacific region have undergone constant growth (Reutter 1987).

Between 1979 and 1985 virtually all trade flows in the Asia-Pacific region grew faster than global trade over the same period, which grew by 19.1 percent. For example, trade between the United States and Canada grew by 63.3 percent; between the United States and Canada and Japan, and Korea and Hong Kong, by 99.1 and 95.5 percent, respectively. Trade between the United States and China grew by 147.5 percent, between the ASEAN countries and China by 193 percent, and between Australia and New Zealand and Japan by 51.6 percent. Other trade flows record even higher growth, such as the trade between China and Japan, which increased by 190.2 percent, and the trade conducted by China through Korea and Hong Kong, which grew a record 309.2 percent.

## Comparison of Some Basic Indicators

Broad comparisons between Latin America and the Asia-Pacific region do not lead to useful conclusions because of the heterogeneous nature of the countries in each region and the differences between the regions as a whole. However, a comparison of Latin America with the Asian NICs and the ASEAN countries may prove interesting. Tironi (1981) has compared trade relations and other indicators in countries of intermediate development in Asia (Hong Kong, Korea, Singapore, and Taiwan) and Latin America (Argentina, Brazil, Chile, Mexico, and Venezuela).

There are significant differences in the level of growth between the Latin American and Asia-Pacific countries. Real gross domestic product (GDP) for the Asian NICs grew at an annual average rate of over 9 percent in the 1960s, over 8 percent in the 1970s, and between 5 and 8 percent in the 1980s (table A.2). In contrast, real GDP growth in Latin America ranged from 2 to 6 percent in the 1960s, 2.5 to 9.0 percent in the 1970s, and −2 to 3 percent in the 1980s. Figures for real GDP growth in the ASEAN countries were also higher than Latin America's, as they are generally for the whole Asia-Pacific region.

As a result of this disparity in growth, the average per capita GDP of the five intermediate developing countries in Latin America, which at a little over US$1,400 in 1977 was almost identical to that of the four Asian NICs fell below that of the Asian NICs (Tironi 1981). In 1986, the per capita GDP in the Asian NICs ranged from US$2,360 in Korea to US$6,801 in Hong Kong. In contrast, real per capita GDP in the Latin American countries barely reached half the figure for the Asian NICs but was slightly higher than the per capita GDP for the ASEAN-4, which in 1986 ranged from US$451 to US$1,711. This trend illustrates the dynamism of the Asian region and the stagnation of Latin America.

According to Tironi's analysis, the degree of openness of the Asian NIC economies to foreign trade, as indicated by the relationship between exports and GDP, was greater than that of comparable countries in Latin America. This conclusion is still valid today. For the Asian NICs, exports represent between 37 and 174 percent of GDP (Wu 1987). For Latin America this figure is considerably smaller, ranging between 12 and 23 percent. In any case, it is worth pointing out that the degree of openness has progressively increased in Latin America. Once again Latin America compares more closely with the resource-rich ASEAN-4 countries where, excluding Indonesia, which is a petroleum-exporting country, exports-to-GDP range between 14 and 21 percent.

Other comparisons in the general trade patterns of the two regions can be made. In the first place, the value of exports for the Asian NICs ranged in 1985 between US$22 and US$30 billion. In the Latin American countries, however, the range was much wider; in 1985 the value of exports ranged from US$3.7 to US$25.6 billion. A similar situation existed in the ASEAN-4 countries, where the value of exports ranged from US$4.6 to US$22.8 billion. The annual growth of exports from 1965 to 1980 was relatively heterogeneous in both regions. In the Asian NICs, export growth ranged from 4.8 percent for Singapore to 27.3 percent for Korea, while in Latin America, it ranged between −9.4 percent for Venezuela and 9.4 percent for Brazil. Clearly, growth has been more significant in the Asian NICs than in Latin America. This trend generally continued from 1980 to 1985. In the Asian NICs, exports grew between 5.9 and 13 percent, and in Latin America, growth of exports ranged from −5.8 to 10.1 percent. The trend of export growth in the Latin American countries is more comparable to that of the ASEAN-4 countries, although the range in export growth is not as wide in the ASEAN-4 countries as it is in Latin America. For instance, from 1965 to 1980, export growth ranged from −2.1 percent for the Philippines to 10.7 percent for Malaysia.

Data on import growth further reflect the Latin American difficulties. In terms of growth of imports, no substantial differences exist between Latin America and the Asian NICs or ASEAN from 1965 to 1980. However, from 1980 to 1985, imports of most Latin American countries dropped, at times sharply. This did not occur in Asia, with the sole exception of the Philippines.

The composition of each region's exports differs from the other's. The NICs primarily export manufactured goods, whereas Latin America mainly exports primary products (Tironi 1981). Naturally enough, the structure of imports is reversed. However, it is worth noting that the percentage distribution of GDP among the different trade sectors in both regions does not differ dramatically. This reconfirms the fact that the most substantial difference between them lies in their degree of openness to foreign trade.

The general conclusion is that the Latin American countries have regressed during the last five years from a position similar to that of the Asian NICs to one resembling that of the ASEAN-4. However, data obtained at a time of crisis should not be taken at face value, since ultimately economic recovery could lead once again to a more dynamic position based on the structure that already exists. Also, over and above the question of structure is the problem of appropriate policies.

## Latin American Trade in the Asia-Pacific Region

The general trend of Latin American trade in the Asia-Pacific region also shows significant growth. From 1979 to 1985, Latin American trade with some Asian countries increased dramatically. For example, trade with China grew 161.1 percent, from US$800 million to US$2 billion, and trade with Korea and Hong Kong increased 130.9 percent, from US$961 million to US$2.2 billion. Trade with Australia and New Zealand increased by 58.9 percent, with Japan by 35.7 percent, and with Canada and the United States by 25.5 percent. No growth in trade was registered for the period with the ASEAN-4 countries (Reutter 1987).

This contrasts with intra-Latin American trade, which decreased by 17.5 percent. In view of this deterioration, the fact that trade within the Asia-Pacific region increased in almost every case is proof of positive trade dynamics. However, on a case-by-case basis, it is also necessary to bear in mind that the value of this trade is not always significant. It undoubtedly is significant with the United States, Canada, and Japan, slightly less so with China, Korea, and Hong Kong, even less so with the ASEAN-4, and barely significant with Australia, New Zealand, and the South Pacific.

As a result of the rapid growth from 1979 to 1985, the percentage of Latin American exports going to Asia-Pacific markets increased in every case. For instance, the share of Latin American exports going to Hong Kong and Korea rose from 0.26 to 0.94 percent of total exports, to the United States and Canada from 37.82 to 43.78 percent, to Japan from 3.88 to 5.10 percent, and to China from 0.84 to 1.60 percent. Consequently, the Asia-Pacific market became a more important market to Latin America (Reutter 1987).

The share of exports from the Asia-Pacific region to Latin America decreased between 1979 and 1985 because of import restrictions in Latin America. For example, the share of exports from Hong Kong and Korea that went to Latin America decreased from 2.49 to 2.16 percent; the share of exports from the United States and Canada to Latin America decreased from 12.72 to 10.77 percent; and the share of exports from Japan to Latin America declined from 5.99 to 4.20 percent. However, for Australia, New Zealand, China, and the Pacific Islands, the share of total exports going to Latin America increased for the same period, although the increase was not very significant. Nevertheless, it is worth noting that the share of exports from the Asia-Pacific region as a whole to Latin America is generally greater than the share of exports from Latin America to those markets. This confirms Tironi's assertion that for the Asian NICs, "Latin America is relatively more important as an export market than as a source of imports" (1981:1414). Data from other sources on Latin American trade also indicate that for Latin America, the Asia-Pacific market is relatively more important as a source of imports than as a destination for exports.

## Influential Countries

Some Latin American countries play a more significant role than others in trade with the Asia-Pacific region. In 1979, Japan's main trading partners with Latin America were, in order of importance, Brazil,

Argentina, Chile, Peru, and Colombia; in 1985, they were Mexico, Brazil, Panama, Argentina, and Chile. In 1979, Hong Kong's and Korea's trading partners with Latin America were Argentina, Chile, Brazil, Mexico, and Panama; but in 1985 the most important trading partners for these Asian NICs were Panama, Brazil, Mexico, Chile, and Argentina.[1]

In 1979, the main Latin American importers of goods from the Asia-Pacific region were Panama (36 percent of total imports from the region), Venezuela (11 percent), Brazil (9 percent), and Chile (7 percent). It is striking that Brazil and Chile were virtually at the same level. The main exporters were Brazil, Argentina, and Chile.

Panama, Mexico, Brazil, and Chile are now the main Latin American trading partners with the Asia-Pacific region. Argentina is no longer a major trade partner. Trade between Argentina and the Pacific declined sharply between 1979 and 1985. During this period Argentine trade with Japan decreased by 33.7 percent, with Hong Kong and Korea by 66.2 percent, and with Australia and New Zealand by 40.5 percent. In contrast, Brazil considerably increased its trade with China, Korea, Hong Kong, Australia, and New Zealand. Mexico, Panama, and Peru also experienced significant trade growth with the Asia-Pacific region from 1979 to 1985.

Chile's exports to the Asia-Pacific region also increased substantially: its exports to the ASEAN-4 increased by 180.7 percent, to Hong Kong and Korea by 34.5 percent, to Australia and New Zealand by 200 percent, to the United States and Canada by 108.8 percent, and to China by 39.4 percent. There was a slight decrease in Chile's exports to Japan (4.9 percent). By 1985, 10.4 percent of Chile's exports were destined for Japan, 3.5 percent to China, and 2.4 percent to Hong Kong and Korea. Although the total volume of exports to the Asia-Pacific market is lower than that of other Latin American countries, Chile's exports to the Asia-Pacific as a share of total Chilean exports is much higher than the corresponding share for the other Latin American countries (Reutter 1987).

## The Concept of the Degree of Openness to the Pacific Basin

Reutter (1987) measures trade in the Pacific using what he calls the "degree of openness," which is calculated by summing the percentages of total exports that each country or group of countries allots to the other Asia-Pacific countries. The degree of openness of trading across the Pacific is also measured. In the case of Latin America, this has the advantage of excluding both intra-Latin American trade and trade with the United States and Canada and reflects only exports to Asia.

For the period 1979–85, Latin America has increased its degree of openness to the Pacific Basin from 64.85 to 66.31 percent, although only 8.34 percent of the trade is carried across the Pacific. In contrast, Japan's degree of openness across the Pacific exceeds 40 percent and Hong Kong's and Korea's exceed 38 percent. It is particularly noteworthy that ASEAN allocates 21 percent of its exports to countries across the Pacific. Thus, the degree of openness of Latin America across the Pacific is among the lowest in the region.

## Latin American Imports

The most significant Latin American imports are manufactured goods, which rose by 10.4 percent during this period to represent 19.8 percent of total Latin American imports. Machinery and transport equipment, vehicles, and clothing are the largest items. The main source of the machinery and transport equipment is Japan, which recorded an import growth to Latin America of 5.8 percent between 1978 and 1983. In fact, Japan was the sole Asian supplier of passenger vehicles to Latin America. Japanese exports of passenger vehicles grew by 29.9 percent between 1978 and 1983, amounting to 48.2 percent of all Latin American imports in this category. Regarding clothing imports, Asian developing countries increased exports to Latin America by 14.5 percent between 1978 and 1983 compared to 10 percent for the Asia-Pacific region as a whole, thereby supplying 23.6 percent of total Latin American imports. Japan, on the other hand, reduced its clothing exports to Latin America by 25 percent during this period.

A similar trend is found in imports of other manufactured goods. While Japanese exports of other manufactured goods to Latin America declined by 38.8 percent, the Asian developing countries increased their exports of these same goods to Latin America by 15.1 percent. Latin American imports from the Asia-Pacific region amounted to 12.7 percent of total imports in this category.

## Latin American Exports

Latin American exports to the Asia-Pacific region consist largely of primary products, both agricultural and mineral, while manufactures constitute a minor share of total exports. Foodstuffs allocated to Asia represent only 7.7 percent of the total Latin American exports of foodstuffs, although between 1978 and 1983 exports of foodstuffs to Japan grew by 25.8 percent, to Australia and New Zealand by 97 percent, to Asian developing economies by 153 percent, and to Asian planned economies by 242 percent. The expansion of foodstuff exports to the region contributed to a general growth of 84.6 percent in that commodity for Latin America—more than twice the world rate of growth for foodstuff exports (32.5 percent).

Cereals, which represent 25 percent of total exports, are an important category in Latin American exports. Cereal exports to the Asia-Pacific region increased 190.6 percent between 1978 and 1983. Raw material exports are also significant, with a 26 percent share of total exports and a 40.8 percent growth rate for the Asia-Pacific region. Raw materials exports increased to Japan (58.8 percent), to Australia and New Zealand (533.3 percent), and to the developing countries (36.9 percent), but decreased to China (28.6 percent). Another important category is textile fibers, with a 37.4 percent share of total exports—which is lower than the 41.2 percent share that it held in 1978. Latin American textile exports decreased to Japan (–41.3 percent), the developing countries (–10.4 percent), and the planned economies (–26.6 percent), with a total decrease of 28.7 percent for the region.

Fertilizers and raw minerals exports increased by 311 percent for the region and amounted to 16.2 percent of Latin American world exports. Minerals exports increased by 119.8 percent, with a 33.2 percent share of the total exports. The export of oils and fats increased by 14.3 percent and amounted to 21.5 percent of the world total. Fuels exports increased dramatically by 3,445 percent, but they represented only 5.5 percent of total Latin American exports. Chemicals exports increased by 421.3 percent, amounting to 11.7 percent of total exports.

Iron and steel exports increased by 397.5 percent and represented 25.0 percent of total exports. Nonferrous metals increased by 155.9 percent and represented 20.7 percent of the total. Other Latin American exports that made up a smaller share of total exports included machinery (3.5 percent), fibers and cloth (6.5 percent), clothing (0.5 percent), and other manufactured goods (12.8 percent).

Clearly there are a number of goods that the Latin American countries do not export to Asia-Pacific countries because of the competition involved, such as cereals to Australia and New Zealand, and textile fibers, fertilizers, and clothing to the Asian developing countries. The degree of competition varies with each country or group of countries. Tironi (1981) has noted that there is greater competition between the Asian NICs and the Latin American intermediate development countries in oil-derived products, shoes, coffee, and nonferrous metals.

Considering the Latin American imports from the Asian NICs and exports to that region, Tironi has concluded that both regions are actually more complementary than competitive. The Asian emphasis on manufactures and the small proportion of Latin American exports that such goods represent, when compounded with the Latin American emphasis on primary products and the small proportion of Asian exports that these represent, signify their complementary nature. On the other hand, Latin American countries are net importers of six out of the sixteen main export products of the Asian NICs, including ships, telecommunications equipment, rubber, electric machinery, toys, and spun textiles. The Asian NICs, in turn, are net importers of thirteen out of the eighteen main products exported by Latin America, among them oil, iron, copper, cereals, and foodstuffs.

It is also necessary to bear in mind that competition does not always mean that different forms of economic interaction between countries is impossible. For example, Australia and New Zealand have invested in Chilean exports with which they actually compete, such as fruit, forest products, mining, and fisheries. The explanation of this phenomenon lies in the need to avoid harmful forms of competition in the Asia-Pacific market and other markets, and to harmonize production and exports to achieve the common good.

## Some Problems

In spite of the growth recorded in trade in the Asia-Pacific region and Latin America's increased share of this trade, Latin America is limited in its ability to take full advantage of the Asian dynamism, since it has not reached the level of activity that characterizes other groups of countries in the region (Tironi 1981). Some of the problems of expanding Latin American trade participation are related to the general characteristics of trade in the Asia-Pacific market, while others are inherent in the Latin American region.

There are serious problems affecting the trade of primary goods in general in the Asia-Pacific market, both within the ASEAN-4 and in Latin America. The report of the Task Force on Trade in agricultural and renewable resource goods established within the framework of the Pacific Economic Cooperation Conference (PECC) in 1983 identifies four main problem areas: trade barriers; price stabilization and certainty of supply; aid and investment; and technical cooperation (PECC 1983).

Regarding trade barriers, there is a need to negotiate tariff reductions for some goods in the food sector, particularly through multilateral negotiations within GATT. This should be done without excluding special nondiscrimination agreements in the region, the liberalization of agricultural quotas approved by GATT, and the widening of the generalized system of preferences for agricultural, fishery, and forestry goods. There is a special emphasis being placed on nontariff barriers, including health and sanitation regulations. There is also a need to avoid sharp changes in prices resulting from certain trade practices, to hold consultations on stocks, and to encourage regional cooperation on some commodity agreements and the promotion of long-term contracts. Of special interest in this connection is the proposal of the Economic and Social Commission for Asia and the Pacific (ESCAP) to create an ASEAN export earnings stabilization scheme (ASEBEX). Even though this set of initiatives was prepared with the situation of ASEAN taken especially into account, it also responds to the difficulties shared by the Latin American trade in primary products. The increase of official aid for development, private joint ventures, and other forms of investment, as well as various other acts of technical cooperation, are additional recommendations to be considered.

Another task force has warned against an increase in protectionism in the Asia-Pacific market and other markets and has emphasized the need to cooperate in order to stem the protectionist tide. It has been suggested that immediate action be taken through GATT, regional agreements, and mechanisms inherent in the PECC (PECC 1985). Developing countries are not the only ones facing problems over their trade in primary products. Australia, New Zealand, Canada, and the

United States face the same problems with their agricultural exports. Since both developing and developed countries share this same problem, cooperation is necessary if solutions are to be found.

The question of trade barriers to primary products has also been discussed in connection with some specific sectors, such as mining and fisheries. In the field of mining, there has been emphasis on the need for safe markets and contractual agreements, for greater access to markets of processed goods, for additional and effective foreign investment, for stabilization of export earnings, and for regional energy safety. The fishing sector presents different problems, namely, access to the exclusive economic zones in the Pacific, specifically including Latin America, and cooperation agreements on highly migratory species of fish (PECC 1983, 1985).

The discussion of problems affecting manufactured goods trade in the Asia-Pacific market has been even more complex because of the diversity of situations to be dealt with. However, problems can be grouped into three main categories: trade barriers, marketing difficulties, and diversity of economic policies (PECC 1983, 1985). Nontariff trade barriers have aroused the most interest, with the suggestion that they be subject to a moratorium, progressively liberalized, and ultimately eliminated. Warnings have also been issued against import controls and discriminatory tariffs on processed raw materials, against the existence of subsidies, and against dumping. They have also emphasized the need for policies that facilitate structural adjustment. In some cases, interest has been voiced in voluntary restrictions on exports and orderly marketing agreements.

Various ideas have been suggested to ease the difficulties in the marketing of manufactured goods that affect the less-experienced developing countries, such as the establishment of trading companies, clear regulations, and special training programs in foreign trade. The issue of policy harmonization would be handled through greater public consultation.

Trade flows allow for the clear identification of some trade patterns. The United States is a big exporter of agricultural products and foodstuffs and a large importer of consumer goods. Japan is a big importer of raw material and foodstuffs and a big exporter of consumer, intermediate, and capital goods. The Asian NICs concentrate on the export of consumer goods to the United States, foodstuffs to Japan, and oil products. These countries, in turn, import intermediate goods and foodstuffs. The ASEAN-4 countries mainly export primary products and import capital goods, even though their manufactured goods exports have risen significantly (Oborne and Fourt 1983).

Clearly, developing countries in the region do not compete among themselves as much as with the industrialized countries of the Asia-Pacific region. As shown earlier, Latin American trade complements that of the Asian NICs and, even though it coincides with ASEAN-4 countries in the export of primary products, they are not in fact as competitive as they might at first appear. This is especially so if the comparison is drawn between the Southern Cone of Latin America and Mexico—the main exporters to the Asia-Pacific region. There is more significant competition with Australia and New Zealand in fruit and forestry products, with Canada in forestry and fishery products, with the United States in foodstuffs, and with several of these countries in mining products. Manufactured goods competition is more complex and involves to some extent the Asian NICs.

## Policy Suggestions

Latin America must now develop a strategy of interacting in the Asia-Pacific region, a strategy that so far has only partially existed in some countries. Through this instrument, common interests and possible action for their harmonization can be identified, and fields of competition and difficulty can be recognized. Identification of common interests has not been systematically pursued, but past experience shows that it goes beyond trade relations and includes policy regarding natural resources and related investments, cooperation in fishing and other aspects of the Law of the Sea, and relations between similar institutions such as the Inter-American Development Bank (IADB) and the Asian Development Bank (ADB), the Economic Commission for Latin America (ECLA), and ESCAP. This strategy has two main components. The first one concerns cooperation possibilities between Latin American countries, with special reference to those in the Southern Cone. The increase of intra-Latin American trade, interconnections in transport and infrastructure, the role of services, and forms of joint action are all aspects to be considered when developing a policy regarding the Asia-Pacific region.

The strategy's second main component concerns the term *Pacific*. Although the term is used in a generic sense, it denotes widely differing situations that should be distinguished and tackled separately. For instance, export policies regarding the United States or Canada vary considerably from those regarding Japan. Equally different are those dealing with China, Australia, New Zealand, the Asian NICs, or the Pacific Islands. All these cases involve different realities that must be taken into account.

Some general suggestions for increasing trade with the countries in the Asia-Pacific region can be made. The Latin American strategy toward Asia-Pacific trade has three general goals: (1) to provide greater market access to the developing countries in the region that have adopted export strategies, especially as they start to concentrate on manufactured goods; (2) to offset the effects of the decline in the rate of growth of developed economies by reorienting trade to the Asia-Pacific region so as to benefit from the trade expansion there; and (3) to promote the structural adjustment that these economies need to achieve the aforementioned goal (Oborne and Fourt 1983). The first goal would help to set the foundation for the industrial development, improve the terms of trade, and expand the exports of the Latin American countries to other markets.

To attain those goals, it would be necessary to give priority to the elimination of tariff and nontariff barriers affecting trade in the region. This concerns particularly Japan and partly the United States, but it also affects the region's other countries. Several actions proposed by the PECC task forces are of clear interest to Latin American trade. They include

❖ The negotiation of tariff reductions for agricultural products, foodstuffs, and fishery and forestry products. This should be considered a priority for GATT and should also be accomplished through regional consultations. Latin America should be part of this process of negotiation at various levels. Ultimately, Latin America's participation in PECC, which up to now has been marginal or nonexistent (with sectoral exceptions), should be strengthened.

❖ Wider access to the generalized system of preferences of Japan and other countries in the region. In this area, some degree of competition with the ASEAN-4 countries, which benefit from traditional links with Japan, may be encountered. Consultations between the ASEAN-4 and Latin America may prove useful in this regard.

❖ The liberalization of the quota system for agricultural imports, regardless of what may be achieved through GATT. It would also be useful to analyze the actual or potential effects of voluntary export restrictions and agreements on the orderly marketing of Latin American exports.

❖ The codification, harmonization, and liberalization of nontariff barriers, particularly Japan's health and sanitation regulations, inspections, and customs procedures. To this end, the establishment of a special task force in which Latin America ought to take part was proposed. These actions are also applicable mutatis mutandis to the export of manufactured goods with special emphasis on the need to remove nontariff barriers, subsidies and dumping, import controls, and discriminatory tariffs on processed raw materials.

Some of these problems and actions have already been discussed by the Latin American countries and through the Latin American Economic System's (SELA) Program of Action. They have specified products whose access to the Japanese market ought to be improved and have begun operation of the Generalized System of Preferences regarding Latin America (Moneta 1987; SELA 1985). This program has also addressed the structure of Latin American trade and proposed specific action regarding Latin America's market.

Still another factor that is critical for Latin America's development is the stabilization of export prices and earnings, especially in agricultural and mineral products. The suggested situations include the following: (1) the avoidance of sharp changes in agricultural, forestry, fishery, and minerals policies, a recommendation that again points to the advantage of holding periodic consultations; (2) the establishment of periodic consultations with the United States regarding the handling of stocks of raw material, an issue that has traditionally attracted the attention of Latin America; (3) the development of regional cooperation in the Asia-Pacific region between members who are partners in agreements on commodities—the same activity may be suggested among members of producer organizations, such as the Intergovernmental Council of Copper-Exporting Nations (CIPEC); (4) the promotion of long-term contracts for natural resources, a recommendation that has already been carried out with some products and in which Latin America is especially interested; and (5) the establishment of a price stabilization scheme for raw material exports, both agricultural and mineral, in the Asia-Pacific markets (ASEBEX), which was proposed by ESCAP (Chintayarangsan 1983), and which would operate on a product-by-product basis with interest-free credits that would be obtained and paid for at the end of each shortage or surplus period. Although Latin America has not been considered under the terms of this proposal, it could be discussed in consultations among the countries involved, especially when and if the restructuring of the Japanese economy makes special financing available.

The establishment of a forum on minerals and energy has been suggested to hold informal talks on trade barriers, conditions of foreign investment, and other related aspects with regard to the mining sector. Latin America's participation in this type of mechanism would be equally appropriate.

These kinds of actions are now part of Japan's emergency economic program and restructuring process to tackle the problems of its financial surplus (Moneta 1987). Generally speaking, the program aims at promoting exports from developing countries through the opening of the Japanese market and providing financial aid to attain that goal. Available resources will be partly channeled through multilateral financial organizations. Thus, the program can provide the right conditions for payment of the foreign debt.

Latin America's share in this scheme demands the development of a special policy whose most significant component is the identification of projects that allow for the selection of new forms of assistance. Trade, investments, and the infrastructure required to increase participation in the Asia-Pacific market may be appropriate projects to this end. Technical cooperation may also fit into this scenario.

Marketing difficulties have also created obstacles to the growth of Latin American exports in the Asia-Pacific market. This is partly due to Latin America's limited experience and partly to differences in style, language, culture, and other factors. The following are, inter alia, some actions proposed within the framework of the PECC to overcome these obstacles:

❖ The promotion of public trading companies to serve private companies, including forms of joint ownership. Likewise, private trading companies, which in some cases have attained considerable success in Latin America, could also participate. The establishment of binational private export consortia has also been quite successful in Latin America. In general, the approach of joint exports has possibilities, as indicated by the positive Chilean-Argentine experience.

❖ The establishment of clear-cut public regulations applicable to private companies.

❖ The establishment of regional training centers in international trade and the eventual establishment of a public business school.

An important proposal put forward by Chilean businessmen participating in the Pacific Basin Economic Committee (PBEC) called for the establishment of a Pacific Chamber of Commerce in which the Latin American countries would be members. The committee could contribute to the aforementioned marketing objectives and help identify trade and investment opportunities in the region.

The actions suggested by PECC and via PBEC are relevant to Latin American trade with the different groups of countries that make up the Asia-Pacific region, regardless of the fact that some of them apply specifically to Japan or other important markets in the region. It is also necessary to take other actions aimed at stimulating South-South trade in the Asia-Pacific market which, in spite of steady growth, is still marginal. As mentioned above, Latin American trade with the NICs and the ASEAN-4 holds interesting potential because of its complementary nature, though at the same time it presents competition problems. Equally promising is trade with Australia and New Zealand. In spite of their tendency to compete with the Southern Cone of Latin America, these two developed countries offer other possibilities of interaction. The Pacific Islands are a special case because of their smaller economies, although they still hold possibilities for trade and other forms of cooperation with Latin America (Vicuña 1982). Likewise, expanding Latin American trade with China must take into account the characteristics of China's economy.

There are two additional actions worthy of suggestion: the identification of successful public and private opportunities, and the facilitation of periodic consultations to achieve greater cooperation and participation of Latin America in Asia-Pacific trade and to provide adequate coordination. Consultations, so far, have occurred only on an isolated and sporadic basis. The presence of Latin American observers at PECC activities and their attendance at meetings of the South Pacific Commission and the South Pacific Forum have been useful to this end.

## Conclusion

There is great potential for economic cooperation between the Latin American countries and those of the Asia-Pacific region in trade, investment, and services. Such cooperation is based on the complementary nature of exports. There is also a certain degree of actual or potential competition with some countries or groups of countries, especially in primary products and manufactured goods. Accordingly, there is a need for consultations and other forms of coordination.

It is necessary, therefore, for the Latin American countries to draft a clear agenda regarding the Asia-Pacific region by identifying interests, problems, and possible solutions. The position of Latin America, which is the newest actor in the Asia-Pacific region, must be clearly stated. So far this has been undertaken only in a rather fragmentary manner. Initial skepticism regarding this approach has been largely overcome, but it is now necessary to define Latin America's position and concerns with greater precision. Latin American participation in the PECC and the Pacific and other organizations in the Asia-Pacific region encourage cooperation in the region, but more should be done to facilitate such cooperation.

# Multilateral Trade Negotiations

Participation by Latin American countries in the Uruguay Round of GATT has been marked by a combination of interest and skepticism. Such negotiations provide Latin American countries with an opportunity to reverse increasingly protectionist action, discrimination, and various forms of graduation that limit trade possibilities in the region.[1] At the same time, their present financial situation raises an obstacle to their effective participation in negotiations. Latin American countries must keep a certain degree of autonomy in order to adjust their trade policies to the demands of their financial, monetary, and fiscal policies, a necessity that makes engaging in multilateral trade commitments more difficult for these countries.

Latin American countries are also worried about the inclusion in the negotiations of so-called new issues, namely trade in services, intellectual property, and investment. In these areas, a set of multilateral policies and the liberalization of the corresponding markets is sought, although the benefits to be derived by Latin American countries through these efforts are not clear. It is in this context, therefore, that the interests and priorities of Latin American countries in the Uruguay Round ought to be considered. These negotiations would be of great interest for Latin America and the Caribbean, if they result in a strengthened international trading system that provides regional exports with safe and stable access to markets and prevents the implementation of the restrictive and discriminatory action that has been widespread lately. However, Latin American countries cannot take full advantage of possible benefits to be derived from negotiations unless the present financial crisis is solved. Likewise, the degree to which regional interests are reflected in the negotiations on the new issues ought to be analyzed.

## General Aims

The Uruguay Round may be of great significance for Latin American countries provided these negotiations result in the creation of a multilateral trade system that responds to their interests and development needs. In this sense, the most interesting aims for the countries in Latin America are related to the following aspects: (1) greater and safer access to markets of industrialized countries consistent with efforts by Latin American countries to expand and diversify their exports; (2) the strengthening of and respect for multilateral policies and nondiscrimination; and (3) full implementation of stipulations and commitments on differential and more favorable treatment for developing countries.

Basically, the aim for Latin America is to develop a system of international trade allowing for the adaptation of productive activities and Latin American trade to changes in world demand, especially in the most dynamic sectors. Comparative advantages in the modern world depend less on resource endowment than on national capability to adapt production and exports to new technology and to the demands of the world market. This requires, in the case of Latin American countries, restructuring the productive machinery.

However, this restructuring of Latin American economies cannot be done without ensuring greater access to the markets of developed countries, so that the achievement of competitive advantages regarding certain products is not thwarted by restrictive action in the main export markets. Access to markets is also essential to provide a steady flow of the resources needed to finance investments in the Latin American industrial sector and to set such investments in the right international framework. The Latin American countries feel that an improved multilateral system of safeguards is required.

From the Latin American perspective, the safeguards system should be considered as a way to reverse the trend toward managed trade that is obvious in the textile and steel sectors. In addition, the system could ensure a significant degree of safe access to markets, particularly for countries lacking retaliatory capabilities, which up to now has constituted the main disciplinary factor in the implementation of safeguards.

The developing countries have been most affected by the weakness of the GATT system of safeguards and by the lack of commitment to such a system by the main developed countries. In fact, an improved and strengthened system of safeguards is essential to the credibility of the system, and its successful negotiation is requisite to the acceptance of new multilateral concessions or other obligations. If the present trend toward managed trade and the adoption of discriminatory action against developing countries cannot be reversed, it is rather useless to search for, let alone offer, new trade concessions.

Likewise, in order to retain the credibility of the Uruguay Round of negotiations at Punta del Este, Latin American countries have insisted that all those taking part comply with the commitment not to introduce new measures aimed at restricting or distorting trade ("stand-still" measures) and at dismantling ("rolling back") the existing ones. Initially, the Latin American countries asserted that a status quo agreement should come before the negotiations, and that in the context of this agreement only those measures strictly consistent with GATT rules were to be adopted. GATT should be informed of all these measures and a follow-up and surveillance mechanism of the status quo commitment ought to be established by the GATT Council.[2] According to the Latin American countries, one of the main purposes of the status quo commitment should be to prevent the implementation of measures in the so-called gray area, specifically the "voluntary agreements of export restriction," and to include the nonimplementation of graduation within the framework of the Generalized System of Preferences (GSP).

The Latin American countries want to ensure that the special and differential treatment in favor of developing countries, which is part of the multilateral commitments adopted within the framework of GATT (Part 4, Enabling Clause), is reflected in every agreement that may be reached during the Uruguay Round and is considered by the different negotiating groups.

## Traditional Issues

The Ministerial Declaration of Punta del Este, which sets the framework for the Uruguay Round of negotiations, consists of two parts. The first part includes questions related to traditional issues of multilateral trade negotiations and to two issues not previously addressed. Traditional issues are the object of negotiations of twelve special groups: tariffs, nontariff measures, tropical products, products derived from natural resources, textiles, agriculture, GATT articles, safeguards, multilateral trade negotiations agreements, subsidies and compensation rights, dispute settlement procedures, and operation of the GATT system. The two new issues, investment and intellectual property rights, are being dealt with in two additional groups. The second part of the declaration is devoted to the question of trade in services. The following questions, related to the aims of negotiation within the framework of the traditional issues, are of most interest to the Latin American countries.

The seven rounds of multilateral negotiations held before the Uruguay Round brought about a substantial reduction in average tariffs. It had been stated, therefore, that the subject of tariffs would not be a priority in the later negotiations. It should be pointed out, however, that the tariff schedules of industrialized countries, and more notably in the field of certain productive sectors, tend to be biased against exports of developing countries. Thus, although the average tariff levels in the United States, the EC, and Japan are 4.8, 5.6, and 5.5 percent, respectively, imports originating in the developing countries must pay, on average, higher customs duties than those originating in the industrialized countries. For some products of special interest to developing countries (foodstuffs and clothing), tariff incidence may range between 16 and 21 percent in the United States, Japan, and the EC.

It should also be pointed out that the GSP is unilaterally implemented by the industrialized countries; it does not cover the whole spectrum of goods, and its effectiveness is impaired by various limitations. Furthermore, some industrialized countries such as the United States have added new restrictions to the system and are seeking to use the GSP as an instrument of negotiation to obtain concessions from the developing countries. Therefore, from the Latin American perspective, insofar as tariffs are concerned, there is reason to continue the liberalization process in the industrialized countries. In the opinion of the countries of the region, negotiations should be aimed at the following: reduction of tariff rates; harmonization of the different tariffs of industrialized countries, which show significant differences; and improvement of the GSP.

The existence of nontariff measures raises another serious obstacle regarding access to the markets of developed countries. This obstacle basically applies to sectors of special interest to Latin America. In fact, the United Nations Conference on Trade and Development (UNCTAD) has estimated that in 1986, 48.9 percent of food imports, 64.2 percent of iron and steel imports, and 67 percent of clothing imports were subject to nontariff measures. It is worth noting that during the last few years protectionism in the case of steel has increased considerably. Trade in steel is now managed through a system of price controls and so-called voluntary export restraints. Various other obstacles (antidumping, countervailing duties, and marketing requirements) have been set with the aim of further restricting the steel trade. As a result, iron and steel exporters in Latin America have been limited to an insignificant percentage of the markets of industrialized countries. To a large extent these markets have been reserved for local producers and for producers in other developed countries.[3]

Thus, for Latin America, it is a priority to ensure the elimination of nontariff barriers that are incompatible with GATT principles and rules. In cases where nontariff barriers are condoned by GATT, it is important to attempt to suppress their distorting effects on trade.

In practice, trade in agricultural products is excluded from full GATT discipline. There are several reasons for this: (1) there are special rules regarding export subsidies and quantitative restrictions on agricultural products; (2) in 1955 the United States obtained a waiver allowing it to keep restrictions on the trade of certain agricultural products; (3) the EC Common Agricultural Policy protects domestic prices by means of variable levies applied on imports and export subsidies (it has been difficult to establish in GATT the illegality of these mechanisms owing to the lack of binding tariffs on these products and to the weakness of rules on agricultural export subsidies); (4) the persistence of residual quantitative restrictions, as in the case of Japan in a manner inconsistent with GATT obligations; and (5) regulations apparently applied for health and sanitary reasons.

Although efforts have been made to solve the problems of agricultural trade within a multilateral framework, no significant progress has been made. The most significant results of the Tokyo Round in this area were limited to price-fixing arrangements on dairy products, an agreement to manage trade in beef, and the consolidation of beef quotas in the United States.

It is up to the Latin American countries to press for a global solution that allows for the stabilization of world trade in agricultural products and for greater access to markets for their exports. Several countries in the region are among the main producers and exporters of agricultural products, which has led to their participation in the Cairns Group.[4] This group was set up at the preliminary stage of the Uruguay Round and has since been very active in agricultural negotiations.

The Cairns Group has proposed that agricultural negotiations should result in: (1) a long-term agreement aimed at the complete liberalization of trade in agricultural products and the elimination of agricultural subsidies; (2) a program of reforms—implemented within a period no longer than ten years—to gradually eliminate measures supporting the agricultural sector; and (3) a series of immediate measures to keep market access and export subsidies at present levels.

The EC and the United States have also put forward specific agricultural proposals. However, negotiations in this area will be extremely difficult owing to existing distortions in world agricultural trade and to the high political sensitivity of government measures in support of the agricultural sector of the main industrialized countries. This is illustrated by the heavy subsidy—around US$65 billion per year—allocated to agricultural production by these countries.

In 1963, the GATT Contracting Parties already decided to take whatever actions were necessary to eliminate all tariff and nontariff measures affecting the trade of tropical products. Later on, the developing countries succeeded in having tropical products recognized as a "special and priority sector" in the Tokyo Declaration, and separate negotiations on these products were carried out at the initial stages of the Tokyo Round. The negotiations were intended to cover tariffs, nontariff barriers, and other measures affecting the trade of tropical products—including manufactured and semimanufactured goods. At the 1982 GATT Ministerial Meeting, there were consultations and negotiations aimed at greater liberalization of the trade of tropical products in their processed and semiprocessed forms.[5] However, no significant improvements have been achieved.

Although some industrialized countries have recently improved market access of certain tropical products within the framework of their GSP, negotiations are not yet over. Latin American countries have insisted on the priority nature of negotiations on tropical products and on the immediate implementation of the agreements reached at the Punta del Este Ministerial Declaration, regardless of the progress made in other areas of negotiations. The aim of Latin American countries is free access to the markets of developed countries for export of all tropical products on a nonreciprocal basis. Nevertheless, negotiations on this issue have become complicated owing to the proposal for wider product coverage put forward by the industrialized countries. According to this proposal, negotiations should encompass not only the products in which developing countries as the main exporters may be interested (for example, coffee, cocoa, and tea), but also other products produced in the industrialized countries themselves (for example, wood). Should this proposal be accepted, the developed countries could demand reciprocity from developing countries regarding the opening of their markets—an issue that has not been raised so far.

Trade of certain natural resource products, such as minerals, nonferrous metals, and forestry and fishery products, is subject to a set of barriers including quantitative restrictions and other tariff measures. Further, escalation of tariff schedules by degree of processing means that effective protection is higher for more processed goods. Therefore, not only do these barriers affect the market access of these products but they also deprive Latin American and other developing countries of the opportunity to export higher value-added goods. In regard to fishery products, some industrialized countries (such as those of the EC) hope to limit access to their markets by granting greater access to products from countries that in turn grant fishery rights to EC ships in the territorial sea of the exporting country. The Latin American countries have energetically rejected this proposal, which would imply giving up sovereignty in return for access to export markets of the industrialized countries.

The aim of the Latin American countries is to integrate textile trade into the GATT framework through the strengthening of GATT rules and policies. This is a question of the utmost importance for Latin American and other developing countries, where the textile sector represents a high percentage of exports, value added, and employment. However, for over two decades the textile trade has been managed by the Multifibre Agreement (MFA), which is contrary to GATT rules and principles because it is based on the negotiation of quantitative restrictions on a discriminatory basis. The MFA is an instrument specifically aimed against the developing countries and was based on the rationale that textile exports from those countries produced serious dislocations in the markets of the industrialized countries. Originally established as a temporary mechanism, the MFA has become a permanent feature restricting textile exports from developing to industrialized countries.

## Multilateral Trade Agreements

One of the main results of the Tokyo Round was the adoption of different codes that interpret or regulate the application of certain provisions to the General Agreement, and agreements on beef, dairy products, and civil aviation. However, certain difficulties have been met regarding the enforcement of these agreements. In some cases, the benefits of these agreements have not been extended to all contracting parties, including Latin American countries, which is in open contradiction to the most-favored-nation treatment stipulated in GATT Article 1 and to the 1979 decision dealing specifically with this issue.[6] Moreover, some developing countries that are signatories to the Code on Subsidies and Counteracting Duties have been denied their benefits unless they accept additional conditions unilaterally imposed by some industrialized countries.

On the other hand, enforcement of the codes has given rise to differences in the levels of rights and obligations of the various contracting parties in important areas such as subsidies and antidumping. In fact, both the regulation and the interpretation of the codes are carried out within the framework of committees of signatories in which only those countries subscribing to the codes participate. Because most developing countries have not signed the codes, they are excluded from these decisions even if they participate in the committees as observers. The guidelines set by the codes have not served to prevent a serious increase in restrictive measures, especially regarding countervailing rights and antidumping duties. Therefore, Latin American countries have proposed to improve special and differential treatment in favor of developing countries and to avoid new negotiations in order to ensure such differential treatment.

As already mentioned, the issue of safeguards is very important for Latin America. An agreement on safeguards is essential for the adequate operation of the international trading system and would provide an additional contractual basis to standstill or rollback commitments. The present system has proved inadequate and has not been able to avoid the proliferation of discriminatory protective measures, most of which are aimed against Latin American countries. Negotiations aimed at the improvement of the multilateral system of safeguards have lasted over a decade, but it has not been possible to attain an agreement on safeguards. Certain developed countries have insisted on amending GATT Section 19 in order to permit a selective (i.e., discriminatory) application of safeguards against suppliers considered harmful to domestic producers. This has been strongly opposed by developing countries. Selectivity is the antithesis of GATT principles and is an expression of the trend towards bilateralism (Sistema Económico Latinoamericano [SELA] 1988). This constitutes the most significant threat to the multilateral trading system and to the possibilities of Latin American countries' increasing their participation in world trade.

For Latin America, a legally binding agreement on safeguards is essential. The agreement should be based on the unconditional clause of the most-favored nation, clearly eliminating every possibility of discrimination in its implementation. The economic criteria of serious injury should be stricter, so that a mere threat of injury is not reason enough to adopt safeguard measures. The measures should be subject to short, fixed limits and to multilateral surveillance. Tariffs and measures that have the same effect as tariffs should be used instead of quantitative restrictions.

The problem with the GATT dispute-settlement procedure is that disputes are often settled by one country withdrawing concessions granted to the transgressing country, that is, by commercial retaliation. Latin American countries do not consider this a viable option when the other party is the EC, the United States, or Japan, because of the differences in power. Therefore, for Latin American countries a strengthening of the dispute-settlement mechanism may be achieved only through: (1) greater political commitment by the larger trading partners with respect to their multilateral obligations; (2) greater provision and binding of the said commitments; and (3) consistency of national law and multilateral obligations and the elimination of inconsistent and even conflicting points between national laws and multilateral commitments.

In the Uruguay Round, new issues (such as trade in services, trade-related investment, and intellectual property measures) have also been included. The last two issues have been included in Part 1 of the Ministerial Declaration of Punta del Este. These are complex issues and their international regulation will have direct and immediate effects on internal policies and laws. That is why these negotiations are so crucial and challenging for the countries involved, especially those of Latin America.

More than any other new issue, discussions on the topic of services have been marked by considerable differences between the countries.[7] Although differences have generally placed industrialized and developing countries on opposite sides, there remain differences within the groups as well. The positions of the various countries are defined, to a large extent, by the relative importance of services in their national economies. In fact, the contribution of services to output, employment, or trade varies considerably across the countries. For example, in the United States the services sector represents two-thirds of its GDP and employs over 70 percent of the labor force (table A.4). In addition, the United States is the main exporter of services (US$35 billion in 1980), and the U.S. services industries have become remarkably international in nature in the last few years (United States Office of Technology Assessment 1986). The situations of Japan and the countries of the EC are quite similar. Services exports of the EC countries as a whole are three times those of the United States (European Economic Community 1984), and Japan is also increasingly turning into a services-oriented economy.

On the other hand, the situation of the developing countries is quite different. Studies undertaken by UNCTAD (1984) and by the Permanent Secretariat of SELA (1985) indicate that the contribution of services to GDP is as important in developing countries as in the industrialized countries. For example, the contribution of services to Latin American gross domestic product amounted to 56 percent in Chile in 1983, and 54 percent in both Mexico in 1985 and Venezuela in 1986, a percentage very similar to that of Japan (table A.4). However, a sectoral analysis reveals that the category Services, which includes, for example, data-processing activities, and is the core of the so-called leading industries, is less important in the developing countries.

There is even greater contrast between developed and developing countries regarding international trade in services. In services trade, the industrialized countries hold a leading position. In 1980, their imports represented 70 percent of total world imports of services, their exports represented over 80 percent, and the services trade balance recorded a surplus of approximately US$10 billion. In contrast, during the same year the deficit in Latin American trade in services was US$9 billion.

These differences regarding the importance of services to each group of countries, in addition to the complexity of the sector, and the limitations on various relevant aspects of negotiations—such as definitions, categories of barriers or obstacles to trade in services, and inaccurate statistics—seem to point to a long and difficult process of discussions within GATT.

In the so-called initial phase of negotiations, the goals of the various countries were clear. The negotiation proposals of industrialized countries were aimed at the adoption of a general framework, so as to make the liberalization of trade in services easier (OECD 1987). This general framework included not only the flow of services from one country to another but also aspects of investment and financial transfers related to these activities. According to the industrialized countries, the principles to be included within this framework would be the following:

❖ Access to markets, so that foreign suppliers of services may compete openly and fairly with local companies. According to this principle, the liberalization of trade in services should not only support such trade but also facilitate the possibility of direct investment.

❖ Transparency regarding the laws, regulations, and actions related to the trade in services, which implies a commitment by the countries to inform other nations of any actual or eventual changes in their legal rules that may affect trade in services.

❖ Same or similar treatment for foreign service companies as domestic ones. Moreover, as a general guideline for negotiations, developed countries have also indicated that the practice adopted for the codes on nontariff barriers negotiated during the Tokyo Round should be followed. In this sense, the general framework would consist of a kind of "umbrella" code, from which sectoral codes may be negotiated for different categories of services.

In contrast, Brazil and India, the two most active countries within the group of developing countries, provided specific proposals that referred to procedures and organization. Because the Latin American countries import services, have negative balances in their services transactions, and have services companies that are not internationally competitive, they at first opposed negotiations regarding services in the belief that they would derive little benefit from them. They expressed little interest in liberalizing their trade in services, since it could further hinder the development of their own new national services industries.

Another problem relates to the inconsistency between international agreements relating to trade in services and existing national sectoral policies and laws. Industrialized countries want to obtain certain uniform commitments on policies and legislation regulating the services sector at a national level. In this way they hope to gain uniform access to markets for their exports and services industries. On the other hand, Latin American countries maintain that the policies and laws in the services sector are not protectionist-oriented. They argue that the policies and laws aim to regulate certain sectors of services for strategic reasons (consumer protection, development of certain sectors of services, and so forth) instead of hindering or preventing activity in these sectors.

Another important difference is the distinction, clear for developing countries and less so for developed ones, between trade in services and investment in them. This distinction arises from the very nature of the services, where production and consumption generally appear simultaneously. Thus, in many cases the sale or trade of services requires the physical presence of the person offering this service in the place of consumption. In other words, trade in services often requires investments in the countries acquiring these services.

The industrialized countries consider liberalization of trade in services to imply certain obligations related to the investment in services, when these are considered necessary, so that trade activities can take place. Initially, the United States, as the originator of the proposal to include trade-related investments in the negotiations, wanted to address problems related to local content requirements and the obligation to export a specific percentage of the production, which some countries demand of foreign investors. In fact, the United States has suggested that barriers and discriminatory measures applied by countries to foreign investment should be reviewed. Therefore, its aim seems to be to broaden the scope of GATT so as to encompass the whole question of foreign investment. If this were to happen, the United States would be able to legitimize at a multilateral level the use of retaliatory measures in the cases considered under section 301 of its 1984 Trade and Tariffs Law. It would also make GATT mechanisms for the settlement of disputes applicable to investment problems, another aim of the United States.

Developing countries do not accept the interpretation of the industrialized countries that whenever a service implying a "presence" in the country is rendered or sold, it should be considered a business transaction. Should this interpretation be accepted, liberalization of trade in services would involve changing all the rules related to foreign investments in developing countries. The most important consequence of this liberalization as it is defined by the developed countries would be to place national and foreign services sector companies on equal footing. In developing countries, however, acceptance of this definition would imply unfair competition between national companies and international services companies.

Latin American countries also insist that the negotiations must be limited to the exchange of services across national borders. It is felt that the establishment of branches or subsidiary companies providing services, such as those in the manufacturing or industrial sector in recipient countries, must follow the laws and regulations governing foreign investments, because these laws have been drafted to ensure that foreign investments contribute to the implementation of the development plans and objectives of the recipient countries.

In negotiations on trade in services, what is at stake is a change in trade relations between the industrialized and the developing countries. The latter, especially those in Latin America, face a great challenge. Their answer to the strategic objectives of the industrialized countries regarding services is vitally important because what is at stake is the establishment of their own policies and mechanisms, which will affect future development of these sectors in their own economies.

The mandate established by the Declaration of Punta del Este in this area was much more limited in scope. First, an analysis of the operation of GATT articles on investment measures, including any restrictive and distorting effects is required. Second, negotiations are expected to develop appropriate future provisions that may be needed to avoid any adverse effects on trade.

During the initial phase of negotiations in 1987, the first part of the mandate was considered, that is, the review of GATT articles relating to foreign investment matters. The investment measures more frequently mentioned are the export performance and local content requirements. Export performance requirements refer to regulations demanding that a specific percentage of the production from foreign investment should be exported. This is one of the most interesting aspects for the United States, and one that has the support of many developed countries, including the EC, Japan, and the Scandinavian countries. Local content requirements refer to rules by which foreign investors are obliged to buy from national suppliers, or by which a specific amount of the production of the investor has to be manufactured in the country.

The United States attaches great significance to measures of this type, and in the 1984 Trade and Tariff Law (section 307) included regulations specifically aimed at reducing or eliminating their implementation by third countries. According to these regulations, the United States Trade Representative (USTR) is directly empowered, without following procedures required under section 301, to impose duties or other import restrictions on products or services of a country imposing export requirements, including prohibiting entry into the United States of products subject to such requirements.

Nevertheless, these matters have already been thoroughly considered within the framework of GATT, and some clear ideas about the subject have thus taken shape. In fact, a panel set up in 1982 to study the complaint of the United States on the enforcement of Canada's Foreign Investment Review Act (FIRA) concluded that GATT does not ban the practice of placing conditions on foreign investment in terms of the sale of goods in foreign markets and of giving preference to the domestic market, and that the agreement does not oblige contracting parties to prevent companies from undertaking dumping operations. Therefore, the panel determined that in this case Canada was not acting in a manner that was incompatible with the principles of nondiscrimination stipulated under the agreement. It was thus clear that if export requirements promote dumping or subsidies, these effects should be managed according to specific regulations under GATT for each particular case.

Moreover, the panel concluded that Canada's practice of awarding more favorable treatment to investments that purchased goods of Canadian origin or from Canadian resources, as compared to investments that purchased imported goods, was incompatible with Article 3:4 (GATT 1984). Nevertheless, it is worth taking into account that in each case only the effects that these measures may have on trade ought to be considered.

Latin American countries have pointed out that a number of the so-called measures presented by some countries are in fact domestic policies, and in that regard, group negotiations should focus only on the instruments used and not on the aims of those policies. For example, one aim is to achieve economies of scale in the developing countries with small national markets.

A specific aspect of intellectual property rights, namely, trade of counterfeit goods has been considered within the GATT framework ever since this matter was discussed for the first time in 1978 by the subgroup on "customs matters" set up by the Tokyo Round. Other aspects of intellectual property rights had only been considered lightly until the United States submitted detailed proposals on the subject in the preparatory stage of the Uruguay Round. The issues submitted by the United States in this area are closely related to the problems of trade of high-technology goods and therefore go beyond traditional discussions on the more limited issue of counterfeit trademarks.

The United States has justified its initiative in GATT on the grounds that current international law on intellectual property, including the Paris Convention on Patents and Trademarks, and the Bern Convention on Copyright, does not grant sufficient protection to intellectual property. It asserts, for example, that the stipulations of the Paris Convention allow for, but do not enforce, embargo or banning of imports of counterfeit goods and are therefore inadequate.

In April 1986, the United States proposed two sets of actions for GATT to consider: (1) to complete and implement an anticounterfeiting code so that imported goods with counterfeit trademarks cannot enter the market; and (2) to conclude a mandatory agreement against distorting trade practices derived from lack of adequate protection of intellectual property. This would also imply legalizing retaliatory measures against goods that have infringed on U.S. international property rights under the U.S. Law of Trade and Tariffs. It has also been suggested that GATT may serve as an international forum to expressly acknowledge the protection of intellectual property rights for new technologies such as computer software and literary works sent by satellite and manufactured microorganisms (Dam 1986).

These comprehensive aims, which are almost tantamount to establishing a new system of intellectual property, go beyond the mandate of the Declaration of Punta del Este. As noted by some developing countries, namely India and Brazil, negotiating means identifying the intellectual property laws that are currently in force and that are implemented in such a way that they restrict trade.

If negotiations are carried out in areas not included under the agreement, the consequences for developing countries may be very important. In developing nations, intellectual property laws were usually set up to prevent artificial obstacles to the transfer of technology and to counteract the excesses of the dominant position of multinational corporations. It would be cause for great concern to developing countries if the technologically leading countries were to impose restrictions on their export markets to avoid any piracy of intellectual property that may occur because of inadvertence or reluctance to enforce rules and regulations originally designed to facilitate the transfer of technology.

## Conclusion

Although negotiations on traditional issues are very interesting for the Latin American countries, the challenge facing Latin America in the Uruguay Round of negotiations is to have its interests regarding new issues adequately expressed and recognized by other members. It is not possible to fully understand the consequences of negotiations on new issues if they are considered separately, and without taking into account their interrelationships. The goals of the industrialized countries in the negotiations are based on a global conception closely linked to the restructuring of international economic relations that has been induced by the momentous technological changes taking place.

Technological progress is transforming the productive process. The international division of labor bears the brunt of technological changes that affect the comparative advantages of the various countries. The struggle to ensure technological control and influence on the world economy explains many of the trade conflicts that have arisen lately between the United States, the EC, and Japan.

The issue of technology also explains the increasing interest of the developed countries in ensuring access to markets in developing countries under conditions that guarantee the growth of their own goods and services industries—sectors in which they have comparative advantage stemming from their technological superiority. For these purposes, developed countries have realized the necessity of having an international contractual framework that follows certain policies and allows these objectives to be achieved. Thus the Uruguay Round was perceived as an adequate framework to favor this new type of institutional support that would adapt to new international conditions. A number of proposals submitted by developed countries regarding new issues respond to this approach.

For example, the proposal to include investment regulations is aimed at guaranteeing the presence of investors wherever the nature of the services rendered, or the marketing of products requires such a presence because of technical, legal, or economic reasons. It has been emphasized that problems relating to intellectual property should be considered. This reflects the need to protect the technological innovations upon which the economic power of the industrialized countries is based and to prevent third-party countries from "expropriating" such technologies.

As mentioned before, the issue of investment bears a close relationship to that of services. In many cases the rendering of services (that is, trade in the services sector) requires investments where the services must be rendered. Therefore, international regulations of trade in services also imply a review of matters related to investments.

The industrialized countries assert that freer trade in services requires the liberalization of stipulations regulating foreign investment when it is necessary to the rendering of the services. In a wider sense, if the new proposals by the United States are followed, liberalization of trade in services and the elimination of obstacles to investment flows generally go hand in hand. This is of great concern to developing countries. The industrialized countries emphasize that the principles of "national treatment" and "right to operate" in the other country ought to be included in the international framework regulating the services sector. This would seem to indicate that the focus of negotiations would be the policies and laws ruling foreign investments in various countries. This may be seen from the review of the different national surveys on services, which a number of industrialized countries have submitted to GATT. When these countries consider obstacles to trade in services in some sectors such as banking, insurance, advertising, and so forth, the obstacles mentioned in the surveys are the policies and stipulations regulating foreign influence on these sectors.

Likewise, the proposals regarding intellectual property are closely related to the need of the producing countries to safeguard their technological power. Therefore, capacity for technological innovation and the control of these innovations are of the utmost importance to the success of the economic strategies of these countries. This is the case for high-technology goods, now the most dynamic component of world trade. These goods are produced in industrialized countries and are the result of large investments in research and development. Such investments can be carried out only if reasonable returns may be expected through the marketing, at a national and international level, of the resulting new products. At the same time, marketing will depend on the adequate protection of property rights of the new products, so that the products are not copied by other countries in violation of patent laws. Thus developing countries, especially those in Latin America, need to recognize and react to this long-held position of industrialized countries in the ongoing negotiations process. The issue at stake in the negotiations of the Uruguay Round is the reorganization of international economic relations as a whole, not simply a discussion of trade concessions.

*Part Five*

# Conclusion

*Miguel Urrutia*

# Asia and Latin America: Main Issues for Further Research

To gain as much benefit as possible from a comparative analysis of Latin American and Asian economic development, it would be useful to have taxonomies that place the different economies of both continents in categories that facilitate meaningful comparisons. This brief chapter suggests some criteria for classifying economies, thus making comparisons more interesting. The three basic criteria for classification are: (1) the degree to which a country is rich in resources on a per capita basis; (2) the size of the market; and (3) the stage of growth in which a country finds itself.

Resource-rich countries are those with high natural resource exports per capita, and large market countries have large- or medium-sized populations with relatively high incomes. Stage of growth refers to whether a country has moved from import substitution to the export phase of industrialization. These characteristics define the way a country responds to different policies. By characterizing Asian and Latin American countries in this way, policy comparisons may become more fruitful.

**Table 13.1**
**Classification of Asian and Latin American Countries by**
**Selected Economic Indicators**

| Country | Export Proportion[a] | Labor Surplus Indicator[b] | Natural Resources[c] | Human Capital Resources[d] | Exports of Manufactured Goods (as % of total exports) | Net Contribution of Manufactured BOP[e] (as % of total imports) |
|---|---|---|---|---|---|---|
| **Large Resource-rich Economies** | | | | | | |
| Argentina | 0.12 | 0.05 | 175 | 70 | 22 | −50 |
| Brazil[f] | 0.09 | 0.25 | 96 | 35[g] | 40 | 8 |
| Mexico | 0.16 | 0.54 | 138 | 55 | 30 | −40 |
| Indonesia | 0.29 | 2.26 | 64 | 39[h] | 22 | −55 |
| **Resource-rich Economies with Limited Markets** | | | | | | |
| Bolivia | 0.15 | 0.41 | 81 | 37[h] | 2 | −86 |
| Chile | 0.26 | 0.27 | 317 | 69 | 8 | −66 |
| Colombia | 0.14 | 0.62 | 145 | 50 | 18 | −58 |
| Costa Rica | 0.29 | 0.62 | 267 | 41 | 36 | −47 |
| Dominican Republic | 0.15 | 1.38 | 77 | 50 | 29 | −53 |
| Jamaica | 0.30 | 0.82 | 88 | 58[g] | 66 | −23 |
| Paraguay | 0.06 | 0.13 | 50 | 31 | 19 | −58 |
| Peru | 0.12 | 1.14 | 102 | 65 | 23 | −63 |
| Trinidad | 0.23 | 0.60 | 783 | 76 | 32 | −28 |
| Venezuela | 0.17 | 0.37 | 444 | 45 | 9 | −73 |
| Malaysia | 0.47 | 0.86 | 560 | 53[h] | 36 | −37 |
| Papua New Guinea | 0.40 | 3.61 | 270 | 14[h] | 6 | −65 |
| Thailand | 0.21 | 1.38 | 97 | 30 | 42 | −34 |
| **Large Excess-labor Economies** | | | | | | |
| China | 0.10 | 4.40 | 11 | 37 | 64 | −41 |
| India[f] | 0.06 | 1.57 | 4 | 35[h] | 72 | −11 |
| Pakistan | 0.10 | 1.17 | 11 | 17[h] | 68 | −19 |
| **Excess-labor Economies with Limited Markets** | | | | | | |
| El Salvador | 0.19 | 1.64 | 116 | 24 | 23 | −59 |
| Guatemala | 0.15 | 1.14 | 94 | 17[g] | 32 | −40 |
| Haiti | 0.19 | 2.18 | 23 | 18[h] | 63 | −33 |
| Honduras | 0.26 | 1.17 | 174 | 36 | 10 | −72 |
| Bangladesh | 0.05 | 3.96 | 2 | 18 | 74 | −27 |
| Burma | 0.04 | 1.73 | 7 | 24[g] | 13 | −85 |
| Korea[f] | 0.35 | 3.66 | 72 | 94 | 91 | 37 |
| Nepal | 0.05 | 3.11 | 3 | 25 | 67 | −60 |
| Philippines | 0.15 | 1.06 | 34 | 65 | 60 | −19 |
| Sri Lanka | 0.19 | 2.27 | 44 | 63 | 42 | −42 |

*Continued on following page*

Table 13.1 Continued

| Country | Export Proportion[a] | Labor Surplus Indicator[b] | Natural Resources[c] | Human Capital Resources[d] | Exports of Manufactured Goods (as % of total exports) | Net Contribution of Manufactured BOP[e] (as % of total imports) |
|---|---|---|---|---|---|---|
| **Small Highly Urbanized Economies** | | | | | | |
| Barbados | 0.21 | 0.75 | 232 | 93[h] | 75 | -37 |
| Panama | 0.07 | 0.45 | 146 | 59 | 14 | -67 |
| Uruguay[f] | 0.19 | 0.14 | 213 | 70[h] | 41 | -12 |
| Hong Kong[f] | 0.95 | 12.72 | 499 | 69[h] | 92 | 11 |
| Singapore[f] | 1.17 | 5.36 | 2,837 | 71[h] | 67 | -7 |
| Taiwan[f] | 0.55 | na | 203 | na | 96 | 63 |

a. Total exports – GNP ratio in U.S. dollars.
b. 1980 agricultural labor force – arable land ratio in hectares.
c. Per capita exports of primary products (agricultural products, minerals, and fuels).
d. 1985 school enrollment ratio for secondary schools.
e. Manufactured exports minus manufactured imports over total imports.
f. Countries that have clearly passed the primary import-substitution stage of industrialization. These countries have an index of –15 or more in column 6, and 40 percent or more of their exports are of manufactured goods.
g. 1983.
h. 1984.
SOURCES: Food and Agriculture Organization (FAO), *Agriculture Towards 2000*, 1987; Food and Agriculture Organization (FAO), *Production Yearbook 1985*, vol. 39; World Bank, *World Development Report*, 1982; World Bank, *World Tables 1987*, 4th ed.

Table 13.1, which presents one possible method of classifying the countries from both regions, shows that, in general, the export orientation of the Asian countries is much higher than that of the Latin American countries. Within each grouping, the ratio of exports to gross national product (GNP) is highest among the Asian countries, and Singapore and Hong Kong clearly stand out with ratios of 1.17 and 0.95. It would appear also that only a few of the Latin American economies have excess labor resources. In contrast, the labor surplus indicator of all of the Asian countries, except Malaysia, is greater than 1.0. Although the Latin American countries generally do not have surplus labor, many of them are rich in natural resources, as indicated by the high value of their per capita exports of primary products. With the exception of Singapore (which serves as an entrepôt for Asian trade), the Asian economies show a lower value of such exports than the Latin American ones.

These conditions imply that a policy package that would facilitate economic development in the Latin American countries would be quite different from that which would be suggested for labor-surplus, resource-poor countries. This chapter highlights some of the policy issues that address these types of situations and may be usefully analyzed in a comparative framework.

## Extent and Quality of Government Intervention

When Latin Americans started to receive news about the phenomenal success of some Asian economies, Western interpreters of those experiences emphasized that the success resulted from free-market policies. It is now known that in Japan, the Asian NICs, and the ASEAN countries, there was pervasive government intervention in the economy. As Chen points out, however, it was neoclassical intervention (see chapter 3, this volume).

Financial sector policies, for example, do not fit the above generalization. It appears that Japan and the Asian NICs have regulated their credit markets very closely. In Japan, Korea, and Singapore there has been virtually no consumer credit. In Latin America, following the advice of eminent First World economists, most countries liberalized their financial sectors, which in the 1970s led in many cases to consumption binges, capital flight, and indebtedness.

Thus, while it is easy to talk about market-facilitating intervention, the realities are more complex. Hence, further research and comparison of the type, extent, and quality of the interventions that were carried out in different development phases would be fruitful.

## Capital Mobilization

The most interesting difference between the NICs and the Latin American quasi-NICs is the difference in saving rates. In 1986, the ratio of gross domestic saving to gross domestic product (GDP) was 40 percent in Singapore, about 35 percent in Korea and Taiwan, and 27 percent in Hong Kong. This was in contrast to the Latin American countries at about the same period, when the ratio of savings to GDP was highest in Mexico at 27 percent and as low as 11 percent in Argentina (table A.5). Understanding this difference in saving behavior between the two regions would be easier if more information about the underlying causes were available.

Many aspects of the difference are intriguing. Examples include (1) the role of forced saving; (2) industrial concentration; and (3) cultural factors and family structure. A comparative analysis of these factors would be well justified.

# The Role of Immigration

Suggestions have been made by Tan about the role of migrants in the economies of the NICs, and by Hughes about migration as a macroeconomic policy tool in Australia (see chapter 14, this volume).

In Latin America, the role of migrants in the rapid growth of the Southern Cone countries in the first half of the century is clear, but there are observers who have suggested that some present-day phenomena of political divisiveness may be related to these early migrations. Nevertheless, some land-rich Latin American countries could absorb migration, but there has been no serious discussion of migration policies in the last decade.

# Policy Stability and Growth

There seems to be a correlation between policy stability and growth if one looks at the Asian NICs and Latin America. Sardi emphasizes the importance of policy stability and discusses the inherent instability of policy in Latin American countries dependent on commodity exports with price volatility (see chapter 4, this volume). It is possible that the greater export diversification in Asia reduces the volatility of export revenues and that this in turn facilitates policy continuity.

Policy stability, however, may also be a function of the political regime. The stability may be substantial in long-lived authoritarian regimes or one-party systems. Of course, in addition to being stable, policies must be correct. Indonesia has had an authoritarian regime; yet it has a pragmatic, well-designed, and flexible set of economic policies that have facilitated growth. The same was not the case for the Philippines during the stable years of the authoritarian Marcos regime.

In Latin America, substantial political changes brought about through democratic processes as well as coups have meant radical changes in economic policies that negatively affected expectations and investment. During the authoritarian period, Brazilian policies were fairly stable and consistent, but the same was true in democratic Colombia. Economic policy stability is, therefore, not related to authoritarianism and democracy but to the particular nature of the authoritarian and democratic regimes in question.

It is interesting, then, to analyze the process of decision making in economic policy formulation in different regimes. Aspects such as the nature of the bureaucracy and its role in decision making may be very crucial. In Asia, the recruitment process and salaries of high-level bureaucrats seem to ensure a relatively high degree of professionalism in the bureaucracy that is largely absent in Latin America. A comparison of the nature and effectiveness of bureaucracies in the two regions may produce important insights.

Finally, in a changing world environment, policy adaptability may be more important that policy stability. What package of policies combines policy stability and adaptability?

In Latin America, some countries adapted too rapidly to international change. In the 1970s, many countries took advantage of world negative real rates of interest and availability of credit too quickly. Colombia, for example, changes policy more slowly than most countries and has had few dramatic growth spurts, but also no dramatic recessions. As a result, in the 1970s, Colombia did not increase its indebtedness as fast as its neighbors did (table A.13). Resistance to some policy innovations is sometimes a virtue.

The complexities of party politics in a democracy may produce policy stability. This was not the case in Chile or Argentina but may be an explanation for policy stability in Colombia, Venezuela, and postwar Japan. Centralization of power may in fact not produce the policy stability experienced in Singapore, Korea, or Taiwan. Centralization may produce instability, as has been the case with military governments in Peru and Argentina.

The role of external political shocks may be important. What role, for instance, did the Allied occupation of Japan, the impact of the Korean War, and the end of the Japanese occupation of Taiwan play in the development of those countries? These external shocks destroyed powerful controlling interests in these countries and facilitated major land reforms and asset redistributions. In contrast, external shocks have not weakened the traditional pressure groups in Latin America.

Certainly, Latin American economists are now more interested in exploring the relationships between economics and politics than ever before. A dialogue on political economy and the politics of economics with Asian experts might suggest much to Latin American economists.

## Economic Integration and East-West Trade

In the area of economic integration, Latin American countries have a richer experience than Asian countries, and the lessons learned might be of great value in Asia. The history of the Andean Pact nations and of ASEAN's attempts at industrial programming at the regional level suggest that this is not a fruitful avenue to follow. This lesson should be instructive to the newly created South Asian Association for Regional Cooperation (SAARC).

## Conclusion

The issues set forth above deserve further exploration. Explaining the causes of economic growth and backwardness in one's own country to economists from another continent adds new insights to the development process. Attempting to compare development experiences often helps to clarify which variables and policies are strategic in the growth process. For these reasons, there should be a continuing dialogue and joint analysis of development problems between Asian and Latin American economists.

# Toward Clarity and Common Sense

An analysis of the comparative experience of Asian and Latin American developing countries since the Second World War must conclude that there are differences to be explained. Whatever growth and development criteria are used, several Asian countries have grown faster and more steadily than any Latin American countries throughout the period.[1] The economic performance of the four most rapidly developing Asian economies (Hong Kong, Korea, Singapore, and Taiwan) and of Thailand has been particularly impressive in both growth and equity terms. Indonesia and Malaysia have also developed strongly, utilizing their rich resource endowment better than most countries with booming sectors. India, Pakistan, and Sri Lanka, though growing weakly by the standards of East and Southeast Asian countries, experienced stronger growth in the 1980s than in the 1970s.

In terms of per capita income growth, the differences between East Asia and Latin America are even clearer because in East and Southeast Asia population growth has declined faster than in most Latin American countries, as a result of effective family planning policies and in response to strong growth in gross domestic product (GDP). China's ability to provide basic needs for a population of more than one billion people stands out as a major achievement of development, although some of China's growth indicators must be treated cautiously because of its lack of statistical infrastructure. Only the Philippines has had poor economic performance in the region.

The Latin American countries, despite having the highest per capita income and human and physical capital endowment among developing countries at the end of the Second World War, and despite favorable natural resource endowments, only doubled their per capita incomes between 1950 and 1980 and then stagnated in the 1980s. In marked contrast, the Asian newly industrializing countries (NICs), doubled their per capita income in every decade since the 1950s. The per capita income of Korea, which in 1951 was devastated by war and was one of the poorest developing countries in the world, in 1987 surpassed that of Argentina, one of the highest-income developing countries forty years ago. In 1900, moreover, together with Australia, Argentina had the highest per capita income in the world (Maddison 1982).

The voluminous literature on development suggests that natural resource endowment, country size, geography, location, and capital inflows (notably of aid) are not the principal causes of differentials in national growth rates. On the contrary, difficulties of appropriate policy formulation and implementation make resource-rich countries the most likely candidates for booming sector crises. When countries are grouped by natural endowments (Chenery and Syrquin 1975), the rapidly growing outliers turn out to be countries with poor natural resource endowments.

Differences in economic performance also do not appear to have cultural origins. The work of Max Weber ([1922] 1965), and R. H. Tawney (1926), and their recent followers in the Confucian school (see Chen, chapter 3, this volume) has demonstrated that various cultures contain the seeds of both growth and economic decline. Protestant, Roman Catholic, Greek Orthodox, Confucian, Buddhist, Hindu, Jewish, and both Shiite and Suni Muslim cultures have seen rapid economic development and no development at all, depending on the economic policy environment that encouraged the various traits within each culture to develop. Several East Asian countries have shown at various times that the Confucian ethic is as conducive to stagnation as to rapid development.

Degrees of democracy, autocracy, and political cohesion vary within and between the South, Southeast, and East Asian and Latin American regions. Focused and careful analyses (Haggard 1980;

Mackie 1988) have not been able to elicit general causal relationships between political systems and economic performance. Rapid economic growth has been an important factor in political stability in Southeast and East Asia, whereas the lack of growth has led to political upheavals in developing and industrial countries; some political regimes, however, have been able to survive despite very poor economic performances. The only constant that seems to emerge from past experience is that political stability is essential to growth. And political stability requires some degree of consensus and popular support for governments, even if they are not elected democratically.

If we draw on the other chapters of this volume as well as on the wider evidence of the debate about the causes of development, economic performance appears to be determined primarily by a country's domestic economic policy framework. Economic policy objectives and administrative rules of the game are molded by political systems. To an important degree, however, the economic climate is affected by the content and the vigor of the debates that take place in university classrooms and how these debates are reflected in the media. The political decisions taken about economic issues reflect a community's intellectual perceptions about the economics of development.

The discussion about development has many common characteristics in Asia and Latin America. Detailed perceptions about economic growth and development continue to vary within and among countries. Over the course of nearly half a century of development experience, fundamental differences of view about the process of development have become more important in economic performance than the similarities. Three principal models have emerged: the statist South Asia-China model; the outward- and private enterprise-oriented East and Southeast Asian model, which aims at rapid growth; and the *dependencia* (dependency) Latin American model.[2] Adherence to these three models appears to account, to an appreciable degree, for the differences in performance among the three broad groupings of countries.

The three models of development overlap in various ways. There is something of dependencia thinking in all developing countries, and the statist and dependencia models encompass growth objectives. Export growth, efficiency in private and public enterprises, and macroeconomic prudence receive lip service in most countries. There are, however, major differences between the statist and dependencia models on the one hand and the growth model on the other. In South Asia and Latin America, economic debate is still strongly influenced by development economics. The behavioral characteristics of developing countries, so the argument goes, are different from those of industrial countries; industrial countries' economic relations with developing countries are biased against them and differ from those of industrial countries' relations with each other. In the growth model, in contrast, producers and consumers in developing countries are thought to behave similarly to those in industrial countries, and the international economic environment is neutral. These fundamental differences of perception have influenced economic policy formulation and hence economic performance.

## Data Biases in International Comparisons

Data limitations complicate intercountry and interregional comparisons. The analytical development of data has slowed since interest in the nature of development peaked in the late 1960s and early 1970s. Comparisons of real GDP and its components have not been pursued as assiduously as they might have been (Kravis 1986). Country data usually still contain three price systems: agricultural prices, which are often below world market prices; services prices, which are largely undervalued in international comparisons because they are measured at domestic wage rates; and prices of manufactured goods, which are overvalued by protection (Balassa and Hughes 1969).

Despite the importance ascribed to barter terms of trade in the dependencia and statist models, indices of capital goods prices still measure the price of products (such as tractors) instead of the prices of the capital services they provide, understating quality changes and hence overstating real prices over time. Barter terms of trade are open to so much error in estimation that not only the extent of change but also the directions of change sometimes vary among different sources. Indicators of long-term trade trends, such as income terms of trade, are rarely calculated.

Facts are loosely used in much of the development literature. Gross domestic product and net material product figures and growth rates are sometimes used interchangeably, notably for China. Nontariff barriers are not differentiated by impact or duration, making the analysis of the real impact of trade barriers on trade trends impossible. Interpretations of growth data vary so widely that the period 1982–88, for example, is being described simultaneously as a period of the longest sustained global growth in history, a period of worldwide recession, and even as a period of crisis.

Many of the persistent problems with facts and data are related to the use of international jargon that substitutes for analysis in development discussion. For example, the terms *cooperation* and *interdependence* are used to give an emotive content to international trade and even to promote capital flows. In each case the objective, analytical relationships that characterize these transactions are blurred, and the differences between the private and social costs and benefits associated with various economic trends are confused. Self-reliance is often regarded as a major policy objective, although it has little economic meaning. It is the countries that sought self-reliance most assiduously, through import substitution regardless of cost, that have experienced the most serious balance-of-payments problems. Regional integration is widely regarded as a desirable economic as well as political end despite its high economic costs and ensuing history of failure, particularly among developing countries. Conclusions based on dependencia and statist models have invaded economic analysis, leading to intellectual muddle and blurring the conclusions that may be sensibly drawn from the available data.

## Role of Government Direction and Regulation

In the spectrum of attitudes represented by the theorists and practitioners of development, the conviction that national government must play a key role in economic development is fairly pervasive. A government's role may be evident by default: nonintervention in the economy has major economic effects. Government is generally regarded as having a role to play in establishing a development culture in which policies promoting growth with equity can thrive. Human resource development is also widely regarded as an essential public responsibility, particularly in the early stages of development. Macroeconomic stability, long ignored by many developing countries, is now recognized as an essential component of growth. But further views on the role of government in development diverge widely.

At one extreme, growth model proponents believe that the principal directions within an economy can be set by macroeconomic and microeconomic policies acting on the prices that individuals, households, and (private or public) enterprises face. The need for administrative intervention is minimized and public employment is limited. Macro-economic and microeconomic policies that seek price stability and openness to international competition result in appropriate resource and factor allocation and utilization. In an open economy there is little danger of market failure in tradables. Where market failure is evident, for example, in persistent dumping, countervailing action can be taken, or in a small economy, such as Hong Kong, dumping may be welcomed. The opening up of services industries to international competition reduces the share of nontradables in the economy. It is central to the growth model approach that rising employment opportunities at higher levels of productivity will ensure that growth will be accompanied by equity. The avoidance of unproductive public employment by limiting direct and indirect public intervention in the economy is an essential component of this model.

Openness is a key concept of the rapid growth model, but it entails uncertainty and risk. Experience suggests that government intervention more often adds uncertainty than it reduces risk. The proper role of government is to maintain a competitive market environment and provide information to reduce uncertainty so that economic units—producers and consumers—can take advantage of that environment. The production of goods and services should be left to private enterprises because public enterprises cannot manage risk. Many private enterprises will succeed by taking risks in the face of uncertainty, but others will fail. The institution of bankruptcy is thus an essential component of an open economic system. Producers also fail in closed systems, but the failed enterprises—public and private—are usually kept in operation by budget subsidies at great cost to the economy.

Market failure is highly correlated with the degree to which an economy is closed. As soon as a part of the economy is protected, it becomes necessary to regulate entry, prices, volumes of output, and quality so that monopolistic exploitation may be avoided. Attempts to stabilize export prices to avoid uncertainty for farmers and governments usually destabilize incomes and revenues. The market has been made to fail. Regulation has unanticipated by-product effects (Corden 1974) and encourages the use of resources in creating and maintaining protection of industries and their profits (Krueger 1974). Administrative costs grow. Administrators join private-enterprise rent seekers. Over time intervention grows until the policy and regulatory framework becomes pervasive. Rules change constantly and their administration becomes increasingly arbitrary and uncertain. The policy framework, far from achieving its objectives, places heavy taxes on economic activities. At worst, combined with macroeconomic instability (marked by double- or even triple-digit inflation), the economy disintegrates into chaos.

The effect of regulations such as tariff and nontariff barriers to trade, subsidies, barriers to entry, price controls, and various licensing arrangements cannot be measured accurately with existing techniques. Partial equilibrium measures, such as "net effective assistance" and "domestic resource cost," are difficult to calculate because of data limitations and must be interpreted cautiously. Partial equilibrium effects can at times be opposite to total effects. General equilibrium analysis is data- and resource-intensive and thus very costly. Even a simple measurement that may be used as a very rough proxy for the extent of regulation, such as the number of public servants employed in economic regulation, is usually difficult to calculate over time and between countries. Without the data to test hypotheses about the effect of regulation on economic efficiency and growth, the debate about regulation continues without resolution. Dependencia and statist-oriented analysts argue that the East Asian successes are the result of government regulation and intervention, whereas the proponents of the outward-oriented rapid growth model believe that if regulation had been even more limited, growth would have been faster and more equitably distributed, with consequent improvements in the quality of life. Japan is perhaps the foremost example of a country at a high income level, but with a low quality of life in terms of housing, hours of travel to work, and access to leisure facilities. The elimination of agricultural protection would be necessary to improve standards of living in these areas in Japan.

## Public versus Private Ownership and Management

Government intervention in the economy through public ownership of enterprises has economic characteristics that tend to reduce the utility of those enterprises in offsetting market failure. Public ownership is widely used to take direct responsibility for those components of social and physical infrastructure that are either most efficiently produced or provided for by one producer (i.e., by a natural monopoly) or where the external benefits cannot be captured by producers, particularly in the early stages of development. Another important component of development is public investment in social and physical infrastructural facilities to produce goods that can be used by many individuals and whose use cannot be discriminated by payment (i.e., public goods).

The dependencia and statist models postulate that, particularly at the early stages of development, governments not only have to supply public goods but also have to intervene where private entrepreneurs are not available, for whatever reasons. Government is thought to be able to improve the allocation and utilization of scarce resources where private entrepreneurs might otherwise waste them by failing in business. By capturing the commanding heights of an economy, governments are thought to be capable of avoiding the monopolistic practices of private firms. By participating directly in natural resource development, they are also thought capable of capturing all the resource rents instead of allowing foreign interests to do so. In most developing countries, the public ownership of goods and services has thus not been confined to public goods that have major externalities. With the exception of a few small economies, notably Hong Kong, where public ownership is confined to the production of public goods that have large external economies—power, transportation, and land development and housing—developing countries built up wide-ranging public sectors from the 1950s to the 1980s. In addition to public utilities, the public sector often included mineral exploitation, some manufacturing, and services such as banking. In countries such as China, public ownership has until recently been all-encompassing, and it still dominates. There are some examples of efficient public enterprises, but in the main, public ownership is characterized by political intervention, nepotism, managerial inefficiency, and high costs to the central budget.

Improving the efficiency of public enterprises has become a policy issue on both sides of the Pacific. But privatization is not a quick and easy option. Achieving efficiency in public goods and natural monopolies such as railways is an intransigent problem even in advanced industrial countries. Public ownership and public management both tend to be inefficient, but so do private ownership and management in a monopolistic situation. Monopolies, whether public or private, tend to exploit consumers. Privately and publicly owned utilities can appear to be efficient by earning high profits and distributing dividends. But in a monopolistic situation such profits may be earned despite great inefficiency. In the monopolistic situations that exist in some areas of telecommunications or in power supply and similar industries, private and public ownership and management has to be subject to surveillance and regulation if it is not to be exploitative.

Investment by public utilities tends to be large-scale. If ownership is public, this can embarrass the government through high public borrowing requirements. Utilities, however, do not have high borrowing requirements, not because they are publicly owned but because they are capital-intensive. The macroeconomic impact on the economy is the same whether borrowing is by the private or public sector. The economic issues concern the efficiency with which investment funds are used, the returns that they earn, and how capital as well as other resources are managed to produce high-quality products at low cost.

The principal argument for privatization is concerned more with management than ownership. Private management tends to be more efficient than public management because it is usually less hampered by limits on hiring and firing and by seniority rules. But private management also tends to be efficient only in the competitive sectors of the economy. There are many examples of poorly managed private firms in monopolistic situations.

The principal advantage of the private ownership and management of enterprises lies in the sanctions imposed by the threat of failure. For this reason alone, it usually makes sense to privatize public enterprises that do not produce public goods. Existing enterprises, however, may be difficult to privatize because their asset base is exaggerated by past management failures and would have to be written down severely to make private investors interested in purchasing them. This usually proves very difficult politically. Privatizing public utilities also requires a review of the regulatory environment to ensure that the new private enterprise will not be able to exploit consumers.

Privatization is thus not a panacea. But it is a major policy issue, particularly for the South Asian countries. Statist policies have led to monumental public-enterprise problems that are likely to take years to resolve. In China, the appropriate form of ownership and organization for manufacturing, services, and even for agriculture is still far from clear. In the rest of East and Southeast Asia and in Latin America, an enterprise-by-enterprise approach may prove to be the least difficult course of reform. Typically, the greater the distortion from a competitive and open environment, the greater the operating costs are likely to be to an economy, as well as the costs of reform.

## Macroeconomic Policies

Macroeconomic policies have now come into prominence in terms of economic development. If domestic prices and the price of foreign exchange remain stable, there is little concern with macroeconomic issues. But if inflation reigns, so that real interest rates fluctuate and the national currency becomes overvalued, sustained economic growth becomes impossible.

The importance of price stability was recognized by the East Asian countries to be an essential step to outward orientation, competitiveness, and growth. Examples include Taiwan and Korea, where price stabilization and devaluation were regarded as key policies when these countries reformed their export policies (Riedel 1988). In South Asia price and exchange-rate stabilization became important targets in the 1960s. Malaysia and Thailand complained in the late 1960s that the imprudent price policies of the industrial countries were leading to the export of inflation to developing countries that had opted for sound macroeconomic policies. In 1965 Indonesia was the last of the ASEAN-4 countries to stabilize its prices.

Several Asian countries experienced episodes of double-digit inflation, sometimes up to 20 percent in the 1970s, primarily as a result of rising petroleum prices. Each time, the governments brought prices under control quickly, often at considerable short-term cost, because they recognized that sustained growth was impossible with inflation. After the industrial countries failed to deal with increasing inflation as an aftermath of petroleum price increases, the Asian governments opted for a recession rather than continuing inflation. That recession had a marked impact on their standards of living. But it was thought worth the cost because price stability cleared the way for a prolonged period of growth, from 1982 to the present. Price stability has important social welfare effects. It is essential to growth with equity. In Asia it is thus widely perceived that taxation through inflation is a sophisticated form of stealing from the poor. In Latin America, average inflation rates have been significantly higher. Although some of the smaller Central American and Caribbean countries have had inflation rates averaging 10 to 20 percent (as did Mexico before 1976), in the larger countries, particularly Argentina and Brazil (and in smaller ones such as Peru and Bolivia), annual inflation rates of more than 100 percent are common. Even in Colombia, where inflation has been held down, inflation rates averaged about 20 percent in the 1970s and 1980s.

Recently, major successful stabilization efforts in Chile, Uruguay, Mexico, and Bolivia have taken place.

The instruments of macroeconomic policy vary among developing countries. Financial markets are less developed and the use of monetary and financial policy instruments are more limited than in industrial countries. Most developing countries, notably in South Asia and Latin America, have financial systems that are tightly controlled by the government. This reduces the usefulness of interest rates and other price signals. Inward-oriented trade policies tend to result in chronic balance-of-payments difficulties, so that capital movements must be carefully controlled. Monetary and financial policies then become distorted and are likely to have little effect on price stabilization.

The other principal instrument of macroeconomic policy—fiscal policy—thus has to carry the main burden of stability in developing countries. This requires not only strong political will but a considerable command of efficient procedures, both in raising revenue and in the management of public expenditures. Fiscal policies thus lie at the heart of effective government intervention in many developing economies. Asian countries (even one as large as India) have been successful in prudent fiscal management. Despite their government-controlled financial systems (in India, Pakistan, Sri Lanka, Indonesia, and Korea), they have succeeded, by and large, in maintaining price stability while expanding their infrastructural sectors. In contrast to most Latin American countries, most Asian countries have been able to maintain stable exchange rates and thus avoid the cycles of devaluation followed by imported inflation and further devaluation that have undermined macroeconomic stability in Latin American countries.

## Microeconomic Policies

The critical difference between the East Asian countries and the other regions lies in their overall growth rates, particularly during the 1980s. However, there is also an important difference between the Latin American and South Asian countries. Whereas Latin American growth rates fell steeply in the 1980s, South Asian countries showed a small but steady increase in the 1970s over the 1960s and a marked increase in the 1980s in comparison to the 1970s. This accelerated growth largely reflected the gradual improvement in agricultural growth rates that followed the liberalization of agricultural policies. Agricultural growth was made possible by underlying macroeconomic stability. South Asia, like East and Southeast Asia, became largely self-sufficient in grains.

In major Latin American countries, in contrast, the stop-go swings of the 1970s continued the dependencia-inspired policy pattern of the 1950s and 1960s. The ability to borrow freely in international capital markets exacerbated the amplitude of economic swings, leading to the very poor performance of the 1980s. Ideological rigidities were not eased by the adoption of some of the economic aspects of the growth model in countries such as Argentina, Chile, and Uruguay. While financial liberalization replaced repression in some countries, fiscal balance could not be achieved overnight in countries that had for decades practiced taxation through inflation. While Brazil had a rapid growth period from 1967–74, guided by growth policies that included indexation to neutralize inflation effects, after the petroleum price rises of 1974 the country reverted to growth through external indebtedness and import substitution.

Although the major differences in economic performance appear to lie in manufacturing, the importance of agriculture also stands out. The East and Southeast Asian countries steadfastly enjoyed a higher rate of agricultural as well as manufacturing growth than either the South Asian or Latin American countries (table 14.1). The principal explanation lies in the stimulus to agriculture in East and Southeast Asia from the 1950s that came from the application of Green Revolution technology, which ironically was initially developed and used in Mexico in the 1940s and 1950s, from policies aimed at "getting the prices right," and by making appropriate infrastructure available. The lower levels of production for manufacturing throughout the period not only encouraged a more efficient and less inward-oriented structure of manufacturing but also permitted a more rapid rate of agricultural growth. Useful services-sector data are unfortunately not available, but it seems that the East and Southeast Asian countries also had a relatively rapid, outward-oriented, and efficient growth of services, notably in such areas as tourism, banking, and in internal as well as external trade.

By the mid-1980s the actual policies that farmers, manufacturers, and other producers and consumers faced were drawing together in several countries. While Hong Kong and Singapore remained the two principal liberal economies, Taiwan, Korea, and Chile were approaching an openness policy. Thailand and Malaysia had always been fairly open, growth-oriented economies, with relatively low

**Table 14.1**
**Real Average Annual Growth of Value Added for Latin American and**
**Asian Regions, by Sector, 1960–86 (% in 1980 US $)**

|  | 1960–70 | 1970–80 | 1980–86 | 1960–86 |
|---|---|---|---|---|
| **Agriculture** | | | | |
| Latin America | — | 3.0 | 1.9 | — |
| Brazil | — | 4.2 | 2.0 | — |
| South Asia[a] | 1.4 | 2.1 | 2.7 | 2.2 |
| India | 0.8 | 1.9 | 2.5 | 2.0 |
| East and Southeast Asia (excluding China) | 3.9 | 3.9 | 3.3 | 3.8 |
| China | 6.7 | 3.0 | 7.9 | 4.6 |
| **Mining** | | | | |
| Latin America | — | 2.6 | 3.4 | — |
| Brazil | — | 5.9 | 9.3 | — |
| South Asia[a] | 4.7 | 6.0 | 8.1 | 5.2 |
| India | 5.2 | 4.2 | 9.7 | 4.7 |
| East and Southeast Asia (excluding China) | 8.7 | 6.5 | 1.8 | 6.8 |
| China | — | — | — | — |
| **Manufacturing** | | | | |
| Latin America | — | 3.8 | -0.4 | — |
| Brazil | — | 8.5 | 1.2 | — |
| South Asia[a] | 3.6 | 4.8 | 6.2 | 4.3 |
| India | 2.9 | 4.6 | 5.9 | 3.9 |
| East and Southeast Asia (excluding China) | 10.6 | 12.0 | 7.0 | 11.1 |
| China | 7.6 | 7.3 | 12.6 | 9.5 |

Dashes indicate data not available.
a. Excludes Bangladesh.
SOURCE: International Economic Data Bank, Australian National University, Canberra.

levels of protection and hence a bias against agriculture. The structure of production in East Asia as compared with the other regions acquired differing characteristics as a result of some thirty years of different government signals. Levels of effective assistance were lowest and had the least variance in open economies such as Singapore and Hong Kong. Taiwan and Korea were moving in the same direction. Over the years the effect was to stimulate entrepreneurs to be efficient and outward-looking.

In the Southeast and East Asian countries, the business culture had developed strongly outward-oriented targets for the individual firm, for industries, and for the economy as a whole. In South Asian and most Latin American countries, in contrast, export orientation remained the exception. The major rewards still came with import substitution. The regulatory frameworks may have appeared to be similar, with protection for import substitution offset by export incentives, but the effectiveness of regulations in terms of openness was different: the ratio of exports to GDP was far higher in most East Asian countries than in other developing countries. The real rate of export growth was similarly higher in East and Southeast Asia. When China changed its economic outlook in the late 1970s, the pursuit of export performance typically became one of its first objectives.

The combination of prudent macroeconomic policies with growth-oriented microeconomic policies has been reflected in relatively high saving and investment ratios in the East and Southeast Asian countries. The countries of Asia and Latin America had reached relatively high investment ratios in the 1960s. All raised investment in the 1970s, with the East and Southeast Asian countries and China registering the largest increases.

Investment in South Asia stabilized in the 1980s. Once the major changes in agricultural policy were completed, there was little incentive to increase investment in the stagnating manufacturing and services sectors, and public resources were not available for increased infrastructural investment. In Latin America, slow growth, high debt service, and political instability led to a decline in the ratio of investment to GDP. In the East and Southeast Asian countries, investment ratios jumped again, reflecting booming economies and rapid growth in public revenue. The growth impetus should thus be maintained unless a major recession reduces world demand or unless political upheavals occur. In China, the freeing up of private and cooperative initiatives, notably in agriculture, has led to very high investment ratios.

East and Southeast Asia's relatively high investment ratios explain only part of their high sectoral and overall growth rates. Policies that lead to relatively small distortions in the production structure have meant better resource allocation and utilization. Capital/labor intensity has been lower and employment growth higher. Shift work tends to be more common, so that although relatively little capital is used, it is used more intensively. Paradoxically, production in export-oriented economies tends to be less imported-input-intensive than in import-substituting ones. Thus not only have more dollars been invested but for each dollar invested the social returns have also been higher in East and Southeast Asia than in other developing economies.

Macroeconomic policies have some microeconomic effects. Financial policies stimulate saving and price stability encourages investment. Similarly, microeconomic policies have macroeconomic effects. Outward-oriented policies in agriculture, manufacturing, and services ease balance-of-payments constraints and require lower levels of intervention in monetary policy. Rapid growth increases public revenues and reduces budget constraints. Macroeconomic and microeconomic policies are thus mutually reinforcing, and the policy framework as a whole has a marked impact on growth. The experience of countries such as Japan and Korea suggests that individual policies can diverge quite considerably from optimal directions without bringing growth to a halt, provided essential directions of openness and growth are maintained by the overall policy framework.

## The International Environment

The international environment plays a role in explaining differences in global growth over time. The protectionism of the 1930s undermined growth, whereas the unprecedented openness of the industrial countries' economies since the Second World War stimulated it, in developing countries as well as in industrial ones. Trade, capital, and labor flows between and into industrial countries have been remarkably free of barriers. Protection against imports from developing countries has largely been limited to clothing, footwear, and textiles, despite the burgeoning of new protectionism in the late 1970s and early 1980s. Migration opportunities have declined. Overall, however, the 1980s have presented developing countries with an opportunity for considerable export growth. In any case, all these countries face the same international environment. The barriers that do exist are mostly directed against the Asian NICs, and yet the latter continue to expand their exports more vigorously than most other developing countries. It seems that the principal obstacles to export growth do not lie in the international economy's biased rules of the game but in the perceptions of the statist and dependencia models that the rules are biased. Uncertainty is engendered, investment is undermined, and exporting fails to take place.

As indicators of long-run as well as short-run export potential and achievement, both the statist and the dependencia models have focused on the movement of the barter terms of trade rather than the

income terms. Barter terms of trade are useful short-term macroeconomic indicators. But for the long run, even if the barter terms could
be measured accurately, they have little analytical value. Countries
seeking to increase exports of agricultural, mineral, and manufactured
goods and services must be concerned with their income terms of
trade—that is, not with relative movements in prices but with the buy-
ing source of export earnings. To increase export earnings, a country
must be highly competitive, and this often means reducing prices
through high productivity, that is, deliberately worsening the barter
terms of trade. This was the approach adopted by the Asian NICs and
other highly motivated exporters such as Thailand and Malaysia. All
these countries focused on increasing efficiency within their export
sectors in order to be able to drop prices against competitors.

From the 1950s onward, the Asian NICs played a seminal role in
the growth of exports of manufactures. By disproving the hypothesis
that developing countries could not compete with industrial countries
in manufactures, they opened the way to rapid growth. By specializing
in highly productive agriculture and in labor-intensive manufactures
along the lines of their comparative advantage, the East and Southeast
Asian countries expanded exports and employment rapidly and reduced balance-of-payments and government budget constraints on
economic growth. By limiting levels of protection, they were able to
welcome private direct foreign investment (DFI) without incurring
high costs. Korea was the principal exception, eschewing private DFI
at considerable cost to its technological development.

Most of the East and Southeast Asian developing countries, like
the Latin American countries, borrowed heavily in international capital markets in the 1970s when world capital markets were liquid and
the real cost of capital was low. Borrowing was, however, very limited
in the South Asian countries, notably in India and China. As an extension of their prudent macroeconomic policies, these countries understood that having chosen repressed financial systems and high
protection with concomitantly low and slowly growing exports, they
had to limit private capital inflows of all types. In Southeast Asia relatively high rates of borrowing caused problems only in the Philippines,
where macroeconomic and microeconomic policy distorted the economy. Several countries experienced liquidity problems when real interest rates rose just as commodity prices were falling in the early 1980s,
but there were no solvency problems. After the difficulties of the 1981–
82 recession, export earnings rose rapidly from a high base. The highly

productive investments of the 1970s brought the benefits of increasing productivity and income. Asia has not experienced debt crises in the 1980s.

Most Latin American countries' experience was more akin to that of the Philippines than to those of the other East and Southeast Asian countries. Repressed financial systems, high protection with low export levels, and low export growth were compounded by capital flight. Inflation continued unabated. Borrowed capital had been used for consumption and, worse still, for unproductive private and public investment. The debt service ratios were much higher than in Asia due to lower export/GDP ratios. Liquidity problems soon turned into solvency crises.

Typically of dependencia postures, policymakers in Latin America blamed international conditions for their debt difficulties and turned toward the industrial countries for the solution to their problems. Taxpayers in industrial countries, however, were not enthusiastic about paying for the debts incurred by extravagant policies. The Latin American debt policies were, not surprisingly, very unsuccessful. Major lenders, whose lack of prudence had contributed markedly to the high level of debt, have finally begun to write off some of their assets, but the action has come late and is still limited. There have been some aid flows to enable countries (notably Bolivia) to write off their debt, but the international initiatives on which much hope has been placed from time to time have not transpired. Sharing the costs of the debt or helping to reduce it by aid flows would at least in part be at the cost of the prudent borrowers of Asia. The cost of the debt burden would thus be transferred from imprudent to prudent borrowers. Attitudes toward the accumulation and servicing of debt thus differ considerably on the two sides of the Pacific.

## Regional Integration and Interregional Relations

In economic terms the role of regional integration is quite clear. The literature abounds with indications that, except in special, narrowly defined circumstances, regional integration is a poor second-best alternative to unilateral and global liberalization such as has taken and is, hopefully, taking place through the General Agreement on Tariffs and Trade (GATT).

The main impetus to regional integration in Europe, Latin America, and Asia has been political. But only very sophisticated countries, such as the members of the Association of Southeast Asian Nations (ASEAN) and, more recently, the South Asian Association for Regional Cooperation (SAARC), have understood this. Even when a regional grouping is largely outward-oriented, as the European Community (EC) has been, inward-oriented policies, such as the community's Common Agricultural Policy, seem irresistible. The truly outward-oriented European Free Trade Agreement (EFTA) has such costs. Some developing countries have benefited partially from the EC's trade diversion policies (Thailand's exports of cassava chips are an example), but the costs in terms of trade foregone for these and other countries have outweighed the benefits by a very considerable margin. And the bureaucratic costs have been enormous. Some 6,000 very highly paid international public servants labor in Brussels, while EFTA is serviced by eighty. It is not clear whether the common market arrangements for the expanded EC to free up all barriers to the movement of capital and labor as well as goods and services will add to global openness or detract from it. The world economy will only benefit if the Uruguay Round can submerge the regional integration aspects in global liberalization.

For developing countries, regional integration has predominantly inward-oriented connotations. It has largely been an outcome of import-substitution policies, which were based on the argument that through import substitution, countries could attain adequate economies of scale. A number of studies have indicated why regional arrangements among developing countries have failed despite considerable and costly inputs by the countries concerned and by the international community. These high costs include the replacement of comparative advantage in external trade by trade diversion within the region (as in the Central American Common Market [CACM]); the inability to share gains equitably among countries at different stages of development, with different economic philosophies and of different size (as in East Africa); the inherent nonviability of industrial plan policies (like those of the Andean Common Market [ANCOM]); and the high cost of complementation schemes (such as the Latin American Free Trade Association's [LAFTA]), whose benefits accrue to transnational corporations. It is not surprising that only ASEAN, which has sought to remain an association for political and economic negotiation and has largely avoided integration, has succeeded. The CACM, the most complete of the developing-country regional schemes, also did the most damage to its constituent countries. Efficient exporting industries were replaced by import substitution for a market of some twenty-three million poor people. The elite—employees in manufacturing and the public service—grew wealthy at the expense of those in rural areas and urban slums, a situation that contributed substantially to the region's wars.

Political cooperation among neighboring (and other) countries is extremely valuable. So is cooperation that facilitates economic flows by unifying customs forms or railway timetables. However, in the face of economic theory and the negative experience of the last thirty years, it is amazing that phrases such as "regional cooperation" or "regional integration" can still start the adrenaline pumping. Taxes squeezed out of the working people in developing and industrial countries continue to be squandered on schemes that have no merit and no future.

What of trade between Asia and Latin America? Is this an economist's question? Goods and services know no nationality. Trade either takes place where goods and services are complementary, exploiting different comparative advantages between or within industries, or where economies of scale and specialization can be achieved by competitive and differentiated products. Trade is taking place for the former reasons to the extent that differences in distance and transport facilities make it feasible and sensible. Trade is not likely to occur for the latter reasons until the countries on both sides of the Pacific liberalize their trade regimes and behave like Hong Kong or Singapore.

# Conclusion

It would be interesting to conjecture about the relative progress of these developing countries—East, Southeast, and South Asia and Latin America—under other conditions. What if East and Southeast Asia had maintained their inward-oriented, highly protected, and inflation-prone policies of the 1950s under the influence of dependencia and statist models? And what if, at the same time, South Asia and Latin America had reformed their economic policies under the influence of the outward-oriented growth model?

The East and Southeast Asian countries would be struggling with poverty. Korea and Thailand would still be among the poorest countries in the world, and these countries would have a heavy burden of debt. Argentines, Brazilians, and other Latin Americans, on the other hand, would be living at standards characteristic of Spain or Singapore. And they would be living ten years longer, on average, than they do now.

The countries of South Asia would have trebled their per capita income. They would no longer be low-income countries. People would be healthier and they would live longer than the forty-five years (Bangladesh) or fifty-six years (India) they tend to live now.

The world economy would be larger and stronger, with greatly increased volumes of international trade, capital, and labor flows. The industrial countries and the NICs (such as India and Brazil) would be able to give greater assistance to the poor countries of East and Southeast Asia and Africa.

# Appendix

## Table A.1
## Population, Area, and Gross Domestic Product (GDP) in Selected Countries, 1986

| | Population (millions) | Area (1,000 km$^2$) | Gross Domestic Product In Millions (US $) | Gross Domestic Product Per Capita[a] (US $) |
|---|---|---|---|---|
| **DEVELOPING COUNTRIES** | | | | |
| **Asia** | | | | |
| Hong Kong | 5.5 | 1 | 37,408 | 6,802 |
| Korea (ROK) | 41.6 | 99 | 98,307 | 2,365 |
| Singapore | 2.6 | 1 | 17,348 | 6,698 |
| Taiwan | 19.4 | 36 | 77,252 | 3,982 |
| Indonesia | 166.9 | 1,919 | 75,232 | 451 |
| Malaysia | 16.1 | 330 | 27,788 | 1,726 |
| Philippines | 56.0 | 300 | 31,009 | 554 |
| Thailand | 52.1 | 542 | 41,766 | 802 |
| Bangladesh | 100.6 | 144 | 15,125 | 150 |
| Burma | 37.3 | 678 | 7,974 | 202 |
| India | 766.1 | 3,288 | 232,170 | 303 |
| Nepal | 17.1 | 147 | 2,361 | 138 |
| Pakistan | 99.2 | 804 | 32,409 | 327 |
| Sri Lanka | 16.1 | 66 | 6,406 | 398 |
| China | 1,050.2 | 9,597 | 225,614[b] | 215[b] |
| **Latin America** | | | | |
| Argentina | 31.0 | 2,767 | 78,798 | 2,542 |
| Barbados | 0.3 | <1 | 1,331 | 5,324 |
| Bolivia | 6.6 | 1,099 | 5,494 | 839 |
| Brazil | 138.5 | 8,512 | 270,026 | 1,950 |

# Table A.1 Continued

| | Population (millions) | Area (1,000 km²) | Gross Domestic Product In Millions (US $) | Gross Domestic Product Per Capita[a] (US $) |
|---|---|---|---|---|
| Chile | 12.3 | 757 | 16,882 | 1,369 |
| Colombia | 29.2 | 1,139 | 34,497 | 1,182 |
| Costa Rica | 2.7 | 51 | 4,425 | 1,657 |
| Dominican Republic | 6.4 | 49 | 5,373 | 837 |
| Ecuador | 9.7 | 284 | 11,128 | 1,153 |
| El Salvador | 4.9 | 21 | 3,953 | 805 |
| Guatemala | 8.2 | 109 | 6,314 | 771 |
| Haiti | 5.4 | 28 | 2,244 | 419 |
| Honduras | 4.5 | 112 | 3,739 | 829 |
| Jamaica | 2.3 | 11 | 2,433 | 1,040 |
| Mexico | 79.6 | 1,973 | 127,136 | 1,598 |
| Panama | 2.2 | 77 | 5,121 | 2,297 |
| Paraguay | 3.8 | 407 | 5,407 | 1,419 |
| Peru | 20.2 | 1,285 | 14,394[c] | 731[c] |
| Trinidad & Tobago | 1.2 | 5 | 5,039[c] | 4,270[c] |
| Uruguay | 3.0 | 176 | 6,218 | 2,086 |
| Venezuela | 17.8 | 912 | 49,962 | 2,808 |
| DEVELOPED COUNTRIES | | | | |
| Japan | 121.5 | 372 | 1,958,913 | 16,124 |
| United States | 241.6 | 9,363 | 4,194,500 | 17,361 |

a. Net material product.
b. 1985.
c. Because of rounding, per capita GDP does not equal GDP (US $ millions) divided by population.
SOURCES: Asian Development Bank, Key Indicators of Developing Member Countries of ADB, July 1987; Hong Kong, Census and Statistics Department, Hong Kong Monthly Digest of Statistics, February 1987; International Monetary Fund, International Financial Statistics, yearbooks 1987 and 1988; Republic of China, Directorate-General of Budget, Accounting and Statistics, Quarterly National Economic Trends; Taiwan Area, Republic of China, February 1987; World Bank, World Development Report, 1987 and 1988.

Table A.2
Growth of Real GDP and Real GDP per Capita in Selected Countries, 1960–86
(compounded annual % change)

| | Real GDP | | | | Real GDP per Capita |
|---|---|---|---|---|---|
| | 1960–70 | 1970–80 | 1980–86 | 1987[a] | 1960–86 |
| **DEVELOPING COUNTRIES** | | | | | |
| **Asia** | | | | | |
| Hong Kong | 9.3 | 8.7 | 6.2 | 13.6 | 5.9 |
| Korea (ROK) | 9.5 | 8.2 | 8.3 | 11.2 | 6.6 |
| Singapore | 9.2 | 9.1 | 5.3 | 8.8 | 6.4 |
| Taiwan | 9.6 | 9.7 | 6.8 | 11.2 | 6.5 |
| Indonesia | 3.8 | 8.0 | 4.3 | 3.5 | 3.1 |
| Malaysia | 6.5 | 7.9 | 4.3 | 4.7 | 3.7 |
| Philippines[b] | 5.2 | 6.3 | -0.6 | 4.6 | 1.5 |
| Thailand | 7.9 | 6.9 | 4.7 | 6.6 | 4.0 |
| Bangladesh | na | 5.8[c] | 3.9 | 4.0[d] | 2.5[e] |
| Burma[f] | 2.8 | 4.2 | 5.0 | 3.0 | 1.8 |
| India[f] | 3.9 | 3.2 | 5.3 | 1.5 | 1.7 |
| Nepal[g] | 2.2 | 2.0 | 3.9 | 2.3 | 0.1 |
| Pakistan[d] | na | 6.9[d] | 6.7 | 7.7 | 2.9[e] |
| Sri Lanka | 5.8 | 4.6 | 5.1 | 3.1 | 3.2 |
| China[h] | 4.0 | 5.7 | 7.6 | 9.3 | 3.6 |

Continued on following page

# Table A.2 Continued

283

| | Real GDP | | | | Real GDP per Capita |
| | 1960–70 | 1970–80 | 1980–86 | 1987[a] | 1960–86 |
|---|---|---|---|---|---|
| **Latin America** | | | | | |
| Argentina | 3.0 | 2.5 | -0.9 | na | 0.2 |
| Barbados | 5.1[i] | 4.7 | -0.6[i] | na | 3.4[k] |
| Bolivia | 5.2 | 4.4 | -2.6 | 1.9 | 0.9 |
| Brazil | na | 8.6 | 2.8[i] | na | 3.6[l] |
| Chile | 4.2 | 2.5 | 0.6 | na | 0.8 |
| Colombia | 5.5 | 5.5 | 2.6 | 5.4 | 2.3 |
| Costa Rica | 6.1 | 5.6 | 1.0 | 3.2 | 1.7 |
| Dominican Republic | 5.0 | 6.9 | 1.6 | 8.1 | 2.0 |
| Ecuador | 5.2 | 8.9 | 2.3 | na | 2.7 |
| El Salvador | 5.6 | 3.2 | -1.4 | 2.7 | 0.3 |
| Guatemala | 5.5 | 5.7 | -0.9 | na | 1.0 |
| Haiti | 0.9 | 4.7 | -0.7 | -0.7 | 0.4 |
| Honduras | 4.9 | 4.6 | 1.3 | 4.2 | 0.4 |
| Jamaica | 4.7 | -0.8 | 0.4 | na | 0.1 |
| Mexico | 7.0 | 6.6 | 0.7 | na | 2.2 |
| Panama | 7.7 | 5.5 | 2.9 | 2.9 | 2.7 |
| Paraguay | 4.3 | 8.6 | 1.9 | 4.3 | 2.2 |
| Peru | 5.7 | 3.5 | -0.5[i] | na | 0.8[m] |
| Trinidad & Tobago | 4.3 | 4.4 | -4.0[i] | na | 1.2[m] |
| Uruguay | 1.7 | 3.0 | -1.6 | 4.9 | 0.8 |
| Venezuela | 6.1 | 4.1 | -0.2 | na | 0.4 |

*Continued on following page*

## Table A.2 Continued

| | Real GDP | | | | Real GDP per Capita |
| --- | --- | --- | --- | --- | --- |
| | 1960–70 | 1970–80 | 1980–86 | 1987[a] | 1960–86 |
| DEVELOPED COUNTRIES | | | | | |
| Japan[b] | 11.7 | 4.7 | 3.7 | 3.7 | 6.0 |
| United States[b] | 3.8 | 2.8 | 2.4 | 2.9 | 1.9 |

na = Not available.
a. Preliminary estimates.
b. GNP.
c. 1973–80.
d. Fiscal year ending June 30.
e. 1973–86.
f. Fiscal year beginning April 1.
g. Fiscal year ending July 15.
h. National income (NI).
i. 1961–70.
j. 1980–85.
k. 1961–85.
l. 1970–85.
m. 1960–85.
SOURCES: Asian Development Bank, Key Indicators of Developing Member Countries of ADB, July 1987; Far Eastern Economic Review, April 14, 1988; International Monetary Fund, International Financial Statistics, yearbooks 1987 and 1988; People's Republic of China, State Statistical Bureau, Statistical Yearbook of China 1987; Republic of China, Directorate-General of Budget, Accounting and Statistics, Statistical Yearbook of the Republic of China, 1987 and 1985 issues; World Bank, World Tables 1980.

## Table A.3
## Projected Real GDP Growth in Selected Countries, 1987–92
### (%)

| | 1987[a] | 1988 | 1989 | 1990 | 1991 | 1992 |
|---|---|---|---|---|---|---|
| | | | Projections (annual rates) | | | |
| WORLD[b] | 3.0 | 2.9 | 2.5 | 2.9 | 3.5 | 3.4 |
| DEVELOPING COUNTRIES[b] | 4.8 | 4.5 | 4.8 | 5.2 | 5.4 | 5.4 |
| **Asia** | | | | | | |
| NICs | | | | | | |
| Hong Kong | 13.6 | 7.7 | 6.5 | 6.1 | 6.6 | 6.9 |
| Korea (ROK)[b] | 12.2 | 8.5 | 6.9 | 7.0 | 7.2 | 7.2 |
| Singapore[b] | 8.8 | 5.4 | 5.2 | 5.0 | 4.8 | 5.5 |
| Taiwan | 12.2 | 7.4 | 6.1 | 7.4 | 7.0 | 7.8 |
| ASEAN-4 | | | | | | |
| Indonesia | 2.9 | 2.9 | 3.0 | 2.6 | 3.6 | 3.0 |
| Malaysia | 2.9 | 2.3 | 1.9 | 2.8 | 3.2 | 4.0 |
| Philippines | 5.0 | 6.2 | 6.5 | 5.1 | 4.9 | 5.0 |
| Thailand | 5.8 | 6.2 | 5.0 | 4.5 | 4.5 | 4.4 |
| South Asia | | | | | | |
| India | 2.4 | 4.9 | 5.3 | 6.0 | 6.3 | 5.5 |
| Pakistan | 5.4 | 4.5 | 4.6 | 4.6 | 4.7 | 4.7 |

*Continued on following page*

# Table A.3 Continued

| | 1987[a] | Projections (annual rates) | | | | |
| | | 1988 | 1989 | 1990 | 1991 | 1992 |
|---|---|---|---|---|---|---|
| **Latin America** | | | | | | |
| Argentina | 1.5 | 3.2 | 3.0 | 2.4 | 3.2 | 3.0 |
| Brazil | 2.7 | 2.7 | 3.5 | 4.6 | 4.7 | 4.6 |
| Chile | 5.4 | 5.5 | 3.3 | 3.1 | 3.9 | 4.9 |
| Colombia | 5.1 | 4.4 | 2.8 | 2.6 | 3.6 | 3.7 |
| Ecuador | -3.0 | 6.1 | 2.8 | 3.0 | 4.0 | 4.0 |
| Mexico | 1.1 | -3.0 | 1.5 | 3.2 | 4.2 | 3.3 |
| Peru | 6.0 | -3.5 | 1.2 | 2.7 | 3.1 | 2.8 |
| Uruguay | 5.6 | 3.5 | 4.1 | 4.0 | 4.2 | 4.1 |
| Venezuela | 3.0 | 0.8 | -1.3 | 1.7 | 2.0 | 3.7 |
| DEVELOPED COUNTRIES[b] | 2.7 | 2.4 | 1.8 | 2.1 | 2.9 | 2.8 |
| Japan | 4.0 | 4.2 | 2.8 | 3.2 | 3.3 | 3.3 |
| United States[b] | 2.9 | 2.4 | 1.3 | 1.6 | 3.4 | 3.0 |

a. Preliminary estimates.
b. GNP.
SOURCE: Lawrence Klein, Peter Pauly, and Kiseok Lee, *Project Link World Outlook*, University of Pennsylvania, April 7, 1988.

## Table A.4
## Structure of GDP in Selected Countries, 1960–86
### (% of GDP at current prices)

| | 1960 | | | | 1970 | | | | 1980 | | | | 1986 | | | |
|---|---|---|---|---|---|---|---|---|---|---|---|---|---|---|---|---|
| | Agr. | Mfg. | Other Ind.[a] | Serv. | Agr. | Mfg. | Other Ind.[a] | Serv. | Agr. | Mfg. | Other Ind.[a] | Serv. | Agr. | Mfg. | Other Ind.[a] | Serv. |
| **DEVELOPING COUNTRIES** | | | | | | | | | | | | | | | | |
| **Asia** | | | | | | | | | | | | | | | | |
| Hong Kong | 3 | 22 | 11 | 61 | 2 | 28 | 7 | 59 | 1 | 22 | 8 | 65 | 1[b] | 22[b] | 8[b] | 70[b] |
| Korea (ROK) | 37 | 14 | 6 | 43 | 26 | 21 | 8 | 45 | 15 | 30 | 11 | 44 | 12 | 30 | 12 | 45 |
| Singapore | 4 | 12 | 6 | 79 | 2 | 20 | 10 | 67 | 1 | 30 | 9 | 60 | 1 | 27 | 11 | 62 |
| Taiwan | 29 | 22 | 7 | 42 | 16 | 34 | 7 | 43 | 8 | 42 | 9 | 41 | 6 | 43 | 12 | 45 |
| Indonesia | 51 | 9 | 6 | 33 | 45 | 10 | 9 | 36 | 24 | 13 | 29 | 34 | 26 | 14 | 18 | 42 |
| Malaysia[c] | 33 | 8 | 10 | 49 | 29 | 12 | 13 | 46 | 22 | 21 | 17 | 40 | 21 | 17 | 20 | 42 |
| Philippines | 26 | 20 | 8 | 46 | 28 | 23 | 7 | 43 | 23 | 24 | 13 | 40 | 26 | 25 | 7 | 42 |
| Thailand | 40 | 13 | 6 | 41 | 28 | 16 | 9 | 46 | 25 | 20 | 9 | 46 | 17 | 21 | 9 | 53 |
| Bangladesh | 57 | 5 | 2 | 36 | 55 | 6 | 3 | 37 | 50 | 10 | 5 | 35 | 47 | 8 | 6 | 39 |
| Burma | 33 | 8 | 4 | 55 | 38 | 10 | 4 | 48 | 47 | 10 | 3 | 41 | 48 | 10 | 3 | 39 |
| India | 47 | 13 | 6 | 28 | 43 | 13 | 7 | 28 | 34 | 15 | 7 | 33 | 27 | 14 | 10 | 39 |
| Nepal | 65[d] | 3[d] | 8[d] | 23[d] | 67 | 4 | 7 | 21 | 58 | 4 | 7 | 25 | 62[e] | 8[e] | 4[e] | 26[e] |
| Pakistan | 44 | 11 | 4 | 36 | 33 | 15 | 5 | 37 | 27 | 14 | 8 | 41 | 22 | 16 | 9 | 43 |
| Sri Lanka | 32 | 15 | 5 | 48 | 27 | 16 | 7 | 46 | 26 | 17 | 11 | 40 | 23 | 13 | 11 | 23 |
| China | 23 | na | 48 | 29 | 35 | 32 | 9 | 24 | 32 | 35 | 13 | 20 | 31 | 34 | 12 | 23 |
| **Latin America** | | | | | | | | | | | | | | | | |
| Argentina | 18 | 27 | 10 | 45 | 11 | 26 | 9 | 42 | 7 | 21 | 10 | 46 | 11 | 27 | 12 | 39 |
| Bolivia | 26 | 15 | 10 | 49 | 20 | 13 | 19 | 48 | 18 | 14 | 15 | 53 | 24 | 13 | 10 | 52 |

Continued on following page

# Table A.4 Continued

| | 1960 | | | | 1970 | | | | 1980 | | | | 1986 | | | |
|---|---|---|---|---|---|---|---|---|---|---|---|---|---|---|---|---|
| | Agr. | Mfg. | Other Ind.[a] | Serv. | Agr. | Mfg. | Other Ind.[a] | Serv. | Agr. | Mfg. | Other Ind.[a] | Serv. | Agr. | Mfg. | Other Ind.[a] | Serv. |
| Brazil | 16 | 23 | 6 | 42 | 10 | 25 | 7 | 41 | 10 | 28 | 9 | 43 | 10[b] | 26[b] | 10[b] | 46[b] |
| Chile | 9 | 21 | 14 | 56 | 7 | 26 | 15 | 52 | 7 | 21 | 16 | 55 | 6[f] | 21[f] | 18[f] | 56[f] |
| Colombia | 31 | 16 | 8 | 40 | 25 | 16 | 7 | 44 | 19 | 17 | 8 | 46 | 18 | 16 | 6 | 50 |
| Costa Rica | 26 | 14 | 6 | 54 | 23 | na | 24 | 53 | 17 | 20 | 9 | 54 | 21 | na | 29 | 50 |
| Dominican Republic | 27 | 17 | 6 | 50 | 20 | 20 | 8 | 51 | 18 | 15 | 12 | 55 | 17 | 16 | 14 | 53 |
| Ecuador | 26 | 16 | 4 | 54 | 24 | 18 | 7 | 51 | 12 | 18 | 20 | 50 | 14[b] | 19[b] | 23[b] | 45[b] |
| El Salvador | 32 | 15 | 4 | 49 | na | na | na | na | 27 | 15 | 6 | 52 | 20 | 15 | 6 | 59 |
| Honduras | 37 | 13 | 6 | 44 | 32 | 14 | 8 | 45 | 31 | 17 | 8 | 44 | 27 | 14 | 11 | 48 |
| Jamaica | 10 | 15 | 21 | 54 | na | na | na | na | 8 | 15 | 22 | 55 | 6 | 22 | 18 | 54 |
| Mexico | 16 | 19 | 10 | 55 | 12 | 24 | 9 | 55 | 8 | 23 | 14 | 54 | 11[b] | na[b] | 35[b] | 54[b] |
| Panama | 23 | 13 | 8 | 56 | 15 | 12 | 9 | 64 | na | na | na | na | 9 | 8 | 10 | 73 |
| Paraguay | 36 | 17 | 3 | 44 | 32 | 17 | 4 | 47 | 30 | 17 | 8 | 45 | 27 | 16 | 10 | 47 |
| Peru | 21 | 20 | 12 | 47 | 20 | 20 | 13 | 47 | 10 | 20 | 22 | 48 | 11[b] | 20[b] | 18[b] | 51[b] |
| Trinidad & Tobago | 8 | 24 | 22 | 46 | na | na | na | na | na | na | na | na | 5 | 8 | 27 | 59 |
| Uruguay | 18 | na | 26 | 49 | 11 | na | 25 | 51 | 10 | na | 28 | 48 | 10 | na | 28 | 48 |
| Venezuela | 6 | 0 | 42 | 52 | 7 | 16 | 23 | 54 | 6 | 16 | 31 | 47 | 9 | 23 | 14 | 54 |
| DEVELOPED COUNTRIES | | | | | | | | | | | | | | | | |
| Japan | 13 | 34 | 11 | 43 | 6 | 36 | 11 | 47 | 4 | 29 | 13 | 54 | 3 | 10 | 11 | 56 |
| United States | 4 | 28 | 10 | 58 | 3 | 25 | 9 | 63 | 3 | 22 | 12 | 64 | 2 | 20 | 11 | 67 |

na = Not available.
a. Includes mining, utilities, and construction.
b. 1985.
c. Constant 1970 or 1978 prices.
d. 1965.
e. 1984.
f. 1983.

SOURCES: Asian Development Bank, Key Indicators of Developing Member Countries of ADB, July 1987; Republic of China, Directorate-General of Budget, Accounting, and Statistics, Statistical Yearbook of the Republic of China, 1987; World Bank, computer data tapes, 1988; World Bank, World Development Report, 1982 and 1988.

## Table A.5
## Domestic Savings and Investment Rates in Selected Countries, 1970 and 1986
### (% of GDP)

| | Gross Domestic Savings | | Gross Domestic Investment | | Resource Gap | |
|---|---|---|---|---|---|---|
| | 1970 | 1986 | 1970 | 1986 | 1970 | 1986 |
| **DEVELOPING COUNTRIES** | | | | | | |
| **Asia** | | | | | | |
| Hong Kong | 25 | 27 | 21 | 23 | 4 | 4 |
| Korea (ROK) | 15 | 35 | 25 | 29 | -10 | 6 |
| Singapore | 18 | 40 | 39 | 40 | -20 | -0 |
| Taiwan | 26 | 36 | 26 | 17 | -0 | 20 |
| Indonesia | 14 | 24 | 16 | 26 | -2 | -2 |
| Malaysia | 27 | 32 | 22 | 25 | 4 | 6 |
| Philippines | 21 | 19 | 21 | 13 | -0 | 6 |
| Thailand | 21 | 25 | 26 | 21 | -5 | 4 |
| Bangladesh | 7 | 3 | 11 | 13 | -4 | -10 |
| Burma | 11 | 12 | 14 | 15 | -4 | -3 |
| India | 17 | 23 | 18 | 25 | -1 | -2 |
| Nepal | 3 | 9 | 6 | 19 | -3 | -10 |
| Pakistan | 9 | 7 | 16 | 17 | -7 | -10 |
| Sri Lanka | 16 | 13 | 19 | 24 | -3 | -11 |
| China | 29 | 36 | 29 | 39 | 0 | -3 |
| **Latin America** | | | | | | |
| Argentina | 22 | 11 | 22 | 9 | 0 | 2 |
| Bolivia | 24 | 5 | 24 | 8 | 0 | -3 |
| Brazil | 20 | 24 | 21 | 21 | -0 | 3 |
| Chile | 17 | 18 | 16 | 15 | 1 | 4 |

*Continued on following page*

# Table A.5 Continued

| | Gross Domestic Savings | | Gross Domestic Investment | | Resource Gap | |
|---|---|---|---|---|---|---|
| | 1970 | 1986 | 1970 | 1986 | 1970 | 1986 |
| Colombia | 18 | 20 | 20 | 18 | -2 | 3 |
| Costa Rica | 14 | 24 | 21 | 23 | -7 | 1 |
| Dominican Republic | 11 | 12[a] | 21 | 18[a] | -10 | -6[a] |
| Ecuador | 14 | 20 | 18 | 20 | -5 | -1 |
| El Savador | 13 | 7 | 13 | 13 | 0 | -6 |
| Guatemala | 14 | 9[a] | 13 | 11[a] | 1 | -2[a] |
| Haiti | 7 | 6 | 11 | 12 | -4 | -6 |
| Honduras | 15 | 13[a] | 21 | 17[a] | -6 | -4[a] |
| Mexico | 21 | 27[a] | 23 | 21[a] | -2 | 5[a] |
| Nicaragua | 16 | -2[a] | 19 | 19[a] | -2 | -21[a] |
| Panama | 24 | 21 | 28 | 17 | -3 | 3 |
| Paraguay | 14 | -4 | 15 | 17 | -1 | -21 |
| Peru | 24 | 18 | 22 | 20 | 2 | -1 |
| Uruguay | 10 | 13 | 11 | 8 | -1 | 5 |
| Venezuela | 34 | 21 | 30 | 20 | 5 | 1 |
| DEVELOPED COUNTRIES | | | | | | |
| Japan | 40 | 32 | 39 | 28 | 1 | 4 |
| United States | 18 | 15 | 18 | 18 | 0 | -3 |

na = Not available.
a. 1985.
SOURCES: Republic of China, Council for Economic Planning and Development, *Taiwan Statistical Data Book 1987*; World Bank, computer data tapes, 1988.

**Table A.6**
**Distribution of World Exports, 1960–86**
**(billions of U.S. dollars and % of world exports)**

| | 1960 | 1970 | 1980 | 1986 |
|---|---|---|---|---|
| WORLD | $120.6 | $290.4 | $1,896.7 | $1,992.1 |
| DEVELOPED COUNTRIES | | | | |
| Japan | 3.4% | 6.7% | 6.9% | 10.6% |
| United States | 17.1 | 14.9 | 11.6 | 10.9 |
| Other Developed Countries | 49.1 | 54.2 | 46.8 | 51.9 |
| DEVELOPING COUNTRIES | | | | |
| Africa | 5.8% | 4.5% | 5.0% | 2.7% |
| Asia | 8.8 | 6.0 | 8.6 | 11.5 |
| NICs | 1.7 | 2.2 | 4.0 | 6.6 |
| ASEAN-4 | 2.5 | 1.6 | 2.5 | 2.1 |
| South Asia | 1.9 | 1.0 | 0.7 | 0.8 |
| China | 2.1 | 0.8 | 1.0 | 1.6 |
| Middle East | 4.0 | 4.5 | 12.6 | 4.7 |
| Western Hemisphere | 7.7 | 5.5 | 5.5 | 4.2 |
| Other Developing Countries | 4.2 | 3.8 | 3.0 | 3.5 |

SOURCE: International Monetary Fund, International Financial Statistics, yearbook 1987 and August 1988.

## Table A.7
## Merchandise Trade Balance in Selected Countries, Selected Years, 1970–86
(millions of U.S. dollars)

| | 1970 | 1975 | 1980 | 1981 | 1982 | 1983 | 1984 | 1985 | 1986 |
|---|---|---|---|---|---|---|---|---|---|
| DEVELOPING COUNTRIES | -6,985 | 5,963 | 80,801 | 17,275 | -15,714 | -15,013 | 5,693 | -8,220 | -25,224 |
| **Asia** | | | | | | | | | |
| Hong Kong | -391 | -739 | -2,679 | -2,957 | -2,569 | -2,059 | -250 | 479 | 74 |
| Korea (ROK) | -1,149 | -2,193 | -4,787 | -4,877 | -2,398 | -1,747 | -1,386 | -846 | 3,130 |
| Singapore | -907 | -2,758 | -4,628 | -6,605 | -7,379 | -6,325 | -4,597 | -3,473 | -3,002 |
| Taiwan | -43 | -643 | 78 | 1,411 | 3,316 | 4,836 | 8,497 | 10,621 | 15,625 |
| Indonesia | 106 | 2,332 | 11,075 | 8,988 | 5,434 | 4,800 | 8,020 | 8,331 | 4,100 |
| Malaysia | 286 | 277 | 2,166 | 220 | -388 | 842 | 2,433 | 3,139 | 3,045 |
| Philippines | -195 | -1,462 | -2,554 | -2,824 | -3,295 | -3,086 | -1,158 | -852 | -624 |
| Thailand | -589 | -1,072 | -2,709 | -2,924 | -1,604 | -3,919 | -2,985 | -2,121 | -384 |
| Bangladesh | na | -994 | -1,841 | -1,908 | -1,694 | -1,441 | -1,894 | -1,773 | -1,822 |
| Brunei | 11 | 776 | 4,009 | 3,443 | 3,063 | 2,645 | 2,561 | 2,328 | na |
| Burma | -61 | -94 | -313 | -348 | -15 | 110 | 140 | 47 | -5 |
| India | -98 | -2,026 | -6,278 | -7,123 | -5,428 | -4,913 | -5,622 | -6,876 | -5,978 |
| Nepal | -33 | -71 | -262 | -229 | -307 | -370 | -288 | -293 | -317 |
| Pakistan | -334 | -1,106 | -2,732 | -2,748 | -3,068 | -2,252 | -3,295 | -3,150 | -1,990 |
| Sri Lanka | -44 | -188 | -995 | -817 | -984 | -872 | -402 | -655 | -733 |
| China | 28 | -237 | -1,842 | -170 | 2,972 | 841 | -1,119 | -15,199 | -12,024 |

*Continued on following page*

## Table A.7 Continued

| | 1970 | 1975 | 1980 | 1981 | 1982 | 1983 | 1984 | 1985 | 1986 |
|---|---|---|---|---|---|---|---|---|---|
| **Latin America** | | | | | | | | | |
| Argentina | 79 | -986 | -2,520 | -287 | 2,288 | 3,332 | 3,522 | 4,582 | na |
| Barbados | -73 | -109 | -296 | -378 | -294 | -300 | -268 | -255 | -312 |
| Bolivia | 31 | -131 | 264 | -63 | 250 | 166 | 233 | 71 | na |
| Brazil | -110 | -4,922 | -4,829 | -786 | -894 | 5,098 | 11,795 | 11,307 | na |
| Chile | 308 | 214 | -453 | -2,458 | 181 | 1,082 | 466 | 1,080 | 1,308 |
| Colombia | -107 | -30 | -718 | -2,243 | -2,383 | -1,887 | -1,036 | -589 | 1,240 |
| Costa Rica | -86 | -201 | -538 | -201 | -19 | -106 | 524 | -122 | -30 |
| Dominican Republic | -55 | 5 | -678 | -480 | -676 | -686 | -578 | -752 | -715 |
| Ecuador | -84 | -13 | 228 | 205 | 139 | 759 | 867 | 1,299 | 368 |
| El Salvador | 22 | -67 | 112 | -188 | -158 | -156 | -252 | -282 | -145 |
| Guatemala | 14 | -92 | -41 | -420 | -235 | 45 | -150 | -115 | 513 |
| Haiti | -15 | -69 | -180 | -306 | -222 | -239 | -271 | -268 | 164 |
| Honduras | -40 | -101 | -190 | -191 | -62 | -124 | -208 | -108 | na |
| Jamaica | -183 | -365 | -208 | -499 | -646 | -767 | -416 | -575 | -368 |
| Mexico | -1,058 | -3,666 | -3,890 | -4,422 | 6,086 | 13,796 | 12,619 | 8,115 | 4,240 |
| Panama | -248 | -606 | -1,089 | -1,212 | -1,194 | -1,091 | -1,147 | -1,057 | 341 |
| Paraguay | -12 | -29 | -305 | -304 | -342 | -277 | -251 | -198 | -343 |
| Peru | 412 | -1,260 | 1,398 | -456 | -447 | -327 | 935 | 956 | -320 |
| Trinidad & Tobago | -62 | 302 | 899 | 636 | -625 | -229 | 254 | 613 | 43 |

*Continued on following page*

**Table A.7 Continued**

| | 1970 | 1975 | 1980 | 1981 | 1982 | 1983 | 1984 | 1985 | 1986 |
|---|---|---|---|---|---|---|---|---|---|
| Uruguay | 2 | -172 | -621 | -426 | -87 | 257 | 148 | 147 | 268 |
| Venezuela | 758 | 2,796 | 7,394 | 7,019 | 3,555 | 6,449 | 6,377 | 4,304 | 540 |
| DEVELOPED COUNTRIES | | | | | | | | | |
| Japan | 437 | -2,041 | -10,855 | 8,629 | 6,886 | 20,528 | 33,524 | 46,676 | 83,204 |
| United States | 546 | 2,232 | -36,198 | -39,613 | -42,608 | -69,340 | -123,289 | -148,483 | -169,774 |

na = Not available.
SOURCES: International Monetary Fund, *International Financial Statistics, yearbook 1987*; Republic of China, Council for Economic Planning and Development, *Taiwan Statistical Data Book 1987*.

**Table A.8**
**Annual Growth of Merchandise Exports in Selected Countries, 1960–86[a] (%)**

| | 1960–70 | 1970–80 | 1980–86 | 1981 | 1982 | 1983 | 1984 | 1985 | 1986 |
|---|---|---|---|---|---|---|---|---|---|
| WORLD | 9.2 | 20.6 | 0.8 | -1.7 | -7.2 | -2.7 | 5.9 | 0.8 | 10.8 |
| DEVELOPING COUNTRIES | 6.5 | 24.9 | -4.4 | -2.3 | -11.4 | -6.3 | 3.6 | -5.1 | -4.2 |
| **Asia** | | | | | | | | | |
| Hong Kong | 13.8 | 22.9 | 10.3 | 10.5 | -3.8 | 4.6 | 29.0 | 6.6 | 17.4 |
| Korea (ROK) | 38.1 | 35.6 | 12.1 | 21.4 | 2.8 | 11.9 | 19.6 | 3.5 | 14.6 |
| Singapore | 3.2 | 28.7 | 2.5 | 8.2 | -0.9 | 5.0 | 10.2 | -5.2 | -1.3 |
| Taiwan | 24.6 | 29.6 | 12.3 | 14.1 | -1.8 | 13.1 | 21.2 | 0.9 | 29.5 |
| Indonesia | 2.8 | 34.8 | -6.3 | 1.6 | 0.1 | -5.1 | 3.5 | -15.1 | -20.3 |
| Malaysia | 3.6 | 22.6 | 1.2 | -9.1 | 2.2 | 17.2 | 16.9 | -6.3 | -10.1 |
| Philippines | 5.3 | 18.6 | -3.0 | -1.5 | -12.1 | -1.6 | 7.9 | -12.6 | 3.5 |
| Thailand | 5.6 | 24.8 | 5.2 | 8.1 | -1.2 | -8.3 | 16.4 | -3.9 | 23.5 |
| Bangladesh | na | 14.3[b] | 2.5 | 4.4 | -2.8 | -5.9 | 28.6 | 7.3 | -11.9 |
| Burma | -7.0 | 15.9 | -7.3 | 1.1 | -17.4 | -4.1 | 0.3 | -12.9 | -9.4 |
| India | 4.3 | 15.5 | 1.4 | -3.4 | 12.8 | -2.2 | 3.2 | -15.3 | 16.9 |
| Nepal | 1.4[c] | 6.7 | 10.0 | 75.0 | -37.1 | 6.8 | 36.2 | 25.0 | -11.3 |
| Pakistan | 0.1 | 20.8 | 4.4 | 10.1 | -16.9 | 28.4 | -16.9 | 7.1 | 23.5 |
| Sri Lanka | -1.2 | 12.0 | 2.3 | 2.4 | -5.2 | 3.1 | 38.0 | -9.1 | -8.9 |
| China | -1.1 | 22.9 | 9.5 | 18.6 | 1.9 | 1.4 | 12.0 | 10.1 | 14.0 |

*Continued on following page*

# Table A.8 Continued

| | 1960–70 | 1970–80 | 1980–86 | 1981 | 1982 | 1983 | 1984 | 1985 | 1986 |
|---|---|---|---|---|---|---|---|---|---|
| **Latin America** | | | | | | | | | |
| Argentina | 5.1 | 16.3 | 0.9[d] | 14.0 | -16.6 | 2.8 | 3.5 | 3.6 | na |
| Barbados | 5.2 | 18.9 | 3.3 | -14.2 | 32.5 | 24.9 | 21.8 | -11.3 | -20.7 |
| Bolivia | 10.6[e] | 17.4 | -8.2 | -3.2 | -9.2 | -8.8 | -4.0 | -14.1 | -9.5 |
| Brazil | 8.0 | 22.1 | 1.8 | 15.7 | -13.4 | 8.5 | 23.3 | -5.1 | -12.7 |
| Chile | 9.9 | 14.1 | -1.7 | -16.4 | -5.0 | 3.4 | -4.7 | 4.5 | 10.4 |
| Colombia | 4.7 | 18.3 | 4.4 | -25.1 | 4.7 | -0.5 | 12.4 | 2.6 | 43.6 |
| Costa Rica | 10.6 | 15.8 | 1.9 | 0.6 | -13.7 | 0.3 | 15.2 | -3.0 | 14.9 |
| Dominican Republic | 3.3 | 14.5 | -4.8 | 23.5 | -35.4 | 2.2 | 10.6 | -15.3 | -2.3 |
| Ecuador | 2.7 | 29.3 | -2.1 | -1.2 | -13.2 | 4.5 | 16.1 | 12.5 | -24.9 |
| El Salvador | 7.3 | 16.4 | -5.7 | -25.8 | -12.3 | 5.2 | -1.4 | -6.3 | 11.5 |
| Guatemala | 9.9 | 18.0 | -5.6 | -19.5 | -8.1 | 3.2 | -4.5 | -7.3 | 4.6 |
| Haiti | 1.9 | 18.9 | -3.2 | -32.7 | 7.2 | -5.5 | 16.2 | -2.8 | 6.9 |
| Honduras | 11.1 | 16.5 | 0.5 | -12.2 | -8.4 | 0.4 | 11.2 | 2.5 | 11.6 |
| Jamaica | 8.0 | 10.9 | -7.7 | 1.1 | -25.5 | -1.8 | 0.1 | -23.1 | 8.6 |
| Mexico | 6.3 | 27.2 | 0.7 | 26.2 | 8.0 | 2.9 | 11.9 | -9.4 | -26.6 |
| Panama | 14.6 | 12.7 | -0.5 | -8.9 | 14.3 | -14.4 | -14.0 | 21.4 | 4.5 |
| Paraguay | 9.0 | 17.1 | -4.6 | -4.5 | 11.5 | -18.5 | 24.5 | -9.3 | -23.0 |
| Peru | 8.8 | 14.2 | -7.1 | -2.5 | -2.1 | -26.8 | 15.6 | -5.3 | -15.8 |
| Trinidad & Tobago | 5.3 | 23.8 | -16.5 | -7.8 | -18.3 | -23.4 | -7.6 | -0.6 | -36.2 |
| Uruguay | 6.1 | 16.3 | 0.5 | 14.7 | -15.8 | 2.2 | -11.5 | -7.6 | 27.3 |
| Venezuela | 1.3 | 22.0 | -10.2 | 4.7 | -18.0 | -8.1 | -7.8 | -10.3 | -19.7 |

*Continued on following page*

# Table A.8 Continued

| | 1960–70 | 1970–80 | 1980–86 | 1981 | 1982 | 1983 | 1984 | 1985 | 1986 |
|---|---|---|---|---|---|---|---|---|---|
| **DEVELOPED COUNTRIES** | | | | | | | | | |
| Japan | 16.9 | 21.0 | 8.3 | 16.1 | -8.7 | 6.2 | 15.5 | 4.4 | 19.0 |
| United States | 7.7 | 17.7 | -0.3 | 5.9 | -9.2 | -5.5 | 8.7 | -2.2 | 2.0 |

na = Not available.
a. Compounded annual growth of merchandise trade expressed in U.S. dollars and current prices.
b. 1972–80.
c. 1963–70.
d. 1980–85.
e. 1966–70.

SOURCES: International Monetary Fund, *International Financial Statistics, yearbook 1987*; Republic of China, Council for Economic Planning and Development, *Taiwan Statistical Data Book, 1987*.

## Table A.9
## Annual Growth of Merchandise Imports in Selected Countries, 1960–86[a] (%)

| | 1960–70 | 1970–80 | 1980–86 | 1981 | 1982 | 1983 | 1984 | 1985 | 1986 |
|---|---|---|---|---|---|---|---|---|---|
| WORLD | 9.2 | 20.4 | 1.0 | -0.9 | -6.3 | -3.0 | 6.3 | 1.8 | 9.0 |
| DEVELOPING COUNTRIES | 6.5 | 22.0 | -1.4 | 8.8 | -6.3 | -6.2 | -0.4 | -2.5 | -0.8 |
| **Asia** | | | | | | | | | |
| Hong Kong | 11.0 | 22.7 | 7.9 | 10.5 | -4.9 | 2.0 | 19.0 | 4.0 | 19.1 |
| Korea (ROK) | 22.4 | 27.0 | 6.0 | 17.2 | -7.2 | 8.0 | 16.9 | 1.6 | 1.5 |
| Singapore | 6.3 | 25.6 | 1.0 | 14.9 | 2.2 | -0.0 | 1.8 | -8.3 | -2.9 |
| Taiwan | 17.8 | 29.2 | 3.4 | 7.4 | -10.9 | 7.4 | 8.2 | -8.5 | 20.2 |
| Indonesia | 5.7 | 26.9 | -0.2 | 22.5 | 27.0 | -3.0 | -15.1 | -26.1 | 4.5 |
| Malaysia | 4.4 | 22.6 | 0.1 | 7.2 | 7.5 | 6.8 | 5.9 | -12.4 | -12.0 |
| Philippines | 5.6 | 21.0 | -6.9 | 2.2 | -2.5 | -3.5 | -19.4 | -15.1 | -1.2 |
| Thailand | 11.3 | 21.6 | -0.1 | 8.0 | -14.1 | 20.3 | 1.1 | -11.1 | -0.7 |
| Bangladesh | na | 18.2[b] | 0.6 | 3.8 | -8.7 | -12.1 | 30.5 | -1.9 | -2.5 |
| Burma | -4.2 | 16.6 | -14.6 | 5.1 | -50.4 | -34.5 | -10.8 | 18.4 | 7.4 |
| India | -0.8 | 21.5 | 0.5 | 3.7 | -4.1 | -4.9 | 7.2 | -1.2 | 3.0 |
| Nepal | -0.7[c] | 16.4 | 5.0 | 7.9 | 7.0 | 17.5 | -10.3 | 8.9 | 1.3 |
| Pakistan | 1.1 | 22.0 | 0.1 | 5.3 | -2.9 | -2.5 | 9.8 | 0.6 | -8.8 |
| Sri Lanka | -0.7 | 18.2 | -0.9 | -7.4 | 5.8 | -4.0 | -3.4 | 6.4 | -2.0 |
| China | -1.5 | 24.2 | 13.7 | 8.5 | -12.6 | 12.9 | 21.6 | 63.9 | 1.5 |

*Continued on following page*

**Table A.9 Continued**

Continued on following page

| | 1960–70 | 1970–80 | 1980–86 | 1981 | 1982 | 1983 | 1984 | 1985 | 1986 |
|---|---|---|---|---|---|---|---|---|---|
| **Latin America** | | | | | | | | | |
| Argentina | 3.1 | 20.1 | -18.4[d] | -10.5 | -43.4 | -15.6 | 1.8 | -16.8 | na |
| Barbados | 8.7 | 16.5 | 2.0 | 9.6 | -3.7 | 12.7 | 6.1 | -7.9 | -3.3 |
| Bolivia | 8.4 | 15.6 | 0.9 | 43.8 | -40.7 | 1.9 | -16.5 | 12.2 | 29.7 |
| Brazil | 6.9 | 24.2 | -10.5[d] | -3.5 | -12.5 | -20.3 | -9.5 | -5.8 | na |
| Chile | 6.4 | 20.6 | -9.0 | 24.2 | -44.5 | -22.0 | 15.9 | -14.0 | 6.2 |
| Colombia | 5.0 | 18.7 | -3.1 | 11.5 | 5.4 | -9.3 | -9.5 | -7.9 | -6.7 |
| Costa Rica | 11.2 | 17.1 | -4.7 | -21.5 | -26.5 | 11.1 | 10.7 | 0.4 | 5.2 |
| Dominican Republic | 11.8 | 18.4 | -2.2 | 1.7 | -13.4 | 1.9 | -1.7 | 2.8 | -3.6 |
| Ecuador | 9.2 | 23.5 | -3.5 | -0.3 | -11.4 | -26.3 | 17.1 | -6.4 | 13.0 |
| El Salvador | 5.8 | 16.2 | -1.1 | 2.4 | -13.0 | 4.0 | 9.7 | -1.6 | -6.1 |
| Guatemala | 8.9 | 18.9 | -14.6 | 4.8 | -17.1 | -18.2 | 12.5 | -8.0 | -47.3 |
| Haiti | 3.2 | 21.2 | 3.3[d] | 22.9 | -13.2 | 1.3 | 11.1 | -1.8 | na |
| Honduras | 11.9 | 16.8 | -2.8 | -6.3 | -24.2 | 11.4 | 15.9 | -6.9 | -1.5 |
| Jamaica | 9.2 | 8.4 | -3.2 | 25.8 | -6.9 | 7.9 | -23.6 | -0.5 | -14.2 |
| Mexico | 7.6 | 23.0 | -7.7 | 23.7 | -37.1 | -47.0 | 46.9 | 18.7 | -14.3 |
| Panama | 11.5 | 15.0 | -2.7 | 6.3 | 1.9 | -10.0 | 0.8 | -2.2 | -11.7 |
| Paraguay | 7.2 | 23.3 | -1.1 | -2.4 | 12.0 | -18.8 | 7.3 | -14.3 | 14.9 |
| Peru | 5.1 | 14.9 | 2.1 | 70.3 | -2.1 | -26.8 | -27.5 | -8.5 | 39.8 |
| Trinidad & Tobago | 6.3 | 19.3 | -13.5 | -1.7 | 18.3 | -30.2 | -25.7 | -16.8 | -16.5 |
| Uruguay | 0.6 | 21.9 | -11.3 | -2.3 | -32.4 | -29.0 | -1.4 | -8.9 | 15.8 |
| Venezuela | 4.6 | 20.3 | -3.5 | 10.8 | -1.2 | -32.7 | -12.8 | 8.4 | 15.7 |

**Table A.9 Continued**

| | 1960–70 | 1970–80 | 1980–86 | 1981 | 1982 | 1983 | 1984 | 1985 | 1986 |
|---|---|---|---|---|---|---|---|---|---|
| DEVELOPED COUNTRIES | | | | | | | | | |
| Japan | 15.4 | 22.3 | –1.7 | 1.1 | –8.0 | –3.8 | 7.7 | –4.2 | –2.2 |
| United States | 10.1 | 19.7 | 7.1 | 6.4 | –6.8 | 5.9 | 26.4 | 6.0 | 7.0 |

na = Not available.
a. Compounded annual growth of merchandise trade expressed in U.S. dollars and current prices.
b. 1972–80.
c. 1963–70.
d. 1980–85.
SOURCES: International Monetary Fund, *International Financial Statistics*, yearbook 1987; Republic of China, Council for Economic Planning and Development, *Taiwan Statistical Data Book, 1987.*

## Table A.10
## Ratio of Exports and Imports to GDP, 1970, 1978, and 1986
### (% at current prices)

| | Exports | | | Imports | | |
|---|---|---|---|---|---|---|
| | 1970 | 1978 | 1986 | 1970 | 1978 | 1986 |
| **DEVELOPING COUNTRIES** | | | | | | |
| **Asia** | | | | | | |
| Hong Kong | 92.9 | 84.6 | 111.3 | 89.4 | 88.1 | 107.0 |
| Korea (ROK) | 14.0 | 30.3 | 40.9 | 23.6 | 33.3 | 35.1 |
| Singapore[a] | 81.9 | 128.9 | 129.8 | 129.8 | 166.0 | 147.0 |
| Taiwan | 29.7 | 52.4 | 60.4 | 29.7 | 45.9 | 40.8 |
| Indonesia | 12.8 | 21.7 | 20.8 | 15.8 | 14.8 | 22.7 |
| Malaysia | 46.1 | 49.1 | 56.8 | 44.4 | 43.5 | 51.1 |
| Philippines | 19.1 | 18.2 | 24.7 | 19.4 | 23.3 | 18.5 |
| Thailand | 16.7 | 21.5 | 28.2 | 21.5 | 25.5 | 25.0 |
| Bangladesh | 6.0[b] | 5.5 | 6.5 | 5.0[b] | 14.0 | 14.5 |
| Burma | 5.6 | 5.8 | 5.0 | 8.2 | 10.1 | 7.7 |
| India | 4.4 | 7.3 | 6.6[c] | 4.5 | 7.6 | 8.0[c] |
| Nepal | 4.9 | 5.6 | 6.0 | 8.7 | 13.6 | 19.5 |
| Pakistan | 7.6 | 9.4 | 11.7 | 10.3 | 18.5 | 19.2 |
| Sri Lanka | 25.5 | 34.8 | 23.7 | 28.6 | 39.5 | 35.3 |
| China[d,e] | 2.9 | 5.6 | 13.9 | 2.9 | 6.2 | 19.2 |

*Continued on following page*

# Table A.10 Continued

|  | Exports | | | Imports | | |
|---|---|---|---|---|---|---|
|  | 1970 | 1978 | 1986 | 1970 | 1978 | 1986 |
| **Latin America** | | | | | | |
| Argentina | na | 11.5 | 14.7[f] | na | 7.7 | 9.8[f] |
| Barbados | na | 58.1 | 59.1 | na | 68.3 | 52.7 |
| Bolivia | 20.2 | 22.6 | 23.8 | 20.2 | 30.1 | 25.6 |
| Brazil | 7.1 | 6.7 | 41.7[d] | 7.7 | 7.9 | 24.2[d] |
| Chile | na | 20.6 | 30.6 | 100.0 | 23.9 | 26.8 |
| Colombia | 13.3 | 16.6 | 19.8 | 14.5 | 13.8 | 13.1 |
| Costa Rica | 28.2 | 28.4 | 31.8 | 35.0 | 36.2 | 31.0 |
| Dominican Republic | 17.2 | 17.5 | 8.7 | 24.5 | 24.4 | 9.6 |
| Ecuador | 14.0 | 21.3 | 23.5 | 18.6 | 27.0 | 23.2 |
| El Salvador | 24.9 | 30.3 | 23.2 | 24.5 | 39.5 | 29.5 |
| Guatemala | 18.6 | 21.5 | 16.1 | 17.8 | 27.3 | 14.6 |
| Haiti | 12.7 | 29.5 | 18.4 | 16.7 | 39.2 | 26.5 |
| Honduras | 27.3 | 36.0 | 26.7 | 33.9 | 40.9 | 29.2 |
| Jamaica | 33.2 | 42.1 | 52.6 | 37.4 | 40.8 | 52.9 |
| Mexico | 7.7 | 10.5 | 17.7[c] | 9.7 | 11.0 | 9.7[c] |
| Panama | 38.0 | 40.2 | 33.9 | 41.4 | 44.9 | 30.6 |
| Paraguay | 14.9 | 18.4 | 16.4 | 16.1 | 22.1 | 20.4 |
| Peru | 19.9 | 22.3 | 25.7[d] | 15.8 | 19.1 | 18.8[d] |
| Trinidad & Tobago | 38.0 | 45.1 | 32.9[d] | 39.5 | 40.5 | 28.8[d] |

*Continued on following page*

**Table A.10 Continued**

| | Exports | | | | Imports | | |
|---|---|---|---|---|---|---|---|
| | 1970 | 1978 | 1986 | | 1970 | 1978 | 1986 |
| Uruguay | 12.1 | 17.9 | 24.0 | | 13.5 | 20.3 | 18.6 |
| Venezuela | 23.7 | 24.8 | 27.3[d] | | 19.1 | 37.9 | 17.5[d] |
| DEVELOPED COUNTRIES | | | | | | | |
| Japan | 11.3 | 11.8 | 13.2 | | 10.2 | 10.0 | 13.2 |
| United States | 5.6 | 8.2 | 6.8 | | 5.5 | 9.4 | 10.2 |

na = not available
a. Merchandise trade only.
b. 1973.
c. 1984.
d. 1985.
e. Percentage of national income.
f. 1983.
SOURCES: Asian Development Bank, *Key Indicators of Developing Member Countries of ADB*, July 1987; Hong Kong, Census and Statistics Department, *Estimates of Gross Domestic Product 1966 to 1983*; Hong Kong, Census and Statistics Department, *Hong Kong Monthly Digest of Statistics*, October 1984 and August 1987; International Monetary Fund, *International Financial Statistics*, yearbook 1987 and August 1988; Republic of China, Council for Economic Planning and Development, *Taiwan Statistical Data Book 1987*.

## Table A.11a
## Destination of Exports for Selected Countries, 1970
### (% of total exports)

| | Total Exports (US $ millions) | DESTINATION COUNTRY | | | | | | | |
| --- | --- | --- | --- | --- | --- | --- | --- | --- | --- |
| | | Developed | | | | Developing | | | |
| | | United States | EC | Japan | Other Developed | Africa | Middle East | Latin America & Caribbean | Asia[a] |
| **DEVELOPING COUNTRIES** | | | | | | | | | |
| **Asia** | | | | | | | | | |
| NICs | 6,376 | 16.0 | 11.7 | 31.8 | na | 3.5 | 1.8 | 1.4 | 18.8 |
| Hong Kong | 2,503 | 21.7 | 7.1 | 35.8 | 10.4 | 4.3 | 2.2 | 2.2 | 11.8 |
| Korea (ROK) | 839 | 7.7 | 28.2 | 47.1 | 3.7 | 2.0 | 0.8 | 0.9 | 7.5 |
| Singapore | 1,533 | 17.4 | 7.6 | 11.1 | 5.9 | 3.4 | 2.3 | 1.7 | 35.5 |
| Taiwan | 1,481 | 9.6 | 14.6 | 38.1 | na | 2.9 | 1.3 | 0.0 | 19.5 |
| ASEAN-4 | 4,548 | 16.0 | 29.9 | 19.6 | 3.4 | 0.7 | 1.1 | 0.7 | 24.2 |
| Indonesia | 1,108 | 14.9 | 40.8 | 13.0 | 3.6 | 0.1 | 0.0 | 0.4 | 23.1 |
| Malaysia | 1,687 | 20.3 | 18.3 | 13.0 | 5.3 | 0.8 | 1.4 | 1.4 | 33.1 |
| Philippines | 1,043 | 8.0 | 40.1 | 41.6 | 1.3 | 0.3 | 0.2 | 0.2 | 7.4 |
| Thailand | 710 | 19.3 | 25.5 | 13.4 | 1.7 | 2.1 | 3.2 | 0.1 | 29.3 |
| South Asia[b] | 2,875 | 20.8 | 11.6 | 12.6 | 5.0 | 5.4 | 9.1 | 1.3 | 13.0 |
| Bangladesh | na | na | na | na | na | na | na | na | na |
| Burma | 106 | 21.1 | 7.6 | 0.3 | 3.1 | 5.4 | 0.2 | 1.0 | 52.2 |
| India | 2,024 | 19.1 | 13.9 | 13.5 | 4.8 | 5.0 | 10.1 | 0.5 | 9.2 |
| Nepal | 21 | 20.3 | 4.8 | 9.7 | 0.5 | 0.0 | 0.0 | 0.0 | 64.3 |
| Pakistan | 724 | 25.6 | 5.9 | 11.7 | 5.9 | 6.8 | 8.0 | 3.6 | 16.6 |
| Sri Lanka | 335 | 33.2 | 3.3 | 7.2 | 8.0 | 4.0 | 5.6 | 0.8 | 17.1 |

**Table A.11a Continued**

| | Total Exports (US $ millions) | Developed | | | | DESTINATION COUNTRY Developing | | | |
|---|---|---|---|---|---|---|---|---|---|
| | | United States | EC | Japan | Other Developed | Africa | Middle East | Latin America & Caribbean | Asia[a] |
| **Other Asia** | | | | | | | | | |
| China | 1,680 | 18.8 | 13.7 | 0.0 | 3.9 | 5.4 | 2.3 | 0.3 | 42.4 |
| **Latin America** | | | | | | | | | |
| Argentina | 1,773 | 53.3 | 6.2 | 8.9 | 2.6 | 0.7 | 1.2 | 21.1 | 0.9 |
| Barbados | 46 | 39.7 | 0.0 | 20.0 | 4.6 | 0.0 | 0.0 | 23.6 | 0.0 |
| Bolivia | 228 | 46.0 | 9.5 | 32.6 | 0.1 | 0.0 | 0.0 | 9.7 | 0.0 |
| Brazil | 2,739 | 39.7 | 5.3 | 24.7 | 7.3 | 2.1 | 0.6 | 11.8 | 1.8 |
| Chile | 1,246 | 56.8 | 12.0 | 14.2 | 3.7 | 0.2 | 0.3 | 12.2 | 0.1 |
| Colombia | 729 | 30.7 | 2.8 | 36.3 | 9.4 | 0.1 | 0.0 | 10.5 | 0.1 |
| Costa Rica | 227 | 19.6 | 5.0 | 42.0 | 6.3 | 0.0 | 0.0 | 24.0 | 0.1 |
| Dominican Republic | 214 | 10.4 | 2.6 | 84.3 | 0.7 | 0.0 | 0.0 | 1.1 | 0.0 |
| Ecuador | 210 | 19.1 | 16.1 | 38.4 | 1.8 | 0.0 | 0.2 | 10.1 | 0.0 |
| El Salvador | 236 | 28.0 | 10.6 | 20.7 | 2.9 | 0.0 | 0.0 | 31.8 | 0.0 |
| Guatemala | 290 | 20.6 | 6.8 | 28.3 | 5.3 | 0.4 | 0.4 | 37.0 | 0.6 |
| Haiti | 41 | 33.3 | 3.1 | 60.4 | 1.2 | 0.0 | 0.0 | 1.9 | 0.0 |
| Honduras | 172 | 22.8 | 1.4 | 54.1 | 0.8 | 0.1 | 0.0 | 20.1 | 0.0 |
| Jamaica | 340 | 16.8 | 0.4 | 52.8 | 18.8 | 2.1 | 0.0 | 7.5 | 0.0 |
| Mexico | 1,313 | 7.4 | 5.2 | 57.0 | 2.3 | 0.1 | 0.1 | 9.8 | 0.3 |

*Continued on following page*

# Table A.11a Continued

| | Total Exports (US $ millions) | DESTINATION COUNTRY | | | | | | | |
| | | Developed | | | | Developing | | | |
| | | United States | EC | Japan | Other Developed | Africa | Middle East | Latin America & Caribbean | Asia[a] |
|---|---|---|---|---|---|---|---|---|---|
| Panama | 106 | 20.5 | 0.3 | 63.6 | 5.6 | 0.0 | 0.0 | 8.0 | 0.0 |
| Paraguay | 64 | 37.6 | 1.8 | 14.3 | na | 0.4 | 0.2 | 38.3 | 0.0 |
| Peru | 1,048 | 38.8 | 13.5 | 33.2 | 1.4 | 0.0 | 0.4 | 6.5 | 0.8 |
| Trinidad & Tobago | 482 | 13.0 | 0.6 | 50.8 | 7.2 | 0.4 | 0.0 | 22.6 | 0.0 |
| Uruguay | 233 | 54.7 | 0.7 | 8.6 | 1.6 | 1.0 | 4.6 | 12.8 | 3.3 |
| Venezuela | 3,204 | 13.2 | 0.8 | 37.9 | 13.1 | 0.5 | 0.0 | 34.1 | 0.0 |
| DEVELOPED COUNTRIES | | | | | | | | | |
| Japan | 19,314 | 12.1 | — | 31.2 | 9.3 | 4.1 | 3.0 | 5.5 | 24.9 |
| United States | 43,247 | 28.6 | 10.8 | — | 27.4 | 3.2 | 3.51 | 5.1 | 7.8 |

Dashed cells indicate not applicable.
na = Not available.
a. Asia includes the NICs, ASEAN-4, South Asia, China, and Brunei.
b. Does not include exports of Bangladesh.
SOURCES: International Monetary Fund, *Direction of Trade Statistics*, computer data tapes 1988 and yearbook 1987; Republic of China, Ministry of Finance, Department of Statistics, *Monthly Statistics of Exports and Imports, the Republic of China*, no. 157 (September 1982) and no. 219 (November 1987).

Table A.11b
**Destination of Exports for Selected Countries, 1986**
(% of total exports)

| | Total Exports (US $ millions) | DESTINATION COUNTRY | | | | | | | |
| | | Developed | | | | Developing | | | |
| | | EC | Japan | United States | Other Developed | Africa | Middle East | Latin America & Caribbean | Asia[a] |
|---|---|---|---|---|---|---|---|---|---|
| **DEVELOPING COUNTRIES** | | | | | | | | | |
| **Asia** | | | | | | | | | |
| NICs | 133,323 | 12.3 | 10.2 | 36.8 | na% | 1.9 | 3.8 | 1.6 | 22.5 |
| Hong Kong | 35,420 | 14.5 | 4.7 | 31.4 | 7.1 | 1.5 | 2.5 | 1.4 | 32.4 |
| Korea | 35,624 | 12.5 | 15.2 | 38.5 | 8.1 | 1.6 | 5.2 | 3.4 | 12.1 |
| Singapore | 22,490 | 11.1 | 8.6 | 23.4 | 5.5 | 2.8 | 4.6 | 2.0 | 37.4 |
| Taiwan | 39,789 | 10.8 | 11.4 | 47.7 | na | 1.9 | 3.2 | 0.0 | 14.4 |
| ASEAN4 | 42,364 | 14.6 | 28.3 | 20.0 | 3.5 | 1.2 | 2.6 | 1.0 | 27.3 |
| Indonesia | 14,824 | 9.3 | 44.8 | 19.6 | 2.2 | 1.0 | 1.6 | 1.2 | 18.9 |
| Malaysia | 13,977 | 14.5 | 23.3 | 16.4 | 3.5 | 0.5 | 1.6 | 0.7 | 38.2 |
| Philippines | 4,787 | 18.3 | 17.8 | 35.7 | 3.9 | 0.5 | 2.0 | 0.9 | 19.4 |
| Thailand | 8,776 | 21.5 | 14.1 | 17.9 | 5.4 | 3.2 | 6.2 | 1.1 | 28.6 |
| South Asia | 15,239 | 22.0 | 10.7 | 18.8 | 5.3 | 4.0 | 9.3 | 0.5 | 12.9 |
| Bangladesh | 889 | 20.7 | 8.0 | 23.7 | 6.8 | 8.0 | 9.5 | 0.9 | 13.2 |
| Burma | 506 | 9.2 | 8.8 | 2.8 | 1.6 | 20.5 | 2.5 | 3.0 | 42.9 |
| India | 10,317 | 20.8 | 11.5 | 21.7 | 4.6 | 2.5 | 7.3 | 0.2 | 9.8 |
| Nepal | 144 | 28.5 | 1.0 | 23.7 | 3.3 | 0.0 | 0.6 | 0.2 | 42.8 |
| Pakistan | 3,383 | 27.9 | 9.8 | 10.8 | 7.3 | 5.2 | 16.8 | 1.1 | 16.2 |
| Sri Lanka | 1,163 | 24.0 | 5.6 | 26.0 | 5.2 | 1.6 | 18.3 | 1.2 | 10.8 |

Continued on following page

# Table A.11b Continued

| | Total Exports (US $ millions) | Developed | | | | Developing | | | |
|---|---|---|---|---|---|---|---|---|---|
| | | EC | Japan | United States | Other Developed | Africa | Middle East | Latin America & Caribbean | Asia[a] |
| **Other Asia** | | | | | | | | | |
| China | 31,366 | 12.8 | 15.1 | 8.4 | 2.8 | 1.8 | 6.7 | 1.2 | 38.9 |
| **Latin America** | | | | | | | | | |
| Argentina | 7,477 | 30.8 | 6.7 | 9.3 | 2.8 | 3.7 | 7.2 | 19.4 | 6.5 |
| Barbados | 274 | 13.9 | 1.2 | 45.2 | 4.5 | 0.0 | 0.0 | 19.1 | 1.8 |
| Bolivia | 590 | 13.6 | 1.4 | 19.5 | 2.7 | 0.0 | 0.0 | 58.9 | 0.4 |
| Brazil | 24,551 | 25.0 | 6.4 | 26.7 | 5.4 | 4.3 | 5.6 | 12.2 | 6.0 |
| Chile | 4,226 | 34.1 | 9.9 | 21.7 | 2.8 | 0.8 | 2.1 | 17.0 | 4.9 |
| Colombia | 5,174 | 34.9 | 4.8 | 35.8 | 10.8 | 1.0 | 0.1 | 9.5 | 0.8 |
| Costa Rica | 1,091 | 28.9 | 0.9 | 42.8 | 6.3 | 0.1 | 0.0 | 17.6 | 0.2 |
| Dominican Republic | 1,218 | 6.7 | 0.8 | 85.0 | 2.9 | 0.7 | 0.0 | 1.8 | 0.1 |
| Ecuador | 2,940 | 7.7 | 2.4 | 49.6 | 3.7 | 0.1 | 0.0 | 9.7 | 10.0 |
| El Salvador | 735 | 28.1 | 3.8 | 49.3 | 2.9 | 0.0 | 0.0 | 14.0 | 0.1 |
| Guatemala | 572 | 16.4 | 4.2 | 45.7 | 3.9 | 0.2 | 4.7 | 22.3 | 0.7 |
| Haiti | 461 | 17.2 | 0.5 | 77.0 | 2.5 | 0.0 | 0.0 | 2.7 | 0.0 |
| Honduras | 902 | 22.9 | 10.1 | 49.1 | 6.8 | 0.5 | 0.6 | 6.5 | 0.6 |
| Jamaica | 583 | 26.2 | 1.1 | 34.7 | 21.0 | 1.1 | 0.0 | 10.3 | 0.0 |
| Mexico | 16,579 | 12.5 | 6.4 | 67.3 | 2.5 | 0.2 | 0.8 | 6.3 | 1.5 |
| Panama | 332 | 14.3 | 0.1 | 67.7 | 2.6 | 0.0 | 0.7 | 14.1 | 0.0 |
| Paraguay | 232 | 20.5 | 0.8 | 4.0 | 4.9 | 1.2 | 0.1 | 67.1 | 0.3 |
| Peru | 2,505 | 24.9 | 10.6 | 30.1 | 3.3 | 0.7 | 1.2 | 14.5 | 5.7 |

DESTINATION COUNTRY

*Continued on following page*

# Table A.11b Continued

DESTINATION COUNTRY

| | Total Exports (US $ millions) | Developed | | | | Developing | | | |
|---|---|---|---|---|---|---|---|---|---|
| | | EC | Japan | United States | Other Developed | Africa | Middle East | Latin America & Caribbean | Asia[a] |
| Trinidad & Tobago | 1,372 | 14.8 | 1.1 | 62.7 | 3.3 | 0.0 | 0.0 | 16.1 | 0.4 |
| Uruguay | 1,355 | 20.6 | 1.3 | 32.6 | 3.9 | 0.7 | 5.5 | 23.1 | 6.0 |
| Venezuela | 8,412 | 15.7 | 3.3 | 44.7 | 4.5 | 0.1 | 0.0 | 20.0 | 0.8 |
| DEVELOPED COUNTRIES | | | | | | | | | |
| Japan | 211,735 | 14.7 | — | 38.7 | 8.5 | 1.5 | 4.5 | 4.0 | 24.3 |
| United States | 217,291 | 24.5 | 12.4 | — | 26.9 | 1.8 | 4.8 | 14.3 | 13.2 |

Dashed cells indicate not applicable.
na = Not available.
a. Asia includes the NICs, ASEAN-4, South Asia, China, and Brunei.
SOURCES: International Monetary Fund, Direction of Trade Statistics, computer data tapes 1988 and yearbook 1987; Republic of China, Ministry of Finance, Department of Statistics, Monthly Statistics of Exports and Imports, the Republic of China, no. 157 (September 1982) and no. 219 (November 1987).

## Table A.12a
## Origin of Imports for Selected Countries, 1970
### (% of total imports)

| | Total Imports (US $ millions) | Developed | | | | | Developing | | |
|---|---|---|---|---|---|---|---|---|---|
| | | EC | Japan | United States | Other Developed | Africa | Middle East | Latin America & Caribbean | Asia[a] |
| **DEVELOPING COUNTRIES** | | | | | | | | | |
| **Asia** | | | | | | | | | |
| NICs | 8,862 | 14.1 | 29.7 | 18.0 | na | 1.2 | 5.4 | 0.9 | 23.0 |
| Hong Kong | 2,896 | 18.4 | 23.9 | 13.2 | 6.9 | 2.4 | 2.4 | 1.7 | 30.2 |
| Korea (ROK) | 1,984 | 10.5 | 41.0 | 29.5 | 2.4 | 0.3 | 5.7 | 0.3 | 9.7 |
| Singapore | 2,458 | 15.7 | 19.4 | 10.8 | 7.6 | 1.5 | 9.3 | 0.9 | 33.0 |
| Taiwan | 1,524 | 8.3 | 42.8 | 23.9 | na | 0.0 | 4.2 | 0.0 | 10.4 |
| ASEAN-4 | 4,905 | 21.0 | 28.4 | 17.3 | 7.6 | 1.2 | 3.4 | 0.6 | 17.8 |
| Indonesia | 1,002 | 21.6 | 29.4 | 17.8 | 2.8 | 2.9 | 0.0 | 0.3 | 19.6 |
| Malaysia | 1,399 | 23.4 | 17.5 | 8.6 | 9.4 | 0.4 | 3.2 | 0.3 | 33.8 |
| Philippines | 1,206 | 15.7 | 30.6 | 29.4 | 9.1 | 0.1 | 6.0 | 0.7 | 8.0 |
| Thailand | 1,299 | 22.8 | 37.4 | 14.9 | 7.9 | 1.8 | 3.9 | 0.9 | 8.1 |
| South Asia[b] | 3,402 | 22.1 | 7.7 | 27.6 | 10.0 | 5.2 | 7.8 | 0.5 | 5.3 |
| Bangladesh | na | na | na | na | na | na | na | na | na |
| Burma | 152 | 25.7 | 26.2 | 5.9 | 7.0 | 0.3 | 0.1 | 0.0 | 25.7 |
| India | 2,095 | 18.0 | 4.6 | 29.3 | 11.3 | 8.3 | 9.6 | 0.9 | 2.1 |
| Nepal | 531 | 0.8 | 10.0 | 2.1 | 0.9 | 0.0 | 0.0 | 0.0 | 76.2 |
| Pakistan | 1,102 | 29.9 | 10.9 | 28.4 | 8.5 | 0.3 | 5.8 | 0.0 | 5.0 |
| Sri Lanka | 389 | 26.8 | 8.4 | 5.7 | 9.3 | 0.2 | 2.4 | 0.0 | 32.6 |

**Table A.12a Continued**

|  | Total Imports (US $ millions) | Developed | | | | COUNTRY OF ORIGIN | Developing | | |
|  |  | EC | Japan | United States | Other Developed | Africa | Middle East | Latin America & Caribbean | Asia[a] |
|---|---|---|---|---|---|---|---|---|---|
| **Other Asia** |  |  |  |  |  |  |  |  |  |
| China | 1,896 | 26.7 | 33.0 | 0.0 | 11.3 | 5.0 | 1.9 | 0.2 | 7.9 |
| **Latin America** |  |  |  |  |  |  |  |  |  |
| Argentina | 1,685 | 33.1 | 5.0 | 24.9 | 9.4 | 0.6 | 0.7 | 22.9 | 2.3 |
| Barbados | 139 | 40.2 | 3.1 | 20.7 | 10.9 | 0.1 | 0.1 | 18.9 | 1.5 |
| Bolivia | 159 | 26.8 | 16.4 | 31.1 | 4.7 | 0.5 | 0.0 | 16.8 | 0.5 |
| Brazil | 2,849 | 30.2 | 6.2 | 32.2 | 8.2 | 2.6 | 5.9 | 12.0 | 0.5 |
| Chile | 931 | 29.8 | 3.0 | 36.9 | 6.4 | 0.0 | 0.0 | 21.7 | 0.0 |
| Colombia | 844 | 25.6 | 6.3 | 47.8 | 6.9 | 0.1 | 0.0 | 10.1 | 0.3 |
| Costa Rica | 317 | 21.2 | 9.0 | 34.8 | 4.3 | 0.1 | 0.1 | 29.1 | 0.5 |
| Dominican Republic | 280 | 21.6 | 9.6 | 47.1 | 8.1 | 0.0 | 0.0 | 11.8 | 1.1 |
| Ecuador | 274 | 24.7 | 9.3 | 43.4 | 6.1 | 0.1 | 0.1 | 13.4 | 0.6 |
| El Salvador | 214 | 21.7 | 10.4 | 29.6 | 3.3 | 0.1 | 0.0 | 34.3 | 0.2 |
| Guatemala | 284 | 21.4 | 10.3 | 35.3 | 3.9 | 0.1 | 0.0 | 28.0 | 0.6 |
| Haiti | 522 | 5.6 | 9.1 | 46.4 | 6.5 | 0.1 | 0.0 | 7.4 | 1.9 |
| Honduras | 221 | 13.2 | 8.1 | 41.5 | 3.1 | 0.0 | 0.0 | 33.2 | 0.3 |
| Jamaica | 524 | 27.5 | 2.6 | 43.1 | 10.2 | 0.1 | 0.0 | 10.5 | 0.9 |
| Mexico | 2,330 | 21.2 | 3.7 | 61.5 | 8.4 | 0.1 | 0.1 | 3.9 | 0.6 |
| Panama | 357 | 12.2 | 6.6 | 40.1 | 3.4 | 0.1 | 0.0 | 24.0 | 1.4 |
| Paraguay | 64 | 30.1 | 6.8 | 23.4 | 4.4 | 6.0 | 0.0 | 26.7 | 0.8 |
| Peru | 619 | 27.8 | 7.9 | 32.2 | 12.0 | 0.2 | 0.1 | 17.7 | 1.5 |

*Continued on following page*

# Table A.12a Continued

COUNTRY OF ORIGIN

| | Total Imports (US $ millions) | Developed | | | | Developing | | | |
|---|---|---|---|---|---|---|---|---|---|
| | | EC | Japan | United States | Other Developed | Africa | Middle East | Latin America & Caribbean | Asia[a] |
| Trinidad & Tobago | 544 | 18.6 | 2.5 | 16.4 | 4.2 | 4.2 | 9.4 | 29.3 | 0.7 |
| Uruguay | 233 | 27.1 | 1.5 | 12.9 | 6.6 | 4.3 | 8.3 | 32.9 | 2.8 |
| Venezuela | 1,958 | 27.8 | 7.9 | 48.5 | 8.6 | 0.4 | 0.1 | 4.5 | 1.0 |
| DEVELOPED COUNTRIES | | | | | | | | | |
| Japan | 18,875 | 8.5 | — | 29.5 | 15.5 | 5.5 | 12.2 | 6.7 | 16.6 |
| United States | 42,711 | 24.3 | 14.6 | — | 32.9 | 2.7 | 1.1 | 14.7 | 8.5 |

Dashed cells indicate not applicable.
na = Not available.
a. Asia includes the NICs, ASEAN-4, South Asia, China, and Brunei.
b. Does not include imports of Bangladesh.
SOURCES: International Monetary Fund, *Direction of Trade Statistics*, computer data tapes 1988 and yearbook 1987; Republic of China, Ministry of Finance, Department of Statistics, *Monthly Statistics of Exports and Imports, the Republic of China*, no. 157 (September 1982) and no. 219 (November 1987).

## Table A.12b
### Origin of Imports for Selected Countries, 1986
### (% of total imports)

| | Total Imports (US $ millions) | COUNTRY OF ORIGIN | | | | | | | |
| | | Developed | | | | Developing | | | |
| | | EC | Japan | United States | Other Developed | Africa | Middle East | Latin America & Caribbean | Asia[a] |
|---|---|---|---|---|---|---|---|---|---|
| **DEVELOPING COUNTRIES** | | | | | | | | | |
| **Asia** | | | | | | | | | |
| NICs | 118,365 | 11.3 | 26.7 | 16.0 | na | 0.8 | 6.4 | 1.6 | 27.2 |
| Hong Kong | 35,360 | 11.5 | 20.4 | 8.4 | 5.0 | 1.1 | 1.0 | 0.6 | 50.7 |
| Korea (ROK) | 33,335 | 10.8 | 33.3 | 20.2 | 8.0 | 1.0 | 5.8 | 4.5 | 10.2 |
| Singapore | 25,506 | 11.6 | 19.9 | 15.0 | 5.2 | 0.9 | 12.7 | 0.7 | 32.9 |
| Taiwan | 24,165 | 11.3 | 34.2 | 22.4 | na | 0.0 | 8.3 | 0.0 | 10.2 |
| ASEAN-4 | 35,921 | 15.0 | 24.1 | 17.1 | 8.1 | 0.9 | 5.4 | 1.5 | 26.3 |
| Indonesia | 10,724 | 17.1 | 29.2 | 13.8 | 9.5 | 0.9 | 6.3 | 1.6 | 20.5 |
| Malaysia | 10,828 | 14.6 | 20.5 | 18.8 | 8.7 | 0.3 | 2.2 | 1.1 | 31.6 |
| Philippines | 5,213 | 10.9 | 17.0 | 24.8 | 6.6 | 0.7 | 10.2 | 2.0 | 28.1 |
| Thailand | 9,155 | 15.1 | 26.4 | 14.4 | 6.7 | 1.6 | 5.2 | 1.7 | 25.8 |
| South Asia | 27,683 | 30.0 | 13.9 | 9.5 | 7.5 | 1.4 | 12.4 | 1.7 | 14.0 |
| Bangladesh | 2,502 | 16.5 | 13.9 | 8.5 | 8.5 | 0.1 | 9.2 | 0.3 | 23.7 |
| Burma | 668 | 20.2 | 35.2 | 2.6 | 4.3 | 0.3 | 0.8 | 0.1 | 23.4 |
| India | 18,830 | 33.2 | 12.4 | 9.0 | 7.5 | 1.4 | 12.8 | 2.0 | 11.4 |
| Nepal | 316 | 13.8 | 23.0 | 2.6 | 2.4 | 0.0 | 0.0 | 0.0 | 58.2 |
| Pakistan | 5,367 | 27.0 | 16.3 | 13.1 | 7.5 | 2.0 | 14.9 | 1.5 | 14.6 |
| Sri Lanka | 1,829 | 15.5 | 17.4 | 6.4 | 7.2 | 3.4 | 10.5 | 2.2 | 36.0 |

*Continued on following page*

# Table A.12b Continued

| | Total Imports (US $ millions) | COUNTRY OF ORIGIN | | | | | | | |
| | | Developed | | | | Developing | | | |
| | | EC | Japan | United States | Other Developed | Africa | Middle East | Latin America & Caribbean | Asia[a] |
|---|---|---|---|---|---|---|---|---|---|
| **Other Asia** | | | | | | | | | |
| China | 43,503 | 17.8 | 28.6 | 10.8 | 9.1 | 0.6 | 0.3 | 3.6 | 16.6 |
| **Latin America** | | | | | | | | | |
| Argentina | 5,067 | 30.8 | 7.4 | 18.5 | 6.5 | 0.5 | 0.4 | 31.5 | 1.9 |
| Barbados | 587 | 20.8 | 5.6 | 40.4 | 10.5 | 0.0 | 0.0 | 18.6 | 2.5 |
| Bolivia | 636 | 13.8 | 5.0 | 19.3 | 3.4 | 0.1 | 0.3 | 53.4 | 1.5 |
| Brazil | 16,390 | 22.3 | 6.5 | 24.6 | 8.6 | 7.1 | 14.2 | 9.7 | 4.0 |
| Chile | 3,132 | 21.5 | 9.5 | 20.5 | 5.0 | 2.8 | 1.2 | 24.9 | 2.7 |
| Colombia | 4,077 | 22.9 | 10.5 | 35.6 | 8.5 | 0.1 | 0.5 | 19.2 | 0.7 |
| Costa Rica | 1,145 | 15.4 | 10.6 | 35.8 | 4.5 | 0.0 | 0.3 | 28.6 | 3.9 |
| Dominican Republic | 1,663 | 9.3 | 7.7 | 55.4 | 4.0 | 0.1 | 0.2 | 19.2 | 4.1 |
| Ecuador | 2,074 | 23.4 | 14.5 | 31.9 | 7.4 | 0.3 | 0.9 | 17.0 | 1.6 |
| El Salvador | 912 | 11.3 | 3.8 | 40.3 | 2.1 | 0.0 | 0.0 | 35.4 | 1.8 |
| Guatemala | 1,157 | 19.4 | 6.1 | 41.2 | 3.7 | 0.1 | 0.5 | 23.3 | 3.5 |
| Haiti | 652 | 11.6 | 4.6 | 65.3 | 3.5 | 0.1 | 0.0 | 9.5 | 5.2 |
| Honduras | 826 | 12.6 | 9.4 | 48.4 | 3.1 | 0.0 | 0.3 | 21.6 | 3.2 |
| Jamaica | 969 | 12.3 | 3.8 | 50.7 | 7.6 | 0.1 | 0.1 | 20.3 | 1.5 |
| Mexico | 12,320 | 14.3 | 6.3 | 67.1 | 5.3 | 0.5 | 0.1 | 3.1 | 1.1 |
| Panama | 1,285 | 9.0 | 8.4 | 34.9 | 5.1 | 0.0 | 0.1 | 36.3 | 31.4 |
| Paraguay | 511 | 18.2 | 5.7 | 13.7 | 2.0 | 7.2 | 0.1 | 47.9 | 5.2 |
| Peru | 1,915 | 21.1 | 9.5 | 27.2 | 11.6 | 0.0 | 0.1 | 26.5 | 2.0 |

Continued on following page

# Table A.12b Continued

|  | Total Imports (US $ millions) | COUNTRY OF ORIGIN | | | | | | | |
|  |  | Developed | | | | Developing | | | |
|  |  | EC | Japan | United States | Other Developed | Africa | Middle East | Latin America & Caribbean | Asia[a] |
| Trinidad & Tobago | 1,332 | 21.0 | 10.7 | 42.9 | 9.3 | 0.3 | 0.1 | 10.8 | 2.4 |
| Uruguay | 1,066 | 22.1 | 3.2 | 10.3 | 4.4 | 6.8 | 4.7 | 43.2 | 1.7 |
| Venezuela | 8,399 | 26.9 | 6.9 | 45.9 | 5.7 | 0.4 | 0.0 | 11.2 | 1.0 |
| DEVELOPED COUNTRIES |  |  |  |  |  |  |  |  |  |
| Japan | 127,660 | 11.1 | — | 23.0 | 13.3 | 2.8 | 14.6 | 4.7 | 28.1 |
| United States | 387,075 | 20.5 | 22.1 | — | 22.2 | 2.8 | 2.3 | 11.4 | 17.5 |

Dashed cells indicate not applicable.
na = Not available.
a. Asia includes the NICs, ASEAN-4, South Asia, China, and Brunei.
SOURCES: International Monetary Fund, Direction of Trade Statistics, computer data tapes 1988 and yearbook 1987; Republic of China, Ministry of Finance, Department of Statistics, Monthly Statistics of Exports and Imports, the Republic of China, no. 157 (September 1982) and no. 219 (November 1987).

## Table A.13
## External Debt Outstanding for Selected Countries, 1978–86[a]

| | 1978 | | 1982 | | 1983 | | 1984 | | 1985 | | 1986 | |
|---|---|---|---|---|---|---|---|---|---|---|---|---|
| | US $ (millions) | Percent of GNP | US $ (millions) | Percent of GNP | US $ (millions) | Percent of GNP | US $ (millions) | Percent of GNP | US $ (millions) | Percent of GNP | US $ (millions) | Percent of GNP |
| **Asia** | | | | | | | | | | | | |
| Hong Kong[b] | 480 | 2.8 | 892 | 2.9 | 1,035 | 3.6 | 1,130 | 3.6 | 1,000 | 3.0 | na | na |
| Korea (ROK) | 17,000 | 34.0 | 36,496 | 52.6 | 39,547 | 52.0 | 41,633 | 50.5 | 46,073 | 55.0 | 43,560 | 45.8 |
| Singapore[b] | 1,227 | 15.8 | 1,521 | 11.7 | 1,563 | 10.3 | 1,729 | 11.3 | 1,753 | 11.6 | 2,113 | 13.6 |
| Indonesia | 17,976 | 36.3 | 26,500 | 29.4 | 29,693 | 38.4 | 31,966 | 39.3 | 35,745 | 43.8 | 42,038 | 58.5 |
| Malaysia | 2,518[b] | 16.9[b] | 11,336 | 44.3 | 14,557 | 51.6 | 16,094 | 50.8 | 18,056 | 62.4 | 19,649 | 76.2 |
| Philippines | 10,222 | 42.5 | 23,483 | 59.8 | 23,116 | 67.8 | 23,837 | 75.5 | 25,155 | 79.1 | 27,000 | 89.7 |
| Thailand | 4,852 | 21.2 | 11,496 | 32.3 | 12,961 | 33.1 | 14,464 | 35.7 | 16,407 | 44.5 | 16,970 | 42.3 |
| Bangladesh | 2,736 | 31.5 | 4,656 | 35.5 | 5,053 | 42.0 | 5,286 | 37.9 | 6,133 | 38.2 | 7,407 | 47.6 |
| Burma | 872 | 18.7 | 1,971 | 33.4 | 2,236 | 36.8 | 2,265 | 36.2 | 3,038 | 43.4 | 3,720 | 44.6 |
| India | 16,438 | 13.8 | 22,817 | 13.3 | 24,750 | 13.2 | 27,857 | 15.5 | 32,476 | 16.4 | 36,814 | 17.1 |
| Nepal | 103 | 6.4 | 337 | 14.0 | 444 | 18.0 | 469 | 18.7 | 584 | 24.9 | 732 | 28.5 |
| Pakistan | 7,814 | 41.0 | 10,069 | 30.9 | 10,274 | 33.0 | 10,469 | 31.2 | 11,483 | 34.6 | 12,584 | 36.0 |
| Sri Lanka | 1,128 | 41.5 | 2,499 | 53.5 | 2,690 | 53.5 | 2,755 | 46.6 | 3,259 | 55.1 | 3,833 | 59.9 |
| China | na | na | 8,358 | 3.2 | 9,607 | 3.5 | 13,000 | 4.6 | 16,548 | 6.2 | 21,993 | 8.5 |
| **Latin America** | | | | | | | | | | | | |
| Argentina | 13,273 | 31.6 | 43,634 | 83.5 | 43,914 | 73.9 | 45,730 | 63.2 | 46,157 | 76.3 | 46,167 | 62.1 |
| Barbados | 99 | 17.8 | 332 | 33.6 | 565 | 54.4 | 387 | 34.1 | 449 | 37.3 | 601 | 46.3 |
| Bolivia | 2,163 | 66.2 | 3,168 | 105.3 | 3,775 | 137.5 | 3,847 | 137.7 | 4,143 | 94.8 | 4,619 | 118.8 |
| Brazil | 53,415 | 26.2 | 91,026 | 35.9 | 95,531 | 49.5 | 101,090 | 51.0 | 102,112 | 47.5 | 106,174 | 39.3 |

# Table A.13 Continued

| | 1978 | | 1982 | | 1983 | | 1984 | | 1985 | | 1986 | |
|---|---|---|---|---|---|---|---|---|---|---|---|---|
| | US $ (millions) | Percent of GNP | US $ (millions) | Percent of GNP | US $ (millions) | Percent of GNP | US $ (millions) | Percent of GNP | US $ (millions) | Percent of GNP | US $ (millions) | Percent of GNP |
| Chile | 7,026 | 46.9 | 17,342 | 77.2 | 17,595 | 97.5 | 19,180 | 111.2 | 19,333 | 137.1 | 19,410 | 129.9 |
| Colombia | 5,097 | 22.2 | 10,302 | 27.0 | 11,409 | 30.2 | 12,274 | 33.4 | 14,031 | 42.6 | 14,619 | 46.8 |
| Costa Rica | 1,683 | 49.2 | 3,449 | 158.5 | 4,246 | 150.9 | 4,031 | 124.3 | 4,434 | 127.2 | 4,453 | 118.7 |
| Dominican Republic | 1,376 | 30.0 | 2,462 | 37.2 | 2,891 | 47.0 | 3,046 | 64.2 | 3,299 | 79.6 | 3,301 | 66.4 |
| Ecuador | 3,976 | 53.9 | 7,862 | 68.2 | 7,331 | 74.8 | 8,205 | 88.8 | 8,147 | 69.7 | 8,467 | 79.0 |
| El Salvador | 914 | 30.2 | 1,423 | 42.2 | 1,682 | 47.2 | 1,710 | 43.6 | 1,740 | 47.2 | 1,680 | 43.7 |
| Guatemala | 813 | 13.4 | 1,537 | 17.9 | 1,799 | 20.1 | 2,379 | 25.7 | 2,579 | 40.5 | 2,601 | 35.7 |
| Haiti | 201 | 20.1 | 536 | 36.5 | 569 | 35.5 | 656 | 36.5 | 704 | 36.7 | 698 | 32.7 |
| Honduras | 935 | 53.7 | 1,799 | 69.5 | 2,085 | 74.7 | 2,321 | 78.1 | 2,711 | 85.6 | 2,863 | 84.0 |
| Jamaica | 1,396 | 58.8 | 2,845 | 102.6 | 3,317 | 108.1 | 3,526 | 174.9 | 3,859 | 227.8 | 3,882 | 197.3 |
| Mexico | 35,363 | 35.2 | 85,890 | 55.4 | 91,704 | 68.9 | 94,076 | 58.3 | 94,165 | 55.7 | 97,662 | 80.5 |
| Panama | 2,318 | 96.4 | 3,923 | 99.0 | 4,388 | 106.4 | 4,406 | 102.7 | 4,755 | 104.8 | 4,802 | 99.9 |
| Paraguay | 615 | 22.3 | 1,298 | 30.3 | 1,407 | 43.7 | 1,495 | 48.7 | 1,779 | 60.7 | 1,960 | 53.8 |
| Peru | 9,329 | 89.1 | 11,636 | 47.1 | 11,588 | 61.5 | 12,399 | 64.4 | 12,925 | 81.6 | 14,575 | 59.4 |
| Trinidad & Tobago | 535 | 14.8 | 1,062 | 13.4 | 1,298 | 17.1 | 1,074 | 14.1 | 1,236 | 17.2 | 1,427 | 30.4 |
| Uruguay | 998 | 19.9 | 2,551 | 28.1 | 3,055 | 60.3 | 3,066 | 62.8 | 3,560 | 74.6 | 3,375 | 56.8 |
| Venezuela | 16,760 | 42.4 | 31,933 | 48.1 | 37,260 | 57.4 | 36,217 | 75.3 | 34,710 | 73.6 | 33,891 | 70.8 |

na = Not available.
a. Includes long-term (public and publicly guaranteed and private long-term debt) and short-term debt.
b. Excludes private nonguaranteed long-term debt.
SOURCE: World Bank, *World Debt Tables*, 1985/86, 1986/87 and 1987/88 editions.

**Table A.14**
**Debt-Service Ratio for Selected Countries, 1970–86[a]**
(% of total exports)

| | 1970 | 1978 | 1982 | 1983 | 1984 | 1985 | 1986 |
|---|---|---|---|---|---|---|---|
| **Asia** | | | | | | | |
| Hong Kong[b] | na | 0.6 | 0.2 | 0.2 | 0.2 | 0.2 | na |
| Korea | 20.4 | 11.8 | 16.1 | 16.2 | 16.3 | 21.4 | 24.4 |
| Singapore[b] | 0.6 | 2.2 | 0.8 | 1.3 | 1.0 | 2.4 | 1.4 |
| Indonesia | 13.9 | 25.0 | 16.5 | 18.4 | 19.0 | 25.1 | 34.9 |
| Malaysia | 4.4 | 10.0[b] | 9.2 | 10.2 | 12.8 | 29.2 | 20.0 |
| Philippines | 22.8 | 26.3 | 23.4 | 22.9 | 17.7 | 19.6 | 21.3 |
| Thailand | 14.0 | 16.0 | 16.0 | 19.1 | 21.5 | 25.4 | 26.3 |
| Bangladesh | na | 12.9 | 12.6 | 13.3 | 15.5 | 17.6 | 25.1 |
| Burma | 17.2 | 15.5 | 25.8 | 32.9 | 40.1 | 46.4 | 55.4 |
| India | 25.1 | 12.3 | 12.9 | 14.8 | 15.3 | 20.5 | 25.0 |
| Nepal | na | 1.4 | 2.0 | 3.2 | 3.9 | 5.3 | 9.2 |
| Pakistan | 23.5 | 21.1 | 18.4 | 31.0 | 25.9 | 31.7 | 27.2 |
| Sri Lanka | 10.8[b] | 9.2 | 10.7 | 12.0 | 11.5 | 14.9 | 18.4 |
| China | na | na | 8.3 | 7.2 | 5.8 | 7.0 | 7.9 |
| **Latin America** | | | | | | | |
| Argentina | 21.6[b] | 27.0[b] | 38.2 | 38.7 | 41.3 | 53.0 | 61.8 |
| Barbados | 0.7 | 2.4 | 3.7 | 4.0 | 3.4 | 5.4 | 7.5 |
| Bolivia | 11.4[b] | 51.2[b] | 34.1 | 34.5 | 43.1 | 44.1 | 30.1 |
| Brazil | 21.8 | 57.6 | 71.7 | 45.9 | 33.0 | 33.2 | 41.8 |
| Chile | 24.4 | 49.3 | 62.1 | 47.7 | 52.2 | 44.4 | 37.1 |

*Continued on following page*

## Table A.14 Continued

| | 1970 | 1978 | 1982 | 1983 | 1984 | 1985 | 1986 |
|---|---|---|---|---|---|---|---|
| Colombia | 19.3 | 11.6 | 22.2 | 30.3 | 24.5 | 35.1 | 31.5 |
| Costa Rica | 19.9 | 37.9 | 20.1 | 56.8 | 29.1 | 38.1 | 28.9 |
| Dominican Republic | 15.2 | 19.7 | 26.7 | 25.4 | 15.1 | 18.1 | 21.7 |
| Ecuador | 14.0 | 11.9 | 70.0 | 26.3 | 34.0 | 31.3 | 33.9 |
| El Salvador | 12.0 | 10.2 | 11.3 | 19.3 | 21.4 | 22.5 | 20.8 |
| Guatemala | 8.2 | 5.8 | 10.3 | 14.7 | 20.5 | 22.6 | 24.3 |
| Haiti | 7.7 | 8.5 | 5.4 | 4.8 | 5.5 | 6.0 | 6.1 |
| Honduras | 5.2 | 16.7 | 26.2 | 22.0 | 20.2 | 20.2 | 22.0 |
| Jamaica | 2.8[b] | 16.9[b] | 21.2 | 21.4 | 21.1 | 32.9 | 32.7 |
| Mexico | 44.3 | 62.4 | 44.5 | 45.4 | 49.0 | 50.0 | 51.5 |
| Panama | 7.7 | 32.5 | 6.6 | 6.6 | 8.2 | 6.6 | 7.6 |
| Paraguay | 11.8[b] | 10.2 | 13.6 | 18.1 | 16.0 | 13.8 | 21.1 |
| Peru | 40.0 | 49.2 | 44.2 | 29.1 | 25.1 | 22.3 | 20.5 |
| Trinidad & Tobago | 4.5 | 1.9 | 2.7 | 8.8 | 4.9 | 7.1 | 15.8 |
| Uruguay | 23.6 | 48.3 | 27.9 | 23.5 | 32.4 | 36.3 | 22.3 |
| Venezuela | 2.9[b] | 6.9[b] | 21.8 | 21.6 | 19.9 | 16.3 | 38.5 |

na = Not available.
a. Includes debt service on public and publicly guaranteed and private nonguaranteed debt.
b. Includes debt service on public and publicly guaranteed debt only.
SOURCE: World Bank, World Debt Tables, 1985/86, 1986/87, and 1987/88 editions.

## Table A.15
## U.S. Direct Foreign Investment, 1976–86
### (millions of U.S. dollars)

| | 1976 | 1977 | 1978 | 1979 | 1980 | 1981 | 1982 | 1983 | 1984 | 1985 | 1986 |
|---|---|---|---|---|---|---|---|---|---|---|---|
| WORLD | 11,949 | 11,893 | 16,056 | 25,222 | 19,222 | 9,624 | -2,369 | 373 | 2,821 | 17,267 | 28,047 |
| DEVELOPED COUNTRIES | 8,919 | 7,866 | 10,555 | 18,191 | 17,893 | 5,965 | -21 | 2,135 | 1,101 | 13,366 | 20,512 |
| Canada | 2,471 | 1,581 | 1,206 | 4,477 | 3,906 | -757 | -2,051 | 604 | 2,259 | -735 | 2,664 |
| Europe[a] | 5,492 | 5,289 | 7,820 | 12,259 | 13,011 | 5,278 | 1,506 | 525 | 47 | 13,713 | 16,452 |
| Japan | 454 | 411 | 725 | 760 | 19 | 488 | 243 | 1,257 | -361 | 1,165 | 1,884 |
| DEVELOPING COUNTRIES | 3,050 | 4,192 | 5,587 | 6,967 | 1,150 | 2,993 | -2,456 | -1,943 | 2,382 | 3,799 | 8,233 |
| Latin America and the Caribbean | 1,762 | 3,949 | 4,014 | 3,362 | 2,833 | -197 | -5,138 | -3,692 | -171 | 3,838 | 7,450 |
| Africa[b] | 370 | -238 | 437 | 499 | 635 | 434 | 565 | 15 | 276 | -3 | -155 |
| Middle East | 757 | 311 | 496 | 1,946 | -3,158 | 232 | 203 | 867 | 607 | -90 | 533 |
| Asia and the Pacific | 160 | 170 | 641 | 1,161 | 839 | 2,523 | 1,913 | 867 | 1,670 | 54 | 405 |

a. Includes all countries in continental Europe, including USSR.
b. Excludes South Africa.

SOURCES: United States, Department of Commerce, Bureau of Economic Analysis, U.S. Direct Investment Abroad, 1966 Final Data; Selected Data on U.S. Direct Investment Abroad, 1950–76; U.S. Direct Investment Abroad, 1977; U.S. Direct Investment Abroad, 1982 Benchmark Survey Data; and Survey of Current Business, November 1984 and August 1987.

## Table A.16
## Japanese Direct Foreign Investment, 1976–86
### (millions of U.S. dollars)

| | 1976 | 1977 | 1978 | 1979 | 1980 | 1981 | 1982 | 1983 | 1984 | 1985 | 1986 |
|---|---|---|---|---|---|---|---|---|---|---|---|
| WORLD | 3,462 | 2,806 | 4,598 | 4,995 | 4,693 | 8,932 | 7,703 | 8,145 | 10,155 | 12,217 | 22,320 |
| DEVELOPED COUNTRIES | | | | | | | | | | | |
| Europe[b] | 337 | 220 | 323 | 495 | 578 | 798 | 876 | 990 | 1,937 | 1,930 | 3,469 |
| North America | 749 | 735 | 1,364 | 1,438 | 1,596 | 2,522 | 2,905 | 2,701 | 3,544 | 5,495 | 10,441 |
| DEVELOPING COUNTRIES | | | | | | | | | | | |
| Latin America and the Caribbean | 420 | 456 | 616 | 1,207 | 588 | 1,181 | 1,503 | 1,878 | 2,290 | 2,616 | 4,737 |
| Africa | 272 | 140 | 225 | 168 | 139 | 573 | 489 | 364 | 326 | 172 | 309 |
| Middle East | 278 | 225 | 492 | 130 | 158 | 96 | 124 | 175 | 273 | 45 | 44 |
| Asia and the Pacific | 1,245 | 865 | 1,340 | 976 | 1,186 | 3,339 | 1,385 | 1,847 | 1,628 | 1,435 | 2,327 |

a. Data reflect DFI approvals and not actual flows for the fiscal year beginning April 1.
b. All countries in continental Europe, including USSR.
SOURCES: Japan, Ministry of Finance, *Zaisei Kinyu Kokei Geppo* [Monthly Bulletin of Fiscal and Monetary Statistics], December 1985 and December 1987.

## Table A.17
## Share of Income of the Lowest 40 Percent of Households
## in Selected Countries

| | Year | Lowest 40 percent (income share) |
|---|---|---|
| **DEVELOPING COUNTRIES** | | |
| **Asia** | | |
| NICs | | |
| Hong Kong | 1980 | 16.2 |
| Korea | 1976 | 16.9 |
| ASEAN-4 | | |
| Indonesia | 1976 | 14.4 |
| Malaysia | 1973 | 11.2 |
| Philippines | 1985 | 14.1 |
| Thailand | 1975–76 | 15.2 |
| South Asia | | |
| Bangladesh | 1981–82 | 17.3 |
| India | 1975–76 | 16.2 |
| Sri Lanka | 1980–81 | 15.9 |
| **Latin America** | | |
| Argentina | 1970 | 14.1 |
| Brazil | 1972 | 7.0 |
| Costa Rica | 1971 | 12.0 |
| El Salvador | 1976–77 | 15.5 |
| Mexico | 1977 | 9.9 |
| Panama | 1973 | 7.2 |

*Continued on following page*

## Table A.17 Continued

| | Year | Lowest 40 percent (income share) |
|---|---|---|
| Peru | 1972 | 7.0 |
| Trinidad & Tobago | 1975–76 | 13.3 |
| Venezuela | 1970 | 10.3 |
| DEVELOPED COUNTRIES | | |
| Japan | 1979 | 21.9 |
| United States | 1980 | 17.2 |

SOURCE: World Bank, *World Development Report 1987*, table 26, pp. 272–73.

# Notes and Works Cited

**Seiji Naya, Suby Roy, and Pearl Imada: "Introduction"**

*Works Cited*

Akamatsu, K. 1962a. "A Historical Pattern of Economic Growth in Developing Countries," *The Developing Economies*, preliminary issues, no. 1 (March-August), pp. 3–25.

———. 1962b. "A Theory of Unbalanced Growth in the World Economy," *Weltwirtschaftliches Archiv*, Vol. 86, No. 2, pp. 196–217.

Kojima, K. 1978. *Direct Foreign Investment: A Japanese Model of Multinational Business Operations.* New York: Praeger.


**1   Kedar N. Kohli: "Economic Trends in Latin America"**

*Works Cited*

Asian Development Bank. 1985. *Improving Domestic Resource Mobilization through Financial Development.* Manila: Asian Development Bank.

———. 1987. *Key Indicators of Developing Member Countries of ADB.* Manila: Asian Development Bank.

Chen, Edward K. Y. 1987. "Technological Revolution and Economic Development." In *Productivity through People in the Age of Changing Technology.* Tokyo: Asian Productivity Organization.

Drucker, Peter. 1986. "The Changed World Economy." *Foreign Affairs*, spring.

Grilli, E. R., and M. C. Yan. 1988. "Primary Commodity Prices, Manufactured Goods Prices, and the Terms of Trade of Developing Countries: What the Long Run Shows." *World Bank Economic Review*, vol. 1, no. 1 (January).

Hughes, Helen. 1987. "Economic Policies for Productivity." In *Productivity through People in the Age of Changing Technology.* Tokyo: Asian Productivity Organization.

Kohli, Kedar N. 1987. "Financing Public Sector Development Expenditure: The Asian Experience." *Asian Development Review*, vol. 5, no. 1.

———. 1987. "Falling Commodity Prices: Implications for Asian and Pacific Developing Countries." *Asian Development Review*, vol. 5, no. 1.

Kohli, Kedar N., and Ifzal Ali. 1986. "Science and Technology for Development: Role of the Bank." *ADB Economic Staff Paper*, no. 32 (December). Manila: Asian Development Bank.

Lee, J., P. B. Rana, and I. Ali. 1986. "Impact of Appreciation of the Yen on Developing Member Countries of the Bank." *ADB Economic Office Report Series*, no. 35 (May). Manila: Asian Development Bank.

Lee, Jungsoo. 1987. "Domestic Adjustment to External Shocks in Developing Asia." *ADB Economic Staff Paper*, no. 39 (October). Manila: Asian Development Bank.

Rhee, Y. N. 1985. "Instruments for Export Policy and Administration: Lessons from the East Asian Experience." *World Bank Staff Working Paper*, no. 775. Washington, D.C.: World Bank.

Sachs, J. D. 1981. "The Current Account and Macroeconomic Adjustment in the 1970s." *Brookings Papers on Economic Activity*, vol. 1.

## 2 Edmar L. Bacha: "Economic Trends in Latin America"

*Notes*

1. The difference between the net financial transfer in table 2.2 and the net resource transfer in table 2.4 corresponds to net foreign reserves accumulation in Latin America.

2. This presumes that nontraded goods prices, which must weigh more heavily in the implicit price deflator of GDP than in that of investment, follow the prices of exports more closely than those of imports.

3. The importance of this effect depends on the weight of imports in consumption, and also on the behavior of the prices of nontraded goods and services entering both the GDP and the domestic consumption deflators.

4. Note also that a maxidevaluation increases the public sector domestic borrowing requirements, when foreign interest payments are higher than the net loans to the government from abroad, which was the case everywhere in Latin America after 1982.

*Works Cited*

Amadeo, E., and T. Banuri. 1987. "The Importance of Institutions and History in Development Policy: A Comparison of Macroeconomic Experience in Asia and Latin America." Paper prepared for the Macroeconomic Policy Group. Rio de Janeiro and Helsinki.

Balassa, Bela, G. M. Bueno, P. P. Kuczynski, and M. H. Simonsen. 1986. *Toward Renewed Economic Growth in Latin America*. Washington, D.C.: Institute for International Economics.

Bianchi, A., R. Devlin, and J. Ramos. 1987. "The Adjustment Process in Latin America, 1981–86." Paper presented at the Symposium on Growth-Oriented Adjustment Programs, sponsored by the World Bank and International Monetary Fund, Washington, D.C., 25–27 February.

Fishlow, A. 1985 "The State of Latin American Economics." In *Inter-American Development Bank, Economic and Social Progress in Latin America—1985 Report*, ch. 5. Washington, D.C.: Inter-American Development Bank.

Inter-American Development Bank (IADB). 1986. *Economic and Economic Progress in Latin America, 1986 Report*. Washington, D.C.: IADB.

International Monetary Fund (IMF). 1987. *World Economic Outlook*, October 1987. Washington, D.C.: IMF.
————. 1988. *International Financial Statistics Yearbook 1987*. Washington, D.C.: IMF.
United Nations Economic Commission for Latin America (ECLA). 1987. *Balance preliminar de la economía latinoamericana 1987*. LC/G.1485 (31 December).
World Bank. 1983. *World Tables: The Third Edition*, Vol. 1, *Economic Data*. Baltimore: Johns Hopkins University Press.
————. 1987. *World Development Report 1987*. New York: Oxford University Press.

## 3   Edward K. Y. Chen: "Trade Policy in Asia"

*Notes*

1. While it is recognized that the smaller the extent of market distortions, the greater the competitiveness and therefore the better the performance in the export of manufactured goods, very few empirical studies have been done to substantiate this correlation. See Agarwala (1983) and Spinanger (1987).

2. It was reported that Japan set a maximum limit of 5 percent for its offshore semiconductor production and European firms set a 20 percent limit (Grunwald and Flamm 1985:85).

*Works Cited*

Agarwala, R. 1983. "Price Distortions and Growth in Developing Countries." *World Bank Staff Working Papers*, no. 575. Washington, D.C.: World Bank.
Balassa, Bela. 1981. *The Newly Industrializing Countries in the World Economy*. New York: Pergamon Press.
Berger, P. 1983. "Secularity: East and West." In *Cultural Identity and Modernization in Asian Countries: Proceedings of Kokugakuin University Centennial Symposium*. Tokyo: Institute for Japanese Culture and Classics, Kokugakuin University.
Brown, G. T. 1973. *Korean Pricing Policies and Economic Development in the 1960s*. Baltimore: The Johns Hopkins University Press.
Chen, E. K. Y. 1976. "The Empirical Relevancy of the Endogenous Technical Progress Function." *Kyklos*, no. 2.
————. 1977. "Domestic Saving and Capital Inflow in Some Asian Countries: A Time-Series Study." *Asian Survey*, July.
————. 1979. *Hyper-Growth in Asian Economies*. London: Macmillan.
————. 1980. "Export Expansion and Economic Growth in Some Asian Countries: A Simultaneous-Equation Model." In R.C.O. Matthews, ed., *Measurement, History, and Factors of Economic Growth*. London: Macmillan.
————. 1984. "The Economic Setting." In David Lethbridge, ed., *Business Environment in Hong Kong*. Hong Kong: Oxford University Press.
Chen, P. S. J., ed. 1983. *Singapore Development Policies and Trends*. Singapore: Oxford University Press.

Chenery, Hollis, and Lance Taylor. 1968. "Development Patterns: Among Countries and Over Time." *Review of Economics and Statistics*, November.
Cline, William. 1982. "Can the East Asian Model of Development Be Generalized?" *World Development*, vol. 10, no. 2.
Davis, W. E., and D. G. Hatano. 1985. "The American Semiconductor Industry and the Ascendancy of East Asia." *California Management Review*. Berkeley: Graduate School of Business Administration, University of California.
Frank, C. R., Jr. 1975. *Foreign Trade Regimes and Economic Development: South Korea*. New York: Columbia University Press.
Grunwald, J., and K. Flamm, eds. 1985. *The Global Factory*. Washington, D.C.: Brookings Institution.
Hasan, P., and D. C. Rao. 1979. *Korea: Policy Issues for Long-Term Development*. Baltimore: Johns Hopkins University Press.
Henderson, J. 1986. "The New International Division of Labour and American Semiconductor Production in Southeast Asia." In C. Dixon et al., eds., *Multinational Corporations and the Third World*. London: Croom Helm.
Ho, Samuel P. S. 1978. *Economic Development of Taiwan, 1860–1970*. New Haven: Yale University Press.
Hsing, Mo-huan. 1971. *Taiwan: Industrialization and Trade Policies*. Oxford: Oxford University Press.
Johnson, Chalmers. 1985. "Political Institutions and Economic Performance: The Government-Business Relationship in Japan, South Korea, and Taiwan." In R. A. Scalapino, ed., *Asian Economic Development*. Berkeley: Institute of East Asian Studies, University of California.
Kahn, Herman. 1979. *World Economic Development: 1979 and Beyond*. Boulder, CO: Westview Press.
Krueger, Anne. 1981. "Export-Led Industrial Growth Reconsidered." In W. Hong and L. B. Krause, eds., *Trade and Growth of the Advanced Developing Countries in the Pacific Basin*. Seoul: Korea Development Institute.
Kuo, Shirley W. Y. 1983. *The Taiwan Economy in Transition*. Boulder, CO: Westview Press.
Lau, L. J., ed. 1986. *Models of Development: A Comparative Study of Economic Growth in South Korea and Taiwan*. San Francisco: Institute for Contemporary Studies.
Lee, Soo Ann. 1973. *Industrialization in Singapore*. Camberwell, Australia: Longman.
Lee, T. H., and K. S. Liang. 1982. "Taiwan." In B. Balassa, ed., *Development Strategy in Semi-Industrialized Countries*. Baltimore: Johns Hopkins University Press.
Lewis, W. A. 1980. "Slowing Down of the Engine of Growth." *American Economic Review*, September.
Li, K. T., and Tzong-shian Yu, eds. 1982. *Experiences and Lessons of Economic Development in Taiwan*. Taipei: Academia Sinica.
Lo, Fu-chen, and B. N. Song. 1986. "Industrial Restructuring of the East and Southeast Asian Economies." Paper presented at the Conference on the Asian-Pacific Economy Towards the Year 2000, Beijing, November.

MacFarquahar, R. 1980. "The Post-Confucian Challenge." *The Economist,* 9 February 1980.

Maizels, A. 1968. *Exports and Economic Growth of Developing Countries.* London: Cambridge University Press.

Myint, H. 1982. "Comparative Analysis of Taiwan's Economic Development with Other Countries." In K. T. Li and Tzong-shian Yu, eds., *Experiences and Lessons of Economic Development in Taiwan.* Taipei: Academia Sinica.

Rana, P. B. 1985. *Exports and Economic Growth in the Asian Region.* ADB Economic Staff Paper, no. 25. Manila: Asian Development Bank.

Ranis, Gustav. 1985. "Can the East Asian Model of Development Be Generalized: A Comment." *World Development,* no. 4.

Riedel, J. 1984. "Trade as the Engine of Growth in Developing Countries, Revisited." *Economic Journal,* March.

Scott, Allen J. 1985. "The Semiconductor Industry in Southeast Asia: Organization, Location, and the International Division of Labour." *UCLA Working Paper.* Los Angeles: Department of Geography, University of California.

Scott, Maurice (1977) "Foreign Trade." In Walter Galenson, ed., *Economic Growth and Structural Change in Taiwan.* Ithaca: Cornell University Press.

Spinanger, Dean. 1987. "Does Trade Performance Say Anything About Efficient Industrialization Policies? Some Evidence from Pacific Rim Countries." *Kiel Working Paper,* no. 302 (October).

Tu, Wei-ming. 1984. *Confucian Ethics Today: The Singapore Challenge.* Singapore: Federal Publications.

Weber, Max. [1905] 1930. *The Protestant Ethic and the Spirit of Capitalism.* New York: Scribner. (First published in 1905.)

## 4    Jorge Ospina Sardi: "Trade Policy in Latin America"

*Notes*

1. Cultural differences have been ignored. The notion that cultural factors explain economic performance can be misused. In the 1950s, economists spoke of cultural barriers to development in Taiwan and Korea. No doubt today they praise the cultures of these countries as favoring their economic development and as superior to those of other developing countries.

2. The inflow of foreign capital during booms and the outflow during crises should not be considered as "perverse" behavior, since it is completely predictable and rational in economic terms.

3. Once capital-intensive investment projects (for instance, electrical power generation plants) have been started, it is extremely difficult to make any significant cutbacks in them on an emergency basis.

4. Due to the nature of the products and the structure of agricultural trade, restrictive government measures are generally more effective.

*Works Cited*

Balassa, Bela. 1984. "Trade Between Developed and Developing Countries—
The Decade Ahead." *World Bank Reprint Series*, no. 321. Washington, D.C.:
World Bank.

Balassa, Bela, Geraldo Bueno, Pedro Pablo Kuczynski, and Mario Henrique
Simonsen. 1986. *Hacia una renovación del crecimiento económico en América
Latina*. Washington, D.C.: Institute for International Economics.

Balassa, Bela, and John Williamson. 1987. "Adjusting to Success." *Policy Analysis in International Economics*, no. 17 (June). Washington, D.C.: Institute
for International Economics.

Economic Commission for Latin America and the Caribbean (ECLAC). 1987a.
"La evolución reciente de las relaciones comerciales internacionales."
LC/R.596 (May). Santiago de Chile: ECLAC.

———. 1987b. "El proteccionismo de los países industrializados: Estrategias
regionales de negociación y defensa." LC/G.1459 (June). Santiago de
Chile: ECLAC.

Grilli, Enzo R., and Maw Cheng Yang. 1988. "Primary Commodity Prices,
Manufactured Goods Prices, and the Terms of Trade of Developing
Countries: What the Long Run Shows." *World Bank Economic Review*,
vol. 1, no. 1 (January).

International Monetary Fund. 1987. "Primary Commodities: Market Development and Outlook." *World Economic and Financial Surveys*, May.

Khan, Moshin H. 1987. "Macroeconomic Adjustment in Developing Countries: A Policy Perspective." *Research Observer*, January. Washington, D.C.:
World Bank.

List, Friedrich. [1841]1955. *Sistema nacional de economía política* (The national
system of political economy). Madrid: Aguilar. (First published in 1841
as *Das Nationale System der politischen oekonomie*.)

Urdinola, Antonio J. 1987. "Política comercial y modelos de desarrollo:
Alternativas para América Latina." In José A. Ocampo and Eduardo
Sarmiento, eds., *Hacia un nuevo modelo de desarrollo? Un debate*. Bogotá:
Tercer Mundo Editores.

Urrutia, Miguel. 1987. "Latin America and the Crisis of the 1980s." In Louis
Emmerij, ed., *Development Policies and the Crisis of the 1980s*. Paris: OCED.

World Bank. 1986. *World Development Report 1986*. Washington, D.C.: World
Bank.

———. 1987. *World Development Report 1987*. Washington, D.C.: World Bank.

## 5   Youngil Lim: "Comparing Brazil and Korea"

*Notes*

1. The BEFIEX (Beneficio Fiscaio a Programas Especiais de Exportacao)
program, which has been in operation since 1972, offers an incentive package
for an export commitment (generally for a period of ten years) that is negotiated between the government agency and exporters. A typical package
includes a 70 to 90 percent tariff and tax reduction on imports and a 50 percent

reduction on import duties for raw materials and intermediate inputs. Only in exceptional cases is a 100 percent exemption allowed. In contrast, the South Korean incentive system offers 100 percent exemptions from all duties and taxes for imports needed for export production.

2. See World Bank 1983:58. Tyler (1983. estimated that the real export growth rate fell by 8.5 percent with each percentage point of increase in the nominal antiexport bias.

3. The data for Korea are not strictly comparable with those for Brazil because the Korean data refer to the business conglomerates called *jaebol* (similar to Japanese *zaibutsu*), which have multiple products in different subsectors, while the Brazilian data appear to be related to single-product firms.

4. It is not clear whether the reported proportion refers only to the sectors in which the public enterprises operate or to the manufacturing sector as a whole.

5. In Brazil, price controls are administered by one government agency, and subsidies to cover the state-owned enterprises' losses by another. This implies that little incentive exists for the state enterprises to take responsibility for making a profit and being efficient. Leibenstein's X- efficiency problem in decision making is particularly relevant in this regard, as the effort-responsibility-consequences chain in the reward system is effectively broken (see Leibenstein 1978).

6. In addition, much of this section is taken and revised from Lim 1986.

7. In a more systematic study of capital utilization, Kwon and Kim (1973:80) report:

> The Korean experience in the past 10 years clearly demonstrates that the increased utilization has been a very important source of economic growth. It was indicated that the growth of output in Korean manufacturing was far in excess of what could be attributable to the growth of investment and employment. During the same period of overall rate of utilization is found to have doubled. Hence, it can safely be concluded that a major source of Korean economic growth in recent years has been the increasing utilization rate of capital stock.

8. For instance, Krueger (1980:289) hypothesizes that "technological economic factors imply an overwhelming superiority for development through export promotion. These factors include such phenomena as minimum size of plan, increasing returns to scale, indivisibilities in the production process, and the necessity for competition."

9. There is some evidence showing that during the 1970s in Korea totalfactor productivity grew faster in small- and medium-scale industry than in large-scale industry. The small- and medium-scale industry of Korea approximates the model of a competitive market (Lim 1986).

10. The last issue is raised pointedly in Baer et al.(1977) and Fuhr (1987). Similar issues are discussed for Asian counterparts in Johnson (1985).

*Works Cited*

Aghevli, Bijan B., and Jorge Márquez-Ruarte. 1985. "A Case of Successful Adjustment: Korea's Experience During 1980–84." *IMF Occasional Paper*, no. 39 (August). Washington, D.C.: IMF.

Baer, W., R. Newfarmer, and T. Trebat. 1977. "On State Capitalism in Brazil: Some New Issues and Questions." *Inter-American Economic Affairs*, vol. 30 (winter).

Baer, Werner. 1987. "The Resurgence of Inflation in Brazil, 1974–86." *World Development*, vol. 15, no. 8.

Balassa, Bela. 1978. "Export Incentives and Export-Performance in Developing Countries: A Comparative Analysis." *Welwirtschaftliches Archiv*, no. 1.

Bank of Korea (various years) *Financial Statements Analyses*, 1976–78 issues.

Caves, Richard E., and Masu Uekusa. 1976. *Industrial Organization in Japan*. Washington, D.C.: Brookings Institution.

Conner, J. M. 1976. "A Quantitative Analysis of the Market Power of United States Multinational Corporations in Brazil and Mexico." Ph.D. diss., University of Wisconsin, Madison.

Economist Intelligence Unit. 1986. *Country Profile: Brazil 1986–87*. London: Economist Intelligence Unit.

Floyd, Robert H., Clive S. Gray, and R. P. Short. 1984. *Public Enterprise in Mixed Economies: Some Macroeconomic Aspects*. Washington, D.C.: IMF.

Fuhr, Harald. 1987. "Economic Restructuring in Latin America: Towards the Promotion of Small-Scale Industry." *IDS Bulletin*, vol. 18, no. 3. University of Sussex: Institute of Development Studies.

Hong, Wontack. 1979. *Trade, Distortions and Employment Growth in Korea*. Seoul: Korea Development Institute.

Il, Sakong. 1979. "The Role of Public Enterprises in the National Economy of Korea." *Korean Development Studies*, vol. 1, no. 2 (June). Published in Korean by the Korea Development Institute, Seoul.

Johnson, Chalmers. 1985. "Political Institutions and Economic Performance: The Government-Business Relationship in Japan, South Korea and Taiwan." In Robert A. Scalapino, Seizaburo Sato, and Jusuf Wanandi, eds., *Asian Economic Development—Present and Future*. Berkeley: Institute of East Asian Studies, University of California.

*Joong-Ang Daily News* [1980]1981. Article of 5 February 1980, as cited in Youngil Lim, *Government Policy and Private Enterprise: Korean Experience in Industrialization*. Berkeley: Institute of East Asian Studies, Center for Korean Studies, University of California.

Krueger, Anne O. 1980. "Trade Policy as an Input to Development." *American Economic Review*, vol. 70, no. 2 (May).

Kwon, Jene K., and Young-Chin Kim. 1973. *Capital Utilization in Korean Manufacturing, 1962–71: Its Level Trend and Structure*. Seoul: Korea Industrial Development Research Institute.

Lee, Kyu Uck. 1980. "Industrial Organization in Korean Manufacturing." *Korea Development Studies*, vol. 2, no. 4 (December).

Leibenstein, Harvey. 1978. *General X-efficiency Theory and Economic Development.* New York: Oxford University Press.

Lim, Youngil. 1981. *Government Policy and Private Enterprise: Korean Experience in Industrialization.* Berkeley: University of California.

———. 1986. "Sources of Manufacturing Efficiency: Some Evidence from East Asian Economies and Implications for Current Reforms in the People's Republic of China." *Industry and Development* (UNIDO Journal), no. 16.

Lin, Ching-Yuan. 1988. *Latin America and East Asia: A Comparative Development Perspective.* Armonk, NY: M. E. Sharpe.

Lloyd's Bank. 1986. *Brazil: Economic Report 1986.* London: Lloyd's Bank.

Luedde-Neurath, Richard. 1986. *Import Controls and Export-Oriented Development: A Reassessment of the South Korean Case.* Boulder, CO and London: Westview Press.

Nam, C. H. 1981. "Trade, Industrial Policies and the Structure of Protection in Korea." In W. Hong and L. B. Krause, eds., *Trade and Growth in the Advanced Developing Countries in the Pacific Basin.* Seoul: Korea Development Institute.

Nishimizu, M., and S. Robinson. 1984. "Trade Policies and Productivity Changes in Semi-industrialized Countries." *Journal of Development Economics,* vol. 16, no. 2 (September/October).

Ranis, Gustav. 1973. "Industrial Sector Labour Absorption." *Economic Development and Cultural Change,* vol. 21, no. 3 (April).

Sachs, Jeffrey D. 1985. "External Debt and Macroeconomic Performance in Latin America and East Asia." *Brookings Papers on Economic Activity,* no. 2.

Song, Dae-Hee. 1986a. "The Performance Evaluation of Korean Public Enterprises: Policy Practice and Experience." *Korea Development Institute Working Paper,* no. 8601 (October).

———. 1986b. "The Role of the Public Enterprise in the Korean Economy." In Kyu-Uck Lee, ed., *Industrial Development Policies and Issues.* Seoul: Korea Development Institute.

Tyler, William G. 1983. "Anti-Export Bias in Commercial Policies and Export Performance: Some Evidence from the Recent Brazilian Experience." *Weltwirtschaftliches Archiv,* vol. 119, no. 1.

United Nations Centre on Transnational Corporations, John Dunning, and John Cantwell. 1987. *IRM Directory of Statistics of International Investment and Production.* New York: New York University Press.

United Nations Industrial Development Organization. 1988. Data bank.

Westphal, Larry E., Linsu Kim, and Carl J. Dahlman. 1985. "Reflections on the Republic of Korea's Acquisition of Technological Capability." In Nathan Rosenberg and Claudio Frinschtak, eds., *International Technology Transfer: Concepts, Measures, and Comparison.* New York: Praeger.

Willmore, L. N. 1986. "The Comparative Performance of Foreign and Domestic Firms in Brazil." *World Development,* vol. 14, no. 4.

World Bank. [1978] 1986. "Consolidated Balance of Payments." Bank release of 19 May 1978, as cited in Ahn Choong-Yong, "Foreign Investment and Trade Promotion Scheme: Some Comparisons between Korea and Latin American Countries." Mimeo, Chungang University, Seoul.
———. 1983. *Brazil: Industrial Policies and Manufactured Exports*. Washington, D.C.: World Bank.
———. 1985. *Brazil: Country Economic Memorandum*. Report No. 5373-BR, vol. 1 (February).
Young, Soogil. 1986. "Import Liberalization and Industrial Adjustment in Korea." *Korea Development Institute Working Paper*, no. 8613 (December).

## 6 John Wong: "The ASEAN Model of Regional Cooperation"

*Notes*

1. For reference to other Third World regional groupings, see El-Agraa (1987) and Robson (1980).

2. The Association of Southeast Asia, or ASA, with Malaysia, the Philippines, and Thailand as members, was a failure (it lasted from 1961 to 1967). The other attempt, the Maphilindo (Malaysia, the Philippines, and Indonesia), was stillborn in 1963.

3. For a more detailed discussion of the economic structures of ASEAN, see Wong (1979).

4. For those key official documents, see ASEAN Secretariat (1978).

5. Back in 1970, ASEAN sought the assistance of several international bodies to organize a United Nations Study Team to look into arrangements for economic cooperation in ASEAN. The team, led by G. Kansu with the eminent British economist E.A.G. Robinson as senior adviser, submitted a report in 1972. The report recommended three principal techniques for economic cooperation: (1) selective trade liberalization for specific commodities, to be implemented through intergovernment negotiations; (2) industrial complementation, to be negotiated through private-sector initiative but with appropriate tariff concessions from governments; and (3) "package deal" arrangements, in the form of joint industrial projects. See *Journal of Development Planning* (1974).

6. It was the Philippines that included snow plows on its list. This was matched by an equally fantastic offer from Indonesia: nuclear reactors. Both exist only in the customs directory and were not traded in the region. See Tan (1982).

7. There have been several more detailed studies on the impact of PTAs over the years. See Naya (1980) and Ooi (1981).

8. For a more detailed discussion of the comparative experiences of ASEAN and the Andean Pact, see Wong (1986).

*Works Cited*

ASEAN Secretariat. 1978. *10 Years ASEAN*. Jakarta: Association of Southeast Asian Nations.

"Economic Co-operation Among Member Countries of ASEAN." 1974. *Journal of Development Planning*, no. 7.

El-Agraa, Ali M., ed. 1987. *International Economic Integration*. 2nd ed. London: Macmillan.

Institute of Strategic and International Studies. 1987. "ASEAN: The Way Forward." Report of the Group of Fourteen on ASEAN Economic Cooperation and Integration, Malaysia.

Naya, Seiji. 1980. "ASEAN Trade and Development Cooperation: Preferential Trading Arrangements and Trade Liberalization." Report prepared for UNCTAD and UNDP, Project RAS/77/015A/40.

———. 1987. "Toward the Establishment of an ASEAN Trade Area." Report prepared for the ASEAN Secretariat and the Committee on Trade and Tourism, Institute for Strategic and International Studies, Kuala Lumpur..

Ooi Guat, Tin. 1981. *ASEAN Preferential Trading Arrangements (PTA): An Analysis of Potential Effects on Intra-ASEAN Trade*. Singapore: Institute of Southeast Asian Studies.

Rieger, Hans Christoph. 1987. "Towards an ASEAN Common Market: A Concrete Proposal." Paper presented at the First ASEAN Economic Congress, held by Institute of Strategic and International Studies, March.

Robson, Peter. 1980. *The Economics of International Integration*, London: Allen & Unwin.

Tan, Gerald. 1982. *Trade Liberalization in ASEAN*. ASEAN Economic Research Unit, Research Notes and Discussion Paper, no. 32. Singapore: Institute of Southeast Asian Studies.

Wong, John. 1979. *ASEAN Economies in Perspective: A Comparative Study of Indonesia, Malaysia, the Philippines, Singapore and Thailand*. London: Macmillan.

———. 1986. *Regional Industrial Cooperation: Experiences and Perspective of ASEAN and the Andean Pact*. Vienna: United Nations Industrial Development Organisation.

## 7    A. R. Bhuyan: "Beginnings of Cooperation in South Asia"

*Notes*

1. Readers wishing further references on the subjects of this chapter may consult, for example, the inaugural issue of *South Asia Journal* (July/September 1987), especially the articles by Malcolm S. Adiseshiah, G. Corea, E. Gonsalves, and Arif A. Waqif.

*Works Cited*

Adiseshiah, Malcolm S. 1987. "The Economic Rationale of SAARC." *South Asia Journal*, vol. 1, no. 1 (July/September).

Agarwal, Govind R. 1984. *Perspective for the Development of Nepalese Himalayan Resources*. Kathmandu, Nepal: CEDA.

Akrasanee, Narongchai. 1984. *ASEAN Economies and ASEAN Economic Coop-eration*. ADB Economic Staff Paper, no. 23. Manila: Asian Development Bank.

Gonsalves, E. 1987. "An Agenda for the Next Decade." *South Asia Journal*, vol. 1, no. 1 (July/September).

Inter-American Development Bank (IADB). 1984. *Inter-American Development 1984 Report: Economic and Social Progress in Latin America*. Washington, D.C.: IADB.

Kappagoda, N. 1987. "Regional Cooperation in South Asia: Current Policy Issues." Paper presented at the Asian Development Bank/East-West Center Symposium on Regional Cooperation in South Asia, Manila, 9–11 March.

United Nations Conference on Trade and Development (UNCTAD). 1982–83. *Economic Cooperation and Integration Among Developing Countries: A Review of Recent Developments in Subregional, Regional and Interregional Organizations and Arrangements*. Vols. 1–3, TD/B/C.7/51 (parts 1–3). New York: UNCTAD.

Waqif, Arif A. 1987. "Exploring Potential Areas of Industrial Cooperation in South Asia." *South Asia Journal*, vol. 1, no. 1 (July/September).

Zehender, W. 1987. "Industrialization and Regional Cooperation in Black Africa." *Economics*, vol. 36.

**8    Ricardo Ffrench-Davis: "Economic Integration in Latin America"**

*Notes*

1. Apart from the formal process of economic integration, there have been several cooperative efforts among the countries in the region. First, the Comisión Especial de Coordinación Latinoamericana [Special Commission for Latin American Coordination] (CECLA), and, then, the Sistema Económico Latinoamericano [Latin American Economic System] (SELA) have had, since 1975, a regional coverage.

2. Three countries not participating in integration agreements—Haiti, the Dominican Republic, and Suriname—have applied for admission to CAR-ICOM.

3. Dutch disease refers to the adverse impact on nonresource exports resulting from an increase in the price of a resource and the subsequent expansion of that resource sector. The increase in investment flows accompanying the resource boom causes a real appreciation of the exchange rate that can lead to a decline in revenue from nonresource exports and increasing expenditure on imports. The term was originally used to describe the decline in industrial exports of the Netherlands as a result of an increase in petroleum prices and exports (Corden 1981).

4. There were nonreciprocal tariff preferences in favor of Bolivia, Ecuador, Paraguay, and (in part) Uruguay, but they proved to be insufficient to achieve a balanced distribution of the benefits of integration among member countries. Uruguay was the more active user of these preferences.

5. Preferences were also valid for less-developed partners, such as Bolivia, Ecuador, and Paraguay.

6. By 1971 the trade to which they gave rise represented a share of 22 percent of reciprocal imports of manufactures benefiting from tariff preferences as compared to 6 percent in 1966 (Ayza et al. 1975: 159). The share in overall reciprocal imports was 1 percent and 7 percent in 1966 and 1971, respectively. By 1980, it had diminished to 4 percent (ECLA 1984: 87).

7. Two significant cases were those of Argentina in 1967 and Chile in 1975 onward. In Chile, by 1979 the general tariff was a uniform 10 percent. The reverse occurred in Peru (1974–77) and Chile (1972–73) where strong nontariff restrictions were applied more strongly to trade with nonmember countries.

8. Data based on SITC categories 5+6+7+8, excluding division 68 (CEPAL 1984).

9. The definitions are not identical with those used by CEPAL (1984). CEPAL's definition of manufactures is narrower.

10. The simple average of the starting internal tariff rate was 44 percent (Aninat 1978).

11. Other foreign trade tools also influence the composition of imports, though in an indirect or a less systematic way—i.e., exchange-rate policy and some nontariff regulations. It must be noted that, of course, other (nontrade) mechanisms, would also have a significant effect on trade as indicated by the post–1982 recessive adjustment in Latin America.

12. Several other programs were sent to the Commission in 1975. Subsequently they were readjusted in order to take account of the withdrawal of Chile, but were not approved.

13. In addition, annual profit remittances which were limited to 14 percent of the equity capital were increased to 20 percent in 1976.

14. In cases in which the state was a stockholder and had determinant powers in the decision-making process, a lower 30 percent share held by the state was set as the minimum requirement for mixed enterprises.

15. Reciprocal exports are equal to reciprocal imports. Since 1982 Latin America was forced to generate trade surpluses with the rest of the world; therefore if the share of reciprocal imports in total imports is measured, the step back in trade is not clearly observed.

16. Part of the drop in reciprocal exports found a market in other regions. The Latin American countries devalued their exchange rates. Within the debtor nations the effects of the devaluations were nullified, but they were effective vis-à-vis other regions. Thus, there was a net incentive to export to creditor countries. The relatively higher aggregate demand of these countries worked in the same direction. However, given the different composition of reciprocal and total exports, the most typical reciprocal exports did not find alternative markets abroad, and their drop contributed to larger domestic recessions.

*Works Cited*

Aninat, A. 1978. "El Programa de Liberación y el Arancel Externo Común en El Acuerdo de Cartagena." In E. Tironi, ed., *El Pacto Andino: Carácter y perspectivas.* Lima: Instituto de Estudios Peruanos.

Aninat, A., R. Ffrench-Davis, and P. Leiva 1984. "La integración andina en el nuevo escenario de los años ochenta." *Apuntes CIEPLAN,* no. 62 (October).

Ayza, J., G. Fichet, and N. González. 1975. *América Latina: Integración económica y sustitución de importaciones.* México: Fondo de Cultura Económica.

Corden, W. M. 1981. "The Exchange Rate, Monetary Policy and the North Sea: The Economic Theory of the Squeeze on Tradeables." *Oxford Economic Papers,* vol. 33 (July supplement).

Economic Commission for Latin America [ECLA] 1984. "Asociación Latinoamericana de Integración: Experiencia de Tres Años de Funcionamiento, Problemas y Perspectivas." Santiago de Chile: ECLA.

Instituto para la Integración de América Latina (INTAL) 1974. *Análisis de los márgenes de preferencia y el comercio intrazonal en el marco de la Asociación Latinoamericana de Libre Comercio.* Buenos Aires: INTAL.

———. 1985–86. *El proceso de integración en América Latina.* Buenos Aires: INTAL.

———. 1986. *Exenciones arancelarias e integración.* Buenos Aires: INTAL.

———. 1987. "Nuevos acuerdos para consolidar la integración argentina-brasileña." *Integración Latinoamericana,* no. 129 (November). Published monthly by el Instituto para la Integración de América Latina, Buenos Aires.

Inter-American Development Bank (IADB). 1984. "Economic Integration in Latin America." *Inter-American Development Report 1984: Economic and Social Progress in Latin America. Part One.* Washington, D.C.: IADB.

———. and INTAL. 1987. *El comercio intralatinoamericano en los años 80s: Estadísticas.* Buenos Aires: INTAL.

Junta del Acuerdo de Cartagena (JUNAC). 1981. "Orientaciones para la elaboración del Arancel Externo Común." In R. Ffrench-Davis, ed., *Intercambio y Desarrollo,* vol. 1, lectura 38. México: Fondo de Cultura Económica.

Lahera, E., and F. Sánchez. 1985. "Estudio comparativo de la Decisión 24 en los países del Grupo Andino: Situación actual y perspectivas." LC/R.422 (October). Santiago de Chile: ECLA.

Latin American Free Trade Association (LAFTA). 1973. *El sistema de pagos y créditos recíprocos y el Acuerdo de Santo Domingo.* ALALC/SEC/ PA/30 (June). Montevideo: LAFTA.

———. 1983. *Evaluación del funcionamiento de convenio de pagos y créditos recíprocos y eventuales medidas destinadas a su perfeccionamiento.* LAIA/CAFM/III/DT.2 (January).

Salgado, G. 1987. "Comercio intraregional e integración económica: crisis y tendencias recientes." Paper presented at Latin America in the World Economy seminar sponsored by Instituto para la Integracíon de América Latina and Economic Commission for Latin America, Buenos Aires, September.

Tironi, E. 1976. Economic Integration and Foreign Direct Investment Policies: The Andean Case. Ph.D. diss., Massachusetts Institute of Technology, Cambridge.

———. 1981. "Teoría de la integración y empresas transnacionales." In R. Ffrench-Davis, ed., *Intercambio y Desarrollo*. México: Fondo de Cultura Económica.

———, ed. 1978. *El Pacto Andino: Carácter y perspectivas*. Lima: Instituto de Estudios Peruanos.

Vacchino, J. M. 1981. *Integración económica regional*. Caracas: Universidad Central de Venezuela.

Vaitsos, C. 1974. *Intercountry Income Distribution and Transnational Enterprises*. Oxford: Clarendon Press.

White, E. 1986. "Las inversiones extranjeras y la crisis económica en América Latina." In R. Ffrench-Davis and R. E. Feinberg, eds., *Debt and Development Crisis in Latin America: Basis for a New Consensus*. Notre Dame, IN: University of Notre Dame Press.

Wionczek, M., ed. 1969. *Economic Cooperation in Latin America, Africa and Asia: A Handbook of Documents*. Cambridge, MA: MIT Press.

## 9 Atsushi Murakami: "Japan and the United States: Roles in Asian Development"

*Notes*

1. Unfortunately, trade figures for Taiwan were not available in the United Nations *Commodity Trade Statistics*. But it should be noted that Taiwan's trade has significantly expanded each year. Today Taiwan has a surplus in its total trade balance, and its reserve of foreign currency amounts to the third highest in the world, after Japan and West Germany.

2. The Japanese government announced that by 1990 it would double its ODA flows from its 1985 level. This would make the total ODA flow more than US$40 billion during the period 1986–92. The ratio of Japanese ODA to GNP would then be 0.36 percent in 1992, which is comparable to the DAC average in 1986. Already, Japanese ODA in fiscal year 1988 is expected to be over US$10 billion, making Japan the world's largest provider of ODA.

*Works Cited*

Japan External Trade Organization (JETRO). *White Papers on Foreign Direct Investment of the World and Japan*. Various issues. Tokyo: JETRO.

Ministry of International Trade and Industry (MITI). 1987. *Present Situation and Problems of Economic Cooperation*. Various issues. Tokyo: MITI.

Nihon Keizai Shinbun, 30 January; 7 and 26 February; 20 and 30 March 1988.

10   Carlos Juan Moneta: Latin American Economic Relations
     with the United States and Japan

*Works Cited*

Bitar, Sergio. 1985. "La inversión estadounidense en el Grupo Andino."
   *Integración Latinoamericana*, no. 98 (February). Buenos Aires: Instituto
   para la Integración de América Latina and IADA.
————. 1986. "La política de los Estados Unidos ante la inversión extranjera
   y sus implicaciones para América Latina." *Capítulos del SELA*, no. 11 (Jan-
   uary-March).
Bradford, Colin, and C. Moneta. 1987. *Situación y perspectivas de las relaciones
   entre América Latina y Japón*, Cuadernos del SELA, p. 58, Edit. La Flor,
   Buenos Aires.
General Agreement on Tariffs and Trade (GATT). 1983–84. *Informe del Com-
   ercio Mundial*.
————. 1987. *Monthly Bulletin of Statistics* (December).
Inter-American Development Bank (IADB). 1987. *Progreso económico y social en
   América Latina, Informe 1987*. Washington, D.C.: IADB.
Japan Tariff Association (JTA). 1987. *The Summary Report: Trade of Japan*. Tokyo:
   JTA.
JEJ. 1987a. 6 June.
————. 1987b. 24 October.
————. "FY 1988 Budget," 2–9 January 1988.
Keizai Koho Center (KKC). 1985. *Smoothing the Way for Imports*. KKC Brief, no.
   26 (February). Tokyo: Japan Institute for Social and Economic Affairs.
————. 1986. *Keidanren Proposals for Widening Market Access and Actual Mea-
   sures Implemented*. KKC Brief, no. 35 (September).
————. 1987. "Keidaren Recommendations on Promoting the Recycling of
   Funds to Developing Countries." *Keidanren Review*, no. 108 (December).
Moneta, C. 1987a. "Las propuestas e ideas japonesas en materia de
   financiamiento y su importancia para América Latina." *Capítulos del
   SELA*, no. 16 (April-June). Caracas: SELA.
————. 1987b. "Japón-América Latina: Reestructuración y mercados." *Nueva
   Sociedad*, no. 91 (September-October).
Morgan Guaranty Trust. 1987. *World Financial Markets*, July.
Sistema Económico Latinoamericano (SELA). 1986. *Relaciones económicas entre
   América Latina y el Japón*. SP/CL/XII.O/DT, no. 13 (August). Buenos
   Aires: SELA.
————. 1987a. *La evolución de la economía mundial y el desarrollo de América
   Latina y el Caribe*. SP/CL/XIII.O/DT, no. 5 (September). Buenos Aires:
   SELA.
————. 1987b. *La dinámica del comercio exterior en América Latina, 1970–86*.
   SP/CL/XIII.O/DI, no. 6 (September). Buenos Aires: SELA.
————. 1987c. *La política industrial de América Latina hacia los fines del siglo XX*.
   SP/CL/XIII.O/DT, no. 12 (September). Buenos Aires: SELA.
————. 1988. *Working paper on the Evolution of the Japanese Economy*. April.
   Buenos Aires: SELA.

Sociedad Latinoamericana. 1986. *Panorama de la industria y la cooperación económica del Japón.* Tokyo: Sociedad Latinoamericano.

United States Department of Commerce. 1981. *U.S. Direct Investment Abroad.* Washington, D.C.: U.S. Government Printing Office.

———. 1976–85. *Survey of Current Business.* Washington, D.C.: U.S. Government Printing Office.

*Washington Trade Report.* 1987. 7–31 December.

Yeutter, Clayton. 1988. "El Caribe debe diversificar su agricultura." USIS cable, Bridgetown, 21 January.

**11  Francisco Orrego Vicuña: "Latin American Trade with the Asia-Pacific Region"**

*Notes*

1. The case of Panama should be considered carefully because of its role as a reexport center.

*Works Cited*

Armanet, Pilar, ed. 1987. *América Latina en la cuenca del Pacífico: Perspectivas y dimensiones de la cooperación.* Santiago de Chile: Institute of International Studies, University of Chile.

Chintayarangsan, Rachain. 1983. "ASEAN's Primary Commodity Exports." In *ASEAN and Pacific Economic Cooperation.* Bangkok, Thailand: United Nations Economic and Social Commission for Asia and the Pacific.

Moneta, Carlos J. 1987. "La reestructuración de la economía japonesa y sus efectos en las relaciones económicas con América Latina." Paper presented at Seminario sobre la Cuenca del Pacífico: Desafíos para América Latina, sponsored by Institute of International Studies, Viña del Mar, 4–6 November.

Oborne, Michael W., and Nicholas Fourt. 1983. *Pacific Basin Economic Cooperation.* Paris: OECD.

Pacific Economic Cooperation Conference (PECC). 1983. "Report of the Task Force on Trade in Agricultural and Renewable Resource Goods." In *Issues for Pacific Economic Cooperation.* Report of the Third Pacific Economic Cooperation Conference, Bali, November.

———. 1985. "Report of the Task Force on Trade Negotiations." In *Pacific Economic Cooperation, Issues and Opportunities.* Report of the Fourth Pacific Economic Cooperation Conference, Seoul, April 29–May 1.

Reutter, Juan. 1980. "Diagnóstico y perspectivas de las relaciones económicas entre la región Asia-Pacífico y América Latina." In Francisco Orrego-Vicuña, ed., *La comunidad del Pacífico en perspectiva.* Santiago de Chile: Institute of International Studies, University of Chile.

———. 1987. "Evolución de los flujos comerciales al interior de la cuenca del Pacífico: 1979–1985." In P. Armanet, ed., *América Latina en la cuenca del Pacífico: Perspectivas y dimensiones de la cooperación.* Santiago de Chile: Institute of International Studies, University of Chile.

Sistema Económico Latinoamericano (SELA) 1985. Annex 1: Presentación del Grupo Latinoamericano ante el Comité de Coordinación de los Directores Generales de Ministerios y Agencias del Gobierno del Japón. "Relaciones Económicas América Latina–Japón." *Documento Informativo SP/CL/XI.0/DI*, no. 7 (June). Caracas: SELA.

Tironi, Ernesto. 1981. "Relaciones comerciales entre los países en desarrollo intermedio de América Latina y Asia." *Comercio Exterior*, vol. 31, no. 12 (December).

Vicuña, Francisco Orrego. 1982a. "Prospects of Co-operation between Latin America and the ASEAN Countries." *Contemporary South East Asia*, vol. 4, No. 1 (June).

————. 1982b. "The Pacific Islands in a Latin American Perspective: Towards a Special Relationship?" In Paul F. Hooper, ed., *Building a Pacific Community*. Honolulu: East-West Center.

————. 1987. "América Latina y el proceso de cooperación en la cuenca del Pacífico: La identificación de intereses." In P. Armanet, ed., *América Latina en la cuenca del Pacífico: Perspectivas y dimensiones de la cooperación*. Santiago de Chile: Institute of International Studies, University of Chile.

Vicuña, Francisco Orrego, ed. 1980. *La comunidad del Pacífico en perspectiva*. Vol. 2. Santiago de Chile: Institute of International Studies, Unviersity of Chile.

Vicuña, Francisco Orrego, and Juan Reutter. 1982. "Latin America's Trade Relations with the ASEAN Countries: Prospects for Interaction." *Contemporary Southeast Asia*, vol. 4, no. 1 (June).

Wu, Rong-J. 1987. "The Economic Development of Newly Industrialized Countries in East Asia." In Philip West and Frans A. M. Alting von Geusau, eds., *The Pacific Rim and the Western World*. Boulder, CO: Westview Press.

**12 Miguel Rodríguez Mendoza: "Multilateral Trade Negotiations"**

*Notes*

1. The growing number of Latin American countries that have joined GATT or are negotiating their incorporation (Bolivia, Costa Rica, El Salvador, Guatemala, Honduras, and Mexico) reflects the rising interest of the Latin American nations in these multilateral negotiations.

2. These assertions were submitted by a group of developing countries, including Argentina, Brazil, Cuba, Nicaragua, and Peru, during the preparatory stage of negotiations.

3. For a more comprehensive discussion of the problems faced by the Latin American steel producers, see SELA (1986a, 1986b).

4. Latin American members in this group are Argentina, Brazil, Chile, Colombia, and Uruguay. Other members include Australia, Canada, Hungary, Indonesia, Malaysia, New Zealand, the Philippines, and Thailand.

5. The following products have been considered: tropical beverages, spices, flowers, plants, etc.; some oilseeds and vegetables oils; tobacco, rice,

and tropical roots; tropical fruits and nuts; tropical wood and rubber; and jute and hard fibers.

6. Under the 28 November 1979 Decision on Action by Contracting Parties on Multilateral Trade Negotiations, the agreements resulting from the negotiations may not affect the rights of the GATT contracting parties under Article 1 of the most-favored-nation clause.

7. Trade in services includes a wide range of activities, namely, transport activities, communications, insurance, banking and financial services, data and information services, and so on. The GATT discussions will not have determined which activities are to be included in the negotiations on services.

*Works Cited*

Dam, Kenneth W. 1986. "Testimony of Kenneth W. Dam, Representing the Intellectual Property Committee, before the U.S. Senate Finance Committee." Washington, D.C.: U.S. Government Printing Office.

European Economic Community. 1984. *Etude sur les Échanges Internationaux des Services*. Report submitted to GATT (October).

General Agreement on Tariffs and Trades (GATT). 1980. *Contracting Parties to the General Agreement on Tariffs and Trade, Basic Instruments and Selected Documents*, Twenty-sixth supplement. Geneva: GATT.

―――. 1984. *Contracting Parties to the General Agreement on Tariffs and Trade, Special Group Report*. L/5504 and IBDD 305/151. Geneva: GATT.

Organisation for Economic Co-operation and Development (OECD). 1987. *Elements of a Conceptual Framework for Trade in Services*. Paris: OECD.

Sistema Económico Latinoamericano (SELA). 1985. *Los servicios y el desarrollo de América Latina*. Buenos Aires: SELA.

―――. 1986a. *La política siderúrgica de la Comunidad Europea y sus implicaciónes para América Latina*. SP/CL/XII.DT, no. 11. Buenos Aires: SELA.

―――. 1986b. *América Latina y el proteccionismo en Estados Unidos: El caso del acero*. SP/CI/XII.O/DT, no. 8. Buenos Aires: SELA.

―――. 1988. *Documento de trabajo sobre la Ronda Uruguay de las negociaciones comerciales multilaterales*. SP/III-RC-NCM/DT, no. 2. (February). Buenos Aires: SELA.

United Nations Conference on Trade and Development (UNCTAD). 1984. *Los servicios y el proceso de desarrollo*. TD/B/1008. (August). Geneva: UNCTAD.

U.S. Office of Technology Assessment. 1986. *Trade in Services, Exports and Foreign Revenues*. Washington, D.C.: U.S. Government Printing Office.

**14   Helen Hughes: "Toward Clarity and Common Sense"**

*Notes*

1. Data for the paper are from the International Economic Bank, Australian National University, Canberra.

2. In the statist South Asia-China model, the public sector is relied on to provide the stimulus to growth. This policy stands in sharp contrast to the

outward- and private enterprise-oriented model of East and Southeast Asia. The Latin American *dependencia* model rests on the belief that the economic development of the weaker, less-developed countries rests on the growth and policies of the economically dominant country.

*Works Cited*

Balassa, Bela, and Helen Hughes. 1969. "Statistical Indicators of Industrial Development," *Economics Department Working Paper*, no. 45 (mimeo). Washington, D.C.: International Bank for Reconstruction and Development.

Corden, W. M. 1974. *Trade Policy and Economic Welfare*. London: Oxford University Press.

Chenery, H. B., and M. Syrquin. 1975. *Patterns of Development, 1950–1970*. London: Oxford University Press.

Haggard, Stephan. 1980. "The Politics of Industrialization in the Republic of Korea and Taiwan." In *Achieving Industrialization in East Asia*, edited by H. Hughes. Sydney: Cambridge University Press.

Kravis, Irving B. 1986. "The Three Faces of the International Comparison Project," *The World Bank Research Observer*, vol. 1, no. 1 (January).

Krueger, Anne O. 1974. "The Political Economy of the Rent Seeking Society," *American Economic Review*, vol. 64, no. 3 (June).

Mackie, J. A. C. 1988. "Economic Growth in the ASEAN Region: The Political Underpinnings." In *Achieving Industrialization in East Asia*, edited by H. Hughes. Sydney: Cambridge University Press.

Maddison, A. 1982. *Phases of Capitalist Development*. New York: Oxford University Press.

Riedel, J. R. (1988) "Economic Development in East Asia: Doing What Comes Naturally?" In *Achieving Industrialization in East Asia*, edited by H. Hughes. Sydney: Cambridge University Press.

Tawney, R. H. 1926. *Religion and the Rise of Capitalism: A Historical Study*. London: John Murray.

Weber, Max. 1965. *Sociology of Religion*. London: Methuen. (First published in German in 1922.)

# Contributors

SEIJI NAYA is currently vice-president for strategic planning at the East-West Center, director of the Resources Systems Institute, East-West Center, and professor of economics at the University of Hawaii, Honolulu. He has served as chief economist at the Asian Development Bank in Manila, director of the Asian Studies Program at the University of Hawaii, and visiting professor at Thammasat University in Thailand. Dr. Naya's research focuses on the international economic problems of Asian countries. He has written many articles and books and in 1975 was awarded the National Distinguished Research Award in Economics by Thailand's National Research Council.

MIGUEL URRUTIA is manager of the Economics and Social Development Department of the Inter-American Development Bank. Previously he has been dean of the United Nations University in Toyko, director of the Fundación para la Educación Superior y el Desarrollo (FEDESARROLLO). In Colombia he has served as director of the National Department of Planning, and minister of Mines and Energy. Dr. Urrutia is the author of numerous articles and books on economic development.

SHELLEY M. MARK is currently emeritus professor of Economics at the University of Hawaii and research fellow at the Resource Systems Institute of the East-West Center. He has previously served as director of the Office of Land Use Coordination at the U.S. Environmental Protection Agency, and before that as director of the Department of Planning and Economic Development for the State of Hawaii. Dr. Mark currently serves on a number of commissions for the State of Hawaii as well as in various other organizations in the United States and U.S. government. His recent writings have been about development issues, Chinese development in particular; he has also written about land use and agriculture.

**ALFREDO FUENTES** is currently economic sector chief at the Institute for the Integration of Latin America (INTAL) of the Inter-American Development Bank in Buenos Aires. He has previously been a researcher for the Fundación para la Educación Superior y el Desarrollo (FEDESARROLLO), director of political economy for the Andean Group, general secretary of the Colombian Association of Agriculturalists, and a university professor. He is the author of numerous books and articles on world economics, regional integration, and the politics of international trade.

**EDMAR L. BACHA** is currently professor of economics at the Pontificia Universidade Catolica do Rio de Janeiro. He has recently been visiting professor at both Stanford University and the University of California, Berkeley, and has also held short-term positions at Yale, Columbia, Harvard, and MIT. Dr. Bacha has previously been president of the Brazilian Institute of Geography and Statistics, and a professor at both the Universidade de Brasilia and the Postgraduate School of Economics at the Fundacao Getulio Vargas in Rio de Janeiro. He has served as an advisor to the World Bank, and currently is an advisor to UNESCO. He has written a number of books and articles on Brazilian and international economics.

**AYUBAR RAHMAN BHUYAN** is professor of economics and director of the Bureau of Economic Research at Dhaka University, Bangladesh. He has served as a consultant to, among others, the government of Bangladesh and the United Nations Commission on Trade and Development (UNCTAD). His research interests are development and international economics and his books include *Economic Integration in South Asia: An Exploratory Study* and *A South Asian Customs Union: Prospects and Problems* (both coauthored with M. Akhlaqur Rahman and S. Reza).

**EDWARD K. Y. CHEN** is professor and director of the Center of Asian Studies and honorary professor of economics at the University of Hong Kong. He has held several short-term visiting positions, served as a consultant to a number of international agencies, and is director of a variety of corporations. Dr. Chen's research interests focus on economic development problems, with special reference to the Asian newly industrializing countries (NICs). His recent work has been on multinational corporations; his books include *Multinational Corporations,*

*Technology, and Employment; The New Multinationals; China: Market in the Asia-Pacific;* and *Small Industry in Asia's Export-Oriented Growth.*

RICARDO FFRENCH-DAVIS is vice-president of the Center for Economic Research on Latin America (CIEPLAN) in Santiago, Chile. He has written a wide variety of books and articles on development, international economics, and Latin American economic politics. He has co-edited *Latin America and the New International Economic Order* and *Development and External Debt in Latin America.*

HELEN HUGHES is professor of economics and executive director of the National Centre for Development Studies in the Research School of Pacific Studies at Australian National University. Prior to this she held a variety of positions at the World Bank, including director of the Development Economics Department, and worked for the United Nations Committee for Development Planning. Dr. Hughes has written on economic development, particularly about East Asia. She authored *Australia in a Developing World,* and co-authored *Capital Utilization in Manufacturing in Developing Countries.* She has edited *Removing Constraints to Economic and Social Development,* and *Success in East Asia: Industrialization in Comparative Perspective.*

KEDAR N. KOHLI is currently an economic consultant based in New Delhi, India. He has worked in various capacities at the Indian Planning Commission between 1950 and 1967 and was involved in the formulation of various aspects of the Five-Year Plans. In 1967 he joined the newly established Asian Development Bank where he rose to the position of chief economist before retiring in late 1988. While at the ADB, he wrote extensively on economic problems in the developing countries of Asia.

YOUNGIL LIM is currently senior industrial development officer at the United Nations Industrial Development Organization (UNIDO) in Vienna, where he is responsible for the *Industry and Development Global Report.* Prior to this he was professor of economics at the University of Hawaii. He has written about Asian economics, especially trade and industrialization in South Korea.

MIGUEL RODRIGUEZ MENDOZA is the presidential representative for International Economic Affairs in Venezuela. He has served as director of the Country Consultation and Coordination Department at the Latin American Economic System (SELA) and is the author of several publications on Latin America and GATT negotiations.

**CARLOS JUAN MONETA** is currently a visiting fellow at the Hoover Institution. Previously, he was interim director of consulting and coordination at the Latin American Economic System (SELA), served on the faculty of political science at the Universidad Nacional de Mar del Plata, and was the director of the international relations department at the Universidad del Salvador in Buenos Aires. He has held short-term positions at UCLA, the Universidad Nacional Autónoma de México (UNAM), and the Universidad Central de Venezuela. Dr. Moneta has been a special fellow at the United Nations Institute for Training and Research (UNITAR) and a researcher at the Center of Third World Economic and Social Studies. He has experience in Argentine foreign policy, the foreign debt crisis, and Latin American regional integration.

**ATSUSHI MURAKAMI** is professor of economics at Kobe University, Japan. He has authored books and articles about development and international economics and has translated economic texts into Japanese.

**JORGE OSPINA SARDI** is professor at the Universidad Javierana in Colombia. He also serves as a consultant to the World Bank, the United Nations, the Organisation for Economic Co-operation and Development (OECD), and the Institute for the Integration of Latin America (INTAL). In Colombia he has served as director of the National Department of Planning and general secretary of the society of agriculturalists. His research interests include the foreign debt crisis, energy, foreign investment, and Colombian economics.

**FRANCISCO ORREGO VICUÑA** is a professor at the Institute of International Studies and Law School at the University of Chile. He is a member of the Research Council Pacific Forum and the Pacific Science Council and has long been involved in Pacific affairs, including Pacific Economic Cooperation Conferences and Pacific Basin Economic Council meetings. He has published various articles and books on Latin American participation.

**JOHN WONG** is currently associate professor of economics at the National University of Singapore and has held short-term visiting positions at a variety of institutions, including Harvard, Yale, and Oxford. He has written extensively on the economies of China, ASEAN, and the Asian NICs. His books include *ASEAN Economics in Perspective: A Comparative Study of Indonesia, Malaysia, the Philippines, Singapore and Thailand* and *The Political Economy of China's Changing Relations with Southeast Asia.*

# Index